ONE GOD, MANY PROPHETS

The Universal Wisdom of Islam

Zachary Markwith

ONE GOD, MANY PROPHETS

The Universal Wisdom of Islam

Foreword by
HUSTON SMITH

SOPHIA PERENNIS
SAN RAFAEL CA

First published in the USA

Sophia Perennis 2013

Series editor, James R. Wetmore

For information, address:
Sophia Perennis, P.O. Box 151011
San Rafael, CA 94915
sophiaperennis.com

Library of Congress Cataloging-in-Publication Data

Markwith, Zachary.
One God, many prophets: the universal wisdom of Islam / Zachary Markwith; foreword by Huston Smith.

p. cm.
Includes bibliographical references.
ISBN 978-1-59731-139-7 (pbk: alk. paper)
1. Islam—Philosophy. 2. Mysticism—Islam. 3. Islamic Philosophy. 4. Philosophy and religion. I. Title
BP165.M313 2013
297—dc23 2013036034

Cover design: Cristy Deming

CONTENTS

Foreword by Huston Smith [1]
Introduction [3]

1: *Muslim Sages and the Perennial Philosophy* [19]

The Perennial Philosophy [23]—The Quran, Sunnah, and the Perennial Philosophy [29]—Classical Muslim Sages and the Perennial Philosophy [40]—Contemporary Muslim Sages and the Perennial Philosophy (*René Guénon, Frithjof Schuon, Titus Burckhardt, Martin Lings, Seyyed Hossein Nasr*) [75]—Some Conclusions [112]

2: *Lovers of Sophia* [118]

Srī Ramakrishna [119]—Muḥyī al-Din ibn ʿArabī [126]—Some Conclusions [136]

3: *Thou art Dhāt* [144]

Advaita Vedānta in Light of the Perennial Philosophy [146]—Non-Dual Metaphysics in the Islamic Tradition [156]—Some Conclusions [190]

4: *Christic Sanctity in Islam* [193]

Christic Sanctity According to Ibn ʿArabī [196]—Ḥusayn ibn ʿAlī [201]—Manṣūr Ḥallāj [211]—Some Conclusions [221]

5: *The Eliatic Function in Islam* [224]

Khiḍr [229]—The Mahdī [241]—Some Conclusions [254]

6: *Hermetic Wisdom in Islam* [257]

Some Conclusions [279]

7: *God's Vicegerent on Earth* [282]
Seyyed Hossein Nasr's Defense of Nature

Life and Writings on Nature [283]—A Critique of Modern Philosophy and Science [287]—A Defense of Nature [293]

8: *The Wisdom and Forms of Islam* [305]

Sources [335]
Index [337]

بسم الله الرحمن الرحيم

In the Name of God, the Infinitely Good, the All-Merciful

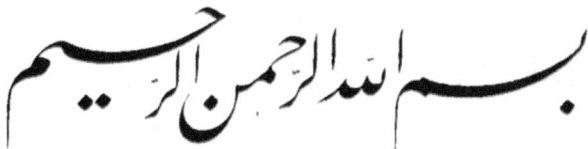

for Sarah

Foreword

I have spent several decades recognizing and validating the eight revealed religions by which God has graced and elevated recorded history: Hinduism, Buddhism, Confucianism, Taoism, Islam, Judaism, Christianity, and the Primal Religions. However, in retrospect it now appears to me that I have not adequately appreciated the contemporary spokesmen of Islam. This realization first dawned on me when I encountered a contemporary Muslim sage, Shaykh 'Īsā Nūr al-Dīn Aḥmad or Frithjof Schuon, and his remarkable successors, among whom I regard Shaykh Abū Bakr or Martin Lings and Seyyed Hossein Nasr as preeminent. It would be wrong to class these men with the plenary founders of the religions, but the heritage that these writers derive from the founding prophets is nothing less than astonishing.

One God, Many Prophets enables my generation's students of Islam and the Perennial Philosophy to relax, take a deep breath of relief, and rejoice, for it is proof positive that this Wisdom is in good hands and that there will be no break in its remarkable history. Zachary Markwith is as competent an heir to Frithjof Schuon, Martin Lings, and Seyyed Hossein Nasr as I can imagine. I have known Zachary for nearly a decade. My regard for him has grown with each meeting and reaches its peak with the appearance of this book.

HUSTON SMITH

Introduction

> And dispute not with the People of the Book, save in the most virtuous manner, unless it be those who have done wrong. And say, "We believe in that which has been sent down unto us and sent down unto you; our God and your God is One, and unto Him do we submit." (Quran 29:46)

At the heart of the Islamic tradition is the principle of Divine Unity (*al-tawḥīd*). The One God (*al-Wāḥid*) is a metaphysical Reality and ubiquitous Presence that transcends and at the same time embraces humanity and the cosmos. The central tenet in Islam, *Lā ilāha illa'Llāh* or "There is no god but God," means that the faithful in all of the world's religions ultimately worship and seek to encounter the same transcendent and immanent Principle, whether they know this Reality as God, Yahweh, Allah, Brahman, Nirvana, the Tao or the Great Spirit. Despite the diverse ways that God is revealed and envisaged in the various traditions, there is One Absolute and Infinite Reality at the summit and center of all of the revealed religions, which is the basis for the Islamic expression, *al-tawḥīdu wāḥidun* or "the doctrine of Unity is unique."

The Quran in fact reminds men and women that the One God sent many messengers and prophets to different human collectivities, including Adam, Noah, Abraham, Moses, David, Jesus, and Muḥammad. We are also told in the Quran, "And for every community there is a messenger..." (10:47) and "...Among them are those whom We have recounted unto thee, and among them are those whom We have not recounted unto thee..." (40:78), which has led a number of Muslim scholars to accept or at least entertain the possibility that Hermes, Pythagoras, Zoroaster, Rama, Krishna, the Buddha, Lao Tzu, Confucius, and others sages, avatars, and shamans from the East and West were Divine messengers or prophets.

The Quran also mentions the Torah, Psalms, and Gospel as Divine revelation, and enjoins Jews and Christians or the "People of the Book" (*ahl al-kitāb*) to follow their revelations, whose protected status has been extended to Zoroastrians, Hindus, Buddhists and others when Muslims ruled over these communities. Moreover, an intelligent and spiritually sensitive Muslim cannot read the Bhagavad Gita or the Tao te Ching, for example, and not see in them Divine inspiration of the highest order, as in fact happened when certain Sufis read these texts in premodern India and China.[1] By reflecting upon other prophets, books, and religions, Muslims embrace their own spiritual inheritance and can recognize and marvel at the signs (*āyāt*) and very Face (*wajh*) of God in other religions. Due to its descent near the end of this cycle of human and cosmic history, the Quran is able to accept and verify previous revelations, prophets and religions in a unique and unprecedented manner. In a world marked by strife and discord, Islam's often neglected emphasis on Divine Unity and religious pluralism can help facilitate greater mutual understanding and peace.

In addition to affirming the doctrine of Divine Unity that is shared by all religions in different forms, Muslims also testify that *Muḥammadun rasūl Allāh* or "Muḥammad is the Messenger of God." The Quran and the *Sunnah* of the Prophet of Islam simultaneously accept and verify previous revelations and religions and establish a particular Sacred Law (*Sharīʿah*), spiritual path (*ṭarīqah*), and theological and philosophical perspective based upon doctrine of Unity for Muslims who accept the veracity of the Prophet of Islam and the Divine origin of the Holy Quran. Throughout this book we are concerned with the principles of both universality and orthodoxy, and posit that men and women can simultaneously accept and appreciate all religions in principle but can best devote themselves to God through one.[2] For Muslims this

1. The Quranic translations throughout this book, unless otherwise noted, are from *HarperCollins Study Qur'ān*, trans. Seyyed Hossein Nasr (San Francisco: HarperOne, forthcoming 2014). Seyyed Hossein Nasr, "Islam and the Encounter of Religions," *Sufi Essays* (Chicago, IL: ABC International Group, Inc., 1999), pp. 123–151.

means that we can accept the Divine origin and learn from aspects of the Indian, Chinese, Persian, Greek, Abrahamic, and Shamanic traditions, following the Prophetic maxim, "Seek knowledge even unto China," while practicing the central rites of Islam. It is precisely through penetrating into the heart of one religion that a spiritual seeker can reach the Divine Reality, which is the common origin of the revealed religions. Among the greatest challenges that humanity faces today is to maintain local, cultural, and religious distinctness alongside a growing awareness of the essential unanimity of our great wisdom traditions. A Muslim need not embrace Trinitarian theology as his own nor pay homage to a Hindu deity to see in Christianity and Hinduism diverse expressions of the principle of Unity in his neighbor's religious forms. Indeed, it is precisely by remaining faithful to the Sacred Law and basic theological doctrines of Islam and benefiting from the Islamic intellectual and spiritual heritage that a Muslim can gain greater awareness of the Unity that embraces all cosmic and human diversity. Moreover, for Divine Unity to become more than a mere theoretical and mental construct, for it to inform one's vision of things, care must be taken to awaken the Intellect (*al-'aql*) or the eye of the heart (*'ayn al-qalb*). It is through this inner faculty of perception that the theoretical knowledge of God outlined and delimited in theology and other

2. There are certainly legitimate exceptions to every rule, including that of exclusive orthopraxy. As discussed in chapter two, Srí Ramakrishna practiced other religious forms, but did so only after attaining realization through Hinduism and with the permission of his celestial guide Kali. The eminent scholar of comparative religion Huston Smith also entered several different religions, but they came in successive stages and he fully indended to practice each new religion fully in their appropriate contexts. In the regard, one can also cite the early Muslim convert Salmān al-Fārsī, who was born a Zoroastrian, entered Christianity, and eventually made his way to Medina to embrace Islam at the hands of the Prophet.While it is not advisable to haphazardly try out each religion as if they were so many interests or hobbies to be collected, the paths of many in our time are marked by such providential turns and experiences. Be that as it may, from our point of view spiritual progress is best made through eventually dedicating oneself to the Divine through a particular religion, without feeling obliged to dismiss all others as heresies. For more on Ramakrishna's special case, see chapter two of the present volume. See also, Zachary Markwith, "Huston Smith's Encounter with the Islamic Tradition," *Sophia* 16, no. 1 (Winter 2010), pp. 81–93.

forms of transmitted knowledge can be transformed into realized gnosis or *ma'rifah*. It is from this more universal vantage point that classical and contemporary Muslim sages and Sufis have been able to accept the diverse revelations and religions of humanity as so many unique expressions of the doctrine of Unity.

The present volume contains reflections on Divine Unity and religious diversity from the Islamic sapiential tradition, which is rooted in the Quran and *Sunnah* (including the *Ḥadīth*) of the Prophet of Islam, where the Arabic word *ḥikmah* or wisdom is frequently employed to denote both Revelation and intellection or Divine wisdom that is sent down from Heaven and that which springs from within.[3] Sapience or the Latin *sapientia* means wisdom and discernment, and is therefore an appropriate translation for the Arabic word *ḥikmah*. The root of *sapientia* (*sapere*) means to taste, and is thus related to that immediate knowledge of the heart expressed by the Sufi terms *dhawq* or taste and *al-'ilm al-ḥuḍūrī* or presential knowledge. After the formative period of Islam it has been especially the Muslim philosophers and Sufis who have inherited and realized this inner wisdom.[4] In the selections that follow

3. For example, we read in the Quran, "These are the signs of the Wise Book *(al-kitāb al-ḥakīm)*" (31:2); and "He grants wisdom *(ḥikmah)* to whomsoever He will. And whosoever is granted wisdom has been granted much good..." (2:269) It is also important to note that one of the Names of God in the Quran is *al-Ḥakīm* or "the Wise." For example, in a prayer of the prophet Abraham narrated in the Quran we read, "Our Lord, raise up in their midst a messenger from among them, who shall recite Thy signs to them, and will teach them the Book and wisdom (*al-ḥikmah*), and purify them. Truly Thou are the Mighty, the Wise (*al-Hakīm*)." (2:129) God is therefore the Source of all wisdom in the form of Revelation or intellection, which are the macrocosmic or objective and microcosmic or subjective manifestations of the transcendent wisdom of God.

4. The centrality of the Islamic sapiential tradition is highlighted by the frequent usage of the term *ḥikmah* and its derivates in the titles of some of the seminal works of both Islamic philosophy and Sufism, including, for example, Shihāb al-Dīn Suhrawardī's *Ḥikmat al-ishrāq* (*The Theosophy of the Orient of Light*), Muḥyī al-Dīn ibn 'Arabī's *Fuṣūṣ al-ḥikam* (*The Ringstones of Wisdom*), Ibn 'Aṭā' Allāh al-Iskandarī's *Kitāb al-ḥikam* (*The Book of Wisdom*), and Ṣadr al-Dīn Shīrāzī's *al-Ḥikmat al-'arshiyyah* (*The Wisdom of the Throne*). See Seyyed Hossein Nasr, "The Meaning and Role of Philosophy in Islam," *Islamic Philosophy from its Origin to the Present* (Albany, NY: State University of New York Press, 2006), pp. 31–47.

we draw from the sources of the Islamic sapiential tradition, including the Quran, *Ḥadīth*, the sayings of the family and companions of the Prophet Muḥammad, Muslim philosophers such as the Ikhwān al-Ṣafā', Shihāb al-Dīn Suhrawardī and Mullā Ṣadrā and Sufis such as Manṣūr Ḥallāj, Jalāl al-Dīn Rūmī and Muḥyī al-Dīn ibn 'Arabī, as well as contemporary Muslim sages.[5]

The relationship between Islam and other religions is a fascinating and timely subject. Few scholars in the modern era have adequately understood or articulated the universal wisdom of Islam. Today Muslim and non-Muslim authors more often than not reduce Islam to fundamentalist or modernist interpretations and expressions. Due to the legacy of European colonialism, as well as the relative decline of the Islamic sapiential tradition, Islamic fundamentalists are generally all too eager to condemn other religions and the people who practice them and even anathematize Muslims who maintain that believers from other religions can attain salvation. Modernists are sometimes more open to other religions, but they are usually more interested in western secular ideologies and forms of technology than the wisdom of Greek philosophy, the Bible or the Bhagavad Gita. Amidst the cacophony of voices writing about Islam and its relation to other religions there are some notable exceptions to these trends. A few Muslim scholars have written about the Unity of God and the multiplicity of prophets and religions while remaining faithful to traditional Islam, including its inner and outer dimensions. Some of the most notable figures who have articulated this perspective in the contemporary period

5. The designation Islamic sapiential tradition is synonymous with the Islamic intellectual tradition frequently used by Seyyed Hossein Nasr and also the *iḥsānī* intellectual tradition recently employed by Joseph Lumbard. Throughout this book we occasionally refer to the Islamic sapiential tradition as the Islamic intellectual and spiritual tradition to denote the wisdom tradition in Islam that has been transmitted by both Muslim philosophers and Sufis. See, for example, Seyyed Hossein Nasr, "Dimensions of the Islamic Intellectual Tradition: *Kalām*, Philosophy, and Spirituality," *Islamic Philosophy from its Origin to the Present*, pp. 119–163; and Joseph E.B. Lumbard, "The Decline of Knowledge and the Rise of Ideology in the Modern Islamic World," in Joseph E.B. Lumbard, ed., *Islam, Fundamentalism, and the Betrayal of Tradition* (Bloomington, IN: World Wisdom, Inc., 2004), pp. 39–77.

include René Guénon, Frithjof Schuon, Titus Burckhardt, Martin Lings and Seyyed Hossein Nasr, whose connection to Islam and the perennial philosophy or *sophia perennis* is discussed in detail in chapter one.

Several studies on Islam and the principle of universality deserve special mention here. Frithjof Schuon's books on this theme, including *Understanding Islam, Dimensions of Islam, Islam and the Perennial Philosophy, Sufism: Veil and Quintessence,* and *Christianity/Islam: Perspectives on Esoteric Ecumenism,* unveil the metaphysical and esoteric dimensions of Islam, while comparing these dimensions to the inner aspects of other religions. All of Seyyed Hossein Nasr's authoritative writings on various aspects of traditional Islam also shed light on this subject. Especially noteworthy in this context are his *The Heart of Islam*, *Sufi Essays, Islam in the Modern World*, and *Three Muslim Sages*. Sachiko Murata and William Chittick have also written a valuable chapter on religious pluralism entitled "Islam and Other Religions" in their book *The Vision of Islam*. Chittick has examined the metaphysics and cosmology of pluralism in Ibn 'Arabī's vision and corpus in his book *Imaginal Worlds: Ibn al-'Arabī and the Problem of Religious Diversity*, while Murata has surveyed the spiritual and historical connections between Islam and Far Eastern philosophy in several groundbreaking volumes, including *The Tao of Islam* and, in collaboration with Chittick and Tu Weiming, *Chinese Gleams of Sufi Light* and *The Sage Learning of Liu Zhi*. Similarly, Reza Shah-Kazemi's penetrating study on the Quran and its Sufi commentaries *The Other in the Light of the One: The Universality of the Qur'ān and Interfaith Dialogue,* as well as his books *The Spirit of Tolerance in Islam*, *Common Ground Between Islam and Buddhism* and *Paths to Transcendence,* open up many previously unexplored vistas for understanding and dialogue. Other volumes on this subject that merit close attention include Muhammad Suheyl Umar's edited book *The Religious Other: Towards a Muslim Theology of Other Religions in a Post-Prophetic Age*, Michael and Judith Fitzgerald's edited text of quotations from the primary Islamic sources, *The Universal Spirit of Islam: From the Quran and Ḥadīth*, and the recent issue of the journal *Studies in Comparative Religion* entitled *Universal Dimensions of Islam* edited by Patrick Laude. To this list one must add the important academic studies by Mohammad Hassan Khalil, *Islam and the Fate of Others: The Salvation Question* and *Between Heaven and Hell: Islam, Salvation, and the Fate of Others*. Another hopeful and encouraging sign in recent years is "A Common Word" statement and initiative led by H.R.H. Prince Ghazi bin Muhammad of Jordan, which has engaged Muslim and Christian leaders and communities from around the world in dialogue based upon the two great commandments: to love God and to love your neighbor as yourself.[6]

6. "A Common Word" began with an open letter to Pope Benedict XVI signed by thirty-eight Muslim scholars and intellectuals in response to the Pope's 2006 Regensburg address where he quoted the Byzantine emperor Manuel II Paleologus as saying, "Show me just what Muhammad brought that was new, and there you will find things only evil and inhuman, such as his command to spread by the sword the faith he preached." The Muslim letter is conciliatory and instructive, reminding us of the goodness and peace at the heart of Islam and Christianity. This initial letter was followed by the statement "A Common Word Between Us and You," which was signed by 138 Muslim scholars and intellectuals. The statement is summarized as follows: "Thus in obedience to the Holy Qur'an, we as Muslims invite Christians to come together with us on the basis of what is common to us, which is also what is most essential to our faith and practice: the Two Commandments of love." Basing this statement on references to the love of God and love of one's neighbor in the Quran and *Ḥadīth*, the author also cites the words of Jesus in the New Testament: "'Hear, O Israel, the Lord our God, the Lord is One. And you shall love the Lord your God with all your heart, with all your soul, with all your mind, and with all your strength.' This is the first commandment. And the second, like it, is this: 'You shall love your neighbor as yourself.' There is no other commandment greater than these." (Mark 12:29–31) "A Common Word" was followed by an outpouring of support from many Christian and Muslim leaders around the world, as well as serious interfaith gatherings held at the Vatican, Yale, Georgetown, and other locations. Theological, spiritual, and socio-political questions were raised at these meetings and given erudite and often inspired responses from leading representatives of these two great faiths. Especially noteworthy are the talks and statements made by Pope Benedict, Rowan Williams, James Cutsinger, Seyyed Hossein Nasr, Habib Ali al-Jifri, and Prince Ghazi himself. These efforts helped to foster greater mutual understanding, an acceptance of differences, and a realization for many that Muslims and Christians worship the same loving God and are called to love one another. See Miroslav Volf, Ghazi bin Muhammad, and Melissa Yarrington, eds., *A Common Word: Muslims and Christians on Loving God and Neighbor* (Grand Rapids: Wm. B. Eerdmans Publishing Co., 2010); Waleed El-Ansary and David K. Linnan, eds., *Muslim and Christian Understanding: Theory and Application of "A Common Word"* (New York: Palgrave Macmillan, 2010); "Pope

We are acutely aware that certain Islamic and western scholars question some of the findings in the above works.[7] Many a devout Muslim is wary of any effort that would compare Islam to other religions except to prove Islam's or rather Muslims' absolute superiority and monopoly of the Truth.Those who share this perspective are dismissive of those who even consider the possibility of non-Muslims attaining salvation through their religion (although some "pardon" those who have never encountered Islam, which begs the question of what an authentic encounter with Islam entails in this

---

Benedict XVI's Remarks at Regensburg and Muslim and Orthodox Responses," *Sophia* 12, no. 2, (Fall/Winter 2006), pp. 5–27; and *Sophia* 14, no. 2 (Winter 2008–9).

7. See for example, Mark Sedgwick, *Against the Modern World* (Oxford: Oxford University Press, 2004); and Muhammad Legenhausen, "Why I am Not a Traditionalist," *Religioscope* (2002), <www.religioscope.com/pdf/esotrad/legenhausen.pdf>. As responses to these selections see the review articles, Michael Fitzgerald, "Against Tradition," *Sacred Web* 13 (July 2004), pp. 137–152; Wilson Eliot Poindexter, "*Against the Modern World*—A Review Essay," *Sophia* 11, no. 1 (Summer 2005), pp. 156–173; and Charles Upton, "What is a 'Traditionalist'?—Some Clarifications," *Sacred Web* 17 (June 2006), pp. 49–99. William Chittick also writes, "It is true that many Muslims believe that the universality of guidance pertains only to pre-Quranic times, but others disagree; there is no 'orthodox' interpretation here that Muslims must accept." *Imaginal Worlds: Ibn al-'Arabī and the Problem of Religious Diversity* (Albany, NY: State University of New York Press, 1994), p. 124. In response to this statement Nuh Ha Mim Keller quotes Imam al-Nawawī as saying, "Someone who does not believe that whoever follows another religion besides Islam is an unbeliever (like Christians), or doubts that such a person is an unbeliever, or considers their sect to be valid, is himself an unbeliever (*kāfir*) even if he manifests Islam and believes in it." Keller goes on to write, "Orthodoxy exists, it is unanimously agreed upon by the scholars of Muslims, and we have conveyed in Nawawī's words above that to believe anything else is unbelief. As for '*others disagree*,' it is true, but is something that has waited for fourteen centuries of Islamic scholarship down to the present century to be first promulgated in Cairo in the 1930s by the French convert to Islam René Guénon, and later by his student Frithjof Schuon and writers under him. Who else said it before? And if no one did, and everyone else considers it *kufr*, on what basis should it be accepted?" Nuh Ha Mim Keller, "A Letter to 'Abd al-Matin: On the Universal Validity of Religions in the thought of Ibn 'Arabī and Emīr 'Abd al-Qādir" (1996), <www.masud.co.uk/ISLAM/nuh/amat.com>. Chapter one of the present volume is in one sense a reply to the question "Who else said it before?," while also responding to a trend among some perennialists who fail to see in Islam and Sufism a primary source of inspiration in the spiritual lives of the five key contemporary Muslim figures surveyed below. It is true that Ibn 'Arabī did not write about this subject in the same way that Frithjof Schuon did, for example, but

day and age?) because this apparently relativizes Islam, its rites and theology as one road to salvation among others. Their perspective is a valid one, but it is not the only one in Islamic history despite attempts to construct a perceived consensus through isolated and sparse selections from a few classical Islamic scholars—none of which carry the weight of the Quran and *Ḥadīth* which themselves are more nuanced about this issue.[8] Our first two chapters in fact

neither did Ibn ʿArabī say exactly the same thing that Suhrawardī or Ḥallāj did on other religions. The writings of Schuon also slightly differ from those of René Guénon or Seyyed Hossein Nasr, for example, in certain places. There are subtle and sometimes not so subtle differences between premodern and modern expositors of pluralism in Islam, but differences in emphasis and even content do not prove the veracity or falsity of the teachings in question. A teaching should be accepted because it is true regardless of who may or may not have said it before in exactly the same way. Moreover, we would argue that the contemporary period necessitates a fuller disclosure of certain esoteric doctrines that were often only alluded to by earlier sages because our faith in God is often challenged when we realize that our particular religious teachings have only been received by a minority of humanity. People of other faiths must still live according to their own religions, however intact they may be, as ways of surrendering to the Will of God that have been revealed and transmitted to them. Even if some wish Islam, Christianity, or Buddhism to be the one universal religion for all of humanity, this is not the case. As such, all people must have access to ethical guidelines and religious rites with a view towards temporal and posthumous justice and accountability. God is also merciful and we maintain that religious diversity and universal salvation for believers of all religions is among the signs of His mercy. Finally, we would argue that the traditionalists have not condradicted the Quran and *Sunnah*, only a limited interpretation and application of these sources. Both the inclusive and exclusive perspectives can still be accepted as valid so long as they do not claim to exhaust the meaning and form of the sources in question.

8. One can find in the traditional sources Sunni scholars who condemned all Shīʿites and Shīʿite scholars who condemned all Sunnis, and even Shāfiʿīs and Ḥanafīs, for example, who cast anathema on one another—all with apparent evidence from the primary Islamic sources. This, however, does not make their rulings on other Muslims or non-Muslims infallible. Important studies on some of the nuanced views of traditional Muslim scholars include Reza Shah-Kazemi, *The Other in the Light of the One: The Universality of the Qur'ān and Interfaith Dialogue* (Cambridge: The Islamic Texts Society, 2006); Mohammad Hassan Khalil, *Islam and the Fate of Others: The Salvation Question* (Oxford: Oxford University Press, 2012); and Asma Afsaruddin, "The Hermeneutics of Interfaith Relations: Retrieving Moderation and Pluralism as Universal Principles in Qur'anic Exegeses," *Journal of Religious Ethics*, vol. 37, issue 2 (June 2009), pp. 331–354.

look at the primary Islamic sources and the writings of Muslim philosophers and Sufis, which offer a wide range of views on this issue, from Muslims who accepted other forms of traditional wisdom for themselves to a full-fledged universalism that accepts pre-Islamic revealed religions as authentic ways to Heaven and the realization of God here on earth. Be that as it may, a Muslim has the right to consider other religions as partial truths or error pure and simple, just as a Christian or Buddhist does. As long as he respects the right of non-Muslims to practice their religion in peace and security—a right enshrined in Islamic Law—then he can believe what he wants, for "...Unto God shall be your return, all together, and He will inform you of that wherein you differed." (5:48) It is our hope that the present volume will allow the Muslim reader to enter into conversation with the Islamic intellectual and spiritual tradition regarding many of these questions—a tradition that has received too little attention compared to the necessary legal and theological schools that delineate the boundaries of Islam, but not those of other religions. If we disagree on some points, perhaps we will find a few that we agree upon. It is my sincere belief that the Prophet's *ummah* embraces us both and that Islam contains exclusive and inclusive perspectives that are simultaneously valid.

Concerning the dismissive attitude held by many western academics to the perspective outlined in this book and also described in detail in the aforementioned volumes, most do not take religion seriously as a phenomenon having its origin in Divine revelation let alone any "subjective" truth claim which is seen as a utilitarian push for social or political influence and power. The scholars in question often play the role of the "objective" unbiased observer, which for all intents and purposes means that they are not intellectually or emotionally invested in the religions they study and therefore see the religions more clearly than those who follow them. A contemporary scholar of Islamic studies can no longer say "We know them better than they know themselves," but this hubris is as pervasive among postmodernists as it was and is among classical orientalists, despite certain cosmetic changes which amount to rejecting Judaism and Christianity along with Islam and other religions from the East. When we turn to the universal dimensions of Islam and religious pluralism in general, postmodernist academics are also wary of any grand narrative that would seek to explain all religions and philosophies, except that of their own grand narrative. We are told to believe that there are no absolute truths, except the absolute "truth" that there are no absolute truths. An attention to detail and the differences of cultures and religions is necessary, but it does not preclude the possibility of a transcendent unity that allows for and in fact demands differences on the formal level. Because the modern scholar cannot access the transcendent through historicism, literary criticism, deconstructionism and other methods at his disposal, we are made to believe that the religions and their followers are reducible to competing political ideologies and factions with a mythological (understood in the negative sense of the word) façade constructed to attract more followers, and therefore wealth, women and power. Rūmī and Ramakrishna are subjected to posthumous Freudian analysis and psychotherapy by observers who know their subjects through the distorted lens of their own secular worldview, despite the violence that this does to their memory and the Muslims and Hindus who venerate them. They cannot entertain the possibility that these sages actually penetrated beyond the veils of cosmic existence to higher levels of being and consciousness because they have projected upon them the limitations that they have imposed upon themselves. It is perhaps even more futile here to try to convince a modern academic of the veracity of religion and especially multiple religions simultaneously, but we can simply request that he suspends his judgment of traditional cultures, including their religions, scriptures, art and mystics, that have provided modes of existence that have proved far more sustainable and meaningful than those secular paradigms responsible for widespread nihilism, the loss of ethics, and the environmental crisis. A measure of humility might also allow the modern scholar to accept the fact that the religious believer is able to penetrate into the depths of his own religion in ways that personal experience and devotion alone afford.

Although it is challenging to step outside of our own perspective and recognize our own biases, we have studied inside and outside of academia with both Muslim and non-Muslim scholars and attempt to recognize the merits and limitations of both. It is impossible for us to do justice to all points of view concerning the various themes addressed in this volume, but there is a cross-section of sources employed, from Muslims to Hindus, Sunnis to Shīʿites, and classical Sufis to sympathetic Catholic orientalists. We naturally favor those that shed some light on the questions we pose and pass over in silence those who maintain that only their school of thought—whether religious or secular—is of any value. We in fact respect the views of the Jew, Christian or Muslim, for example, who thinks that only his religion is true because for a religion to be efficacious its adherents must attach themselves to it and take its claims seriously, but maintain that men and women of faith can simultaneously practice their religion alone, while also accepting that other religions lead to the same God manifested or revealed differently to other communities.

Our prevailing thesis throughout this book—the Unity of God and the multiplicity of prophets and religions—is especially pronounced in the first two chapters, and prolonged in those later selections that examine the presence and influence of pre-Islamic wisdom and prophets in the very fabric of the Islamic tradition. We maintain that the themes and principles discussed in the various chapters, including Divine Unity, religious pluralism, love of the divine feminine, the metaphysics of the Self, Christic, Eliatic and Hermetic wisdom, and a sacred cosmology of nature are among the most accessible openings to the Islamic tradition for western audiences. We believe that the Islamic tradition as a whole can be better understood through reflecting upon its intellectual and spiritual dimensions alongside those of other wisdom traditions that are better known in the West. These selections may also introduce a few Muslims to some of the hidden treasures housed in their own tradition. It is our hope that this book will provide a few keys for both Muslims and non-Muslims to appreciate the underlying unity that embraces religious, cultural and cosmic diversity. It is a humble effort to present the universal and tolerant spirit of Islam which has received too little attention, one that can help us to not only tolerate our differences, but to accept them as necessary expressions of the Divine Will and Nature, which is Infinite, Merciful and Just. As such, God cannot disclose the fullness of His Truth and Light to one community alone and leave the vast majority of humanity in abject error and darkness. The diverse revealed religions reflect diverse aspects of God, all of which lead to salvation, sanctification and knowledge of the One that transcends and at the same time embraces the many. This book may also serve as a corrective to the distorted image of Islam in the West which fails to accurately convey the universal spirit of the religion that has inspired and shaped the lives of the vast majority of Muslims from the seventh century to the present.

It must be stressed at the outset that while the first two chapters are about the Islamic understanding of other religions, the later selections are not primarily about Advaita Vedānta, Christianity, Judaism or Hermeticism, but rather a special kind of non-dual, Christic, Eliatic and Hermetic wisdom that is found in the very nature and form of the Quran and *Sunnah* of the Prophet of Islam.[9] While classical Islamic philosophers and Sufis occasionally integrated foreign terms and symbols, their fundamental characteristics, impetus and goal were determined by the doctrine of *tawḥīd*,

9. The study of Hermetic texts, cosmology, symbolism, astrology and alchemy by Muslim scholars is a special case that we describe in more detail in chapter six. Suffice it to say, the metaphysics and theology of those Muslims who studied Hermeticism derived primarily from the Quran and *Ḥadīth*, while finding parallels in the primary Islamic sources and the books of nature and the soul for the teachings attributed to Hermes, who they considered to be the prophet Idrīs and therefore also the recipient of Divine revelation. Muslims were able to integrate and Islamicize the cosmological and mathematical sciences, certain forms of art and medicine, and the philosophical language of other traditional civilizations without taking from their theologies or pantheons, except in as much as these could be seen as expressions of *tawḥīd* and *nubuwwah*. For example, for Muslims Jesus is not the second hypostasis of the Trinity and Hermes or Mercury is not a Greek or Roman god, but prophets of the One God. As such, the wisdom and sanctity that illuminated these Muslim sages derived first and foremost from the Quran and soul of the Prophet of Islam, without denying the vestiges of wisdom that pre-Islamic prophets left or their living presence in the Islamic spiritual universe. While Muslims claimed these figures and their wisdom as their own, they also recognized the protected status of Jews, Christians, Sabians, Zoroastrians, Hindus, and Buddhists, and therefore acknowledged at least the partial veracity and efficacy of pre-Islamic revealed religions in forms that differed, sometimes radically, from those of Islam.

the Quran and *Sunnah*, which synthesize all pre-Islamic wisdom in a particular revealed form. The unmistakable similarities that we highlight between Advaita Vedānta and the doctrine of *tawḥīd* or Jesus and Ḥallāj, for example, are due to the universal nature of metaphysics and the prophetic structure of the Islamic tradition, and not primarily to Muslim contact with Hindus or Christians. While we draw attention to and celebrate those eminent Muslim sages who studied and appreciated other religions and schools of philosophy, their intellectual and spiritual lives were rooted in the Islamic tradition.[10]

Most of the essays that appear in this book were written under the direction of Prof. Seyyed Hossein Nasr while I was a graduate student at the George Washington University. I am especially grateful to Nasr, whose lectures, books, and guidance inspired and enabled me to approach the ideas dealt with in this volume, although I remain entirely responsible for any mistakes. I am obliged to also acknowledge that, in addition to theses and copious citations, I also took the book's title from Nasr's opening chapter in *The Heart of Islam.*[11]Special thanks are due to Prof. Huston Smith for lending his name and generous endorsement to this volume. I should note I am the least among the students of Nasr and others that Smith mentioned in his foreword. A brief perusal of the names and sources cited in chapter one demonstrates that this is not false humility, but a boast to count myself among them. It is my pleasure to thank Farah Michelle Kimball for introducing me to the key

10. There is a tendency in the West to either completely deny the intellectually open and tolerant spirit of Islam and Muslims throughout history or to suggest that all wisdom, love and sanctity among Muslim philosophers and Sufis resulted from foreign sources, such as Greek philosophy, Christianity, Zoroastrianism or Hinduism. The absurdity of these two prejudices becomes even more apparent when they are juxtaposed. Rarely have the positive qualities of Islam and Muslims, including an openness to revealed wisdom from the East and the West, been attributed to the Quranic revelation and the Prophet Muḥammad—the primary sources of Islam that have determined the unfolding of Islamic philosophy and spirituality from the seventh century to the present.

11. Seyyed Hossein Nasr, "One God, Many Prophets: The Unity of Truth and the Multiplicity of Revelations," *The Heart of Islam* (San Francisco: HarperCollins Publishers, 2002), pp. 1–54.

principles and figures discussed in this book, editing its content, and for her counsel and friendship over the years. I also wish to express my appreciation to my other teachers who have supported my studies and research inside and outside of academia, including Prof. Mohammad Faghfoory, Prof. Ibrahim Farajajé, Prof. Sister Marianne Farina, Prof. G. Reginald Daniel, Imam Bilal Hyde, Dan Kimball, and especially the late Shaykh Abdoulaye Dieye.

A debt of gratitude is owed to my chief editors Adam Vogtman and Desmond Meraz for lending their extensive knowledge, attention to detail, and encouragement to the text and author. I also wish to thank my friends and colleagues for their assistance on this project, including Nigel Jackson, Dr. Hasan Awan, Kareem Monib, Aasim Hasany, Benjamin Merson, Ryan Sawyer, Saleem Andrew McGroarty, Richard North, Dr. Reza Shah-Kazemi, Dr. Leonard Lewisohn, Dr. Tom Cheetham, and Dr. Pir Zia Inayat-Khan. I am also grateful for the help I received from two friends who will remain anonymous. I appreciate the support from Katherine O'Brien at *Sophia*, M. Ali Lakhani at *Sacred Web*, Dr. Gholām Rezā A'vānī, Dr. Shahīn A'vānī and Nicholas Boylston at *Jāvīdān Khirad*, and Farasha Euker at *Luvah* for initially publishing some of the chapters that appear in this volume and for their permission to reproduce them here. I am particularly grateful to James Wetmore and Charles Upton at *Sophia Perennis* for having the courage and kindness to publish this work. James also deserves my thanks and recognition for typesetting the entire text and his meticulous work with all of the transliterated terms. Special mention and thanks are also due to my parents, Lincoln and Patricia Markwith. Finally, I would like to express my gratitude and affection to my wife Sarah Hernandez for her love and support, including her frequent editorial advice, without which this book would not have been possible.

wa'l-ḥamdu li'Llāhi waḥdahu
ZACHARY MARKWITH

1

Muslim Sages and the Perennial Philosophy

> The Messenger believes in what was sent down to him from his Lord, as do the believers. Each believes in God, His angels, His Books, and His messengers. "We make no distinction between any of His messengers." And they say, "We hear and obey. Thy forgiveness, our Lord! And unto Thee is the journey's end."
>
> (Quran 2:285)

> Earnest for truth, I thought on the religions:
> They are, I found, one root with many a branch.
> Therefore impose on no man a religion,
> Lest it should bar him from the firm-set root.
> Let the root claim him, a root wherein all heights
> And meanings are made clear, for him to grasp.[1]
>
> Manṣūr Ḥallāj

The inner ecumenical spirit of Islam, which sees in Islam and other revealed religions the same perennial wisdom in diverse forms, is often marginalized or entirely denied by modern Muslims and non-Muslims who neglect this vital aspect of the Quran and the *Sunnah*, as well as the intellectual and spiritual legacy of Muslim philosophers and Sufis. However, a prominent circle of contemporary Muslim sages, as a result of their attachment to the doctrine of Divine Unity (*tawḥīd*), the Quran, *Sunnah* of the Prophet Muḥammad, and the doctrines and methods of Sufism, as well as an attentive and penetrating study of other religions, were largely responsible for restating the perennial philosophy in the twentieth

1. Martin Lings, *Sufi Poems: A Mediaeval Anthology* (Cambridge: UK: The Islamic Texts Society, 2004), p. 34.

century. It is not an accident that the majority of those responsible for affirming the Unity of God and the multiplicity of religions in the modern era, including René Guénon, Frithjof Schuon, Titus Burckhardt, Martin Lings and Seyyed Hossein Nasr, approached the Divine Reality through the doctrines and rites of Islam.[2] The Quran insists that there is One God who sent a chain of messengers and prophets to humanity with the same essential message. This is in fact also the basis of the *sophia perennis* or perennial philosophy, *sophia* meaning Divine wisdom and *perennis* or perennial relating to the multiplicity of prophets, revealed books, sages and saints, who manifest and transmit this wisdom in different historical and cultural contexts.

At the heart of the perennial philosophy is metaphysics or gnosis, which is the direct knowledge of God and the means of accessing that knowledge. It is from this vantage point that the prophets, avatars, sages and saints have spoken about the essential unity of religions. For the religions only truly meet in the Divine Principle and not on the formal or exoteric level where we sometimes find considerable differences. Below we will look at the origin of the term the "perennial philosophy" or *philosophia perennis* in the West from men such as Agostino Steuco and Gottfried von Leibnitz, who understood and appreciated the perennial wisdom in the various religions that they encountered. We will also examine equivalents to this term in Islamic languages, such as *al-ḥikmat al-khālidah* in Arabic and *jāvīdān khirad* in Persian.

Islam, like the perennial philosophy, is governed and shaped by the principle of Divine Unity (*tawḥīd*). God, as the Absolute and Infinite Reality, is One (*al-Wāḥid*). In Islam, man, religion,

2. While most scholars have overlooked this phenomenon, a few serious studies can be cited, including Seyyed Hossein Nasr, *Islam in the Modern World: Challenged by the West, Threatened by Fundamentalism, Keeping Faith with Tradition* (New York: HarperCollins Publishers, 2010), pp. 361–402; Marcia Hermansen, "The Academic Study of Sufism at American Universities," *The American Journal of Islamic Social Sciences* 24, no. 3 (2007), pp. 24–45; and Carl Ernst, "Traditionalism, the Perennial Philosophy, and Islamic Studies," *Middle East Studies Association Bulletin* 28, no. 2 (December 1994), pp. 176–181.

philosophy, art, nature, and the whole of the cosmos all reflect the principle of Divine Unity through their various forms. Each messenger and prophet came to revive the doctrine of Divine Unity. Within the Quran itself, as well as the *Sunnah* or Wont of the Prophet Muḥammad, one finds some of the most universal expressions of the *religio perennis* or perennial religion. Indeed, the Prophet Muḥammad simply revived the primordial religion (*al-dīn al-ḥanīf*) of Adam and Abraham. More than anything else, we maintain that it was direct knowledge of the doctrine of Divine Unity and the diversity of the divinely sent messengers and prophets which inspired the writings of Guénon, Schuon, Burckhardt, Lings, and Nasr. This is true of not only their works that speak directly about Islam, but also of those that appreciate the Divine Truth and Presence in other religions, and also point to what Schuon referred to as "the transcendent unity of religions," a unity which only truly exists in God and not on the human and cosmic levels which demand diversity. For without religious diversity and distinctness here below, there would be no Islam, Christianity or Buddhism, for example, but only an inefficacious, manmade amalgam consisting of certain features from each religion. The transcendent unity that we have in mind is expressed here below as the diversity and harmony of religions.

While the esoteric knowledge that these contemporary sages articulated is rare and virtually unknown and forgotten in the modern West, the aforementioned sages were not the first Muslims to appreciate sacred knowledge in other religions and civilizations. There is vast precedent for the study of the perennial philosophy among classical Muslim philosophers and Sufis who saw wisdom and expressions of Divine Unity in the Greek philosophical heritage, Zoroastrianism, Hinduism, Buddhism, the Chinese tradition, Judaism and Christianity. When one recalls the principle of universality in Islam, one is immediately reminded of Avicenna and the Muslim peripatetics, Shihāb al-Dīn Suhrawardī and the *Ishrāqī* school, Muḥyī al-Dīn ibn 'Arabī and the *Akbarī* school—which all found a synthesis in the writings and perspective of Mullā Ṣadrā. Likewise, the poetry and prose of the Sufis, which culminated in Persian Sufi poetry and the writings of Farīd al-Dīn 'Aṭṭār, Jalāl al-

Dīn Rūmī, Maḥmūd Shabistarī, Ḥāfiẓ Shīrāzī, and others clearly emphasizes the transcendent unity of religions. Also relevant is the tradition of *futuwwah* or spiritual chivalry and the metaphysical and ethical teachings and examples of Muslims warriors, from Imam 'Alī ibn Abī Ṭālib to the Amīr 'Abd al-Qādir al-Jazā'irī. All of these streams in the Islamic intellectual and spiritual tradition prove that Muslims took other philosophical and religious traditions seriously before the modern era.[3]

After establishing the imperative link between classical Islam and the perennial philosophy, we also examine the lives, writings, and intellectual contributions of Guénon, Schuon, Burckhardt, Lings, and Nasr. Not only did they help more than any other group of scholars to bring the teachings of the Islamic intellectual and spiritual tradition and the perennial philosophy to the attention of the West, but perhaps more importantly they benefited from the initiation, doctrine, and methods of Islam and Sufism. These Muslim sages were not simply concerned with theoretical metaphysics alone, but gained—through the inner reality of the Quran and soul of the Prophet—a Way to Divine Wisdom—the eternal Sophia contained at the center of the Intellect, which transcends and is at the same time the source of our rational faculty. Therefore, it must be stated that their immense contributions to the fields of the perennial philosophy, which includes metaphysics, cosmology, symbolism, art, science, comparative religion, as well as a critique of modernity, scientism, and secularism and their consequences, was

3. More recent trends towards exclusivism relate to the legacy of European colonialism in the Muslim world, which forced many Muslims into more insular and extreme politicized positions or led to an indiscriminate acceptance of modern western philosophy, science and technology, as well as various political and social models. These two general reactions—that is fundamentalism and modernism—have formed various amalgams that freely reduce Islam to its most outward dimensions alone and fill the intellectual lacuna in Muslim societies and minds with modern theories that have almost nothing in common with traditional Islam or other revealed religions.This has led to a general spiritual decline among those fundamentalist or modernist Muslims that feel obliged to dismiss or marginalize Islam's intellectual and esoteric dimensions wherein one finds greater links to other religions, in favor of their various utilitarian and utopian goals.

made possible because of their attachment to the exoteric and esoteric dimensions of the Islamic tradition. While all of these men wrote about other traditions and knew that all orthodox religions lead to salvation and the Truth,[4] they believed in and practiced the religion of Islam, which enabled them to know the transcendent Unity of Being (*waḥdat al-wujūd*), as well as the transcendent unity of religions (*waḥdat al-adyān*).[5]

The contributions of these sages demonstrate the providential link between Islam and the perennial philosophy in the twentieth century, while defending the role that orthodoxy and orthopraxy play in any authentic expression of the perennial philosophy, with a particular emphasis on Islamic doctrines and rites. For one cannot realize the One who transcends forms except by adhering to a form that the One has revealed. Most of the leading perennialists or traditionalists in the twentieth century came to know God through the Islamic tradition and as a result their message was universal and helped to revive an authentic appreciation and understanding of other religions, which are also paths that lead to salvation and sanctification for different individuals and communities.

The Perennial Philosophy

The essence of the perennial philosophy is metaphysics, which is direct knowledge of God and the means of realizing that knowledge. Every religion begins with a descent of the Logos from Heaven, a descent which allows man to ascend vertically from the relative to the Absolute and have a direct taste of principial knowledge.[6] For example, the Logos or Word of God in Christianity is

4. The fact that all religions originally provided access to salvation and sanctification does not mean that all religions are equally accessible or intact, especially their esoteric and contemplative dimensions.

5. These two doctrines, along with the Universal Man (*al-insān al-kāmil*) are perhaps the most important esoteric commentaries on the Quran and *Sunnah* in the Islamic intellectual tradition.

6. The ascent in question is analogous to discerning between the relative and the Absolute through the faculty of the Intellect or the eye of the heart. It is Revelation that catalyzes this ascent or discernment, which are two ways of describing the same transfiguration.

Jesus and in Islam the Quran, which provide paths to salvation and sanctification or an encounter with the Absolute in the hereafter and the present.[7] The primary concern for any person who approaches the perennial philosophy is the vertical axis of a particular religion or that which enables men and women to return to their Source. Yet when a sage encounters the multiplicity of religious forms and senses the Sacred in these forms—which he has first discovered through his own tradition—he cannot ignore that at the heart of all religions is a universal and perennial Truth. While many scholars mistakenly attribute this unity to historical borrowing, each revealed religion is in fact a unique and direct manifestation of Divine wisdom or *sophia*. Therefore, sages who recognize and articulate the perennial philosophy are concerned with knowing the absolute Truth through a particular religion, and the perennial manifestations of the Truth in various religions.

While it was commonly believed that Gottfried von Leibnitz was the first to use the term *philosophia perennis* or "the perennial philosophy" in 1714, according to Seyyed Hossein Nasr, "the term was probably employed for the first time by Agostino Steuco (1497–1548), a Renaissance philosopher, theologian, and Augustinian."[8] Nasr also states,

> The work of Steuco *De perenni philosophia* was influenced by Ficino, Pico, and even Nicholas of Cusa, especially the *De pace fidei* which speaks of harmony between various religions. Steuco, who knew Arabic and other Semitic languages and was a librarian of the Vatican Library where he had access to the "wisdom of the ages" as far as this was possible in the Occident at that time, followed the ideas of these earlier figures concerning the presence

7. Sanctification is expressed in Christian terms by St. Irenaeus as, "God became man in order that man might become God," and in Islam through the descent of the Quran on the Night of Power (*laylat al-qadr*) and the ascent (*mi'rāj*) of the Prophet Muḥammad through the heavens to the Divine Presence or as the Quran states, "two bows' length or nearer." (53:9) The two bows' length symbolizes the arc of descent and the arc of ascent. "Truly we are God's, and unto Him we return." (Quran 2:156)

8. Seyyed Hossein Nasr, *Knowledge and the Sacred* (Albany, NY: State University of New York Press, 1989), p. 69.

of an ancient wisdom which had existed from the dawn of history.[9]

Steuco and the earlier perennialists in the West believed this wisdom extended beyond Christianity and was also present in the ancient Egyptian tradition, the Greek philosophical heritage, Zoroastrianism, Judaism, and Islam.[10] While the perennial philosophy has been articulated in important religious and philosophical texts, its appearance does not always come in the same form. The greatest masterpieces of traditional art and architecture are clear signs of a living intellectual tradition, even if religious or philosophical manuscripts are absent. In addition, many esoteric traditions continue to be transmitted orally, including the practical dimensions of Islamic spirituality or Sufism. The perennial philosophy has existed as long as man has. While the great works of traditional prose and poetry, and especially sacred art and architecture, aid in our return to the Source, not all of these arose in every tradition. For example, wisdom in the heart of a Native American shaman is not dependent upon its written articulation, and in many cases nature or the cosmic revelation serves as a support for intellection.

In addition to an awareness of the *philosophia perennis* in the premodern West, there are direct equivalents to the term the perennial philosophy in other religions, such as *sanatāna dharma* in Hindu-

9. Ibid., p. 70. Nicholas of Cusa wrote in his *De pace fidei*: "There is therefore one sole religion and one sole worship for all beings endowed with understanding, and this is presupposed through a variety of rites. To different countries Thou hast sent different prophets and different masters, the ones at one time, the others at another time. But it is a law of our condition as men of this earth that a long habit becomes for us second nature, that it is taken for a truth and defended as such. It is from this that great dissensions arise, when each community opposes its own faith to other faiths. And if it should be that it is impossible to remove this difference as to rites, and that this difference should even seem desirable in order to increase devotion (each religion attaching itself with more devotion to its ceremonies as if they had the more to please Thy Majesty), nevertheless . . . as Thou art unique, there is but one religion and one worship." Similarly, Marsilio Ficino states, "Among all peoples, in all times, God is worshiped because it is natural to do so, though not with the same rites and methods." Mateus Soares de Azevedo, ed., *Ye Shall Know the Truth: Christianity and the Perennial Philosophy* (Bloomington, IN: World Wisdom, 2005), pp. 211–212.

10. *Knowledge and the Sacred*, p. 70.

ism and *al-ḥikmat al-khālidah* and *jāvīdān khirad* in Islam, which pre-date its use in the West and may have also influenced its formal construction.[11] It was not until the twentieth century, however, that the meaning of the perennial philosophy was expounded with such clarity and depth by the traditionalists or perennialists, including René Guénon, Ananda K. Coomaraswamy, and Frithjof Schuon. According to Schuon:

> "*Philosophia perennis*" is generally understood as referring to that metaphysical truth which has no beginning, and which remains the same in all expressions of wisdom. Perhaps it would here be better or more prudent to speak of a "*Sophia perennis*", since it is not a question of artificial mental constructions, as is all too often the case in philosophy; or again, the primordial wisdom that always remains true to itself could be called "*Religio perennis*", given that by its nature it in a sense involves worship and spiritual realization. . . .[12]

When referring to the perennial philosophy Schuon and other traditionalists use several terms interchangeably. While these terms possess different shades of meaning, they all refer to the essential wisdom that lies at the heart of all authentic expressions of the Truth, whether religious or philosophical. One must keep in mind that the original meaning of the latter term is "the love of wisdom," which modern and postmodern philosophy has forgotten. In any case, Schuon preferred the terms *sophia perennis* or "perennial wisdom" and *religio perennis* or "perennial religion," by which he specifically meant: "discernment between the Real and the illusory, and a unifying and permanent concentration on the Real," as well as, "intrinsic orthodoxy for every religion and all spirituality."[13] His

11. Ibid., p. 68.

12. Seyyed Hossein Nasr, ed., *The Essential Frithjof Schuon* (Bloomington, IN: World Wisdom, 2005), p. 534.

13. Frithjof Schuon, "*Religio Perennis*," *Light on the Ancient Worlds*, trans. Lord Northbourne (Lahore: Suhail Academy, 2004), pp. 137; and "*Sophia Perennis*," *The Essential Frithjof Schuon*, pp. 534–539. All revealed religions are based on the principle of Unity (*al-tawḥīd*) or the One Reality and provide diverse methods of discernment, prayer and contemplation meant to orient men and women towards the Real. The metaphysical discernment at the heart of religion can be envisaged differently as the distinction between illusion and Reality, the relative and the Absolute, the world and

magnum opus and perhaps the greatest work written on the perennial philosophy in the contemporary era is *The Transcendent Unity of Religions.*[14] A.K. Coomaraswamy employed the term *philosophia perennis et universalis* or "the perennial and universal philosophy," and also penned the seminal essay "Paths That Lead to the Same Summit."[15] Guénon used the term "Tradition" throughout his writings because of the negative connotations of the word religion in the France of his time.[16] Moreover, for Guénon the word and reality of Tradition embraces not only religion as it is generally understood in the modern West, but in addition metaphysical principles, symbolism, initiatic doctrines and rites, written and oral transmitted knowledge, social institutions and all the various features of premodern civilizations.[17]

God, the ego and the Self, suffering and Deliverance, forgetfulness and remembrance or ignorance and knowledge, but the transcendent Principle that is the goal of this discernment is One. In Islamic terms this discernment is succintcly expressed by the first *shahādah* or testimonty of faith, *Lā ilāha illa'Llāh* (lit. "There is no god but God"), which distinguishes the illusory aspects of the world and the soul from Ultimate Reality and whose affirmation and repetition constitutes the essential method of discernment and contemplation in Islam. Moreover, just as God is envisaged in a unique manner in each religion, the revealed modes of worship and methods of concentration in the world's religions are also diverse, yet they each lead to knowledge of the One and intimacy with the Beloved or Union. The unitary perspective of Islam and the perennial philosophy demands an appreciation of divinely willed diversity. We read in the Quran, "And We sent no messenger before thee [Muhammad], save that We revealed unto him, 'Verily, there is no god but I, so worship Me.'" (Quran 21:25)

14. Frithjof Schuon, *The Transcendent Unity of Religions* (Wheaton: IL: Quest Books, 2005).

15. Ananda K. Coomaraswamy, *The Bugbear of Literacy* (Bedfont, Middlesex: Perennial Books Ltd., 1979), pp. 50–79.

16. René Guénon, "What is Meant by Tradition?," *Introduction to the Study of the Hindu Doctrines* trans. Marco Pallis (Hillsdale, NY: Sophia Perennis, 2004), pp. 54–57; and Seyyed Hossein Nasr, "What is Tradition?," *Knowledge and the Sacred*, pp. 65–92.

17. Nasr writes, "Tradition . . . means truths or principles of a divine origin revealed or unveiled to mankind and, in fact, a whole cosmic sector through various figures envisaged as messengers, prophets, *avatāras*, the Logos or other transmitting agencies, along with all the ramifications and applications of these principles in different realms including law and social structure, art, symbolism, the sciences, and embracing of course Supreme Knowledge along with the means for its attainment." *Knowledge and the Sacred*, pp. 67–68.

The perennial philosophy also finds expression in the term and reality "the Primordial Tradition." S.H. Nasr writes,

> In one sense, *sanatāna dharma* or *sophia perennis* is related to the Primordial Tradition and therefore to the Origin of human existence. But this view should not in any way detract from or destroy the authenticity of later messages from Heaven in the form of various revelations, each of which begins with *an* origin which is *the* Origin and which marks the beginning of a tradition that is at once *the* Primordial Tradition and its adaptation to a particular humanity, the adaptation being a Divine Possibility manifested on the human plane.[18]

Therefore, while the perennial philosophy is directly related to the Primordial Tradition and its various manifestations or prolongations, it is also the understanding and preservation of particular manifestations of tradition, each of which contains in its heart the Primordial Tradition. The perennial philosophy is not syncretism or an attempt to create a meta-religion devoid of revealed forms, such as the doctrines, rites, and laws of a particular religion. The sages who have articulated the perennial philosophy throughout history have recognized the common wisdom at the heart of all revealed religions, but they have been rooted in one. It is only by attaching oneself to a specific Revelation and tradition from Heaven that one can reach the transcendent Source of all religions. Unlike pseudo-theosophical and New Age constructs that deny the validity of any one religion in the name of universalism, traditionalists who have articulated the perennial philosophy generally live in one religious universe while also seeking to understand and appreciate other religions.

Furthermore, in their original form all religions contain exoteric or outer and esoteric or inner dimensions.[19] The exoteric doctrines, rites, and laws of a religion provide a means of salvation in the here-

18. Ibid., pp. 68–69.

19. In Islam, the exoteric is identified with the *Sharīʿah* (Divine Law), while the esoteric is both the *ṭarīqah* (spiritual path) and the *ḥaqīqah* (Truth). Schuon and others have pointed out that not all religions manifest the initial two dimensions in the same manner.

after for the faithful.Those who wish to see God here and now must also embark on the initiatic and spiritual path, which is synonymous with esoterism.The mistake of many is to attempt to practice esoterism without the necessary doctrines, rites, and laws of a particular tradition, which provide the necessary foundation and protection for those on the spiritual path. We should not confuse the perennial philosophy or the transcendent unity of religions with a false uniformity that strips all religions of their unique doctrines and methods that make the journey to the One possible. Moreover, it is only at the level of the esoteric that the religions begin to converge, and finally meet in the common Principle, wherein we find the transcendent unity of religions. Only the gnostic whose heart has been illuminated by sacred knowledge, which is the goal of esoterism, can perceive the One True Reality as it reveals itself through all orthodox religions, in nature, and the heart of man.

The perennial philosophy is essentially that reoccurring Divine wisdom that manifests in all revealed religions and traditional schools of philosophy that can reawaken the innate wisdom within man. Here *sophia* or wisdom is metaphysics or principial knowledge and the means of attaining knowledge of the Divine or the True, the Good and the Beautiful. However, because metaphysics embraces all that is, the perennial philosophy is also related to traditional cosmology, symbolism, anthropology, psychology, theology, spiritual practice, the virtues, ethics, and art, as well as a critique of those modern and postmodern aberrations such as secularism, humanism, rationalism, scientism, the idea of progress, relativism, nationalism, modern war and the destruction of the natural world. As people of faith become increasingly inundated with these errors and their proponents who are often hostile towards religion and the Sacred, there is nothing more significant than an awareness of the unanimous wisdom and heritage of humanity that is the perennial philosophy.

The Quran, Sunnah, and the Perennial Philosophy

Perhaps more than other religions, Hinduism and Islam are able to accept the multiplicity of religions that lead to the Divine Reality because they stand at the alpha and omega points in this cycle of creation. In the case of Islam, one simply has to examine the writings of Jalāl al-Dīn Rūmī or Muḥyī al-Dīn ibn ʿArabī to see how awareness of Divine Unity and religious diversity has permeated Islamic civilization throughout history, even if the perennial philosophy was not fully elaborated until the twentieth century by leading Muslim traditionalists. The writings of the great Muslim sages, philosophers, and poets are rooted in the Quranic revelation and *Sunnah* of the Prophet Muḥammad, which emphasize the unity of the Divine Principle (*tawḥīd*), as well as the chain of messengers and prophets sent by Heaven to restore the message of Divine Unity. To understand why the restating of the perennial philosophy in the twentieth century came primarily from Muslim sages, it is necessary to understand the essential link between Islam and the perennial philosophy. According to Seyyed Hossein Nasr:

> Islam sees the doctrine of unity (*al-tawḥīd*) not only as the essence of its own message but as the heart of every religion. Revelation for Islam means the assertion of *al-tawḥīd* and all religions are seen as so many repetitions in different climes and languages of the doctrine of unity. Moreover, wherever the doctrine of unity was found, it is considered to be of divine origin.[20]

Muslims believe that the One God sent 124,000 prophets to different communities. The Quran affirms, "And for every community there is a messenger. . . ." (10:47); and ". . . . Among them are those whom We have recounted unto thee, and among them are those whom We have not recounted unto thee. . . ." (40:78) Numerous prophets whose sacred stories are also found in the Bible are extensively referred to in the Quran, such as Adam, Noah, Abraham, Moses, David, Mary and Jesus. For example it is stated,

> Verily We have revealed unto thee, as We have revealed unto Noah and the prophets after him, and as We revealed unto Abraham and Ishmael and Isaac and Jacob and the Tribes, and Jesus and Job and Jonah and Aaron and Solomon, and unto David We gave the Psalms, And messengers We have recounted unto thee before, and

20. *Knowledge and the Sacred*, p. 71.

> messengers We have not recounted unto thee; and unto Moses God spoke directly. . . . (Quran 4:163–164)

The Quran also calls on Muslims to accept the "books" and not only the book. The Arabic revelation mentions the Torah, the Psalms and the Gospel as Divine revelation and in fact refers to Jews and Christians as the "People of the Book" (*ahl al-kitāb*). Under Islamic Law, Muslims are required to respect and even protect the People of the Book, as well as their property and places of worship—a precedent that has been extended to Zoroastrians, Hindus, Buddhists and other religious communities outside of the Abrahamic family throughout history.[21] While the Quran does not explicitly name the prophets or books from the Iranian, Indian, Chinese or Shamanic traditions, it explicitly ensures salvation for all who believe in God and the Day of Judgment and do righteous deeds.[22] According to the Quran:

> Truly those who believe, and those who are Jews, and the Christians, and the Sabeans—whosoever believes in God and the Last Day and works righteousness shall have their reward with their Lord. No fear shall come upon them, nor shall they grieve.[23] (2:62)

Therefore, we can assert that the Quran confirms the validity of all revealed religions as paths that lead to the Transcendent Reality

21. Nasr states, "[Not] only have some of the most authoritative Muslim scholars of the sub-continent during Moghul period called the Hindus '*ahl al-kitāb*', belonging to the chain of prophets preceding Islam and beginning with Adam, but also some of the Muslim Indian commentators have considered the prophet Dhu'l-Kifl mentioned in the Quran to be the Buddha of Kifl (Kapilavasta) and the 'Fig Tree' of surah 95 to be the bodi Tree under which the Buddha received illumination." *Sufi Essays*, p. 132.

22. For an excellent discussion of this topic see Reza Shah-Kazemi, "The Metaphysics of Interfaith Dialogue: Sufi Perspectives on the Universality of the Quranic Message," in James Cutsinger, ed., *Paths to the Heart: Sufism and the Christian East* (Bloomington, IN: World Wisdom, Inc., 2002), pp. 140–189.

23. See Tayeb Chouiref, "The Shaykh Ahmad al-'Alawī and the Universalism of the Qur'ān: A Presentation and Translation of His Commentary of Verse 2:62," in Patrick Laude, ed., *Universal Dimensions of Islam: Studies in Comparative Religion* (Bloomington, IN: World Wisdom, 2011), pp. 42–48.

for different communities. It has been stated by some that this verse and others like it were abrogated, and that Islam only accepts other religions in their original form.[24] While it is true that many religions that predate Islam have decayed, not to mention some modernist and fundamentalist currents within Islam itself, the Quran does not expect other religions to be carbon copies of Islam:

> [For] each among you We have appointed a law and a way. And had God willed, He would have made you a single community, but [He willed otherwise], that He might try you in that which He has given you. So vie with one another in good deeds. Unto God shall be your return, all together, and He will inform you of that wherein you differed. (5:48)

24. On the question of abrogation Ibn 'Arabī states, "All the revealed religions are lights. Among these religions, the revealed religion of Muḥammad is like the light of the sun among the lights of the stars. When the sun appears, the lights of the stars are hidden, and their lights are included in the light of the sun. Their being hidden is like the abrogation of the other revealed religions that takes place through Muḥammad's revealed religion. Nevertheless, they do in fact exist, just as the existence of the lights of the stars is actualized. This explains why we have been required in our all-inclusive religion to have faith in the truth of all the messengers and all the revealed religions. They are not rendered null [*bātil*] by abrogation—that is the opinion of the ignorant." William Chittick, *Imaginal Worlds*, p. 125. Zaid Shakir and Hamza Yusuf also write: "According to some scholars, the position that all aspects of previous religions are not invalid is affirmed by the Qur'an and *Sunnah*. God mentions in the Qur'an, concerning judgments on the basis of the Jewish and Christian scriptures, 'Let the People of the Gospel judge by what God has revealed therein. If any do fail to judge by what God has revealed, they are rebellious profligates.' (5:50) In this and related verses (5:47–49) God affirms the validity of judgments issued on the basis of the scriptures present with the Jewish and Christian communities during the lifetime of the Prophet Muḥammad. Scholars who hold that the law of the communities who preceded the community of the Prophet Muḥammad is a valid source of law for the Muslim community, usher these verses as proof for that position. In the *Sunnah*, the Prophet Muḥammad accepted the judgment of the Torah (Deuteronomy 20:12), as issued by Sa'd b. Mu'ādh, against the Jewish tribe Banī Qurayẓah. The Prophet Muḥammad described that judgment as 'the judgment of God from above the seven heavens.' See Ibn Hishām, *al-Sīrah al-Nabawiyyah* (Beirut: Dār al-Fikr, 1994/1415), 3:181. These and similar narrations support the idea that there is validity in the previous religions. Surely God knows best." Joseph Lumbard, *Submission Faith, and Beauty: The Religion of Islam* (Berkeley, CA: Zaytuna Institute, 2008), p. xxii.

The Quran defines all of the prophets, including Adam, Abraham, Moses, and Jesus, as *muslims* or those who surrender to the Divine Reality. *Islām* or submission to God is seen as the universal essence of all prophetic messages, while at the same time corresponding to the specific religious message inaugurated by descent of the Quran to the Prophet Muḥammad and his community beginning in 610. In the mind of most Muslims there is not a clear line of demarcation between the religion of Islam in the universal and specific meanings of the term. Therefore, some Muslims expect the submission (*islām*) of Christ or the Buddha as practiced among their followers to look exactly like the Islam that is practiced in Mecca in the twenty-first century, while others are more comfortable with the various modes of submission that exist among the religions.[25] Be that as it may, all Muslims understand Islam as the

25. For example, as mentioned above the essence of all prophetic messages is summarized in the Quran as follows, "And We sent no messenger before thee [Muḥammad], save that We revealed unto him, 'Verily, there is no god but I, so worship Me.'" (Quran 21:25) The fundamental discernment at the heart of religion is thus expressed in Islam through the first *shahādah*, "There is no god but God," with the Name of God sometimes replaced by a pronoun such as "I," "He," or "You." When reading the Quranic verse, "And We have sent no messenger, save in the language of his people. . . ." (14:4), however, one must understand the variations in question to be more than a direct translation of the *shahādah* into English, Chinese or Sanskrit, for example, might suggest. A language of a people describes their particular way of envisaging man, the world and God, and therefore begins to explain the differences in psychology, cosmology, and theology that exist in different civilizations and religions. The Divine Word or signs that constitute a Revelation must therefore take into account these differences and may manifest in the form of a book, a man, or the cosmos. In the Quran itself we read an account of the sacred story where God pronounces a variation of the *shahādah* through the burning bush to Moses: "Truly I am God, there is no god but I. So worship Me, and perform the prayer for My remembrance." (20:14) From a certain point of view, the burning bush, Jesus, or the Quran are like avatars in the Abrahamic universe, although from the Islamic perspective only the Absolute is God—a Reality and Presence before which all relativity is effaced and consequently subsumed. Such a perspective begins to explain the diverse modes of revelation in Hinduism, Buddhism, Taoism, and the Shamanic traditions, which are also based on the Reality of the One God, but through revelations and languages that are sometimes poles apart from the Arabic revelation.

perennial religion of submission that God bestowed to humanity through a chain of prophets from Adam to Muḥammad. The only question is whether or not they accept the validity of earlier manifestations of religion after the descent of the Quran to the Prophet of Islam for non-Muslim communities. Even those Muslims who believe that other revealed religions have decayed or been superseded by Islam—and thus rendered entirely inefficacious—are reminded in Quran that, "There is no coercion in religion. . . ." (2:256) As such, the freedom of religion is enshrined in Islamic Law because true faith and devotion must come from within and cannot be imposed by an external source.

While the form of the Quran is clearly situated in the Abrahamic universe, it is only by examining the symbolism and inner reality (*ḥaqīqah*) of the Quran that one can find close correspondences with other religions from the East, and also the Shamanic traditions. According to the Quran, "And upon the earth are signs for those possessing certitude, and within yourselves. Do you not then behold?" (51:20–21) If the Quran represents the central theophany of the Divine Reality in a manner similar to the Torah in Judaism, it also draws our attention to the books of the cosmos and the soul of man. The cosmos or nature as Divine revelation is clearly emphasized among the Native American, Aboriginal, and Shinto traditions, and well as in Taoism. The soul and Spirit of man as revelation, which is central in Christianity as well as the Indian religions, is also found in the Quran. Jesus is in fact honored as the "Spirit of God" (*rūḥ Allāh)* in the Quran, in addition to being the "Word of God" (*kalimat Allāh*). Jesus, and by analogy the avatars in Hinduism and the inner being of each prophet and man, is a direct revelation from the Absolute in a manner similar to the book in Judaism and Islam. By emphasizing the three grand revelations—the book, the cosmos, and man—the Quran helps Muslims to see the signs of the Divine Reality in other religions. Indeed, in the Quran God reveals His signs *(āyāt)* to humanity through Jesus and the Virgin (23:50), the she-camel of the prophet Ṣāliḥ (17:59), the burning bush to Moses (20:23), the Ka'bah in Mecca (3:97), and the variety of wonders observed in the order of nature. It therefore should not be difficult for intelligent Muslims to see the manifestation of the signs of God in other human, animal, plant and even mineral forms in other religions—not to mention higher levels of existence populated by the angels and other celestial beings—without equating these signs with the Absolute itself or reducing their veneration to so many forms of polytheism or idolatry. Polytheism is the positing of more than one Absolute, while idolatry is the reduction of the Absolute to the relative or the worshipping of manmade idols pure and simple, neither of which refer to the sacred function revealed signs have in the various religions of humanity. Hinduism, for example, is a rich tradition wherein God reveals Himself through an almost infinite variety of forms, without being reduced to these forms alone. If God can say through the theophany of the burning bush, "Truly I am God, there is no god but I. . . ." (Quran 20:14) or "I am That I am" (Exodus 3:14), then members of the Abrahamic family should not scoff at the manifestations of Unity in the diverse revealed forms of other religions. The uncreated Quran itself makes use of the created form of the Arabic tongue, as well as the written form of the Book through calligraphy, including paper and ink. Thus, the locus of manifestation for Divine Unity must out of necessity be a created form, without being exhausted by that form.

There are also various terms in the Quran that directly correspond to the perennial philosophy and the Primordial Tradition, which is the common origin of all of the revealed religions. From the Islamic perspective, the Quranic revelation and the Prophet of Islam simply renewed the primordial religion (*al-dīn al-ḥanīf*) that is associated with the prophets Adam and Abraham.[26] The primordial religion in the Quran is also closely related to man's primordial nature (*fiṭrah*), which is hidden by forgetfulness and made accessible through religion and the remembrance (*dhikr*) of God. There is thus an innate purity and wisdom in the human being, which religion serves to remind us of and reconnect us to rather than superimpose upon the soul.

It is true that the Quran has a number of verses that critique

26. Quran 2:135.

some of the beliefs of certain Jews and Christians.[27] For example, the Quran warns Muslims not to believe, as some Jews and Christians do, that only they will go to Heaven. Regarding other points of law and creed, the exoteric forms of the revealed religions necessarily differ in significant ways and Islam has its own perspective that is best suited for those who embrace it. Out of necessity the Quran and the *Sunnah* established a particular Law and theological perspective that differ in important ways from the *Halakhah* in Judaism or the Trinity in Christianity. Every religion is distinct from others on the exoteric level, while in greater accord on the esoteric level, and ultimately in agreement concerning the Unity of the Supreme Principle. The Quran simultaneously articulates a distinct religious perspective for Muslims and reminds us that all revealed religions issue from and lead to the One God. Even though the Quran and the Prophet of Islam inaugurated a distinct religious dispensation for Muslims that differs from other religions, the Book affirms the authentic and protected status of those who follow other revealed religions:

> They are not all alike. Among the People of the Book is an upright community who recite God's signs in the watches of the night, while they prostrate. They believe in God and the Last Day, enjoin right and forbid wrong, and vie with one another in good deeds. And they are among the righteous. Whatsoever good they do, they will not be denied it. And God knows the reverent. (3:113–115)

> [A]nd thou wilt find the nearest of them in affection toward those who believe to be those who say, "We are Christians." That is because among them are priests and monks, and because they are not arrogant. (5:82)

27. Zaid Shakir and Hamza Yusuf write, "Many Muslims unfortunately read the Qur'an as a condemnation of previous religious peoples as opposed to a method to understand their flaws inherent in all of humanity, and as a warning. The Prophet Muḥammad told many stories that involved righteous Jews and Christians of the past whose exemplary behavior elucidated his points. Abū Dharr once quoted a verse about hoarding wealth and the governor of Syria, Mu'āwiyyah replied, 'That was revealed about the People of the Book!' To which Abū Dharr said, 'Yes, but for our reflection!'" *Submission, Faith, and Beauty*, p. 39.

And among the people of Moses there is a community that guides by the truth and does justice thereby. (7:159)

Those who were expelled from their homes without right, only for saying, "Our Lord is God." And were it not for God's repelling people, some by means of others, monasteries, churches, synagogues, and mosques wherein God's Name is mentioned much would have been destroyed. And God will surely help those who help Him. Truly God is Strong, Mighty. (22:40)

The perennial philosophy and the principle of universality is also expressed in the *Sunnah* or Wont of the Prophet Muḥammad (570–632), which complements and acts as a commentary upon the Quran. The Prophet is reported to have said, "The word of wisdom is the stray camel of the believer; wherever he finds it, he has the greatest right to it." And also, "Seek knowledge even unto China." According to an account of the Prophet Muhammad's life when he ordered all of the pre-Islamic idols in the Ka'bah to be smashed:

Apart from the icon of the Virgin Mary and the child Jesus, and a painting of an old man, said to be Abraham, the walls inside had been covered with pictures of pagan deities. Placing his hands protectively over the icon, the Prophet told 'Uthmān to see that all the other paintings, except that of Abraham, were effaced.[28]

There is a major difference between the idolatry practiced in Arabia in the pre-Islamic age of ignorance (*jāhiliyyah*), and the sacred art and symbols of other revealed religions, which the Prophet Muḥammad respected. As the spiritual and political leader of the new Muslim community (*ummah*), he maintained that all of the earlier revealed books, messengers and religions were of Divine origin and therefore Sacred. In response to a conflict between a Jew and a zealous Muslim who wanted to assert the superiority of the Prophet over other prophets, the Prophet Muḥammad stated, "Say

28. Martin Lings, *Muhammad: His Life Based on the Earliest Sources* (Rochester, VT: Inner Traditions International, 1983), p. 300.

not that I am better than Moses," and "Say not that I am better than Jonah."[29] The Prophet also related, "Among men I am the closest to Jesus son of Mary in this world and the next. The prophets are brothers; although they have different mothers, their religion is one."[30] The Prophet also married a Jewish and a Christian woman, who were not forced to convert to Islam, although they both embraced the religion. He also consulted with a Christian monk, who was related to his wife Khadījah, after first receiving the Revelation. Throughout the life of the Prophet, Jews and Christians in Arabia were not forced to convert to Islam, but were allowed to practice their religion in peace and security as long as they did not harm the Muslim community. The Prophet even established a treaty with the Arab and Jewish tribes in Medina known as the Constitution of Medina, which guaranteed and outlined certain basic rights and responsibilities for both Arabs and Jews.[31] As mentioned above, the Quran and various decrees of the Prophet also call upon Muslims to respect the autonomy of and even defend synagogues and churches. A notable example of this is found in the Prophet's

29. Martin Lings, *A Return to the Spirit: Questions and Answers* (Louisville, KY: Fons Vitae, 2005), p. 28.

30. *The Sayings of Muhammad*, trans. Neal Robinson (Hopewell, NJ: The Ecco Press, 1991), p. 36.

31. The Constitution of Medina contains the following points: "This is a document from Muḥammad the Prophet [governing the relations] between the believers and Muslims of Quraysh and Yathrib [Medina], and those who followed them and joined them and laboured with them.... To the Jew who follows us belong help and equality. He shall not be wronged nor shall his enemies be aided.... The Jews of the B. 'Auf are one community with the believers (the Jews have their religion and the Muslims have theirs), their freedmen and their persons except those who behave unjustly and sinfully, for they hurt themselves and their families. The same applies to the Jews of the B. al-Najjār, B. al-Ḥārith, B. Sā'ida, B. Jusham, B. al-Aus, B. Tha'laba, and the Jafna, a clan of the Tha'laba and the B. al-Shuṭayba. Loyalty is a protection against treachery. The freedmen of Tha'laba are as themselves. The close friends of the Jews are as themselves.... The Jews of al-Aus, their freedmen and themselves have the same standing with the people of this document in pure loyalty from the people of this document." Trans. A. Guillaume, *The Life of Muḥammad—A Translation of Ibn Isḥāq's Sīrat Rasūl Allāh* (Karachi: Oxford University Press, 2004), pp. 231–233.

letter to St. Catherine's Monastery at Mt. Sinai.[32] Moreover, a Christian congregation was also allowed to pray in the Prophet's home—the Medina mosque—according to their own rites.[33]

For Muslims, the Prophet of Islam is at once the Logos and, like other prophets in the Islamic universe, a particular manifestation of the Logos. He represents the plenitude of the prophetic function, as well as the human norm, which cannot be reduced to the modern standards that define Promethean man.[34] By walking in the footsteps of the Prophet (or any prophet whose religion has survived) believers rediscover their own pure and primordial nature through which the Divine Truth and Presence can be known. The pinnacle of the Prophet's spiritual life was his miraculous Night Journey. Guided by the Angel Gabriel (Jibra'īl) and seated upon a celestial steed named *burāq*, the Prophet traveled from Mecca to Jerusalem where he led a congregation of various prophets in prayer and from there made a vertical ascension (*mi'rāj*) through the heavens, meeting various prophets and angels along the way, to the Divine Empyrean and Presence.[35] It was here that the final form of the canonical prayer was revealed. The Prophet in fact said, "The daily prayer (*ṣalāh*) is the *mi'rāj* of the believer." One therefore finds a direct

32. Reza Shah-Kazemi writes, "The document itself goes beyond merely granting formal protection. It states that wherever monks or hermits are to be found: 'on any mountain, hill, village, or other habitable place, on the sea or in the deserts or in any convent, church or house of prayer, I shall be watching over them as their protector, with all my soul, together with all my *ummah*; because they [the monks and hermits] are a part of my own people, and part of those protected by me.' It goes on to state their exemption from taxes and warns of stern retribution if the injunctions of the charter are broken by Muslims. Also, most significantly, it makes it incumbent on the Muslims not only to protect the monks, but also, in regard to Christians generally, to 'consolidate their worship at Church.'" "Illumination and Non-Delimitation: Lessons for Inter and Intra Faith Dialogue from the Wisdom of the Prophet of Islam" in Muhammad Suheyl Umar, ed., *The Religious Other: Towards a Muslim Theology of Other Religions in a Post-Prophetic Age* (Lahore: Iqbal Academy, 2008), p. 164.

33. *Muhammad: His Life Based on the Earliest Sources*, p. 324.

34. *Knowledge and the Sacred*, pp. 160–183.

35. Seyyed Hossein Nasr, *Muhammad: Man of God* (Chicago: Kazi Publications, Inc., 1995), pp. 29–36.

correlation and symbiosis between the exoteric rites and the quintessential esoterism of Islam. It is by adhering to his own tradition, and specifically the *Sunnah* of the Prophet, that a Muslim can enter the Divine Stratosphere and gain a direct vision of the Supreme Reality, as well as the countless prophets and angelic beings, and directly witness the transcendent Source of all that is.

Within the Quran and the *Sunnah* of the Prophet of Islam may be found some of the clearest expressions of the perennial philosophy and the transcendent unity of religions, which Muslim sages throughout history and in the twentieth century drew from to convey the perennial philosophy. By referring and adhering to their own traditional doctrines and methods, they drew from the Source of Wisdom which is peerless in Its expression of the Truth:

> Say, "We believe in God, and in what was sent down to us, and in what was sent down to Abraham, Ishmael, Isaac, Jacob, and the Tribes, and in what Moses and Jesus were given, and in what the prophets were given from their Lord. We make no distinction among any of them, and unto Him we submit." (Quran 2:136)

Classical Muslim Sages and the Perennial Philosophy

Following the Quran and *Sunnah*, the writings of Muslim sages from the Islamic sapiential tradition shed considerable light on the perennial philosophy. Less than a century after the death of the Prophet, Arab rule extended from the Iberian Peninsula to the Indus River and thus afforded Muslim philosophers, scientists, and Sufis opportunities to interact with men and women of learning and piety from other religions. Wherever Muslims found traces of prophetic wisdom *(ḥikmah)* they considered it their rightful inheritance and were therefore able to integrate the wisdom of ancient Greece, Egypt, Persia, India and China into their own Abrahamic worldview and civilization. References to other revealed books, prophets and religions are replete throughout the writings of Muslim philosophers and Sufis such as Ibn Sīnā, Suhrawardī, Ibn 'Arabī, and Rūmī, precisely because their twin sources of guidance—the Quran and the *Sunnah*—confirm the validity of previous messages and prophets.[36] What is remarkable about the Muslim sages of the twentieth century we survey below is that they were responsible for not only restating the perennial philosophy, but for also preserving and demonstrating the significance of the Islamic intellectual and spiritual tradition. Seyyed Hossein Nasr writes,

> For [Muslims] the sages of antiquity such as Pythagoras and Plato were "Unitarians" (*muwaḥḥidūn*) who expressed the truth which lies at the heart of all religions. They, therefore, belonged to the Islamic universe and were not considered as alien to it. The Islamic intellectual tradition in both its gnostic (*maʿrifah or ʿirfān*) and philosophical and theosophical (*falsafah-ḥikmah*) aspects saw the source of this unique truth which is the "Religion of the Truth" (*dīn al-ḥaqq*) in the teachings of the ancient prophets going back to Adam and considered Idrīs, whom is identified with Hermes, as the "father of philosophers" (*Abu'l-ḥukamāʾ*).[37]

From al-Kindī to Mullā Ṣadrā,[38] Muslim philosophers and gnostics preserved and transformed Greek philosophy, as well as Persian and Indian philosophy, and followed a different trajectory from the West after the Renaissance because of their attachment to a living

36. Islamic philosophy and Sufism developed along similar lines and the students of both streams of Islamic sapience ultimately made use of the same intellectual faculties, although Muslim philosophers and Sufis have expressed their knowledge of the Sacred in different ways. Unlike the West, where philosophy has become divorced from the Intellect (*al-ʿaql*) or the eye of the heart (*ʿayn al-qalb*) and reduced to the rational faculty alone, in the Islamic world philosophy is wed to Revelation and intellection. In a similar manner, Muslim gnostics and Sufis describe a vision of Reality that is based on the inner reality of Revelation and intellectual intuition and not simply a sentimental form of love that is detached from sacred knowledge, although Divine and human love have always played a central role in Sufism and Islam in general. Therefore, the expressions of the perennial philosophy from Muslim sages in the Islamic intellectual and spiritual tradition derive from objective visions of Reality that are based on the Quran, *Sunnah*, and the central doctrine of Divine Unity, and are not simply theoretical metaphysics or romantic imagery, which may in fact be the symbolic languages or outward forms through which a vision of the Real is conveyed.

37. *Knowledge and the Sacred*, pp. 71–72.

38. Of course Islamic philosophy, and specifically the perennial philosophy in Islam, did not begin with al-Kindī or end with Mullā Ṣadrā, as this study intends to demonstrate.

tradition and Revelation that could help them discern between those sages and schools that were guided by higher principles and those trends in the West and the East that were opposed to sacred knowledge. Most Islamic philosophers relied first and foremost upon the Quran and *Sunnah*, and used the wisdom of ancient philosophers to describe their intellectual vision of Reality that resulted from their attachment to Islam and Islamic esoterism. Abū Yūsuf Ya'qūb al-Kindī (801–866) states,

> We should not be ashamed to acknowledge truth and assimilate it from whatever source it comes to us, even if it be by former generations and foreign peoples. For him who seeks the truth there is nothing of higher value than truth itself; it never cheapens or abases him who reaches for it, but ennobles and honors him.[39]

The Prophet Muḥammad established this principle when he said, "Seek knowledge even unto China." Therefore, the wisdom of the ages, including sacred and inspired texts, philosophy, and the writings of sages from around the world, was considered the rightful inheritance of Muslims and was easily incorporated into Islamic philosophy, esoterism, and a general worldview dominated by *tawḥīd*. Indeed, there is a marked emphasis on the principle of Unity in the teachings of Hermes, Pythagoras, Plato, and Plotinus, for example, which made their assimilation into Islamic philosophy natural and even providential.

Abū Naṣr al-Fārābī (d. 950) wrote a treatise entitled *A Reconciliation of the Opinions of the Two Sages, the Divine Plato and Aristotle* (*al-Kitāb al-jam' bayn ra'yay al-ḥakīmayn, Aflāṭūn al-ilāhī wa Arisṭū*). According to S.H. Nasr, "[Al-Fārābī] considered the wisdom expounded by these men to have come ultimately from Divine revelation, and could not therefore be completely contradictory."[40] In al-Fārābī's *Principles of the Opinion of the People of the Virtuous City* (*Mabādī āra' ahl-madīnat al-fāḍilah*) he also lays out a political philosophy by combining Plato's views in *The Republic*

39. Seyyed Hossein Nasr, *Three Muslim Sages* (Delmar, NY: Caravan Books, 1976), p. 11.

40. Ibid., p. 15.

with the ideals of Islam. In a manner similar to *The Republic*, this treatise is in fact also a discourse on spiritual psychology, as the various cities and their components and characteristics correspond to different aspects within the human microcosm. For example, the philosopher-king of the virtuous city is like the Intellect, while the virtuous city, the ignorant city, the wicked city, and the erring city correspond to the sublime and the base elements of the soul.[41] Al-Fārābī and many Muslim philosophers were also initiated into Sufi orders. The sacred knowledge that they gained through Sufism helped them establish an epistemology that privileged higher modes of knowing—especially Revelation and intellectual intuition—without denying the importance of logic and reason and those pre-Islamic currents of philosophy that according to the early Muslim philosophers were also the result of Revelation and gnosis.[42]

During this extremely fecund intellectual period of cross-fertilization in Islamic and world history we also discover the vestiges of the enigmatic Ikhwān al-Ṣafā' or Brethren of Purity. While most likely being centered in Baṣra in the 10th century, the identity of all of the individuals who comprised this group remains uncertain. The Ikhwān al-Ṣafā' can be categorized as an esoteric circle of Muslim philosophers with Shī'ite and Sufi affiliations.[43] They drew from the primary Islamic sources, Pythagoras, Nicomachus, the Hermetic and alchemical teachings of Jābir ibn Ḥayyān, and other sources to write their encyclopedic work the *Rasā'il*. The fifty-two treatises that constitute the *Rasā'il* deal with almost every science and art cultivated at the time, including, for example, gnosis, theology, cosmology, mathematics, logic, music, as well as other religious, natural,

41. Abū Naṣr Fārābī, *The Perfect State* (*Mabādī ārā' ahl-madīnat al-fāḍilah*), trans. R. Walzer, in S.H. Nasr & M. Aminrazavi, eds., *An Anthology of Philosophy in Persia, vol. I: From Zoroaster to 'Umar Khayyām* (London: I.B. Tauris Publishers, 2008), pp. 134–136, 164–179.

42. *Three Muslim Sages*, p. 16. The recent studies of Peter Kingsley and Algis Uždavinys also show that Greek philosophy has its origins in Revelation and gnosis. See, for example, Peter Kingsley, *Reality* (Inverness, CA: The Golden Sufi Center, 1999); and Algis Uždavinys, *Philosophy as a Rite of Rebirth: From Ancient Egypt to Neoplatonism* (Dorset, UK: Prometheus Truth, 2008).

and arcane sciences.[44] While it is impossible for us to summarize their doctrines here, they drew from various Islamic and pre-Islamic sources, as well as their own innate wisdom, to describe virtually everything under the Sun in view of a thing's relation to the Divine Principle. According to A. L. Ṭībāwī, "The Brethren of Purity believe that the Truth is one without it being the private work of anyone. God has sent His Spirit to all men, to Christians as to Muslims, to blacks as to whites."[45] The Ikhwān al-Ṣafā' themselves state that the perfect man is of,

> East Persian derivation, Arabic in faith, of 'Irāqī, that is Babylonian education, a Hebrew in astuteness, a disciple of Christ in conduct, as pious as a Syrian monk, a Greek in the individual sciences, an Indian in the interpretation of all mysteries, but lastly and especially, a Ṣūfī in his whole spiritual life.[46]

43. The Ismā'īlīs believe the Ikhwān al-Ṣafā' were Ismā'īlīs, although this thesis has not been proved. Be that as it may, we should note the immense contribution to Islamic esoterism and the perennial philosophy that Ismā'īlī philosophers have made. Some of the most eminent Ismā'īlī philosophers include Abū Ḥātim Rāzī, Nāṣir-i Khusraw, Abū Ya'qūb al-Sijistānī, and Ḥamīd al-Dīn al-Kirmānī. Rāzī (d. 933) states, "Whoever is just and is not arrogant, and reflects on the differences by his intellect and examines the contradictions of the prophets and what they have revealed in their *sharāyi'* and the parables which they have struck and have been revealed from God the exalted and glorified,—[he will perceive] that the literal words of the prophets in their symbols (*amthāl*) differ but in the inner content (or intentions, *ma'ānī*) they are consistent. They have not differed in the core value of religion, such as the Divine Unity. They unanimously agree that God, glory be to His remembrance, is One God. . . ." See Latimah-Parvin Peerwani's "Abū Ḥātim Rāzī On The Essential Unity of Religions", in Mohammad H. Faghfoory, ed., *Beacon of Knowledge: Essays in Honor of Seyyed Hossein Nasr* (Louisville, KY: Fons Vitae, 2003), pp. 269–287.

44. Seyyed Hossein Nasr, *An Introduction to Islamic Cosmological Doctrines: Conceptions of Nature and Methods used for its study by the Ikhwān al-Ṣafā', al-Bīrūnī, and Ibn Sīnā* (Albany, NY: State University of New York Press, 1993), pp. 25–43.

45. Ibid., p. 32.

46. Ibid., p. 31. The Ikhwān also state: "We have drawn our knowledge from four books. The first is composed of the mathematical and natural sciences established by the sages and philosophers. The second consists of the revealed books of the Torah, the Gospels and the Quran and the other Tablets brought by the prophets through angelic Revelation. The third is the books of Nature which are the ideas (*ṣuwar*) in the Platonic sense of the forms (*ashkāl*) of creatures actually existing,

As mentioned above, one also finds direct equivalents to the terms the perennial philosophy in Islamic philosophy, such as *al-ḥikmat al-khālidah* in Arabic and *jāvīdān khirad* in Persian, which may have influenced the formulation of the term *philosophia perennis* by Steuco and Leibnitz.[47] *Al-Ḥikmat al-khālidah* or *Jāvīdān khirad* is the title of a book by the Persian Muslim philosopher Abū 'Alī Aḥmad ibn Miskawayh (d. 1030), which contains spiritual and ethical sayings from Abrahamic, Persian, Greek, and Indian sages.[48] One letter in Ibn Miskawayh's collection from the Sassanid minister Būzarjumihr to the Persian emperor Khusraw reads:

> [Do] not be shy in acquiring knowledge and learning . . . do not become bored by the study of books, for their study is a perusal of the minds of all people, and knowledge of the virtues of those who had wisdom in the past, the prophets, and all nations (*umam*) and all the people of the various religious communities (*ahl al-milal*). However, most of that which they described and recorded consists of branches whose roots and causes they did not make clear, and the reason for which they did not unveil. These are praiseworthy things, except that they are numerous and the memory cannot retain and learning cannot encompass knowledge of all of them. But the wise have busied themselves with the roots of these branches and shown their causes and reasons and have subsumed the particulars under the universals. Whoever masters these roots extracts the treasures of truth from every object of investigation, and uncovers the secrets of wisdom from all that is concealed. He who acts like this has a long life even if his days are short.[49]

from the composition of the celestial spheres, the division of the Zodiac, the movement of the stars, and so on . . . to the transformation of the elements, the production of the members of the mineral, plant and animal kingdoms and the rich variety of human industry. . . . The fourth consists of the Divine books which touch only the purified men and which are the angels who are in intimacy with the chosen beings, the noble and purified souls." Ibid., p. 39.

47. Ibn Miskawayh's (d. 1030) text predated Steuco's (d. 1548) use of the term *philosophia perennis* by approximately five hundred years.

48. *Knowledge and the Sacred*, p. 87.

49. Abū 'Alī Aḥmad ibn Muḥammad Miskawayh, *Perennial Philosophy (al-Ḥikmat al-khālidah or Jāwīdān-khirad)*, trans. Alma Giese, in *An Anthology of Philosophy in Persia*, vol. I, p. 344.

The accumulated and essential wisdom of the ages, as well as direct knowledge of the Sacred is also clearly seen in the life and writings of Avicenna or Abū ʿAlī Ḥusayn ibn Sīnā (d. 1037), who was not only a Muslim philosopher and metaphysician, deeply attached to the Quran (which he had memorized), but also a scientist, physician, mathematician, and psychologist, who, like al-Fārābī and the Ikhwān al-Ṣafā', wrote about the theory of music.[50] Ibn Sīnā drew from the primary Islamic sources, Platonism, Aristotelianism, Neoplatonism, Galenism and the writings of the early Muslim philosophers such as al-Fārābī to help compose such classic works of his as *The Book of Healing* (*Kitāb al-shifā'*), *The Canon of Medicine* (*al-Qānūn fi'l-ṭibb*), and *The Book of Directives* (*al-Ishārāt wa'l-tanbīhāt*). S.H. Nasr states,

> But it was essentially the "esoteric" or "Oriental Philosophy" of Avicenna that had the greatest import in the Orient. It was his cosmology supported by his angelology that was elaborated by Suhrawardī and, after being divorced from the rationalistic and syllogistic mesh in whose matrix it was at first placed, became integrated into certain schools of Sufism.[51]

While being firmly rooted in the Revelation and gnosis, Avicenna, as well as Aristotle and the Greek philosophers were later misappropriated to promote rationalism, which was then critiqued by Ashʿarite theologians, Abū Ḥāmid al-Ghazzālī, and Fakhr al-Dīn al-Rāzī, despite certain excesses on their part.[52] For reason has a place in the hierarchy of knowledge in Islam provided that is it subordinate to Revelation and gnosis and does not lead to rationalism or the belief that reason or the mind alone leads to true knowledge. In response to his critics Avicenna or al-Shaykh al-Ra'īs (the Master among wise men) wrote,

50. *Three Muslim Sages*, pp. 16, 20–43.

51. Ibid., p. 50.

52. Ibid., p. 46. Islamic theologians themselves make ample use of reason and logic. Moreover, the great Sufi and theologian Abū Ḥāmid al-Ghazzālī did not object to philosophy as a whole, but to certain theses attributed to various philosophers that contradicted the Quran. In this regard, he also had more than a few warnings for the theologians of his time.

It is not so easy and trifling to call me a heretic
No belief in religion is firmer than mine own.
I am the unique person in the world and if I am a heretic
Then there is not a single Muslim anywhere in the world.[53]

The wisdom of Avicenna and the early Muslim philosophers, which included ancient Greek and Iranian philosophy, was incorporated into Suhrawardī's *Ishrāqī* school, which is based on pure intellection or illumination of the heart, as well as the Quran and *Sunnah*, which are objective and macrocosmic reflections of the Intellect. S.H. Nasr writes,

> Suhrawardī considered himself as the reunifier of what he calls *al-ḥikmat al-ladunīyah*, or Divine Wisdom, and *al-ḥikmat al-'atīqah*, or ancient wisdom. He believed that this wisdom is universal and perennial, the *philosophia perennis* and *universalis*, which existed in various forms among ancient Hindus and Persians, Babylonians and Egyptians, and among the Greeks up to the time of Aristotle. . . .[54]

Shihāb al-Dīn Suhrawardī (d. 1191) or al-Shaykh al-Ishrāq (the Master of Illumination) taught that philosophy began with Hermes or the prophet Idrīs in the Quran and therefore has its origin in prophecy and cannot be divorced from Revelation in the name of rationalism. He believed that he inherited this ancient wisdom from two schools in ancient Egypt and Persia, which both trace their chains of transmission back to Hermes. These chains contain the names of Greek philosophers such as Pythagoras, Empedocles, and Plato, Persian kings and philosophers, and early Sufis from the western and eastern Islamic lands such as Dhu'l-Nūn Miṣrī, Sahl Tustarī, Bāyazīd Basṭāmī and Manṣūr Ḥallāj.[55] Suhrawardī states,

> Whoever is a traveler on the road to Truth is my companion and aid on this path. The procedure of the master of philosophy and *imām* of wisdom, the Divine Plato, was the same, and the sages who preceded Plato in time like Hermes, the father of philosophy, followed

53. Ibid., p. 41.
54. Ibid., p. 61.
55. Ibid., p. 62.

the same path. Since sages of the past, because of the ignorance of the masses, expressed their sayings in secret symbols, the refutations which have been made against them have concerned the exterior of these sayings not their real intentions. And the *Ishrāqī* wisdom, whose foundation and basis are the two principles of light and darkness as established by the Persian sages like Jāmāsp, Frashādshūr, and Būzarjumihr, are among these hidden, secret symbols.[56]

The principles of Suhrawardī's *Ishrāqī* school are found in the Quran, and in all authentic revelations. The Master of Illumination made use of the verse of light in the Quran (24:35)—which includes the Divine Name *al-Nūr* (the Light)—and the commentaries on this verse by al-Ghazzalī in his *The Niche of Lights* (*Mishkāt al-anwār*). He also relied on the writings of Muslim philosophers and Sufis, and the vast intellectual heritage that he inherited from Hermeticism, Pythagoreanism, Platonism, and Zoroastrianism to describe the metaphysics, cosmology, and symbolism of Divine Light in his magnum opus *The Theosophy of the Orient of Light* (*Ḥikmat al-ishrāq*) and numerous other works.[57]

Suhrawardī believed that all of reality consists of degrees of light and darkness. Ultimately, all light finds its origin in the Light of lights (*Nūr al-anwār*) or the Divine Essence, which is like the Sun of existence. This Light then radiates and reflects into the cosmos and in the hearts of men and women through a hierarchy of angels, which are like stars in the night sky. Our goal is to discover our higher self or the angel of one's being, which is the luminous source of the immanent Intellect. Suhrawardī identifies the angel of humanity with Gabriel (Jibra'īl), as well as the Holy Spirit (*rūḥ al-qudus*) and the Muḥammadan Spirit (*al-rūḥ al-muḥammadiyyah*). He establishes a symbolic geography where the material world is seen as the Occident and the spiritual or angelic world as the Orient. With the aid of God and our angelic guide, one must seek to return from this occidental exile here below to the Abode of Light beyond, which is symbolized by the rising of the Sun in the East.[58]

56. Ibid., p. 63.
57. Ibid., p. 60.
58. Ibid., pp. 69–74

Although Suhrawardī was martyred at the age of thirty-eight, the light of his teachings and legacy grew stronger and became an essential element in later branches of Islamic philosophy and gnosis such as the transcendent theosophy of Mullā Ṣadrā, which is discussed below. According to S.H. Nasr,

> The perennial wisdom which the Master of *Ishrāq* had sought to establish, or rather to re-establish, in his short terrestrial life thus became not only a dominant intellectual perspective in Shī'ism, and more generally in the eastern lands of Islam, but also overflowed the banks of the Islamic world to reach other traditions.[59]

Another major light in the firmament of the Islamic intellectual universe is Muḥyī al-Dīn ibn 'Arabī (d. 1240), who made use of the legacy of Divine wisdom or *ḥikmah* that his predecessors preserved and transmitted and also added his own immense contributions. The great Andalusian gnostic, known as al-Shaykh al-Akbar (the Greatest Master), drew from the Quran, *Ḥadīth* literature, Islamic theology and philosophy, and Sufi prose and poetry, to describe his theophanic visions of Reality. His major works, *The Meccan Revelations* (*al-Futūhāt al-makkiyyah*) and *The Ringstones of Wisdom* (*Fuṣūṣ al-ḥikam*), are among the masterpieces of theoretical Sufism or what Joseph Lumbard has called the "*iḥsānī* intellectual tradition."[60] He is famously known in the West for his poem *The Interpreter of Desires* (*Tarjumān al-ashwāq*) in which he describes the beauty of a young Persian maiden Niẓām who becomes a symbol of the Beloved. According to S.H. Nasr, Niẓām is "the embodiment of the eternal *sophia* for [Ibn 'Arabī] and fulfilled a role in his life which resembles that of Beatrice in the life of Dante."[61]

Indeed, the symbol of the feminine beloved is a common feature in the writings of some of the greatest Sufi masters and, as we examine in detail in chapter two, plays an important role in Hinduism and other religions. The archetypal Sophia, which is none other

59. Ibid., p. 82.

60. Joseph Lumbard, "The Decline of Knowledge and the Rise of Ideology in the Modern Islamic World", in *Islam, Fundamentalism, and the Betrayal of Tradition*, pp. 39–77.

61. *Three Muslim Sages*, p. 96

than the Infinite Wisdom and Beauty of God, is reflected in various feminine forms in Islam, such as the Virgin Mary and Fāṭimah the daughter of the Prophet. The beatific vision of Sophia allows man to recognize wisdom and beauty in the various religions, the cosmos, and in his own heart. It is only after seeing the archetype of Wisdom and Beauty that one can recognize its diverse reflections in the world of forms. After seeing Niẓām, Ibn ʿArabī wrote one of the most powerful set of verses, which describes what Frithjof Schuon has called the *religio cordis* or religion of the heart:

Receptive now my heart is for each form;
For gazelles pasture, for monks a monastery,
Temple for idols, Kaʿbah to be rounded,
Tables of Torah and script of Quran.
My religion is love's religion; where'er turn
Her camels, that religion my religion is, my faith.
An example is set us by Bishr, lover
Of Hind and her sister, and likewise the loves
Of Qays and Laylā, of Mayya and Ghaylān.[62]

In Islamic esoterism, the goal of the spiritual path is Union and knowledge that unites, and there is no better symbol for this than love of and union with the beloved. Ibn ʿArabī's poetry and Sufi poetry in general, however, is not based on eroticism or a sentimental love that engenders attachment to transient forms, but on love and knowledge of the Divine Reality—the true Identity of everything that is loved in this world. What also must be kept in mind is that Ibn ʿArabī saw the Divine Reality and Names within all forms and religions, but came to this realization as a result of his attachment to Islam and Sufism, which finds its source in the inner reality of the Quran and soul of the Prophet Muḥammad. It is precisely through the perpetual remembrance (*dhikr*) of God that the Archetypes or Divine Names can be seen in and through the forms of the world. Therefore, as with all of the Muslim sages cited in this chapter, a serious attachment to Islam and Islamic esoterism was what led to and facilitated Ibn ʿArabī's appreciation of other religions.

62. *Sufi Poems*, p. 62.

Ibn ʿArabī and his heirs in the *Akbarī* school of gnosis elucidated the inner meaning of the central doctrine of Divine Unity (*tawḥīd*) in Islam, which is based on the first *shahādah*, *Lā ilāha illa'Llāh* or "There is no god but God," through what became known as the transcendent Unity of Being (*waḥdat al-wujūd*).[63] Ibn ʿArabī, along with ʿAbd al-Karīm Jīlī, was also responsible for explaining the esoteric meaning of the second *shahādah*, *Muḥammadun rasūl Allāh* or "Muḥammad is the Messenger of God," through the doctrine of the Universal or Perfect Man (*al-insān al-kāmil*). It would not be an exaggeration to say that the whole of Islamic esoterism is based on the inner meaning of the *shahādah*, which Ibn ʿArabī wrote about with remarkable insight and erudition.[64] The realization of this inner meaning, however, is not dependent upon its written articulation, especially during the early centuries of Islam. Conversely, the theoretical knowledge that is gained by reading the works of Ibn ʿArabī—which was the fruit of realization for Ibn ʿArabī—is not the same as realized knowledge, which requires a living tradition and the guidance of a spiritual master.

Ibn Arabī's *Fuṣūṣ al-ḥikam* and *al-Futūḥāt al-makkiyyah* also deserve special attention. Concerning the *Fuṣūṣ*, S.H. Nasr writes:

> The work was composed in 627/1229, and according to Ibn ʿArabī's own words, stated in the introduction, it was inspired by a vision of the Prophet holding a book in his hand which he ordered the Shaykh to "take" and to transmit to the world so that men might benefit by it. The very title, *Bezels of Wisdom*, symbolizes the content of the book in that each "bezel" contains a precious jewel which symbolizes as aspect of Divine wisdom, each bezel is the human and spiritual nature of a prophet which serves as a vehicle for the particular aspect of Divine wisdom revealed to that prophet.[65]

63. Ibn ʿArabī, however, never uses the term *waḥdat al-wujūd* in his writings, although he unveiled the inner meaning of *tawḥīd* that would later be known as *waḥdat al-wujūd* by inheritors of the *Akbarī* sciences.

64. On the transcendent Unity of Being and the Universal Man, see S.H. Nasr, *Three Muslim Sages*, pp. 104–108, 110–111.

65. *Three Muslim Sages*, p. 99.

Each chapter is named after a prophet, such as Adam, Seth, Abraham, Moses, Jesus and Muhammad, and contains the archetypal wisdom of that prophet and the universal wisdom of the Divine Word.[66] Written completely within the Islamic universe, the *Fuṣūṣ al-ḥikam* is a summary of Islamic esoterism, as well as the *sophia perennis*, which each prophet manifests in his own way.[67] *Al-Futūḥāt al-makkiyyah* is a vast ocean of wisdom, which also contains some of the most important expressions of the perennial philosophy in the Islamic tradition. The Shaykh al-Akbar writes,

> The People of Unveiling have been given an all-inclusive overview of all religions, creeds, sects, and doctrines concerning God. They are not ignorant of any of these. Adherents follow creeds, sects conform to specific laws, and doctrines are held concerning God or something in the engendered universe. Some of these contradict, some diverge, and some are similar. In every case the Possessor of Unveiling knows from where the doctrine, the creed, or the sect are taken, and he ascribes it to its place. He offers an excuse for everyone who holds a doctrine and does not declare him in error. He does not consider the doctrine to be vain, for God *did not create the heaven and the earth and what is between them for unreality* [Quran 38:27] and He did not create the human being *in vain* [Quran 23:115]. On the contrary, He created him alone to be in His form. . . .[68]

Ibn 'Arabī understood that the diversity of religious forms is based on the infinite possibilities manifested through the Divine Names and Nature, while adhering to the religion of Islam, which provided him with a path to realization and made his universal understanding of forms and the Formless possible. His emphasis on Islamic orthodoxy and even a literal reading of the Quran led him to some of the most universal and esoteric observations about the nature of God, the world, man and religion. Ibn 'Arabī's insights into the transcendent unity of religions and his articulation of quintessential esoterism is also clearly illustrated in the following passage:

66. Ibid., p. 99.
67. *Knowledge and the Sacred*, p. 279.
68. *Imaginal Worlds*, p. 154.

> [Do] not attach yourself to any particular creed exclusively, so that you disbelieve in all the rest; otherwise, you will lose much good, nay, you will fail to recognize the real truth of the matter. God, the omnipresent and omnipotent, is not limited by any one creed, for He says, (Quran 2:109), "Wheresoever ye turn, there is the face of Allah."[69]

In his *al-Futūḥāt al-makkiyyah* Ibn 'Arabi also describes the Islamic perspective on sacred art in other religions, stating that "The Byzantines developed the art of painting to perfection because, for them, the singular nature (*fardāniyyah*) of our Lord Jesus (Sayyidnā 'Īsā), as expressed in his image, is the supreme support of concentration upon Divine Unity."[70] This passage reflects the Prophet Muḥammad's respect for the icon of the Virgin and Christ referred to above. Ibn 'Arabī adhered strictly to the principles and forms of Islamic Law (*Sharī'ah*) and theology (*kalām*) and knew that icons are not meant for Muslims who have aniconic art, but he also clearly understood their importance for other religious communities and believed that God sanctioned them. Such an understanding of Christian iconography can be easily transposed to the sacred art of other religions, such as Hinduism and Buddhism, whose contemplative beauty and refinement cannot be reduced to the crass idolatry of some pre-Islamic Arabs.

Some of the passages cited above tell us more about Ibn 'Arabī's all-inclusive vision of God than they do about his views on the posthumous status of non-Muslims. In other words, he is able to see the signs and Names of God in and through creation, including the diverse religions, because of his spiritual station as a Muslim and an accomplished Sufi. In other places, Ibn 'Arabī critiques some of the beliefs and practices of non-Muslims among the People of the Book. However, his soteriology is centered on Divine mercy (*raḥ-*

69. Reynold A. Nicholson, *The Mystics of Islam* (London: Routledge, Kegal Paul, 1914), pp. 87–88.

70. Titus Burckhardt, *Art of Islam: Language and Meaning*, trans. J. Peter Hobson (London: World of Islam Festival Trust, 1976), p. 30. Burckhardt goes on to write, "It will be seen that this interpretation of the icon, although it is far removed from Muslim theology as generally accepted, is nevertheless at home in the perspective of *tawḥīd*, the doctrine of Divine Unity." Ibid., p. 30.

mah) and, following the Quran, he maintains that "mercy embraces all things" (7:156), including those with flawed beliefs, individuals who have not received personal proof of the veracity of Islam, and even the inhabitants of hell. Moreover, all human beings have a limited understanding of God and take their idea of the Divine for the Reality Itself. Thus, both Muslims and non-Muslims have certain natural limitations and errors that necessitate the Mercy of God—both in this world and the hereafter—for a more comprehensive disclosure of the Truth. For Ibn 'Arabī, salvation is best assured through the inclusive teachings of the Quran and *Sunnah*, but all things ultimately return to God and are embraced by His Mercy.[71]

Muḥyī al-Dīn ibn 'Arabī remains one of the supreme expositors of the perennial philosophy in Islamic history, even if he articulated these teachings in a particular context and manner that differ in important ways from our own. His presence and teachings have nourished generations of Muslim philosophers, gnostics, and aspirants on the Sufi path. He helped pave the way for the great Muslim philosophers and Sufis of later generations, such as Ṣadr al-Dīn Qūnawī, Maḥmūd Shabistarī, 'Abd al-Karīm Jīlī, Mullā Ṣadrā, and the Amīr 'Abd al-Qādir al-Jazā'irī. 'Abd al-Karīm Jīlī (d. 1428) writes in an important passage in his treatise *al-Insān al-kāmil*,

> Ten sects are the sources for all of the religious differences (which are too numerous to count), and all differences revolve around these ten. They are: Polytheists, Naturalists, Philosophers, Dualists, Magians, Materialists, [Hindus], Jews, Christians, and Muslims. For every one of these sects God has created people whose destiny is Heaven and people whose destiny is the Fire. Have you not seen how the polytheists of past ages who lived in regions not reached by the prophet of that time are divided into those who do good, whom God rewards, and those who do evil, whom God recompenses with fire? Each of these sects worships God, as God desires to be worshipped, for He created them for Himself, not for themselves. Thus, they exist just as they were fashioned. [God] may He be glorified and exalted, manifests His Names and Attributes to

71. See Mohammad Hassan Khalil, *Islam and the Fate of Others: The Question of Salvation.*

> these sects by means of His Essence and all of the sects worship Him [in their own way].[72]

Vincent Cornell comments:

> Later on in the text, when he discusses how "each sect finds pleasure in its tenets" (Quran 30:32) he does not absolve the unbelievers of their errors. For Jīlī, religions are not equal in value. However, when the Quran commands, "There is no compulsion in religion" (2:256), this means that even false religions should be respected by Muslims because all religions, including those that are in error, exist by God's will.[73]

Ibn 'Arabī's *Akbarī* school, Suhrawardī's *Ishrāqī* school, Avicenna and other Muslim philosophers all found a harmonious union in the Shī'ite world through the teachings of Mullā Ṣadrā, who represents one of the peaks of the Islamic sapiential tradition and the perennial philosophy. Mullā Ṣadrā or Ṣadr al-Dīn Shīrāzī (d. 1640) was born in Shiraz during Safavid rule of Iran. He created a synthesis between the disciplines and paths of Islamic philosophy, theology, illumination, and gnosis with the help of his eminent predecessors, such as Naṣīr al-Dīn Ṭūsī, Quṭb al-Dīn Shīrāzī, Sayyid Ḥaydar Āmulī, Ibn Turkah Iṣfahānī, and Ibn Abī Jumhūr Aḥsā'ī, as well as his teachers Mīr Dāmād and Shaykh Bahā' al-Dīn 'Āmilī.[74] One of Mullā Ṣadrā's other teachers Mīr Findiriskī also taught the works of Avicenna from Isfahan and studied Sufism and spiritual alchemy. Moreover, Mīr Findiriskī traveled to India where he studied and appreciated Hinduism and wrote a commentary on the *Yoga Vasíshtha*.[75]

Mullā Ṣadrā was versed in traditional philosophy and the religious and intellectual sciences, which had an important impact on his life and writings. Throughout his treatises he refers to the doc-

72. Vincent J. Cornell, "Practical Sufism: An Akbarian Basis for a Liberal Theology of Difference," *Sophia* 15, vol. 2 (Winter 2010), p. 109.

73. Ibid., p. 110.

74. Seyyed Hossein Nasr, *Ṣadr al-Dīn Shīrāzī and his Transcendent Theosophy* (Tehran: Institute for Humanities and Cultural Studies, 1997), p. 24.

75. Seyyed Hossein Nasr, *Islamic Philosophy from its Origin to the Present*, pp. 216–218

trines of Hermes, Plato, Aristotle, Avicenna, al-Ghazzālī, Suhrawardī, and Ibn 'Arabī, for example, while copiously citing the Quran and the sayings of the Prophet and the Shī'ite Imams. He writes in his *Risālah fi'l-ḥudūth*,

> Know that wisdom (*ḥikmah*) began originally with Adam and his progeny Seth and Hermes, i.e., Idrīs, and Noah because the world is never deprived of a person upon whom the science of Unity and eschatology rests. And it is the greatest Hermes who propagated it (*ḥikmah*) throughout the regions of the world and different countries and manifested it and made it emanate upon the "true worshippers." He is the "Father of philosophers (*Abu'l-ḥukamā'*) and the master of those who are the masters of the sciences.[76]

In addition to his vast theoretical knowledge of the Islamic intellectual tradition, including Greek philosophy, he may have been initiated into practical Sufism or *'irfān* by one of his aforementioned teachers or received guidance directly from Khiḍr or the Hidden Imam.[77] We do know that he spent several years in retreat where he focused on quintessential prayer and returned as a realized sage.[78] Therefore, whether he had a regular initiation or received guidance from one of the hidden masters of Islamic esoterism, his knowledge was the fruit of spiritual discipline and gnosis and not simply the result of the rational faculty and theoretical knowledge alone.

Mullā Ṣadrā is best known for his book *The Transcendent Theosophy concerning the Four Intellectual Journeys of the Soul* (*al-Ḥikmat al-muta'āliyah fi'l-asfār al-'aqliyyat al-arba'ah*), also known simply as *Asfār (Journeys)*, but his corpus includes nearly fifty manuscripts on subjects that include Quran and *Ḥadīth* commentary, Imamology, Shī'ite esoterism, philosophy, metaphysics, ontology, cosmogony, eschatology, symbolism, free will and predestination, epistemology, logic, and poetry.[79] In breadth and depth few philosophers in Islamic history can compare to Mullā Ṣadrā, whose

76. Seyyed Hossein Nasr, *Islamic Life and Thought* (Chicago: ABC International Group, Inc., 2001), p. 106.
77. *Ṣadr al-Dīn Shīrāzī and his Transcendent Theosophy*, p. 36.
78. Ibid., p. 37.
79. Ibid., pp. 40–50.

perspective has become known as *al-ḥikmat al-muta'āliyah* or transcendent theosophy, not to be confused with certain pseudo-theosophical movements in the West. S.H. Nasr writes about Mullā Ṣadrā's *Asfār*:

> The symbolism of wayfaring is universal and found in nearly all religions and the flight of the soul to God is often expressed in terms of a journey. The very name Taoism is derived from the Tao or the "way", while in Islam the names for both the Divine Law or *Sharī'ah* and the esoteric way or *ṭarīqah* mean literally road and path. The Sufis especially emphasized in their works the symbolism of traveling. Some Sufi works such as the *Conference of the Birds* (*Manṭiq al-ṭayr*) of 'Aṭṭār are based wholly on this symbolism. Ibn 'Arabī even wrote a treatise whose title includes the name "*al-asfār*" and he discusses the meaning of its singular form, *safar*, in his *al-Iṣṭilāhāt al-ṣūfiyyah*. Mullā Ṣadrā was fully conscious of this tradition and in fact in the introduction of the *Asfār* mentions that the gnostics undertake four journeys. . . .[80]

The four journeys that Mullā Ṣadrā elucidated and experienced are the journey from creation (*al-khalq*) to the Truth (*al-Ḥaqq*), the journey from the Truth to the Truth by the Truth, the journey from the Truth to creation with the Truth, and the journey from creation to creation with the Truth, all of which recall the aforementioned *mi'rāj* of the Prophet of Islam, as well as the Sufi concepts of *fanā'* and *baqā'* or annihilation in and subsistence through God.[81] The path to sacred knowledge that Mullā Ṣadrā writes about in his *Asfār*, as well as his other treatises on metaphysics and ontology, was inspired by his own journey through the Divine Intellect and returns to us as a precious jewel of the Islamic intellectual tradition and the perennial philosophy, reflecting the light and wisdom of the Revelation, intellectual intuition, and reason or the Quran, *'irfān*, and *burhān*. The teachings of Mullā Ṣadrā continue to be studied and cultivated throughout the Islamic world, as well as in India and

80. Ibid., p. 57.

81. Ibid., pp. 55–60; and Seyyed Hossein Nasr, *The Garden of Truth: The Vision and Promise of Sufism, Islam's Mystical Tradition* (New York: HarperCollins, 2007), pp. 128–129.

the West, and constitute a living philosophical tradition that is wed to Revelation and gnosis.

The poetry and prose of Sufi masters, especially Persian Sufi poetry, contain some of the most sublime and explicit references to the *sophia perennis* and the transcendent unity of religions in world history.[82] At the head of this group of Muslim gnostics and aesthetes is Farīd al-Dīn ʿAṭṭār (d. 1220), author of the celebrated masterpiece of Persian literature *The Conference of the Birds* (*Manṭiq al-ṭayr*), the title of which is derived from a Quranic reference to the prophet Solomon who is said to have known "the language of the birds" (27:16). While the metaphysics, autology, and symbolism of the thirty birds (*sī murgh*) and the Supreme Sīmurgh in the *Manṭiq al-ṭayr* are discussed in chapter three, ʿAṭṭār's fascinating story of Shaykh-i Ṣanʿān and the Christian maiden merits close attention here. S.H. Nasr writes, "No page of Persian literature is more moving than the description of the love of the venerable Sufi master for the beautiful Christian maiden."[83]

In ʿAṭṭār's rendition of the story, Shaykh-i Ṣanʿān is the foremost Muslim scholar and Sufi of his time who carefully observes the conditions of Islamic Law and the spiritual path. For fifty years he has led a host of disciples in Mecca when he is haunted by a dream indicating that he will leave Mecca for Rome where he will worship an idol. Troubled and perplexed by this omen, he leaves for Rome with his disciples to decipher its true meaning. ʿAṭṭār writes,

They left the Kaʿbah for Rome's boundaries.
A gentle landscape of low hills and trees,
Where, infinitely lovelier than the view,
There sat a girl, a Christian girl who knew
The secrets of her faith's theology.
A fairer child no man could hope to see—
In beauty's mansion she was like a sun

82. For this reason, it is often difficult for interpreters and readers of Rūmī and Ḥāfiẓ in the West to see their essential link to the Quran and the Prophet of Islam, and falsely attribute to them a universalism that stands opposed to tradition and orthodoxy.

83. Seyyed Hossein Nasr, *Islamic Art and Spirituality* (Albany, NY: State University of New York Press, 1987), p. 106.

> That never set—indeed the spoils she won
> Were headed by the sun himself, whose face
> Was pale with jealousy and sour disgrace
> The man about whose heart her ringlets curled
> Became a Christian and renounced the world...
> In turn the Shaykh's disciples had their say,
> Love has no cure, and he could not obey.[84]

The beauty of the Christian girl has a debilitating affect on the Shaykh, but she will only reciprocate his love if he completely abandons Islam and agrees to drink wine, herd pigs, worship an idol, and burn the Quran! 'Aṭṭār uses these incendiary images and the Shaykh's devotion to the Christian girl to remind the reader or potential wayfarer the degree of devotion, fervor, and trust they must have on the path to the Beloved. The Christian maiden is simultaneously a symbol for the guide on the spiritual path and the Supreme Beloved, while the Shaykh becomes the perfect disciple and lover through resigning his will to the will of his beloved. The Shaykh's apostasy is intentionally blasphemous from the exoteric point of view, while illuminating the nature of esoterism. 'Aṭṭār is boldly highlighting that there is, in the domain of esoterism, no essential difference between Islam and Christianity. He in fact uses the Christian maiden and Christianity to instruct his readers about the nature of the spiritual path and the Truth, as well as the relativity of outward religious forms. S.H. Nasr writes,

> The Shaykh's attraction to a Christian woman in such a shocking manner alludes obviously to the 'iconoclastic' and 'scandalous' character of all that concerns the supraformal Essence *vis-à-vis* the world of forms. But it also indicates clearly the crossing of religious boundaries through esoterism. Here, the maiden is not just the symbol of love, even of a 'scandalous' kind, but as a Christian she represents a being belonging to a different religious universe. Through the attraction of love—which here represents realized gnosis—the Sufi master is not only carried from the world of forms to that of the Essence, but is also transported across reli-

84. Farīd al-Dīn 'Aṭṭār, *The Conference of the Birds* (*Manṭiq al-ṭayr*), trans. Afkham Darbandi and Dick Davis (London: Penguin Books, 1984), pp. 58–60.

> gious frontiers. In 'Aṭṭār's incomparable story is to be found not only a highly poetic treatment of the theme of the love which attracts, consumes, and transforms but also a powerful statement of the role of esoterism in making possible the crossing of the frontiers of religious universes. It is as if 'Aṭṭār wanted to state in the classical language of Sufi poetry that veritable ecumenism is essentially of an esoteric nature and that it is only through the esoteric that man is able to penetrate into the meaning of other formal universes.[85]

It is precisely through penetrating into the depths of Islamic esoterism or Sufism that 'Aṭṭār could see in the Christian girl and Christianity superlative symbols for the spiritual path and its Summit. 'Aṭṭār does acknowledge the social upheaval that the Shaykh's conversion caused and eventually returns him to Islam through a disciple who remained faithful, and in a dream with the Prophet Muḥammad pleaded on behalf of the Shaykh for the Prophet's intercession.[86] 'Aṭṭār's description of the beauty and spiritual influence of the Prophet of Islam closely resembles his initial description of the Christian maiden, who serve the same function at different points in the story. Indeed, the entirety of the poem is a description of the spiritual path in Islam, while incorporating certain symbols from Christianity and ancient Persia, such as the Sīmurgh, to highlight the universality of esoterism and the Oneness of the Divine Reality.

Following closely in the footsteps of 'Aṭṭār is the Sulṭān-i 'Ishq or King of Love, Jalāl al-Dīn Rūmī (d. 1273). S.H. Nasr writes,

> It is by making the distinction between *ṣūrat* and *ma'nā* that Rūmī is able to offer a hermeneutical interpretation of all of reality, of both the 'cosmic Quran' and the 'revealed Quran' and to unveil the transcendent unity of being and of religions. Jalāl al-Dīn is, along with Ibn 'Arabī, perhaps the foremost expositor of the transcendent unity of religions in the annals of Sufism as well as one of the

85. *Islamic Art and Spirituality*, p. 107.

86. The Christian girl also eventually embraces Islam and travels to find the Shaykh.

grand expositors of the cardinal doctrine of the unity of being (*waḥdat al-wujūd*).

The great Persian Sufi poet Rūmī did not discard or circumvent the *ṣūrat* or form of religion, but revealed the *maʿnā* or meaning within the variety of forms that exist in this world, especially religion. Following the Quran, Rūmī saw the signs of the God upon near and distant horizons, including nature, poetry, sacred music and dance, his companions Shams al-Dīn and Ḥusām al-Dīn, Islam and all of the religions he encountered. He was extremely receptive to Divine Beauty and saw the Face of the Beloved everywhere he turned.[87] Mawlānā (lit. our Master), as Rūmī is known in the Islamic world, wrote extensively about the prophets mentioned in the Quran and in fact provided an esoteric commentary on the Revelation with his *Mathnawī*, which led the Persian poet Jāmī to write, "The spiritual couplets of Mawlānā are the Quran in the Persian tongue."[88] Rūmī is so insistent on his attachment to the Arabic revelation and Prophet that he writes in his *Dīwān-i kabīr*:

I am a slave of the Quran if I have a soul
I am the dust of the road of Muḥammad, the Chosen
If anyone quotes from my sayings other than this
I have nothing to do with him and I have nothing to do with his words.[89]

Therefore, we can assert without hesitation that his appreciation for the various prophets and other religions was the result of his knowledge of the inner meaning and the outer form of the Quran and the *Sunnah*. Referring to the prophets, Rūmī states,

87. Frithjof Schuon remarks, "[To] be sensitive to the metaphysical transparency of beauty, to the radiation of forms and sounds, is already to possess—in common with a Rūmī or a Rāmakrishna—a visual and auditative intuition capable of ascending through phenomena right up to the essences and the eternal melodies. "Concerning the Proofs of God", *Studies in Comparative Religion* (Winter 1973), p. 8.

88. Annemarie Schimmel, *Rumi's World: The Life and Work of the Great Sufi Poet* (Boston: Shambhala, 1992), p. 114.

89. Michelle Kimball, "Jalalo'd-Din Rumi's Views on the *Shari'at*," *Sufi* 17 (1993), p. 25.

> If ten lamps are present in (one) place, each differs in form from the other:
> To distinguish without any doubt the light of each, when you turn your face toward their light, is impossible.
> In things spiritual there is no division and no numbers; in things spiritual there is no partition and no individuals.[90]

The above passage highlights that the multiplicity of prophets does not detract from, but is rather an expression of the Unity of God. Due to the intense degree of devotion and fervor that religion inspires, men and women naturally develop a certain amount of partiality for their prophet and religion. This is positive to the extent that one must approach God through a particular manifestation of the Logos, but negative if it leads to the categorical rejection of other revealed books, prophets and religions for other communities. After following a particular tradition, there is nothing more important than Jews, Christians, and Muslims, for example, seeing Moses, Jesus and Muḥammad as manifesting the same Divine Light in different hues. Speaking of those from other religions, Rūmī writes,

> I was speaking one day amongst a group of people, and a party of non-Muslims was present. In the middle of my address they began to weep and to register emotion and ecstasy. Someone asked: What do they understand and what do they know? Only one Muslim in a thousand understands this kind of talk. What did they understand, that they should weep? The Master [i.e. Rūmī himself] answered: It is not necessary that they should understand the form of the discourse; that which constitutes the root and principle of the discourse, that they understand. After all, everyone acknowledges the Oneness of God, that He is the Creator and Provider, that He controls everything, that to Him all things return, and that it is He who punishes and forgives. When anyone hears these words, which are a description and commemoration (*dhikr*) of God, a universal commotion and ecstatic passion supervenes, since out of these words come the scent of their Beloved and their Quest.[91]

90. Jalāl al-Dīn Rūmī, *Mathnawī,* book I, trans. R.A. Nicholson (Warminster, Wiltshire: E.J.W. Gibb Memorial Trust, 1990), p. 39.

91. Reza Shah-Kazemi, *The Other in the Light of the One*, p. 265.

He states elsewhere, "The religion of love is apart from all religions; for lovers, the (only) religion and creed is God."[92] Ultimately, the object of devotion for the gnostics is God alone. The sacred forms of religion issue from and lead to the Absolute, but their outer forms do not exhaust the Absolute. When meaning is not perceived through the forms of religion they can obscure rather than communicate the Presence of God. Rūmī seems well aware of this and is occasionally forced to shock his readers into remembering that the Beloved is the *raison d'être* of religion. With that said, he certainly saw the Quran and the *Sunnah* of the Prophet of Islam as expressing the Will of the Beloved for Muslims. Referring to the universality of sacred knowledge and the connection that exists between mystics of all religions Rūmī writes in his *Mathnawī:*

> Having the same tongue is kinship and affinity,
> With those with whom no intimacy exists, a man is in prison.
> There are many Hindus and Turks with the same tongue,
> And oh, many a pair of Turks, strangers to each other.
> Hence the tongue of intimacy is something else,
> It is better to be of one heart than of one tongue.
> Without speech, without oath, without register,
> A hundred thousand interpreters from the heart arise.[93]

We find numerous examples of the essential, not to be confused with the formal, unity of religions in the writings of almost all Persian Sufi poets. The transcendent unity of religions is almost taken for granted by anyone who has read and appreciated these Muslim sages. In *The Garden of Mystery* (*Gulshan-i rāz)*, Maḥmūd Shabistarī (d. 1340) demonstrates that the inner meaning of Christianity runs parallel to and resembles the esoteric dimensions of Islam or Sufism. While Jesus is seen as a prophet in Islam, the crystallization of his teachings in the Christian world also point to the spiritual path (*ṭarīqah*) and the sole Truth (*al-Ḥaqq*), which is the common goal of all religions. Shabistarī writes:

92. *Mathnawī*, book II, p. 312.

93. Seyyed Hossein Nasr, *The Pilgrimage of Life and the Wisdom of Rumi* (Oakton, VA: The Foundation for Traditional Studies, 2007), pp. 96–97.

I have seen that Christianity's aim is real detachment;
I've seen it as the breaking of the bonds of imitation.
Sacred Unity's courtyard in the monastery of Spirit
where the Sīmurgh of the Everlasting makes Its nest.
From God's Spirit, Jesus, this work of detachment appeared,
since he was manifested from the sacred Spirit.
There is also a spirit from God within you;
in which is found a trace of the Most Holy.
If you should seek extinction of the earthly self,
come into the chamber of the Holy Presence.
Anyone who, angel-like, has detached from the earthly soul
Will be risen, Jesus-like, to the fourth celestial realm.[94]

These lines illustrate that understanding between various religions is best achieved through what Frithjof Schuon has called "esoteric ecumenism" or knowledge of the inner dimension of one's own religion through which one can find common ground with other religions. For the religions begin to converge and resemble one another in their esoteric doctrines and ways and not on the exoteric level, which demands greater diversity. Thus, ecumenism between religions cannot be achieved on the outward level where their forms necessarily diverge and even contradict, but through witnessing their affinity on the inward or esoteric level, which a Christian or Muslim, for example, discovers by remaining devoted to God through both the inner and outer dimensions of his or her own religion.[95] The great Sufi poet Ḥāfiẓ Shīrāzī (d. 1389) writes: "In love no difference there is between monastery and Sufi tavern of ruins,

94. Maḥmūd Shabistarī, *The Garden of Mystery* (*Gulshan-i rāz*), trans. Robert Darr (Sausalito, CA: Real Impressions, 1998), pp. 106–107. See also Leonard Lewisohn's penetrating article, "The Transcendental Unity of Polytheism and Monotheism in the Sufism of Shabistarī," in L. Lewisohn, ed., *The Heritage of Sufism: Classical Persian Sufism from its Origins to Rumi (700–1300)*, vol. I (Oxford: Oneworld Publications, 1999), pp. 379–406.

95. From this point of view, a Christian cannot truly know the transcendent love or knowledge of God that is common to all religions except through the very forms of his or her religion, including Trinitarian theology, the Christian sacraments, and other features of Christianity that are foreign to Islam. Similarly, a Muslim must follow Islamic Law and Sufism to begin to see that inner and transcendent nexus that exists between religions. First and foremost, that nexus or unity is God,

wheresoever it be, there is the glow of the light of the Beloved's Face."[96] Similary, Hātif Iṣfahānī (d. 1783) writes in his *Tarjīʿ band*:

In the church I said to a Christian charmer of hearts,
"O thou in whose net the heart is captive!
O thou to the warp of whose girdle each hair-tip
of mine is separately attached!
How long wilt thou continue not to find the way
to Divine Unity? How long wilt thou impose
on the One the shame of the Trinity?
How can it be right to name the One True God 'Father',
'Son', and 'Holy Ghost'?"
She parted her sweet lips and said to me, while
with sweet laughter she poured sugar from her lips:
"If thou art aware of the Secret of the Divine Unity,
do not cast on us the stigma of infidelity!
In three mirrors the Eternal Beauty cast a ray
from His effulgent countenance.
Silk does not become three things
if thou callest it *parniyān*, *ḥarīr*, and *parand*."
While we were thus speaking, this chant
rose up beside us from the church bell:
"He is One and there is naught save He:
There is no God save Him alone!"[97]

While a number of Persian Sufi poets wrote about the essential unity of Sufism and Christianity, the inner affinity of all religions was not fully elaborated by Muslims until the twentieth century because most religious communities only encountered a few of the

but there is also greater accord when it comes to esoteric practices, such as the invocation of the Name of God in Hesychasm and Sufism. Ecumenism sought on the outward level would try to achieve a false unity between necessarily disparate elements, which must remain distinct to provide the various religious communities with paths to salvation and sanctification and, if possible, esoteric ecumenism. See Frithjof Schuon, *Christianity/Islam: Perspectives on Esoteric Ecumenism*, trans. Mark Perry, Jean-Pierre Lafouge, and James S. Cutsinger (Bloomington, IN: World Wisdom, 2008); and *Paths to the Heart: Sufism and the Christian East.*

96. Seyyed Hossein Nasr, *The Heart of Islam*, p. 316.

97. *Sufi Essays*, p. 136.

world's other great religions and the Quran itself is formally situated in the Abrahamic universe. Similar expressions were however made by Sufis when they encountered Judaism, Zoroastrianism, the Greek philosophical heritage, Hinduism, Buddhism, Confucianism, and Taoism.[98]

One of the most eloquent references to the transcendent unity of religions in Arabic Sufi poetry comes from Manṣūr Ḥallāj (d. 922). Ḥallāj was a Christ-like Sufi who was martyred for uttering *Ana'l-Ḥaqq* or "I am the Truth," which is discussed in more detail in chapter four. The following narration and poem is a brilliant summary of the universal message of Islam and illustrates that the spiritual elite among the early Muslims were well aware of the formal diversity and underlying unity of the revealed religions, which was not simply constructed by a few contemporary thinkers. According to 'Abd Allāh ibn Tāhir Azdī:

> I was quarreling with a Jew in the market of Baghdad, and I blurted out "dog!" Passing then by my side [Ḥallāj] regarded me with an angry air and told me: "Don't make your dog bark so!" and he withdrew in haste. My quarrel ended, I went to find him and entered his home; but he looked away from me. I apologized and he calmed down. Then he said to me "My son, the religious faiths, all of them, arise from God the Most High; He assigned to each group a creed, not of their own choice, but of His choice imposed on them. . . . I would have you know that Judaism, Christianity, Islam, and the other religious denominations may be different names and contrasting appellations, but that their Goal, Himself, suffers neither difference nor contrast."[99]

Then Ḥallāj recited the following poem:

> Earnest for truth, I thought on the religions:
> They are, I found, one root with many a branch.
> Therefore impose on no man a religion,
> Lest it should bar him from the firm-set root.

98. See S.H. Nasr's valuable chapter, "Islam and the Encounter of Religions" in *Sufi Essays*, pp. 123–151.

99. Louis Massignon, *Hallāj: Mystic and Martyr*, trans. by Herbert Mason (Princeton, NJ: Princeton University Press, 1994) p. 104.

Let the root claim him, a root wherein all heights
And meanings are made clear, for him to grasp.[100]

It is not a coincidence that some of the greatest gnostics in Islamic history, figures such as Ḥallāj, Suhrawardī, Ibn 'Arabī, and Rūmī, also knew and disclosed, each in their own way, the transcendent unity of religions, and that some Muslim jurists and theologians were unable to comprehend their statements about both God and other religions. These classical Muslim sages did not base their knowledge on imitation and transmitted knowledge alone, but attained degrees of proximity to the transcendent Reality where the mysteries of God and creation were unveiled. Those Muslims who have not followed the spiritual path to the supraformal Truth, or do not at least possess a measure of intellectual intuition, will find it difficult or impossible to understand the esoteric meaning of *tawḥīd*, which is none other than the transcendent Unity of Being and religions (*waḥdat al-wujūd wa'l-adyān*). Due to the fact that not all believers naturally incline towards metaphysics and the spiritual path, conflicts can arise. In light of this dilemma we should all heed the aforementioned Quranic verse,

> For each among you We have appointed a law and a way. And had God willed, He would have made you a single community, but [He willed otherwise], that He might try you in that which He has given you. So vie with one another in good deeds. Unto God shall be your return, all together, and He will inform you of that wherein you differed. (5:48)

Closely connected to the Quran, *Sunnah* and Sufism is the tradition of *futuwwah* or spiritual chivalry. The term *futuwwah* in Arabic or *javānmardī* in Persian, implies courage, honor, nobility, generosity, and beauty, and traces its origin to the prophet Abraham. According to S.H. Nasr,

> Abraham was therefore the initiator of the cycle of *futuwwah*, which according to later authors such as Wā'iẓ Kāshifī was transmitted like prophecy (*nubuwwah*) itself. Abraham passed it to Ishmael and Isaac, Isaac to Jacob, and Jacob to Joseph, one of the

100. *Sufi Poems*, p. 34.

chief exemplars of *futuwwah.* Then it was transmitted to Christianity and finally Islam. The Prophet of Islam received through the "Muḥammadan Light" the truth and power of *futuwwah,* which he transmitted to 'Alī, who henceforth became the supreme source of *futuwwah* in Islam for both Sunnis and Shī'ites.[101]

The virtues of *futuwwah* are summarized in the life and teachings 'Alī ibn Abī Ṭālib, who is the fourth Caliph in Sunnism and the first Imam in Shī'ism. The saying of the Prophet, "There is no *fatā* (chivalrous youth) except 'Alī and no sword except *Dhu'l-fiqār,*" refers to the chivalry 'Alī displayed on the battlefield and his sword *Dhu'l-fiqār.* On one occasion, the indomitable warrior had overtaken his adversary on the battlefield when the latter spit on his face. At that moment the Imam felt a measure of anger come over him and instead of acting upon that anger decided to show mercy to the man who eventually embraced Islam. Rūmī retells this story in his *Mathnawī*:

He spat on the face of 'Alī
The pride of every prophet and saint. . . .
And 'Alī responded,
He said, "I wield the sword for the sake of Truth,
I am the servant of the Truth, not commanded by the body.
I am the Lion of the Truth, not the lion of the passion,
My action is witness to my religion.
In war I am (manifesting the truth of) *thou didst not throw*
When thou threwest: I am (but) as the sword, and the wielder is
the (Divine) Sun.
I have removed the baggage of self out of the way, I have
deemed (what is) other than God to be non-existence.
I am a shadow, the Sun is my lord; I am the chamberlain,
I am not the curtain (which prevents approach) to Him.
I am filled with the pearls of union, like a (jeweled) sword:
In battle I make (men) living, not slain. . . ."[102]

As a result of his purity and selflessness 'Alī was able to act as an instrument of the Divine and embody the qualities of mercy and self-

101. Seyyed Hossein Nasr, "Spiritual Chivalry" in Seyyed Hossein Nasr, ed., *Encyclopaedia of Islamic Spirituality,* vol. II (Lahore: Suhail Academy, 2000), p. 305.

102. *Mathnawī,* book I, pp. 202–205.

restraint on the battlefield. Modern warfare has fallen from the forbearance, magnanimity, and self-discipline that 'Alī displayed, which is also reminiscent of certain legends of the great knights of Christendom, the Hindu kshatriya caste of India, the Buddhist Shaolin monks of China and the samurai of Japan. We have numerous examples of noble warriors of the past who upheld the tradition of chivalry because their actions were guided by contemplation and tempered by a spiritual discipline that led to the refinement of the soul.

An outstanding example of a relatively recent Muslim sage who also combined metaphysical realization with correct action is the Amīr 'Abd al-Qādir al-Jazā'irī (d. 1883). In the Amīr 'Abd al-Qādir, the universal principles of the Quran and the *Sunnah*, including a deep reverence for other religions and of humanity, come to life. The Amīr was initiated into the Qādiriyyah, Shādhiliyyah, and Naqshbandiyyah Sufi orders, and also received an *Akbarī* investiture from his father, Sīdī Muḥyī al-Dīn. All of these paths played an important role in his spiritual and intellectual development, but it was his connection to the metaphysical teachings and spiritual influence of Ibn 'Arabī that most clearly shaped his life and teachings. Like Ibn 'Arabī, the Amīr understood that the variety of beliefs and religions does not detract from the Unity of God. He writes in his *Book of Stages* (*Kitāb al-Mawāqif*):

> Your God is One God; there is no god but He. (Quran 2:163)
>
> Say: It has been revealed unto me that your God is One God. (Quran 21:108)
>
> Say: I am only a man like you; it is revealed to me that your God is One God. (Quran 18:110)
>
> Proclaim that there is no god but Me. (Quran 16:2)
>
> In these verses and in other analogous verses, God addresses all those who have been reached by the Quranic revelation or earlier revelations—Jews, Christians, Mazdeans, idolaters, Manicheans and other groups professing varied opinions and beliefs with respect to Him—to teach them that their God is One is spite of the divergences of their doctrines and creeds concerning Him. For His Essence is unique, and the divisions in relation to Him do not involve divisions of His Essential Reality. All the beliefs which are

> professed about Him are for Him just different names. Now, the multiplicity of names does not imply multiplicity of the Named! He has a Name in all languages, which are infinite in number, but that does not affect His unicity.
>
> The preceding verses allude to that which is taught by the elite—that is, the Sufis—namely the transcendent unity of Being (*waḥdat al-wujūd*) and the fact that He is the Essence of everything "worshipped" and that, consequently, whatever he may take as the object of his worship, every worshipper worships only Him, as is proved by the following verse: "And your Lord has decreed that you will worship only Him." (Quran 17:23). . . .[103]

It is striking that the Amīr ʿAbd al-Qādir connects the transcendent unity of religions to the transcendent Unity of Being, which he finds justification for in the literal meaning of the Quran. For the unity of religions only truly resides in God and more precisely in the Divine Essence beyond the determined God of the revealed religions. These various determinations are based on particular aspects or Names of God that, in their form and manifestation in the cosmic order, necessarily differ from and exclude others. However, the particular aspects or Names of God accentuated in each of the revealed religions are certainly embraced by and issue from the Oneness of God. It is in fact the Quran and the Prophet's emphasis on the all-embracing Unity of God that makes it possible for Muslims to see the Face of God in the diverse revelations of humanity, even if this possibility does not always occur. In the same section of the *Mawāqif*, the Amīr states:

> If what you think and believe is the same as what the people of the *Sunnah* say, know that He is that—and other than that! If you think and believe that He is what all the schools of Islam profess and believe—He is that, and He is other than that! If you think that He is what the diverse communities believe—Muslims, Christians, Jews, Mazdeans, polytheists and others—He is that and He is other than that! And if you think and believe what is professed by the Knowers

103. Michel Chodkiewicz, *The Spiritual Writings of Amir ʿAbd al-Kader*, trans. James Chrestensen and Tom Manning (Albany, NY: State University of New York Press, 1995), pp. 125–126.

> *par excellence*—prophets, saints and angels—He is that! He is other than that! None of His creatures worships Him in all His aspects; none is unfaithful to Him in all His aspects. No one knows Him in all His aspects; no one is ignorant of Him in all His aspects. . . .[104]

While privileging the Islamic tradition in his own life and teachings, the Amīr simultaneously affirms the veracity and the limitations of all of the revealed religions. He discloses the doctrine of the transcendent unity of religions, but cautions that, "All of this is part of the secrets which it is proper to conceal from those who are not of our way. . . ."[105] In traditional societies it was unnecessary for all believers to have a detailed knowledge of metaphysics and various religions because fulfilling the basic demands of exoteric religion was—and remains—a sufficient condition for salvation. It was enough for spiritual leaders of the caliber of the Amīr ʿAbd al-Qādir to direct sincere believers in appropriate ways based upon their esoteric and exoteric knowledge. Today, however, conditions have changed and secular forces and arguments—including postmodernism and relativism—pull many away from the shelter of faith. This makes metaphysics and a true understanding of comparative religion imperative because the believer and the secular philosopher alike cannot make sense of apparently mutually exclusive truth claims that the various religions advance. Therefore, the writings of the Amīr ʿAbd al-Qādir and of other sages mentioned throughout this work are treasures that grow in value and significance for an increasingly secularized world.

The Amīr translated his erudition and wisdom into what have become legendary acts of chivalry intelligible to the pious believer and metaphysician alike. In addition to the teachings of Ibn ʿArabī, the Amīr also inherited from his father the responsibility of leading the Algerian resistance against the French colonial army beginning in 1832. He was given the titles "Sultan of the Arabs" and "Commander of the Faithful" at the age of twenty-five, and led the struggle against France's brutal occupation and scorched earth military policy. Reza Shah-Kazemi writes,

104. Ibid., pp. 130–131.
105. Ibid., p. 132.

> At a time when the French were indiscriminately massacring entire tribes, when they were offering their soldiers a ten-franc reward for every pair of Arab ears, and when severed Arab heads were regarded as trophies of war, the Amīr manifested his magnanimity, his unflinching adherence to Islamic principles, and his refusal to stoop to the level of his "civilized" adversaries by issuing the following edict:
>
> "Every Arab who has in his possession a Frenchman is bound to treat him well and to conduct him to either the Khalīfah or the Amīr himself, as soon as possible. In cases where the prisoner complains of ill treatment, the Arab will have no right to any reward."[106]

Due to his exemplary conduct and leadership the Amīr ʿAbd al-Qādir was respected and even venerated by his adversaries.[107] After a series of victories and defeats, he was finally forced to surrender to the French authorities in 1847. Despite a promise from the French to allow him to stay in Muslim lands, the Amīr was imprisoned in France until 1852. He was eventually freed by Louis Napoleon Bonaparte, but exiled to Istanbul, Bursa, and finally Damascus in 1856. Remarkably, he settled in the home that Ibn ʿArabī died in, where he focused on family life, teaching and the spiritual path.[108]

In an event that would crown the Amīr's temporal achievements, he risked his life and the lives of his closest companions to protect

106. Reza Shah-Kazemi, "Recollecting the Spirit of *Jihād*," in *Islam, Fundamentalism, and the Betrayal of Tradition*, pp. 131–132. Shah-Kazemi goes on to write, "When asked what the reward was for a live French soldier, the Amīr replied: 'eight douros.' When asked what the reward was for a severed French head, the reply was: 'twenty-five blows of the baton on the soles of the feet.' Many in his ranks, including within the council of the khalīfas, were keen to respond in kind to the French atrocities, to 'fight fire with fire'; but the Amīr could not be swayed from what he knew was right, and resisted all calls for revenge." Ibid, p. 132

107. The French Governor-General of Algeria, Thomas Robert Bugeaud (d. 1849), said, "He is pale and somewhat resembles the way that Jesus Christ is often portrayed," and "He is a kind of prophet, the hope of all fervent Muslims." *The Spiritual Writings of Amir ʿAbd al-Kader*, p. 2.

108. Ibid., pp. 1–6; and Vincent J. Cornell, " ʿAbd al-Qādir" in John L. Esposito, ed., *The Oxford Encyclopedia of the Modern Islamic World*, vol. I (Oxford: Oxford University Press, 1995), pp. 3–6.

the Christians living in Damascus from a bloodthirsty Druze mob. Shah-Kazemi writes, "He wrote letters to all of the Druze shaykhs, requesting them not to 'make offensive movements against a place with the inhabitants of which you have never before been at enmity.'"[109] When the Amīr's diplomatic efforts failed, he addressed the approaching mob as follows:

> Wretches, is this the way that you honor the Prophet? May his curses be upon you! Shame upon you, shame! You will live to repent. You think you can do as you please with the Christians; but the day of retribution will come. The French will yet turn your mosques into churches. Not a Christian will I give up. They are my brothers. Stand back, or I will give my men the order to fire.[110]

In the year 1860, the Amīr took local Christians into his home, and eventually safeguarded fifteen thousand Christians in the citadel, including some Europeans. Imam Shāmil of Dagestan, the French government, and even the U.S. President Abraham Lincoln praised the Amīr's act of self-sacrifice and valor.[111] An observer Charles Henry Churchill wrote,

> All the representatives of the Christian powers then residing in Damascus, without one single exception, had owed their lives to him. Strange and unparalleled destiny! An Arab had thrown his guardian aegis over the outraged majesty of Europe. A descendent of the Prophet had sheltered and protected the Spouse of Christ.[112]

The Amīr suffered the most brutal attacks, imprisonment and exile at the hands of the French colonialists, and returned their injustices and cruelty with impartiality and benevolence for the Christian population living in Damascus. He was able to clearly discern between the French army who had occupied his land and murdered his countrymen, and those innocent Christian non-combatants who

109. "Recollecting the Spirit of *Jihād*," p. 132.

110. Charles Henry Churchill, *The Druzes and the Maronites under the Turkish Rule from* 1840 *to* 1860 (London: Bernard Quaritch, 1862), pp. 207–215.

111. "Recollecting the Spirit of *Jihād*," p. 133.

112. Ibid., p. 133.

are protected under Islamic Law.[113] For all those who belittle the significance of metaphysics, the perennial philosophy and all efforts towards greater interfaith understanding and fellowship, let them recall the Christian lives that the Amīr saved and perhaps consider how much easier it is for modern soldiers and militants to take innocent life if they believe that their enemy is practicing a heretical religion and falls outside of Divine Mercy and salvation.[114] Even the Amīr's fidelity to Islamic Law alone, which the great Sufis remained faithful to, made it incumbent upon him to protect the Christians living in Damascus. The Amīr 'Abd al-Qādir is a premodern Muslim expositor of the doctrine of the transcendent unity of religions who in fact foreshadows the appearance of the Muslim traditionalists in the twentieth century and proves that their knowledge has traditional precedence in Islam and incalculable relevance in the modern world. In this regard, his presence and teachings are comparable to those of Srī Ramakrishna in nineteenth century India, who is discussed in chapter two. After the Prophet of Islam, there have been numerous Muslim saints whose presence and teachings continue to inspire and guide serious seekers. One of the greatest proofs of the *sophia perennis* in Islam is the vast number of saints and sages that it has produced, and, as we shall see, continues to produce.

The Islamic intellectual and spiritual heritage, which derives from the inner and outer reality of the Quran and soul of the Prophet, is an ocean of sacred knowledge. Reviewing this tradition in light of the *sophia* or *religio perennis* helps explain why Muslim sages were largely responsible for restating the perennial philosophy in the

113. This episode in the Amīr's life is a living embodiment and reminder of the Quranic verse: ". . . . whosoever slays a soul—unless it be for another soul or working corruption on the earth—it is as though he slew all mankind, and whosoever saves the life of one, it is as though he saved the life of all mankind. . . ." (5:32)

114. Charles Le Gai Eaton writes, "'Abd al-Qādir fought the Christians who invaded his land, Algeria, because he was a Muslim. Exiled in Damascus, he protected the Christians against massacre by taking them into his own home because he understood. Those who would challenge him or accuse him of heresy should be prepared to face his sword and accept death from its blade since small men risk their necks when they challenge great ones." *Islam and the Destiny of Man* (Albany, NY: State University of New York Press, 1985), p. 38.

twentieth century. Indeed, for a Muslim sage who knows the Quran, *Ḥadīth* literature and the Islamic sapiential tradition, and has followed the spiritual path (*ṭarīqah*) that leads to intimacy with the Divine Reality, the *sophia perennis* is ubiquitous. Without knowing something about the primary Islamic sources, classical Muslim philosophers and Sufis, and their relationship to the perennial philosophy, the connection between contemporary Muslim traditionalists and the perennial philosophy, as described below, is unintelligible.

Contemporary Muslim Sages and the Perennial Philosophy

René Guénon (1886–1951), or Shaykh 'Abd al-Wāḥid Yaḥyā as he is known in the Islamic world, lived the last twenty years of his life in Cairo as a practicing Muslim. He is the reviver of Tradition in the West and a fierce critic of modernity in all of its facets. He wrote extensively about metaphysics, initiation, and symbolism in the context of Hinduism, Taoism, Islam, Christianity, Judaism and Hermeticism. His critique of modernity, including scientism, materialism, secularism, and various precursors to the New Age movement, was like a sword that discerned truth from falsehood, and a powerful and necessary complement to his appreciation of Tradition. Indeed, Guénon's *The Crisis of the Modern World* proves the famous saying, "The pen is mightier than the sword." He is responsible for expounding the principles of Tradition in the modern West where the esoteric dimensions of religion and the supreme science of metaphysics had been forgotten or marginalized. Guénon made the tactical decision to first express himself through writing about the Hindu tradition in his *Introduction to the Study of the Hindu Doctrines* and *Man and His Becoming according to the Vedānta* because he thought that many in the West would not accept traditional principles if they came in Islamic garb, which is closely related to the Jewish and Christian traditions that many had already rejected. This, as well as the fact that Guénon preferred privacy and moved to Egypt, concealed the fact that Guénon lived and died as a traditional Muslim in the fullest sense of the term.

It is evident that Guénon's Catholic upbringing and his encounters with people knowledgeable of other traditions, especially Hinduism and Taoism, enabled him to appreciate the Truth in these religions and further understand the essential unity of all traditions. But what is often overlooked is Guénon's providential acceptance of Islam—both its exoteric shell and esoteric kernel—and how the universality of the Islamic tradition provided a foundation and framework for Guénon's understanding and existential realization of the Divine Reality at the heart of all revealed religions. Guénon writes in his article "*At-Tawḥīd*":

> The doctrine of Unity, that is, the affirmation that the Principle of all existence is essentially One, is a fundamental point common to all orthodox traditions, and we could even say that it is on this point that their basic identity appears most clearly, conveying itself in its very expression. Indeed, wherever there is Unity, all diversity disappears, and it is only in descending toward multiplicity that differences of form appear, the modes of expression themselves then being as multiple as that to which they refer, and susceptible of indefinite variation in adapting themselves to the circumstances of time and place. But 'the doctrine of Unity is unique' (according to the Arabic formula *at-tawḥīdu wāḥidun*), which is to say that it is everywhere and always the same, invariable like the Principle, independent of multiplicity and change, which can only affect applications of a contingent order...This affirmation [of Unity] is nowhere expressed so explicitly and with such insistence as in Islam....[115]

Islam is a central theme in several of Guénon's works including *Insights into Islamic Esoterism and Taoism* and *The Symbolism of the Cross*, which is dedicated to Shaykh 'Abd al-Raḥmān 'Ilaysh al–Kabīr of the Shādhiliyyah order. Guénon's essay "Islamic Esoterism" in *Islamic Esoterism and Taoism* is an essential prerequisite for anyone interested in the inner dimension of Islam because of its insistence on the necessity of Islamic Law (*Sharī'ah*) and a regular initiatic chain (*silsilah*) that goes back to the Prophet Muḥammad. He also continuously reminds us of the goal of all wayfaring, which is knowledge of the One True Reality. These writings on Islam reveal

115. René Guénon, *Insights into Islamic Esoterism and Taoism*, trans. by Henry D. Fohr (Hillsdale, NY: Sophia Perennis, 2004), p. 14–15.

Guénon's own tradition and the spiritual path he followed to reach the Supreme Identity.

In 1912, Guénon was initiated into the Shādhiliyyah order by a Swedish Muslim, Ivan Gustaf Aguéli or 'Abd al-Hādī, who was a disciple of Shaykh 'Abd al-Raḥmān 'Ilaysh al-Kabīr.[116] Shaykh 'Abd al-Raḥmān emphasized the teachings of the great Sufi gnostic Ibn 'Arabī, which can be seen in Guénon's *The Symbolism of the Cross.* This text is essentially about the Universal Man (*al-insān al-kāmil*), which as we have seen is a central doctrine in the *Akbarī* school. While in Egypt Guénon also frequented spiritual gatherings led by Shaykh Salāmah ibn Ḥasan al-Raḍī, founder of the Ḥāmidiyyah branch of the Shādhiliyyah order, from whom Guénon may have also received an initiation.[117] These connections to Shaykh 'Abd al-Raḥmān and Shaykh Salāmah, and by extension the Prophet Muḥammad, connected Guénon to the heart of the Islamic tradition. Yet, according to Guénon, the acceptance of another tradition for initiatic reasons,

> [has] absolutely nothing in common with any kind of exterior and contingent change, whether arising simply from the 'moral' domain. . . . Contrary to what takes place in 'conversion,' nothing here implies the attribution of the superiority of one traditional form over another. It is merely a question of what one might call reasons of spiritual expediency, which is altogether different from simple individual 'preference'.[118]

116. 'Abd al-Hādī, "Universality in Islam," trans. Farid Nur ad-Din in *Universal Dimensions of Islam: Studies in Comparative Religion*, pp. 134–147. 'Abd al-Hādī writes, ". . . . as the Muslims say, '*At-Tawḥīdu wāḥidun*', which means literally, according to the commentary: 'The doctrine of the Supreme Identity is, in essence, everywhere the same. . . .'" Ibid., p. 138.

117. *Islam in the Modern World*, p. 364. Guénon also married the daughter of another Sufi master Shaykh Muḥammad Ibrāhīm. With his wife Fāṭimah, Guénon had four children: Khadījah, Laylā, Aḥmad and 'Abd al-Wāḥid. R. Waterfield, *René Guénon and the Future of the West* (Hillsdale, NY: Sophia Perennis, 2002), pp. 44–45.

118. René Guénon, *Initiation and Spiritual Realization*, trans. Henry Fohr (Ghent, NY: Sophia Perennis, 2001), pp. 61–63. This quote nevertheless raises more questions than it answers. Guénon may not have felt that Islam was inherently superior to other religions, but he did feel that in the twentieth century the esoteric kernel of religion was more accessible to westerners through Islam than through other religions.

Guénon clearly understood the essential identity of all traditions, yet he writes elsewhere that, "the Islamic tradition is . . . the ultimate form of traditional orthodoxy for the present cycle."[119] He realized the necessity of both exoteric and esoteric forms to know the Supreme Identity and the vitality of the outer and inner dimensions of Islam in the contemporary period. Muslim and non-Muslim traditionalists continue to benefit from his exposition of the perennial philosophy. S. H. Nasr writes:

> The central figure who was most responsible for the presentation of the traditional doctrines of the Orient in their fullness in the modern West was René Guénon, a man who was chosen for this task by Tradition itself and who fulfilled an intellectual function of a supra-individual nature.[120]

Guénon's eminent friend Frithjof Schuon also remarks, "[Guénon] had heroically crossed a bridge, and he was the first to do so; after him, others crossed the bridge; the way had been opened."[121] In addition to the leading Muslim traditionalists surveyed below, Guénon influenced a number of other intellectuals and luminaries from the West and the East, including Mircea Eliade, Huston Smith, Marco Pallis, Michel Vâlsan, Muḥammad Ḥasan 'Askarī, 'Abd al-Wahid Pallavicini, and Rusmir Mahmutcehajic, to name but a few. Ananda K. Coomaraswamy wrote:

> No living writer in modern Europe is more significant than René Guénon, whose task it has been to expound the universal metaphysical tradition that has been the essential foundation of every past culture, and which represents the indispensable basis for any civilization deserving to be called so.[122]

The late Rector of Al-Azhar University in Cairo and Sufi master Shaykh 'Abd al-Ḥalīm Maḥmūd authored the small booklet *al-Fay-*

119. René Guénon, *Symbols of Sacred Science*, trans. Henry D. Fohr (Hillsdale, NY: Sophia Perennis, 2004), p. 156.

120. *Knowledge and the Sacred*, p. 100.

121. Frithjof Schuon, *René Guénon: Some Observations* (Hillsdale, NY: Sophia Perennis, 2004), p. 48.

122. Roger Lipsey, *Coomaraswamy; His Life and Work* (Princeton: Princeton University Press, 1977), p. 170.

lasūf al-muslim: 'Abd al-Wāḥid Yaḥyā aw René Guénon. In another book on the Shādhiliyyah order he refers to Guénon as an "*'ārif bi'Llāh*" or gnostic (lit. he who knows by God) and states that, "Muslims place him close to al-Ghazzālī and his like."[123] These selections illustrate that Guénon and his writings were held in high esteem by one of the most influential Muslim scholars of his time. Moreover, in addition to being read by certain Muslim intellectuals and Sufis in the Arab world, Guénon's intellectual influence is even more pervasive in Bosnia, Turkey, Iran, Pakistan, Malaysia and Indonesia.[124]

In addition to the aforementioned books, some of Guénon's most important works include *The Reign of Quantity & the Signs of the Times, The Multiple States of the Being, Symbols of Sacred Science* and *Perspectives on Initiation.* Guénon restored the meaning of the word Tradition through an authentic understanding and inspired exposition of metaphysics, initiation, symbolism, the traditional sciences, and various religious doctrines and rites. He used the term Tradition to designate all of the above realities in a way that had not been necessary before.[125] He also rightfully condemned various precursors to the New Age movement, as can be seen in his *Theosophy: History of a Pseudo-Religion* and *The Spiritist Fallacy.* Finally, he defended Tradition against the most powerful ideologies of the modern world, including scientism, materialism, secularism, and individualism. Guénon is an intellectual and spiritual renewer and reviver of religion comparable to the great classical Sufis, such as al-Ghazzālī, Suhrawardī and Ibn 'Arabī, and in fact fulfilled this function at a time when Tradition had become almost entirely eclipsed in the West by modernism. With the westernization of most parts of the globe, including the Islamic world—which means the spread of secularism and not the Gospel or Plato's *Republic*—Guénon's

123. 'Abd al-Ḥalīm Maḥmūd, *Qaḍiyyat al-taṣawwuf—al-Madrasat al-Shādhiliyyah* (Cairo: Dār al-Ma'ārif, 1999), pp. 281–362; *The Other in the Light of the One*, p. 364.

124. *Islam in the Modern World*, pp. 362–376.

125. On the meaning of Tradition, see René Guénon, "What is Meant by Tradition?," *Introduction to the Study of the Hindu Doctrines* trans. Marco Pallis (Hillsdale, NY: Sophia Perennis, 2004), pp. 54–57; and Seyyed Hossein Nasr, "What is Tradition?," *Knowledge and the Sacred*, pp. 65–92.

critque of modernism and resuscitation of Tradition only grows in relevance.

* * *

Frithjof Schuon (1907–1998) or Shaykh 'Īsā Nūr al-Dīn Aḥmad unveiled universal and esoteric truths that were directed to spiritual seekers with the necessary aptitude and intelligence to understand. Among his greatest achievements is his treatise *The Transcendent Unity of Religions*, which demonstrates the essential unity of all religions, East and West, through metaphysics, symbolism, logic, art, the perennial wisdom contained in the sacred texts and the writings of sages and saints. This book issues from and points to the transcendent Reality that is common to all authentic religions, while recognizing and demonstrating the need for religious differences. Schuon writes:

> [It] must be emphasized that the unity of the different religions is not only unrealizable on the external level, that of the forms themselves, but ought not to be realized at that level, even were this possible, for in that case the revealed forms would be deprived of their sufficient reason. The very fact that they are revealed shows that they are willed by the Divine Word. If the expression "transcendent unity" is used, it means that the unity of religious forms must be realized in a purely inward and spiritual way and without prejudice to any particular form. The antagonisms between these forms no more affect the one universal Truth than the antagonisms between opposing colors affect the transmission of the one uncolored light.... Just as every color, by its negation of darkness and its affirmation of light, provides the possibility of discovering the ray that makes it visible and of tracing this ray back to its luminous source, so all forms, all symbols, all religions, all dogmas, by their negation of error and their affirmation of Truth, make it possible to follow the ray of Revelation, which is none other than the ray of the Intellect, back to its Divine Source.[126]

All of Schuon's writings contain expressions of pure metaphysics that help to resolve some of the enigmas and apparent contradic-

126. Frithjof Schuon, *The Transcendent Unity of Religions* (Wheaton, IL: Quest Books, 2005), p. xxxiv.

tions of the world's religions by providing another option beyond the false choice of asserting the supremacy and ultimate Truth of one religion alone or of denying the veracity of all religions because they outwardly contradict each other. These options fail to convince the intelligent and pious man because he cannot imagine God limiting His Truth, Presence and Mercy to one segment of humanity alone or that the sacred and inspired books, art and saints throughout history were the products of deception, error or chance. Schuon's thesis demonstrates that religious differences are necessary on the level of outward forms, which cannot possibly exhaust the Truth, but in fact lead to the Transcendent Reality wherein alone the religions meet and are fully reconciled. From this point of view, one can accept—in principle—the diverse theologies, laws and rites of the various religions as so many relative determinations of the Absolute for different communities, while fully dedicating oneself to only one of these religions with the knowledge that it communicates a necessary and sufficient measure of the Truth to lead to the Absolute and Infinite Reality that is beyond all limitations. Only a descent from Heaven or a particular Divine revelation, which is naturally limited in its formal manifestation, can ensure the felicitous ascent of man back to his celestial abode.[127] In addition to *The Transcendent Unity of Religion*, some of Schuon's other notable titles on the perennial philosophy include *Esoterism as Principle and as Way*, *Logic and Transcendence*, *Language of the Self*, *Stations of Wisdom* and *Form and Substance in the Religions*.

127. According to Schuon, each religion contains a relatively-Absolute determination of the Absolute or a particular Face of the ineffable and apophatic Reality that transcends all relativity. These include, for example, the Trinity in Christianity and the Names through which God reveals Himself in the Quran. Schuon writes that the relative-Absolute is, "Being as creator, revealer, and savior, who is absolute for the world, but not for the Essence: 'Beyond-Being' or 'Non-Being'." *Form and Substance in the Religions*, trans. Mark Perry and Jean-Pierre LaFouge (Bloomington, IN: World Wisdom, 2002), p. 248. In order for God to communicate with and even create humanity, He must enter into the domain of relativity, while transcending this plane in His supraformal Essence or Self. It is precisely the relative-Absolute, Being or the Face that God turns towards creation that allows man to move from the relative to the Absolute, Beyond-Being or the Divine Essence. Moreover, the relative-Absolute is communicated to humanity by the Logos or the Word of

Schuon has been read and appreciated by some of the most influential Muslim and non-Muslim religious scholars of our time. In his book on the Shādhiliyyah order Shaykh ʿAbd al-Ḥalīm Maḥmūd refers to Schuon as "an overwhelmingly authoritative knower (*ʿālim ḍalīʿ*)."[128] Annemarie Schimmel, an expert in the field of Islamic studies and Sufism, wrote, "[Schuon is] the leading philosopher of Islamic theosophical mysticism."[129] As discussed below Schuon also influenced other contemporary Muslim intellectuals, including Titus Burckhardt, Martin Lings, Charles Le Gai Eaton, Seyyed Hossein Nasr, and Reza Shah-Kazemi. A leading academic authority in the field of comparative religion, Huston Smith, wrote, "The man is a living wonder; intellectually apropos religion, equally in depth and breadth, the paragon of our time. I know of no living thinker who begins to rival him."[130] Similarly, T.S. Elliot commented regarding Schuon's *The Transcendent Unity of Religions*, "I have met with no more impressive work in the comparative study of Oriental and Occidental religion."[131] To this list can be added the names of Thomas Merton, Joseph Epes Brown, Kathleen Raine, Jacob Needleman, James Cutsinger and many others who have been influenced by Schuon's work and perspective.

God. While Jesus in Christianity and the Quran in Islam necessarily differ from one another, they nevertheless fulfill the same salvific and sanctifying function in each religion. On the one hand the modes of Self-disclosure in the various religions are necessarily limited and diverse aspects of God, while on the other they exist as pathways towards and openings to the same Absolute and Infinite Reality. The outward and relative forms of the religions are not simply impediments on the way to the Formless, but necessary keys forged in Heaven that unlock the door to the Divine mysteries, especially when complemented by the esoteric and contemplative dimensions of religion. Schuon knew that God is not exhausted by any one religion, while at the same time he maintained that a particular religion and the personal God of that religion is necessary to attain some measure of awareness of the infinite plenitude of God that is beyond the delimitations and approximations of theology.

128. *A Return to the Spirit*, p. 10.

129. Frithjof Schuon, *Christianity/Islam: Perspectives on Esoteric Ecumenism*, back cover.

130. *Form and Substance in the Religions*, back cover.

131. *The Transcendent Unity of Religions*, back cover.

In a manner similar to Guénon, Schuon did not publicly reveal his Muslim identity and wrote exceptional and inspired works on Hinduism, Buddhism, Native American traditions, Shintoism, Judaism, Christianity and Islam. He wrote about metaphysics, cosmology, philosophy, theology, epistemology, aesthetics, anthropology, psychology, eschatology, and sacred art in a way that is meaningful for all people with the intelligence and will to understand.[132] He restated the essential universality of religions and also wrote scathing critiques of the modern world. What is sometimes obscured for a reader is that Schuon's universal perspective was inseparable from his attachment to a particular religion—Islam—and not simply a sentimental appreciation of ancient wisdom or an attempt to create a meta-religion that discarded the forms of any one religion. Schuon, more than anyone, understood that there are different paths to the mountain's summit, but he also followed one of those paths to reach it, and it was through this path that his theoretical knowledge and innate intuition became fully realized gnosis.[133] Moreover, Schuon's exposition of the transcendent unity of religions also finds precedence in his spiritual master's understanding of other revealed

132. *The Essential Frithjof Schuon.*

133. Admittedly Schuon writes, "Our starting point is Advaita Vedānta, and not a voluntarist, individualist, and moralist anthropology, with which ordinary Sufism is unquestionably identified; and this is true, whether or not it is to the liking of those who wish our 'orthodoxy' to consist in feigning an Arabo-Semitic mentality, or falling in love with it." Jean-Baptiste Aymard and Patrick Laude, *Frithjof Schuon: Life and Teachings* (Albany, New York: State University of New York Press, 2004), p. 46. However, one must keep in mind that there is also an ordinary Hinduism and a quintessential Islam or Sufism, the latter of which Shaykh Aḥmad al-'Alawī and Shaykh 'Īsā Nūr al-Dīn Aḥmad represent, as well as countless other Muslims cited throughout this book. Schuon would not have dreamed, as some of his interpreters have, of relegating Islam and Sufism as a whole to "ordinary Sufism," as is witnessed in his numerous books on the Islamic tradition; or of imagining that only Advaita Vedānta speaks of the centrality of the Self. If the *sophia perennis* is based on the doctrine of non-duality it should go without saying that this doctrine must be present in all religions otherwise it is not perennial. Schuon writes, "'inwardly' every religion is the doctrine of the one Self and its earthly manifestation. . . ." *Gnosis: Divine Wisdom* (Bedford, Middlesex: Perennial Books, 1959) p. 79. On the metaphysics of Advaita Vedānta and quintessential Islam or Sufism, see chapter three of this book. Schuon himself writes, for example, "The Doctrine (and the Way) of Unity is unique" (*al-tawḥīdu wāḥid*): this classical formula expresses in concise

religions. Shaykh al-'Alawī cites the following Quranic verse and then adds his own commentary:

> Truly those who believe, and those who are Jews, and the Christians, and the Sabeans—whosoever believes in God and the Last Day and works righteousness shall have their reward with their Lord. No fear shall come upon them, nor shall they grieve. (2:62)

> [The] fact of mentioning side-by-side the different traditional communities while not distinguishing Muslim believers from other believers must lead us to consider that no one, be he a Muslim, or an infidel (*kāfir*), pious or sinful, as being inferior to us, and this throughout our entire life. In fact, our destiny is unknown to us and it is our state at the moment of death that matters: such is the lot of mankind.

---

manner the essentiality, primordiality and universality of Islamic esoterism as well as of esoterism as such; and we might even say that all wisdom or gnosis—all the Advaita Vedānta, if one prefers—is for Islam, contained within the *shahādah* alone, the two fold Testimony of faith." *Sufism: Veil and Quintessence*, trans. Mark Perry, Jean-Pierre Lafouge, and James Cutsinger (Bloomington, IN: World Wisdom Books, 2006), p. 132. Schuon also states, "The Islamic formula *Lā ilāha illā'Llāh* means, according to gnosis, that "there is no 'me' except it be 'I'"—therefore no real or positive ego except the Self—a meaning which also springs from expressions such as the *Anā'l-Ḥaqq* ("I am the Truth") of al-Ḥallāj or the *Subḥānī* ("Glory to Me") of Bāyazīd. The Prophet himself enunciated the same mystery in the following terms: "He who has seen me, has seen the Truth (God)." *Language of the Self* (Bloomington, IN: World Wisdom Books, Inc., 1999), p. 206. Finally and perhaps most decisively, Schuon writes, "In the first place we cannot but love the *shahādah*, which is an unsurpassable formulation of metaphysical Truth. . . ." *Christianity/ Islam*, p. 192. Only someone who has poorly understood and greatly underestimated the doctrine of Unity in Islam could place it below that of the doctrine of Advaita Vedānta in Hinduism. Therefore, we do not hesitate in identifying Schuon's perspective—and the perennial philosophy as such—with the doctrine and way of Unity in Islam, while insisting that this metaphysical doctrine is shared by all religions in different forms, not the least of which is Advaita Vedānta and Hinduism. If we emphasize the Islamic identity of Schuon it is not because Islam is inherently superior to other forms, but because this essential aspect of his metaphysical perspective, corpus, and spiritual life has been marginalized in some studies. It is true that the Formless Essence—by any name—is the ultimate concern of the esoterist, but this Essence is inaccessible without concomitant exoteric and esoteric forms, which is why Schuon embraced Islam and received an Islamic initiation. Had another initiation been accessible, perhaps he would have chosen differently? However, God also chose Islam and a Sufi initiation for Schuon. *Wa'Llāhu a'lam.*

> Thus I have understood from this enigmatic verse that all aforementioned traditional communities possess a genuine validity in Religion (*makāna fi'l-Dīn*). One may draw from the order of enumeration a certain preeminence of the first over the last, but it remains nonetheless that a traditional community will always be of an incomparably higher rank than pagan cults.[134]

Thus Schuon, while elucidating the principle of universality with unparalleled clarity and precision, wrote in perfect accord with the teachings he had received from traditional sages in the Muslim world and those of the Quran itself. Schuon's Muslim name 'Īsā (Jesus in Arabic) suggests a particular affinity with Christ, who also championed the esoteric and the universal at a time when many people had neglected the Spirit of the Law. Yet Schuon clearly lived and died in the Islamic tradition and practiced the rites and basic laws of the *Sharī'ah*, while also directly benefiting from an Islamic initiation at the hands of the great Algerian Sufi master Shaykh Aḥmad al-'Alawī. Schuon was most of all concerned with quintessential prayer, but it was the quintessential prayer of the Quran—*dhikr Allāh*—supported by the daily prayers, fasting, charity, and all of the necessary pillars and laws of Islam, that constituted his spiritual practice.

Even before meeting Shaykh Aḥmad al-'Alawī, as a young man Schuon met a Muslim saint from Senegal who greatly influenced his perspective. While the exact identity of this man is unknown, Sufi masters from Senegal are reputed for their esoteric knowledge and religious tolerance.[135] Jean-Baptiste Aymard and Patrick Laude write,

134. See Tayeb Chouiref, "The Shaykh Ahmad al-'Alawī and the Universalism of the Qur'ān: A Presentation and Translation of His Commentary of Verse 2:62," in Patrick Laude, ed., *Universal Dimensions of Islam: Studies in Comparative Religion*, pp. 47–48.

135. We can personally attest to the presence of a contemporary Muslim from Senegal who also articulated the transcendent unity of religions in a symbolic manner. Shaykh Abdoulaye Dieye (d. 2002) of the Murīdiyyah Sufi order spoke about the variety of animals and flowers in the natural world as mirroring the diversity that one finds among religions, races and cultures. His hometown St. Louis, Senegal, of which he was the deputy mayor, is reputed for its religious tolerance. While

> It may be that the notion of the "transcendent unity of religions" was evoked in him one day when, walking in the Zoological Gardens in Basel . . . , he met an elderly Senegalese marabout, with whom he conversed for a moment. The marabout, in order to make himself better understood, drew in the sand a circle with radii and added, pointing at the center, "God is the Center, all paths lead to Him."[136]

The essential unity of the traditional forms was also clear to Schuon at an early age when he read the Bible, the Quran, the writings of Plato, the Vedas, and the Bhagavad Gita. Moreover, the seminal works of René Guénon mirrored and gave precision and form to Schuon's own intuitions. Yet the greatest spiritual and intellectual influence upon Schuon came from Shaykh Aḥmad al-'Alawī of the Shādhiliyyah Sufi order. It was from Shaykh al-'Alawī that Schuon received an initiation and a spiritual method—all within the context of orthodox Islam—which was to sustain and nourish him spiritually to the end of his life. In a letter Schuon wrote,

> I wished not only to love God, I also wished to know him, and the Christianity of our time teaches only the love of God, never the knowledge. . . . And so, with regard to the knowledge of God which I was seeking—because it is a need of my nature, and God wishes to be worshipped by every man according to the nature He gave him—I found this sacred knowledge through a holy man of the Arab people, whose name was Aḥmad al-'Alawī. He was a spiritual Master and had many disciples. There I found what I was searching for: the knowledge of God, and the means to realize God.[137]

---

having memorized the Quran, he also spoke of seeing the Truth in the Bible, Bhagavad Gita, Tao te Ching and other books. He also frequently met and prayed with a number of Jewish Rabbis from around the world and articulated a spiritual and non-violent solution to the crisis in Israel and Palestine catalyzed by esoteric representatives of Judaism and Islam and the non-violent example of Shaykh Aḥmadū Bāmbā (d. 1927). Shaykh Abdoulaye Dieye, "The Declaration of La Jolla" (unpublished, 2002); and Michelle Kimball, "Shaykh Ahmadu Bamba's Nonviolent Jihad of the Pen," *Sophia* 15, no. 1 (Summer 2009), pp. 122–141.

136. *Frithjof Schuon: Life and Teachings*, p. 8.

137. Ibid., p. 62.

Schuon was well aware that God can also be known through other traditions, including Christianity, especially through Orthodoxy and Hesychasm.[138] He was particularly attracted to the metaphysical perspective of Advaita Vedānta from India, which is discussed in chapter three. However, he maintained that Hinduism was inaccessible because he was not a born Hindu and therefore without recognized caste. Islam therefore provided Schuon with an analogous metaphysical doctrine and contemplative path, which he followed to know God. The connection between Schuon and Islam has already been brought out in Seyyed Hossein Nasr's essay "Frithjof Schuon and the Islamic Tradition," where Nasr discusses Schuon's acceptance of Islam in Paris in 1932, as well as his study of Arabic and the Quran with the Persian scholar, Sayyid Ḥasan Imāmī.[139] Nasr writes,

> His journey to Algeria in 1932 where he spent several months and most important of all where he met Shaykh Aḥmad al-'Alawī, who initiated the young Schuon into Sufism, only strengthened his bond to the Islamic tradition in general and the traditional ambience of the Maghrib in particular.[140]

Schuon was also made a representative of the Shādhiliyyah 'Alawiyyah order in the West and later received a vision of the Virgin Mary (Maryam al-Batūl) who blessed a new branch of the Shādhiliyyah order.[141] S.H. Nasr states,

> It was Islam and the Muḥammadan *barakah* that allowed him to become a spiritual teacher and a shaykh of the Shādhiliyyah Order, to found a *ṭarīqah*, the Shādhiliyyah 'Alawiyyah Maryamiyyah, and

138. Schuon writes, "Even though Christianity is a *bhakti* by virtue of the general form that defines it, it nonetheless possesses a dimension of *jnāna*, or gnosis, and this is necessarily so since it is an integral and autonomous tradition. The Christian esoterism is founded upon the idea of the immanent Christ, that is, the Intellect—or the "Heart"—which is at once "Light and "Love": for "I am the Light of the world", and "God is Love". Now the intellect is essentially identified with the Self; it is *aliquid increatum et increabile*." *Christianity/Islam*, pp. 68–69.

139. Seyyed Hossein Nasr, "Frithjof Schuon and the Islamic Tradition," *Sophia* 5, no. 1 (Summer 1999), pp. 27–48. See also, *Islam in the Modern World*, pp. 376–390.

140. "Frithjof Schuon and the Islamic Tradition," p. 30

141. *Frithjof Schuon: Life and Teachings*, pp. 17–22, 41–43, 75–76.

to reach spiritual states and stations from whose perspective he was to write his remarkable and incomparable works.[142]

Among Schuon's writings are the most salient works on Islam and the perennial philosophy in a European language. His *Understanding Islam* unveils the metaphysical significance of the *shahādah*, which he describes elsewhere as "an unsurpassable formulation of metaphysical Truth."[143] Perhaps Schuon's most important selection on the Prophet Muḥammad is his essay featured in the edited volume *Islamic Spirituality: Foundations* entitled "The Spiritual Significance of the Substance of the Prophet," about which S.H. Nasr wrote, "Speaking as a spiritual authority, Schuon deals with a subject that has not been treated in such an explicit manner even in traditional Islamic sources."[144] Schuon was also responsible for formulating what might be called the transcendent unity of Sunnism and Shīʿism[145] in his essay "Seeds of a Divergence" in the book *Islam and the Perennial Philosophy*. In *Sufism: Veil and Quintessence*, Schuon looks at the heart of the Islamic tradition and is not afraid to critique some of his eminent predecessors on certain issues. If one examines the writings of Schuon on Islam and Sufism alone, which also include *Dimensions of Islam* and many unpublished manuscripts, one discovers some of the most important writings of the Islamic sapiential tradition that have emerged from the West. His texts elaborated the principles of Islam and Islamic esoterism, which Titus Burckhardt, Martin Lings, Seyyed Hossein Nasr and others later brought to fruition. Schuon dealt with all of the

142. "Frithjof Schuon and the Islamic Tradition," p. 44. Victor Danner also states with regard to both Guénon and Schuon, "This entire current of Western intellectual and spiritual life, which continues to vibrate at the present day and to produce many important formulations of doctrine, could not have existed without an initial Shādhilī impetus and guidance." "The Shādhiliyyah and North African Sufism" in Seyyed Hossein Nasr, ed., *Encyclopaedia of Islamic Spirituality*, vol. II (Lahore: Suhail Academy, 2000), p. 47.

143. *Christianity/Islam*, p. 192.

144. Frithjof Schuon, "The Spiritual Significance of the Substance of the Prophet," in Seyyed Hossein Nasr, ed., *Islamic Spirituality: Foundations* (New York: The Crossroad Publishing Company, 1997), pp. xxvi, 48–63.

145. This is not a completely accurate description, as Sunnis and Shīʿites also agree on most exoteric religious principles.

essential aspects of the Islamic tradition including the Quran, the *Sunnah* of the Prophet Muḥammad, Islamic Law, the spiritual path, theology, eschatology, the doctrine of Divine Unity (*tawḥīd*), and the relationship between Islam and the perennial philosophy, while always differentiating between the relative and the Absolute. Schuon writes in *Islam and the Perennial Philosophy*,

> Revelation is present still, but it is hidden away beneath a sheet of ice which necessitates that intervention of outward Revelation; but these cannot have the perfection of what might be termed "innate Religion" or the immanent *philosophia perennis*. Esoterism by definition takes account of this situation; heretics and philosophers are often aware of it too, in their fragmentary way, but clearly they do not wish to understand that the religions in fact provide the key to pure and universal Truth. That we should say this might well appear paradoxical, but every religious world not only renews the lost Paradise after its own fashion but also bears, in one way or the other, the stigmata of the fall, from which only supraformal Truth is exempt; and this inward Truth is, we repeat, de facto inaccessible without the help of outward manifestations, objective and prophetic.[146]

Schuon asserts the absolute perfection of the Divine Principle alone and the relativity of everything else, but emphasizes that man requires the forms of a particular religion, both outward and inward, to know the Truth. He bases his perspective on the *sophia* or *religio perennis*, which has been defined as "discernment between the Real and illusory, and a unifying and permanent concentration on the Real."[147] There is no doubt that a measure of this discernment was present in Schuon before he formally entered Islam and that he initially encountered metaphysics through reading the Bhagavad Gita and other sacred and inspired texts. However, Islam and Sufism provided Schuon with a metaphysical doctrine and spiritual path based upon the *shahādah* and the Supreme Name of God through which he could discern between the Real and the illusory and concentrate on the Real in a practical manner. Schuon also

146. Frithjof Schuon, *Islam and the Perennial Philosophy*, trans. J. Peter Hobson (World of Islam Festival Publishing Company Ltd, 1976), pp. 194–195.
147. *Light on the Ancient Worlds*, p. 137.

found in the Islamic tradition an orthodox religious framework and spiritual guidance and an initiation at the hands of Shaykh Aḥmad al-ʿAlawī. Moreover, though Schuon sensed the Sacred in the various religions that he encountered at an early age, the doctrine of the transcendent unity of religions was first disclosed to him by a Muslim shaykh from Senegal. While he wrote about the transcendent unity of religions and saw the Divine Truth in all of religious forms he encountered, Shaykh ʿĪsā Nūr al-Dīn Aḥmad approached and fully realized the Truth (*al-Ḥaqq*) through the exoteric and esoteric doctrines and rites of the Islamic tradition, which he practiced for more than sixty years until his passing in 1998.[148]

148. There are some ambiguities and enigmas that surrounded Frithjof Schuon towards the end of his life. These can be and have been interpreted in various ways. At present, we do not have an unbiased survey of these phenomena, but Mark Sedgwick's intellectual history *Against the Modern World*, which relies almost solely upon the reports and opinions of detractors, and Jean-Baptiste Aymard and Patrick Laude's *Frithjof Schuon: Life and Teachings* based upon Schuon's writings and those of his supporters. While both of these studies are helpful in certain respects, a more complete biography would take into account the views of his supporters, detractors, and others not connected to either group. In any case, we are primarily concerned with Schuon's understanding, as expressed in his writings, of Islam and the perennial philosophy in this chapter. Moreover, we believe that Schuon's theses deserve to be considered alongside the greater Islamic and Sufi tradition, as well as those traditionalists who preceded and followed him. *Ad hominem* attacks, based in reality or not, against a particular figure do not undermine or even acknowledge his or her ideas and arguments. Even if one were able to prove that Schuon was unreliable on certain counts, this would not alter the awareness and exposition of the perennial philosophy among many other classical and contemporary Muslim sages. The questions that arise concerning Schuon during his last years, however, do deserve some attention by discerning scholars. Seyyed Hossein Nasr writes, "No matter how much some might seek to aggrandize some of the deviant currents and eddys and aberrations that surrounded him in his very old age and try to present him as a figure that had gone 'beyond' the Islamic form, Schuon was and remained rooted in the Islamic tradition to the moment of his death. . . ." "Frithjof Schuon and the Islamic Tradition," pp. 44–45. The late Charles Le Gai Eaton also remarked, "Schuon . . . was a controversial figure as are a number of Sheikhs, particularly among those living in the West. Perhaps he saw too much and saw too deeply. So far as his teachings are concerned, not only those in his books but also in the great number of texts written for his disciples, it would take a comparable intelligence to fault him and I have never met anyone of comparable intelligence." *A Bad Beginning and the Path to Islam* (Cambridge: Archetype, 2010), p. 348.

* * *

Titus Burckhardt (1908–1984) or Sīdī Ibrāhīm 'Izz al-Dīn was one of Schuon's most eminent disciples who applied the principles expounded by Guénon, Coomaraswamy and Schuon to various intellectual and aesthetic domains, including metaphysics, cosmology, sacred art, symbolism, and also traditional astrology and alchemy. He also wrote about many modern fallacies, including scientism, empiricism, psychological reductionism, and Darwinian evolution. Sīdī Ibrāhīm, as his Muslim friends knew him, smashed these modern idols, but was wiser than many contemporary iconoclasts in that he saw wisdom and beauty in the world's religions, especially in their sacred art.[149] Burckhardt writes with authority in his "A Letter on Spiritual Method":

> There is no spiritual method without these two basic elements: discernment between the real and the unreal, and concentration on the real. The first of these two elements, discernment or discrimination (*vijñāna* in Sanskrit), does not depend on any special religious form; it only presupposes metaphysical understanding. The second element, however, requires a support of a sacred character, and this means that it can only be achieved within the framework of a normal tradition. The aim of method is perpetual concentration on the Real, and this cannot be achieved by purely human means or on the basis of individual initiative; it presupposes a regular transmission such as exists only within a normal tradition. For what is man? What is his puny will? How can he possibly adhere to the Absolute without first integrating his whole being into a non-individual (i.e., supra-individual) form? To be precise: there is no spiritual path outside the following traditions or religions: Judaism, Christianity, Islam, Buddhism, Hinduism

149. Burckhardt wrote that Islamic art was aniconic and not iconoclastic. Therefore, while Muslims do not use naturalistic human or animal forms to represent the Divine Reality, but rather the sonoral and visual forms of the Quran, Islam accepts and respects the various sacred forms revealed by Heaven to other communities. Moreover, the created forms of nature itself, as opposed to artistic imitations of them, are among the Divine signs Muslims are called to reflect upon to know the Creator.

and Taoism; but Hinduism is closed for those who have not been born into a Hindu caste, and Taoism is inaccessible.[150]

Burckhardt is perhaps best known for his book *Sacred Art in East and West*, which beautifully exhibits the perennial wisdom in Hinduism, Christianity, Islam, Buddhism, and Taoism through images and inspired analysis of the sacred art in each tradition. A reader unfamiliar with the central role of sacred art in the world's religions will discover the intellectual and aesthetic principles of each religion through Burckhardt's penetrating vision and mastery of the subject. In his text *Mirror of the Intellect* one finds important expressions of the *sophia perennis*, including an important section dealing with what Burckhardt called the "*cosmologia perennis*." There is also an essay in this text called "Perennial Values in Islamic Art", which reminds us of the principle of Divine Unity in Islamic art and ultimately all traditions. Burckhardt writes,

> Islamic art is fundamentally derived from *tawḥīd*, that is, from an assent to or a contemplation of Divine Unity. The essence of *al-tawḥīd* is beyond words; it reveals itself in the Quran by sudden and discontinuous flashes. Striking the plane of the visual imagination, these flashes congeal into crystalline forms, and it is these forms in their turn that constitute the essence of Islamic art.[151]

Burckhardt has written about the arts of Quranic recitation and calligraphy, geometry, the arabesque, the void, the alchemy of light, and the mosque. He also demonstrated the connection between these forms of art and the inner reality of the Quran, the soul of the Prophet and the principle of Divine Unity. Burckhardt did for Islamic art what A.K. Coomaraswamy did for Hindu and Buddhist art by demonstrating its profound metaphysical and cosmological symbolism, which like other forms of sacred art can only be discerned by the Intellect or the eye of the heart. Huston Smith remarks, "No one since the legendary A.K. Coomaraswamy has been able to demonstrate how entire civilizations define themselves

150. Titus Burckhardt, *Mirror of the Intellect*, trans. William Stoddart (Albany, NY: State University of New York Press, 1987), p. 251.
151. Ibid., p. 230.

through their art with the precision of Titus Burckhardt."[152] Titus Burckhardt and his work have also been praised by Keith Critchlow, Brian Keeble, Annemarie Schimmel, William Stoddart, and the Sufi saint Sayyidah Fāṭimah al-Yashruṭiyyah.[153] Seyyed Hossein Nasr writes,

> He was not a Western scholar of Islam in the usual sense but a person of exceptional intellectual and spiritual gifts who went to the Islamic world as a young man to master the Islamic disciplines from within at the feet of masters of both the exoteric and esoteric sciences. He was providentially chosen to express the truths of the Islamic tradition, and in fact tradition in its universal sense, to the modern world and in a language comprehensible to contemporary man. His writings in fact represent one of the major formulations and statements of traditional Islam in the modern world.[154]

His *Art of Islam* is among the few books on the subject that highlight the intellectual and spiritual nature of sacred and traditional art in Islam. Burckhardt's *Fez: City of Islam* and *Moorish Culture in Spain* demonstrate his vast knowledge of and love for art in the western Islamic lands, which he knew so well. His writings on Islamic art are widely studied throughout the Islamic world, especially in Iran, Turkey, Jordan and Morocco. Burckhardt can in fact

152. William Stoddart, ed., *The Essential Titus Burckhardt: Reflections on Sacred Art, Faiths, and Civilizations* (Bloomington, IN: World Wisdom, 2003). Keith Critchlow also writes, "Burckhardt has done more than any other single author in the past 50, if not 100, years to recover the essential principles of the purpose of the arts. His breadth and depth of scholarship is awe-inspiring. He will emerge in due time as one of the most important writers on the recovery of the true value of art in the twentieth century and even in the twenty-first century." Titus Burckhardt, *Siena: City of the Virgin*, trans. by Margaret McDonough Brown (Bloomington, IN: World Wisdom, 2008), back cover.

153. Fāṭimah al-Yashruṭiyyah writes, "Another of the visitors was a great scholar who has also become a Muslim and followed the Sufi way. He was known as Sīdī Ibrāhīm. This learned man deserves much honor for his translation of the *Fuṣūṣ al-ḥikam* by Shaykh Muḥyī al-Dīn ibn 'Arabī (may God be pleased with him!)." Leslie Cadavid, *Two Who Attained: Twentieth-Century Sufi Saints: Shaykh Ahmad al-'Alawi & Fatima al-Yashrutiyya* (Louisville, KY: Fons Vitae, 2005), p. 178.

154. Seyyed Hossein Nasr, *Traditional Islam in the Modern World* (New York: Kegan Paul International, 1990), pp. 291–292. See also, *Islam in the Modern World*, pp. 390–395.

be considered the most important and discerning writer on Islamic art from the West.

Burckhardt unveiled the true significance of the arcane sciences as can be seen in his penetrating treatises *Alchemy: Science of the Cosmos, Science of the Soul* and *Mystical Astrology According to Ibn 'Arabī*. He also wrote his own treatise on Islamic esoterism entitled *An Introduction to Sufi Doctrine* and translated selections from some of the most important classical books on Sufism into French, including Ibn 'Arabī's *Fuṣūṣ al-ḥikam*, 'Abd al-Karīm Jīlī's *al-Insān al-kāmil* and Mūlay al-'Arabī al-Darqāwī's *Rasā'il*. This last selection contains practical spiritual counsel from a master in Burckhardt's own spiritual lineage (*silsilah*). Darqāwī writes about the Universal or Perfect Man,

> Discriminative knowledge does not hide unitive knowledge from such a man, neither does the unitive hide the discriminative. From him, the effect does not hide the cause, nor the cause the effect; from him, religious law (*Sharī'ah*) does not hide spiritual truth (*ḥaqīqah*) nor spiritual truth religious law; from him, method (*sulūk*) does not hide inner attraction (*jadhb*), nor inner attraction method; and so on. He has attained the aim; he is the perfect one, the gnostic; whereas his opposite is the man who is lost. . . .[155]

This letter stresses the need for both the Divine Law and the spiritual path that leads to the Truth, further demonstrating that the message of the *sophia perennis* is always wed to a particular religious form. Prior to receiving an initiation and spiritual guidance from Schuon, Burckhardt also received an initiation in Morocco, where he also learned Arabic and studied classical Sufi texts and the Islamic arts and sciences. Therefore, like Guénon and Schuon, Burckhardt's writings on the perennial philosophy were the fruit of realized knowledge, which he attained through the Islamic tradition. Concerning this knowledge Burckhardt writes,

155. The Shaykh ad-Darqāwī, *Letters of a Sufi Master*, trans. Titus Burckhardt (Louisville, KY: Fons Vitae, 1998), p. 20.

> Though Islamic mysticism, as it persists in Morocco down to the present day, may be compared in many respects with Christian mysticism—and in other respects with Hindu and Far-Eastern mysticism—it is nevertheless founded entirely on the religious form specific to Islam. Its point of departure is *tawḥīd*, the doctrine of Divine Unity. If Islamic Law demands, as the first duty of every believer, that he "testify" to the unity of God, Islamic mysticism requires that this attestation (*shahādah*), should not be merely with the lips, nor even merely with the mind, but that, beyond all reflections and sentiments, it should be a total and immediate act of testimony or witness (*shahādah*); this means nothing other than the Knowledge of God.[156]

Burckhardt was a visionary figure who could, through the light of the Intellect, penetrate into the sacred forms of all traditions and see them as symbols that suggest and even embody the Divine Archetypes of the True, the Good and the Beautiful. While he wrote about and even helped to revive the study of sacred and traditional Christian art, as can be seen in his *Siena, City of the Virgin* and *Chartres and the Birth of the Cathedral*, his life was molded after the model of the Prophet of Islam and the Will of God as expressed in the Holy Quran. Therefore, his understanding of the principle of Unity and his profound appreciation for the world's great religions and their metaphysical doctrines, cosmologies, sacred art, and symbolism was a result of his connection to the inner dimensions and sacred forms of Islam.

* * *

Martin Lings (1909–2005) or Shaykh Abū Bakr Sirāj al-Dīn was also a disciple of Frithjof Schuon and a guiding light representing Islam and the perennial wisdom of the ages in the darkness that characterizes the modern world. Lings wrote about the *sophia perennis* in the context of Islam, Sufism and even the plays of Shakespeare. Like his predecessors he was deeply concerned with metaphysics, cosmology, symbolism, sacred art, and the crisis of the modern world. Lings is perhaps the most celebrated and widely read European

156. *The Essential Titus Burckhardt*, p. 259.

Muslim scholar. He was born in a Protestant family in Lancashire, England. In 1935, Lings went to Oxford to study English Literature with C.S. Lewis.[157] According to S.H. Nasr,

> Lings reminisced about his days at the University and he told me how disappointed Lewis was when the young Lings left Christianity for Islam and told Lings, "What a loss for Christianity!" As it was, Lings embraced Islam not to deny but to reconfirm the deepest and oft-forgotten truths of Christianity as his works reveal amply and he made great contributions to that religion.[158]

In the 1930's Lings became interested in the perennial philosophy through the writings of René Guénon and Frithjof Schuon, and in 1938 he embraced Islam through Titus Burckhardt.[159] Lings also spent time with Guénon in Egypt, but his most influential teacher was Frithjof Schuon, who initiated and guided him on the spiritual path and later made him a guide for others.[160] Lings' connection to Guénon and Schuon is important because it shaped the rest of his life and writings, and influenced a great number of people in the West and in the Islamic world. The *In Memoriam* section in Lings' last book *A Return to the Spirit* contains moving tributes from Huston Smith, Charles Le Gai Eaton, Jean-Louis Michon, Seyyed Hossein Nasr, Mohamed Zakariyah, Abdallah Schleifer, Shems Friedlander, Virginia Gray Henry-Blakemore, Peter Kingsley, Hamza Yusuf, and Reza Shah-Kazemi. The Grand Mufti of Egypt, Shaykh 'Alī Juma'a, wrote the following in a tribute to Lings after his passing in 2005, which demonstrates the influence of Lings and Guénon in the heart of the Islamic world:

157. Shaykh Ali Juma'a, "The Departure of Shaykh Abū Bakr Sirāj al-Dīn," *Sophia* 11, no. 1 (Summer 2005), p. 38.

158. Seyyed Hossein Nasr, "Shaykh Abū Bakr Sirāj al-Dīn (Martin Lings): A Tribute," *Sophia* 11, no. 1 (Summer 2005), p. 31. See also, *Islam in the Modern World*, pp. 395–402.

159. "Shaykh Abū Bakr Sirāj al-Dīn (Martin Lings): A Tribute," p. 31.

160. "How Did I Come to Put first Things First?," *A Return to the Spirit*, pp. 1–16. Lings begins this selection with the words, "If this question were to be worded: "To whom am I most indebted for the knowledge of how to put first things first?" the answer would be, beyond any doubt, to Frithjof Schuon." Ibid., p. 1.

> The meeting between Martin Lings and René Guénon had the most profound impact on the emergence of the light of guidance which became known as the Traditionalist School (*Madrasat al-Turāth*). One of its most conclusive results was a critique of the modern world which is dominated by materialism and the rediscovery of the wisdom which is at the heart of all religions, whether Zoroastrianism or Buddhism or Hinduism, as well as Judaism, Christianity, and Islam. This wisdom is the primordial light (*fiṭrah*) that God created in the hearts of all people, through which He guides them to the Truth (*al-Ḥaqq*).[161]

Lings' essay "Why 'With All Thy Mind'?" in *A Return to the Spirit* articulates the doctrine of the transcendent unity of religions as clearly and cogently as anything we have read. In this rich volume there are five other chapters on various aspects of the perennial philosophy and Islamic spirituality, as well as a talk on the spiritual meaning and symbolism of the words and postures of the Islamic canonical prayer. This book as a whole reveals Lings' function as a Sufi master. Among Lings' most significant works is undoubtedly his *Symbol & Archetype*, which masterfully expounds the doctrine

161. "The Departure of Shaykh Abū Bakr Sirāj al-Dīn," p. 40; and *A Return to the Spirit*, p. 89. Elsewhere Shaykh 'Alī Juma'a states, "The Muslim also understands from the concept of "the community" (*ummah*) that humanity from the first of creation constitutes one community. 'And, verily, this community of yours is one single community, since I am the Sustainer of you all: remain, then, conscious of Me! (23:52).' Because of this, Muslims accept pluralism, even if some may view non-Muslims as being mistaken. The judgment of this error, however, is for God to make on the Day of Resurrection. The Muslim cooperates and coexists in this worldly life with the people around him, and the history of Islam testifies to the truth of this. Muslims never exterminated peoples or compelled them to enter Islam by force. All religions had a place within the bosom of Islam from Hinduism to Zoroastrianism, to Christianity, to Judaism, and others. Many people are nevertheless too obstinate to accept this fact and would deny it, but it is a fact as obvious as the sun and requires no proof—*res ipsa loquitur*. . . . At the beginning of the twentieth century, Shaykh 'Abd al-Raḥmān 'Ilaysh expressed the view that there could be an interpretation of the law specifically for Muslim minorities, and that western Muslim scholars could constitute a new school of thought, in parallel with their Eastern counterparts, that would perhaps seem foreign to Eastern scholars. . . . This endeavor found a firm basis in the writings of Martin Lings, René Guénon, and Frithjof Schuon—all Western Muslims—among others of the same school. . . ." "Questions from America," *Al Ahram* (March–April 2006).

of symbolism in an unparalleled manner. Another book *The Eleventh Hour* examines the end of this cycle of cosmic existence and the signs that precede it with reference to prophecies and wisdom from the world's religions. With Clinton Minnaar, Lings also selected and edited the essays featured in the book *The Underlying Religion*, which many experts consider the definitive introductory volume to the perennial philosophy. Commenting upon a passage by Schuon, Lings writes,

> As regards what Schuon says about pastoral teaching that is no longer effective, the dogma that there is only one valid religion, namely 'ours', may serve as an example of an argument that is 'psychologically somewhat outworn'. Such teachings 'fail to satisfy certain requirements of causality' because they are now seen to defeat one of the mains ends of religion which is to bestow a sense of the Glory of God. Modern man cannot help having a broader view of the world than his ancestors had, partly through the destruction of the protective walls of the different traditional civilizations—in itself a tragedy—and partly through the enormously increased facilities of travel and the corresponding increase of information which is poured into his mind through various channels. This broader view may enable him to be impressed by religions other than his own, and at the very least it compels him to see that their existence makes the world-wide spread of his own religion impossible. If they were false, what of the Glory of Him who allowed them to establish themselves, with their millennial roots, over so vast an area?[162]

Lings also made some of the most significant contributions to the study of Islam and Sufism in the West. One of Lings' masterpieces is his celebrated biography of the Prophet Muḥammad entitled *Muhammad: His Life Based on the Earliest Sources*, which communicates something of the spiritual grace (*barakah*) of the Prophet and inculcates the love of the beloved of God that has perfumed Muslim believers since the seventh century. Lings' biography conveys accounts of the Prophet's respect for other prophets and religions, his own magnanimous character and teachings and the eternal wis-

162. Martin Lings, *The Eleventh Hour* (Cambridge, UK: Archetype, 2002), p. 56.

dom he received from God as Revelation. This biography in particular, in addition to the numerous other works cited throughout this chapter, highlights the immense contributions traditionalists have made to the study of Islam in European languages. It would not be an exaggeration to state that their works on Islam and Islamic spirituality are the most serious studies on the religion in the West. In Lings' *A Return to the Spirit*, he refers to and then quotes a verse from the Quran, "They believe, all of them, in God and His Angels and His Books and His Messengers. And say: 'We make no distinction between any of His Messengers.'" (2:285) Lings understood the primary Islamic sources well and saw in them the transcendent unity of religions.[163] Lings also began translating the Quran, which regrettably he was unable to complete before his passing. As his partial translation *The Holy Quran: Translations of Selected Verses* indicates, he was gifted with a penetrating understanding of the Book and a sublime command of the English language.

Lings also refused to separate Sufism from Islam, which is a common error in the West. In *What is Sufism?* Lings writes, "Sufism is nothing other than Islamic mysticism, which means that it is the central and most powerful current of that tidal wave which constitutes the Revelation of Islam."[164] Along with the Quran, Lings states that Sufism is based on the *Sunnah* or Wont of the Prophet Muḥammad. This challenges the assumptions of early orientalists, who attempted to demonstrate the Hindu, Buddhist, Neo-Platonic, Zoroastrian, and/or Christian origins of Sufism. While we find parallels between various religions and Islam throughout this volume, the origin of Islamic spirituality is the Quran and *Sunnah* of the Prophet. In addition to introducing some of the fundamental aspects of Sufism in the aforementioned book, Lings also wrote an advanced Sufi treatise entitled *The Book of Certainty: The Sufi Doctrine of Faith, Vision and Gnosis*, wherein he describes the three levels of certainty on the spiritual path based upon the Quran and Sufi commentaries. Lings summarizes this doctrine as follows:

163. *A Return to the Spirit*, p. 28.

164. Martin Lings, *What is Sufism?* (Cambridge: The Islamic Texts Society, 1993), p. 15.

> The Divine Truth is symbolized by the element fire. The three degrees, in ascending order are the Lore of Certainty (*'ilm al-yaqīn*), the Eye of Certainty (*'ayn al-yaqīn*) and the Truth of Certainty (*ḥaqq al-yaqīn*). The Lore is the certainty that comes from hearing the fire described; the Eye is the certainty that comes from seeing its flames; the Truth is the certainty which comes from being consumed in it. This last degree is the extinction (*fanā'*) of all otherness which alone gives realization of the Supreme Identity. The second degree is that of Heart-knowledge, for the Eye which sees is the Heart. As to the Lore, it is a mental understanding which has been raised to the level of certainty by the faculties of intuition which surround the Heart; and it is one of the functions of the doctrine to awaken these faculties and make them operative.[165]

One of Lings' other gems is his biography of Shaykh Aḥmad al-'Alawī entitled *A Sufi Saint of the Twentieth Century.* We not only learn about the saintly figure who initiated Schuon into Sufism and as a result catalyzed the revival of Tradition in the West, but also about the doctrines, methods, and goal of Sufism, such as the transcendent Unity of Being (*waḥdat al-wujūd*), symbolism, ritual purification (*wuḍū'*), prayer (*ṣalāh*), invocation (*dhikr*) and gnosis (*ma'rifah*). This volume also contains selections of Shaykh al-'Alawī's own poetry rendered into masterful English verse. A section of one of these poems entitled "The Path" reads:

> [Alone] God was, and with Him naught else.
> He is now as He was, lastly as firstly,
> Essentially One, with naught beside Himself,
> Inwardly Hidden, Outwardly Manifest,
> Without beginning, without end, Whate'er thou seest,
> Seest thou His Being, Absolute Oneness
> No 'but' hath and no 'except.' How should God's Essence
> Be confined with a veil? No veil there but His Light.[166]

Lings translated a book of exquisite Arabic poetry entitled *Sufi Poems: A Mediaeval Anthology,* which is one of the richest collec-

165. Ibid., pp. 61–62.

166. Martin Lings, *A Sufi Saint of the Twentieth Century: Shaikh Aḥmad al-'Alawī, His Spiritual Heritage and Legacy* (Cambridge: The Islamic Texts Society, 2001), p. 217.

tions of Arabic Sufi poetry in English. He also wrote beautiful poems of his own which have been published in a volume entitled *Collected Poems*. In addition to the art of poetry, Lings was deeply interested in the art of Quranic calligraphy and illumination. From 1970–73, he was Keeper of Oriental Manuscripts at the British Museum. Lings wrote a book on the subject, which has stunning selections from the treasury of this sacred Islamic art, entitled *Splendors of Qur'an Calligraphy and Illumination*. The new edition of this book is truly an epiphany to behold. This work contains a foreword by the H.R.H The Prince of Wales, which illustrates how vast Lings' influence has been.

Lings found expressions of perennial wisdom in places that one would not typically expect from a Muslim. In his *The Secret of Shakespeare*, Lings demonstrated the spiritual meaning of many of Shakespeare's plays and how the characters in each play correspond to aspects of the human soul. Lings' mastery of Elizabethan English permeates all of his works, while it can also be said that his understanding of Sufi psychology and spirituality helped him shed light on the meaning of Shakespeare's characters. The Prince of Wales writes in the foreword to *A Return to the Spirit*:

> One of Martin Lings' greatest legacies—apart from his insights into the true significance of many of Shakespeare's plays and his remarkable biography of the Prophet Muḥammad—must surely be his timely reminder to us that Sufism, of which he was such a distinguished proponent, has always been at the spiritual heart of Islam, constantly reiterating the unshakable and sacred truths of love, compassion and forgiveness which seem to lie at the very sources of the light that lightens our darkness and which, if it illuminates our hearts, can engender that peace we all seek.[167]

Shaykh Abū Bakr will be remembered as a traditional Muslim sage and Sufi master who helped revive perennial wisdom in the twentieth century through his intimate knowledge and understanding of Islam, Sufism, sacred art, symbolism and Shakespeare. His words are illuminating rays from a heart that clearly perceived and

167. *A Return to the Spirit*, p. vii.

faithfully reflected the eternal wisdom of God. Many students of Islam, Sufism, and even Shakespeare continue to benefit from his substantial contributions to the study of traditional spirituality, philosophy and literature.

* * *

Seyyed Hossein Nasr (1933–present) was influenced by all of the above Muslim sages, especially Frithjof Schuon, to whom he pays tribute to in *Knowledge and the Sacred*. He was born in Tehran into a family of educators and physicians. He is a descendent of the Prophet Muḥammad, as his name Seyyed suggests, and also a famous Sufi from Kāshān, Mullā Seyyed Moḥammad Taqī Posht-mashhadī. At a young age he studied the Quran, classical Islamic texts and Persian Sufi poetry, including the works of Firdawsī, Niẓamī, Sa'dī, Rūmī and Ḥāfiẓ, which undoubtedly shaped the rest of his life.[168] At the age of twelve he embarked for the United States to begin an illustrious academic career.

Nasr graduated from M.I.T with a B.S. in physics and did his postgraduate work at Harvard, earning his M.S. in geology and geophysics and his Ph.D. in the history of science and philosophy with an emphasis in Islamic science and philosophy. His dissertation was later published in 1964 as *An Introduction to Islamic Cosmological Doctrines*, which remains the only text of its kind in European languages. His advanced knowledge of the natural and physical sciences is unique among traditionalist writers, except for A.K. Coomaraswamy who began his career as a geologist. Nasr therefore has greater credibility among mainstream scientists and philosophers when he raises objections to the modern worldview, which is based on scientism, materialism and Darwinian evolution—subjects that he knows well.

He has been teaching in universities in the United States, Iran and Lebanon since 1955, and continues to teach courses at the George

168. Seyyed Hossein Nasr, "An Intellectual Autobiography" in Lewis Edwin Hahn, Randall E. Auxier, and Lucian W. Stone Jr., eds., *The Philosophy of Seyyed Hossein Nasr: The Library of Living Philosophers* vol. XXVIII (Peru, Illinois: Open Court Publishing Company, 2001), p. 7.

Washington University on subjects that include Islam, Islamic theology and philosophy, Islamic art, Sufism, Persian Sufi poetry, mysticism East and West, man and nature, and the perennial philosophy. He has helped to train some of the most important intellectuals and academics in Islamic studies and comparative religion, such as William Chittick, Sachiko Murata, James Morris, Naṣrollāh Pourjavādī, Osman Bakar, Gholām Rezā A'vānī, Mehdī Amīnrazavī, Zailan Moris, Ibrahim Kalin, David Dakake, Joseph Lumbard, Caner Dagli, and Waleed El-Ansary, to name but a few. One of Nasr's greatest legacies is the vast number of advanced students that he has trained in his over fifty years of teaching. He also influenced and had the opportunity to work closely with Henry Corbin, Toshihiko Izutsu, Huston Smith, Jacob Needleman, and Keith Critchlow. Moreover, he has studied or been acquainted with some of the most eminent Iranian scholars of the twentieth century, such as Abu'l-Ḥasan Qazwīnī, Muḥammad Kāẓim 'Aṣṣār, Murtaḍā Muṭahharī, Jalāl al-Dīn Āshtiyānī, and most notably 'Allāmah Ṭabāṭabā'ī. Nasr writes,

> During these years we have studied with 'Allāmah Ṭabāṭabā'ī not only the classical [Islamic] texts of divine wisdom and gnosis but also a whole cycle of what might be called comparative gnosis, in which in each session the sacred texts of one of the major religions, containing mystical and gnostic teachings, such as the *Tao te Ching*, the *Upanishads* and the *Gospel of John*, were discussed and compared with Sufism and Islamic gnostic doctrines in general.[169]

Nasr's meetings with Ṭabāṭabā'ī illustrate that one of the greatest Shī'ite scholars of the twentieth century took the esoteric doctrines of other religions seriously, much like the aforementioned Sunni scholars from Al-Azhar that Guénon and Lings met with in Egypt, as well as the Muslim sages that Schuon encountered from Senegal and Algeria. 'Allāmah Ṭabāṭabā'ī himself states,

> [Such] men as Zoroastrians, Jews, Christians, and Muslims follow the "high path" in this life for they believe in God and in man's

169. Allāmah Ṭabāṭabā'ī, *Shi'ite Islam*, trans. by S.H. Nasr (Albany, NY: State University of New York Press, 1975), p. 24.

> eternal life, and consider man to be responsible for his good and evil acts. As a result they accept as proven the existence of a day of judgment (*qiyāmat*) and follow a path that leads to felicity in both this world and the next.[170]

Even more convincingly he writes,

> [We] must not consider gnosis as a religion among others, but as the heart of all religions. Gnosis is one of the paths of worship, a path based on knowledge combined with love, rather than fear. It is the path for realizing the inner truth of religion rather than remaining satisfied only with its external form and rational thought. Every revealed religion and even those that appear in the form of idol-worship have certain followers who march upon the path of gnosis. The polytheistic religions and Judaism, Christianity, Zoroastrianism, and Islam all have believers who are gnostics.[171]

In addition to the eminent representatives of the Islamic sapiential tradition that Nasr studied with in Iran, he also took the poetry of Persian Sufi masters with his mother's milk. An understanding of the universality of the Truth is so ubiquitous in Persian Sufi poetry, and consequently most of the cultures shaped in part by this poetry, that one is not surprised to see Nasr focus on the question of religious pluralism in his own life and writings, applying his own intellectual vision and gifts to the unique circumstances that humanity faces. Moreover, he was also profoundly influenced by the teachings of René Guénon, Ananda K. Coomaraswamy, and especially Frithjof Schuon.[172] In his magnum opus *Knowledge and the Sacred*, Nasr writes,

> If Guénon was the master expositor of metaphysical doctrines and Coomaraswamy the peerless scholar and connoisseur of Oriental art who began his exposition of metaphysics through recourse to the language of artistic forms, Schuon seems like the cosmic intellect itself impregnated by the energy of divine grace surveying the whole of reality surrounding man and elucidating all the concerns of human existence in the light of sacred knowledge.[173]

170. Ibid., pp. 32–33.
171. Ibid., pp. 112–113.
172. "An Intellectual Autobiography," pp. 3–85.
173. *Knowledge and the Sacred*, p. 107.

Nasr has received some of the highest honors in the academic study of religion and philosophy, which he has taken advantage of to restate the perennial philosophy and the transcendent unity of religions. His *Knowledge and the Sacred* was delivered as the Gifford lectures in 1981 at the University of Edinburgh, which are the most prestigious lectures held in the West on the study of religion. This text deals with Tradition and its decline and subsequent revival in the West, metaphysics, traditional anthropology, cosmology, time and Eternity, traditional art, the multiplicity of religions, and spiritual realization, all from a sapiential perspective. Huston Smith once told us that *Knowledge and the Sacred* is among the three most important works written on religion in the twentieth century, the other two being William James' *Varieties of Religious Experience* and Schuon's *The Transcendent Unity of Religions*. Nasr's *Religion and the Order of Nature* was also prepared for the prominent Cadbury Lectures in 1994. An immense volume, *The Philosophy of Seyyed Hossein Nasr*, was dedicated to him in the Library of Living Philosophers series in 2001, which is one of the most prestigious honors an academic can receive in the field of philosophy. These texts signaled the arrival of the perennial philosophy in academia and more mainstream religious and philosophical circles in the West.

Nasr has also written other key texts on the perennial philosophy such as *The Need for a Sacred Science* and edited *The Essential Frithjof Schuon*, which is a valuable collection of Schuon's writings, endorsed by Schuon himself. Nasr also helped edit the volume *Religion of the Heart: Essays Presented to Frithjof Schuon on his Eightieth Birthday* and translated Schuon's *Understanding Islam* into Arabic with Ṣalāh al-Ṣāwī. He has appeared in numerous collections that deal directly with Tradition, modernity, and the perennial philosophy. Nasr also supports and oversees the publication of *Sophia*, the leading traditionalist journal in English, which contains articles by all of the traditionalists mentioned in this chapter, as well as esteemed scholars from various religions. With Katherine O'Brien, the editor of *Sophia*, Nasr has also edited the volumes *In Quest of the Sacred* and *The Essential Sophia*, the latter of which contains many pertinent articles that have appeared in the journal *Sophia*. Nasr's numerous essays and works in Persian, Arabic, Turkish, and other

Islamic languages represent a major contribution to the study of the perennial philosophy in the Islamic world. In *Knowledge and the Sacred*, which is perhaps the most comprehensive treatment of the various dimensions of the perennial philosophy by any one scholar, Nasr writes:

> The unity of religions is to be found first and foremost in the Absolute which is at once Truth and Reality and the origin of all revelations and of all truth. When the Sufis exclaim that the doctrine of Unity is unique (*al-tawḥīdu wāḥidun*), they are asserting this fundamental but often forgotten principle. Only at the level of the Absolute are the teachings of the religions the same. Below that level there are correspondences of the most profound order but not identity. The different religions are like so many languages speaking of that unique Truth as it manifests itself in different worlds according to its inner archetypal possibilities, but the syntax of these languages is not the same. Yet, because each religion comes from the Truth, everything in the religion in question which is revealed by the Logos is sacred and must be respected and cherished while being elucidated rather than being discarded and reduced to insignificance in the name of some kind of abstract universality.[174]

In addition to restating the perennial philosophy in so many academic domains, Nasr has also written some of the clearest and most accessible works in the West on the nature of Islam, Islamic philosophy, science, spirituality, and art. His *Ideals and Realities of Islam*, which was first published in 1966, is still used as a core textbook in many undergraduate and graduate university courses on Islam. His *The Heart of Islam* complements the previous text and deals with the essence of the Islamic tradition, as well as crucial issues that people of all faiths encounter. Nasr's spiritual biography on the Prophet of Islam entitled *Muhammad: Man of God* is a summary of the inner life and qualities of the Prophet. Despite its brevity, this book includes important events in the Prophet's life that are missing in many of his biographies in European languages. With a group of scholars Nasr has also recently translated the Quran into clear

174. Ibid., p. 293.

and eloquent English. This new translation, entitled *HarperCollins Study Qur'ān,* includes a traditional commentary and a number of essays dealing with various themes in the Quran. Its publication crowns Nasr's achievements as one of the leading scholars of Islam in the contemporary period.

Also highly significant regarding Nasr's contributions to the study of Islam is his definition of traditional Islam, which was unnecessary in the premodern Muslim world because both modernist and "fundamentalist" Islam—which he sees as two sides of the same coin—had not emerged in the various forms that we see in the contemporary world. In "What is Traditional Islam?," the prologue to *Islam in the Modern World*, Nasr sharply distinguishes traditional Islam from both modernist and fundamentalist aberrations of the religion. While traditional Islam has numerous and diverse expressions, its main features consist of the Quran and its traditional outer and inner interpretations, the *Ḥadīth*, the Divine Law (*Sharī'ah*), the classical schools of jurisprudence in both the Sunni and Shī'ite worlds, Sufism, the various schools of theology and philosophy, traditional social institutions and forms of governance, and last, but certainly not least, the study and cultivation of sacred and traditional Islamic art and architecture. Nasr's understanding of traditional Islam permeates all of his works on the religion and is among the most helpful interpretive frameworks that both Muslims and non-Muslims can employ to recognize and distinguish authentic manifestations of Islam from its revisionist and reductionist parodies. Charles Le Gai Eaton wrote,

> Who speaks for traditional Islam: the Islam lived for centuries by theologians and jurists, by philosophers and scientists, by artists and poets, by Sufis and simple people of faith throughout the Islamic world during fourteen centuries of Islamic history—the Islam which is in fact still followed by the vast majority of Muslims from the Atlantic to the Pacific? There may be still many who speak privately for this tradition but there are only a few writers and, among these few, Seyyed Hossein Nasr is pre-eminent.[175]

175. William Chittick, ed., *The Essential Seyyed Hossein Nasr* (Bloomington, IN: World Wisdom, Inc., 2007), front material.

Nasr's writings on Islamic philosophy and science are among the most comprehensive and challenging works on the subject to appear in English. In addition to *An Introduction to Islamic Cosmological Doctrines*, some of his other celebrated and influential works include *Three Muslims Sages*, which is concerned with Avicenna, Suhrawardī and Ibn 'Arabī and the perspectives and schools that they represent, *Ṣadr al-Dīn Shīrāzī and his Transcendent Theosophy*, *Islamic Science: An Illustrated Study*, and *Science and Civilization in Islam*. Nasr has also published *Islamic Philosophy from its Origin to the Present: Philosophy in the Land of Prophecy*, which is perhaps the definitive introductory work on the subject that not only lists the main figures, texts and schools of Islamic philosophy, but also discusses the fundamental principles and ideas that have occupied Muslim sages from the first Islamic century to the present.

Nasr's works on Islamic esoterism deal with the most essential aspects of the spiritual path, as well as the intellectual history of Sufism. These include *Sufi Essays*, the two-volume collection he edited entitled *Islamic Spirituality*, which contains selections from some of the leading contemporary authorities on Sufism from both the Muslim world and the West, and a treatise on Sufism entitled *The Garden of Truth*. Nasr's remark regarding Schuon's *Sufism: Veil and Quintessence* that, "It is not only a book about Sufism, but also a Sufi book," also applies to *The Garden of Truth*.[176] Speaking as a spiritual authority and not only an academic, Nasr writes, "The present book is the result of over fifty years of both scholarly study and of existential participation in Sufism. . . ."[177]

Not unrelated to Sufism are his books on Shī'ism, the most famous of which is the volume *Shi'ite Islam* by 'Allāmah Ṭabāṭabā'ī, which Nasr translated and edited. He always reminds his readers of the orthodoxy of both Shī'ism and Sunnism, and has contributed to the authentic presentation and preservation of both branches of the Islamic tradition. It is rare to find such a prominent Muslim scholar who respects the contributions of both Sunnis and Shī'ites and is

176. *Sufism: Veil and Quintessence*, p. ix. See also, Zachary Markwith, "*The Garden of Truth* review article," *Sophia* 14, no. 2 (Winter 2008–2009), pp. 185–195.

177. *The Garden of Truth*, p. xiii.

unwilling to champion one branch alone to the detriment of the other. Nasr writes in his chapter "Sunnism and Shī'ism" in *Ideals and Realities of Islam*:

> [It] can be said that Sunnism and Shī'ism are two orthodox dimensions of Islam providentially placed in this tradition to enable collectivities of different psychological and spiritual temperament to become integrated within the Islamic community. Being each an affirmation of the doctrine of Unity, they do not in themselves destroy the profound unity of Islam, whatever their formal differences may be. They are rather two ways of asserting the truth of the *shahādah, Lā ilāha illa'Llāh.* They are two streams which originate from the same fountain, which is their unique source, namely, the Quranic revelation. And they finally pour into a single sea which is the Divine Unity whose means of realization each contains within itself. To have lived either of them fully is to have lived fully as a Muslim and to have realized that Truth for the sake of whose revelation the Quran was made known to men through the Prophet of Islam.[178]

Nasr has also made unique contributions to the study of sacred and traditional Islamic art. Along with Titus Burckhardt's corpus, Nasr's *Islamic Art and Spirituality* is among the few books on the subject that penetrate into the symbolic structure of Islamic art to reveal the very principles of the religion and the Presence of the One. In this book he writes with elegance and erudition about the intellectual dimensions of Islamic calligraphy and architecture, sacred art in Persian culture, 'Aṭṭār's *Conference of the Birds*, the poetry of Rūmī, the influence of Sufism on traditional Persian music, the Persian miniature, and the void. Nasr has also published two volumes of his own poetry entitled *Poems of the Way* and *The Pilgrimage of Life and the Wisdom of Rumi,* which reveal the artist and gnostic behind the scholar. In the first volume, Nasr writes in a poem entitled "Ode to the One":

> [We] bear witness to Thy Oneness.
> Yet, who are we this Oneness to behold?

178. Seyyed Hossein Nasr, *Ideals and Realities of Islam* (Chicago: ABC International Group, Inc., 2000), pp. 173–174.

It is Thou within us who testifies,
Who bears witness to Thy Oneness pure.
Our selves are but veils hiding Thee from Thee,
But Thy Self resides in our heart of hearts
And our substance, pure and primordial,
Reflects now and forever the glory of Thy Oneness.[179]

Perhaps Nasr's most important intellectual contribution to the world at large is his work on the spiritual nature of the environmental crisis. In a manner similar to Guénon's *The Crisis of the Modern World*, Nasr perceived the spiritual roots of this crisis years before the world took notice. He deserves credit for bringing more attention—and especially wisdom—to one of the most crucial issues of our time. His *Man and Nature* was first published in 1968, followed by the aforementioned *Religion and the Order of Nature* in 1996, and most recently *The Spiritual and Religious Dimension of the Environmental Crisis* in 1999. It is easy to overlook this key aspect of Nasr's corpus because he is such a prolific writer on Islam and the perennial philosophy. Yet he also points out that the ecological disaster we are heading towards and are already experiencing can only be averted by our attachment to a living Revelation and tradition, which provide the necessary means and grace from Heaven for the human being to live in harmony with the earth. Therefore, there is an intimate relationship between the Islamic tradition, the perennial philosophy as it manifests in Islam and other traditions, and Nasr's pertinent and urgent message for the world. This crucial subject is analyzed and discussed in more detail in chapter seven.

In our estimation, there is no living scholar of Islamic studies or the perennial philosophy who matches Nasr's knowledge and insight. The synthesizing quality and encyclopedic quantity to his corpus reveal the depth and breadth of his knowledge. Yet we would be mistaken if we think Nasr's interest in Islam and the *sophia perennis* is limited to the academic domain. He writes in his intellectual autobiography,

179. Seyyed Hossein Nasr, *Poems of the Way* (Oakton, VA: The Foundation for Traditional Studies, 1999), p. 14.

> I also spent much of the summer of 1957 and 1958 in Morocco. Those years were crucial to my whole intellectual and spiritual life. It was at this time that my intellectual and philosophical orientation received its final and enduring formation and I embraced Sufism not only intellectually but also existentially in a form linked to the Maghrib and more particularly to the spiritual lineage of the great Algerian master Shaykh Aḥmad al-'Alawī and Shaykh 'Īsā Nūr al-Dīn Aḥmad. These intellectual and existential experiences not only rooted my mind and soul for the rest of my life in the world of tradition, intellectual certitude, and faith, but also led to the discovery of inner illumination, the harmonious wedding of "logic and transcendence," to use the title of one of the works of Schuon, and intellectual lucidity and rigor combined with love for the truth and beauty.[180]

Therefore, the philosophy that Nasr espouses is philosophy in the original sense of the term—the love of wisdom—combined with an operative tradition in its exoteric and esoteric dimensions, and not simply the academic study of the history of philosophy and religion. Nasr is able to write with such wisdom, authority and beauty about Islam, the Islamic sapiential tradition, and the perennial philosophy because he has gone beyond mere theoretical knowledge of religion and philosophy, and gained sacred knowledge through the inner dimension of Islam.

It has become all too easy in the West to believe in an abstract unity of religions, which denies the importance of any one religion and therefore the possibility of attaining true knowledge of the One Reality. Nasr has defended Tradition in general and his own tradition in particular because he understands the tendency in the West to reject forms in the name of the Formless. Yet those who reject forms, which include some misleading interpreters of Guénon, Coomaraswamy and Schuon, have rejected the means of knowing the Formless. One cannot truly know the transcendent unity of religions unless one knows the Transcendent, and one cannot truly know the Transcendent unless one knows and practices a revealed religion. Nasr has preserved Tradition and championed sacred

180. "An Intellectual Autobiography," p. 27.

knowledge. This is an immense service for all people concerned with the *sophia perennis.*

Finally, he has encouraged people of all faiths to practice their traditions more fully. Like his predecessors, Nasr is a colossal intellectual and spiritual figure, who is also responsible for bringing the light of the *sophia perennis* and Tradition to the modern world. Nasr applied the principles of the perennial philosophy to various intellectual, philosophical and religious domains it had not yet reached. He is also responsible for preserving the tradition of Islam, including Islamic philosophy, science, art, Sufism, Shīʿism and Sunnism. There is no one scholar concerned with the perennial philosophy who has written as many quality works on Islam in all of its facets. Nasr has thereby preserved a unique manifestation of the perennial philosophy for future generations. His knowledge of Islam and other traditions, which he applied so aptly to modernism, scientism, and the environmental crisis, was also the result of his connection to the inner reality and *barakah* of the Quran and the Prophet Muḥammad, who is his biological and spiritual ancestor. This oriental sage in exile helped to transmit the knowledge of the East to the West, and, like the other sages examined, helped to revive the *sophia perennis* and the tradition of Islam in the twentieth century. As we have demonstrated, this was possible because as a Muslim, Nasr understands the doctrine of Divine Unity, the essential unity of the revealed books and messengers, as well as the Islamic intellectual and spiritual tradition, and has explained these principles and heritage in a manner that is intelligible to contemporary men and women.

Some Conclusions

While a further study of this topic is needed to examine other important Muslim and non-Muslim contributions to the study and rearticulation of the perennial philosophy in the twentieth and twenty-first centuries, the names of some of the other major Muslim traditionalists from the West include Victor Danner, Lord Northbourne, Tage Lindbom, Michel Vâlsan, Whitall Perry, Charles Le Gai Eaton, Jean-Louis Michon, Virginia Gray Henry-Blakemore, M. Ali Lakhani, and Reza Shah-Kazemi. While Joseph Epes Brown studied Native American traditions and Leo Schaya penned some penetrating works on Judaism and the Kabbalah, both men practiced the religion of Islam. A number of contemporary Islamic scholars and intellectuals from the Muslim world have also supported the traditionalists and their views. The most notable names among this group include 'Allāmah Ṭabāṭabā'ī, 'Abd al-Ḥalīm Maḥmūd, 'Alī Juma'a, Fāṭimah al-Yashruṭiyyah, Muḥammad Ḥasan 'Askarī, Muhammad Suheyl Umar, Gholām Rezā A'vānī, Osman Bakar, Zailan Moris, Rusmir Mahmutcehajic, Feisal Abdul Rauf, Ali Allawi, and Samer Akkach. Moreover, a number of leading Muslim teachers and authors from the West were also influenced by the writings of the traditionalists, while not necessarily accepting all of their views, including Hamza Yusuf, Nuh Ha Mim Keller, Maryam Jameelah, 'Abd al-Wahid Pallavicini, Mahmoud Shelton, Charles Upton and Rodney Blackhirst.[181] In this context, one can also mention contemporary Sufi masters who have helped introduce Islamic spirituality to the West and accepted the efficacy of other revealed

181. There is a whole new generation of Muslim scholars and intellectuals from the West and the Muslim world who have been influenced by the earlier generations of Muslim traditionalists. Among this new group of Muslim intellectuals are several students of Seyyed Hossein Nasr, including David Dakake, Joseph Lumbard, Ibrahim Kalin, Walid El-Ansari, Caner Dagli and the author of the present volume. A number of leading Muslim scholars from the West also first encountered Islam through the writings of the traditionalists, including Shaykh Hamza Yusuf and Shaykh Nuh Ha Mim Keller, despite not fully accepting their views on other religions.Yusuf writes, "I remember purchasing a small metaphysical treatise by an author with a foreign name way back in 1976 as I was browsing the shelves in a small spiritual bookstore located amidst a beautiful garden in Ojai, California. The title was *The Book of Certainty: The Sufi Doctrine of Faith, Vision and Gnosis*, and the author was Abū Bakr Sirāj al-Dīn [Martin Lings]. At the time, I knew nothing of Islam let alone who the author was, yet the title intrigued me. It was, in essence, what I was searching for—certainty... my curiosity had been piqued and shortly thereafter, in a life-altering transaction, I purchased a Quran and began to read a very personal revelation that would compel me to convert to the religion of Islam." Hamza Yusuf, "A Gentle Soul," in Martin Lings, *A Return to the Spirit*, pp. 112–113. Keller also writes in his translation *Reliance of the Traveller*, "[Seyyed Hossein Nasr] is the author of a number of works that are among the best available in English on the relevance of traditional Islamic sciences and mystical disciples to the situation of modern man, including *Ideals and Realities of Islam*, *Man and Nature*, *Islamic*

religions for non-Muslims, including Ivan Aguéli, Hazrat Inayat Khan, M.R. Bawa Muhaiyaddeen, Muzaffer Ozak, Lex Hixon, Javad Nurbakhsh, Nazim al-Haqqani, Abdoulaye Dieye, Bilal Hyde, Fadhlalla Haeri, Henry Bayman, and Kabir and Camille Helminski, for example.[182] Moreover, some of the leading academic scholars of Islamic and Sufi studies have either been influenced by the traditionalists and their views or have shown some sympathy for them, including Annemarie Schimmel, Toshihiko Izutsu, William Chittick, Sachiko Murata, James Morris, Michel Chodkiewicz, Laleh Bakhtiar, Vincent Cornell, Alan Godlas, Leonard Lewisohn, Éric Geoffroy, Patrick Laude, and Samuel Zinner.[183] It is difficult to

---

Science: An Illustrated Study, and *Sufi Essays*. The translator is indebted to his writings for being among the reasons he became a Muslim." Aḥmad ibn Naqīb al-Miṣrī, *Reliance of the Traveller* (*'Umdat al-sālik*), trans. Nuh Ha Mim Keller (Beltsville: MD: Amana Publications, 1994) p. 1095. It should be noted that while Keller has written against some of the views of Guénon, Schuon and the traditionalists, Yusuf has shown greater sympathy for other religions in recent years. See for example his essay, "Buddha in the Qur'ān?" in Reza Shah-Kazemi, *Common Ground Between Islam and Buddhism* (Louisville, KY: Fons Vitae, 2010), pp. 113–136. The writings of 'Abd al-Wahid Pallavicini, Mahmoud Shelton, Charles Upton, and Rodney Blackhirst are all more or less in accord with those of the traditionalists and may even be considered as creative and critical extensions of the same perspective. These scholars, together with Hamza Yusuf, Nuh Keller, and Maryam Jameelah indicate something of the vast and diverse influence of the traditionalists upon Muslims from the West who have accepted all, most, or only some of their views.

182. Some of these sages have emphasized the universal dimensions of Islam and Sufism more than others, but all of them have transmitted authentic Sufi teachings to the West based upon traditional initiatic chains and precedents. Even though our own perspective on Islamic spirituality is more or less in accord with the traditionalists surveyed in this chapter, the different emphases and approaches of the aforementioned Sufi teachers have provided different souls access to the wisdom and guidance of Islam and Sufism. It should be noted that some Sufi masters have accepted both Muslim and non-Muslim disciples, while others have had only Muslim disciples, but often non-Muslim admirers. I would like to thank Dr. Pir Zia Inayat-Khan for helping me to understand and appreciate these different possibilities.

183. We would add Henry Corbin's name to this list because of his close association with Seyyed Hossein Nasr and the Imperial Iranian Academy of Philosophy, but his writings do not otherwise reflect the perspectives of Guénon, Schuon, Burckhardt or Lings, except in as much as any two studies on Islamic esoterism might naturally coincide.

imagine what Islamic studies in academia or even Islam as a religion in the West would look like without the writings and influence of the traditionalists studied in this chapter.

It would be an inexcusable omission not to mention Ananda K. Coomaraswamy and other leading traditionalists from the world's other religions who were also responsible for restating the perennial philosophy in the modern era. René Guénon's complement in the first half of the twentieth century was A.K. Coomaraswamy (1877–1947), who in his own way revived the study of Tradition through his study of metaphysics, cosmology, symbolism, and especially sacred and traditional art. A.K. Coomaraswamy dealt extensively with the excesses of modernity and was the most important non-Muslim traditionalist responsible for restating the perennial philosophy. Coomaraswamy represents the perennial wisdom of the Hindu tradition, which like Islam is more inclined to accept the validity of other faiths. His writings on traditional Hindu, Buddhist, Christian, and Islamic art and spirituality, as well as the vicissitudes of modernity, represent an intellectual peak in the modern era. We must also mention in summary the eminent Buddhist traditionalist Marco Pallis, the Catholic traditionalists Elémire Zolla, Rama Coomaraswamy, and Wolfgang Smith, and the Orthodox Christian traditionalists Philip Sherrard and James Cutsinger. The great Catholic mystic and author Thomas Merton was in close contact and correspondence with leading traditionalists of his time and also showed sympathy and respect for their writings and perspectives on both Islam and the perennial philosophy.[184] The pioneering studies of Peter Kingsley and Algis Uždavinys on early Greek philosophy also reflect aspects of the traditionalist perspective. Moreover, some of leading scholars of comparative religion in the West embraced the perennial philosophy as their own approach to the study of religion or have been directly influenced by the writings of Guénon, Coomaraswamy, or Schuon, including Mircea Eliade,

184. Rob Baker, "Merton, Marco Pallis, and the Traditionalists," in Rob Baker and Gray Henry, eds., *Merton and Sufism: The Untold Story* (Louisville, KY: Fons Vitae, 1999), pp. 193–265.

Huston Smith, Jacob Needleman, and Harry Oldmeadow.[185] Without question, these perceptive scholars were also responsible, each in their own way, for restating the *sophia perennis* in the twentieth century, which by its nature embraces all divinely revealed religions that issue from and lead to the One. The presence of these sages and their writings demonstrate the universal nature of the perennial philosophy and its message for people of all religions.

However, we cannot ignore the fact that the vast majority of the leading traditionalists in the twentieth century, as well as two of the three founders of the school, practiced the religion of Islam. This was not accidental, but the result of the message of Divine Unity at the heart of the Quran, *Sunnah*, and the Islamic sapiential tradition, which guided and inspired their lives and writings. It is evident that they were also influenced by other religions and teachings of non-Islamic origin, however, the perennial philosophy was restated in the twentieth century to a large extent because of the vibrancy of the Islamic tradition, which was the hidden source of guidance and inspiration in the spiritual lives and writings of these eminent Muslim sages. What must be kept in mind is that when Guénon wrote *The Crisis of the Modern World*, Schuon wrote *The Transcendent Unity of Religions*, Burckhardt wrote *Sacred Art in East and West*, Lings wrote *The Secret of Shakespeare*, and Nasr wrote *Knowledge and the Sacred* they were all praying five times a day in the direction of Mecca, consulting the Quran, following the *Sunnah* of the Prophet Muḥammad, and meditating on and invoking the Supreme Name of God in Arabic. They were not pseudo-universalists who denied Revelation and tradition, but practicing Muslims who also appreciated the multiple manifestations of the *sophia perennis* in the world's religions. They knew that these diverse religions were suited for people of different temperaments and civilizations and brought this knowledge to the attention of the West. Many spiritual

185. William W. Quinn, Jr., "Mircea Eliade and the Sacred Tradition (A Personal Account)," *Nova Religio* 3, no. 1 (1999), pp. 147–153; Zachary Markwith, "Huston Smith's Encounter with the Islamic Tradition," *Sophia* 16, no. 1 (2010), pp. 81–93; Jacob Needleman, ed., *The Sword of Gnosis* (Boston: Arkana, 1986); and Kenneth Oldmeadow, *Traditionalism: Religion in the light of the Perennial Philosophy* (Colombo: The Sri Lanka Institute of Traditional Studies, 2000).

teachers in the contemporary era have spoken about the unity of religions, but few have done so while also insisting that this unity only resides in God and can be best approached through attaching oneself to a particular orthodox religion. Conversely, most religious scholars who insist upon orthodoxy usually deny the principle of universality.

The fact that those most responsible for restating the perennial philosophy in the twentieth century were Muslims sheds light on the universality of Islam. At a time in history when Islam is accused of promoting intolerance and fanaticism because of the actions of some Muslims, it is important to examine the Islamic tradition through the writings of its contemporary sages. In the writings of these scholars, and other luminaries in Islamic history such as Suhrawardī, Rūmī and Ibn ʿArabī, concrete examples of universal and perennial wisdom may be found. These Muslim intellectuals were responsible for demonstrating that all religions issue from the One Transcendent Reality and constitute diverse expressions of Divine Wisdom, Love and Beauty. While this has become common knowledge in many circles, it would be a mistake to overlook the origin of this sacred knowledge. As a relatively recent and living tradition, Islam is able to provide a framework for the spiritual and contemplative life. Our Muslim sages in the twentieth century took this path and shared the fruits of their realization with the world. So while their knowledge and efforts affirm the transcendent unity of religions and helped to revive so many expressions of perennial wisdom for people of all faiths, the Islamic tradition was the fertile soil for the reemergence of the *sophia perennis* in the contemporary era.

2

Lovers of Sophia

When I took up a particular *sadhana* (spiritual practice) and asked Divine Mother importunately with a glowing eagerness of heart for the realization of its result, She benignly crowned me with success in three days only.[1] —Ramakrishna

Receptive now my heart is for each form;
For gazelles pasture, for monks a monastery,
Temple for idols, Ka'bah to be rounded,
Tables of Torah and script of Quran.
My religion is love's religion: where'er turn
Her camels, that religion my religion is, my faith.
An example is set us by Bishr, lover
Of Hind and her sister, and likewise the loves
Of Qays and Laylā, of Mayya and Ghaylān.[2]
—Ibn 'Arabī

When one looks at the lives of some of the greatest sages and expositors Divine Unity and religious pluralism in the history of Islam and other traditions, a curious and reoccurring phenomenon is often present: namely, a celestial or earthly feminine manifestation of Divine wisdom or *sophia*. In this chapter we examine love and devotion to a feminine theophany of the Divine in the lives and teachings of Srī Ramakrishna and Muḥyī al-Dīn ibn 'Arabī, keeping in mind from the outset that there is not an exact one-to-one correlation between the Goddess in Hinduism and the earthly reflection of the Beloved in the lives of the Sufis. Ramakrishna worshipped the

1. Claude Alan Stark, *God of All, Sri Ramakrishna's Approach to Religious Plurality* (Cape Cod, MA: Claude Stark, Inc., 1974), p. 47.
2. Martin Lings, *Sufi Poems*, p. 62.

Hindu Goddess Kali, while Ibn 'Arabī saw the Persian girl Niẓām as a symbol of the Infinite Reality that is beyond forms. Remarkably, both sages were able to appreciate other religions after witnessing a manifestation or symbol of Divine majesty and beauty in the feminine form. While Ramakrishna and Ibn 'Arabī came from different religious, historical, and cultural contexts they arrived at a strikingly similar understanding of the universality of religions by contemplating God through the form of the feminine. This is a reoccurring theme in the lives and teachings of many mystics because the feminine theophany is a direct manifestation or reflection of the infinitude of God, the knowledge of which makes all sacred forms intelligible. It was a beatific vision of the Infinite through the feminine that enabled Ramakrishna and Ibn 'Arabī to appreciate, albeit in different ways, the various sacred forms that they encountered as so many "unique repetitions" of Divine wisdom and beauty.

Srī Ramakrishna

Srī Ramakrishna (1836–1886) also known as *paramahamsa* or "the Great Swan," was born in the village Kumarpukar in Bengal.[3] He was devoted to the Hindu Goddess Kali and other Hindu deities and avatars, but also expressed his love and devotion to the Divine Reality or Brahman through sacred forms from other religious universes, which are not always seen as alien forms in Hinduism. This universal understanding of religious forms in Hinduism can be traced to what in Sanskrit is termed *sanatāna dharma* or the eternal teaching, which has also been translated as perennial wisdom or *sophia perennis*.[4] Ramakrishna has become known in the West mostly through the text *The Gospel of Sri Ramakrishna* recorded by his disciple Mahendranath Gupta, as well as the popular devotional centers established by another disciple Vivekananda.[5] The following analysis will rely primarily on Ramakrishna's own experiences and

3. I.H. Azad Faruqi, *Sufism and Bhakti: Mawlānā Rūm and Srī Rāmakrishna* (New Delhi: Abhinav Publications, 1984), p. 69.

4. Seyyed Hossein Nasr, *Knowledge and the Sacred*, p. 71.

5. Mahendranath Gupta, *The Gospel of Sri Ramakrishna*, trans. Swami Nikhilananda (New York: Ramakrishna-Vivekananda Center, 1992).

teachings, as well as secondary sources which help to elucidate the meaning of his life, teachings and practices in the context of nineteenth century India.

Regarding the place of the Goddess in Hinduism, Alf Hiltebeitel and Kathleen Erndl observe,

> Of all the world's great religions Hinduism has the most elaborate living Goddess traditions. Hindu conceptions of female deities and the over-arching Great Goddess stem from the supreme cosmic power, *Shakti*, from whom all creation emerges and by whom it is sustained. The worship of the Goddess, of the divine as female, has a long history in India and continues to become more popular today. By virtue of their common feminine nature, women are in some contexts regarded as special manifestations of the Goddess, sharing in her powers. . . .[6]

Beginning in 1855, Ramakrishna served as a priest in the Kali temple of Dakshineshwar.[7] Ramakrishna was first and foremost devoted to the Divine Mother or the Goddess Kali, which means black or dark colored. As the consort of Shiva, Kali is the *ādyā-shakti* or primordial power. Along with other deities in the Hindu Pantheon, Shiva and Kali manifest the masculine and feminine principles of existence or *purusha* and *prakṛiki*. Kali is associated with destruction and renewal, which are symbols for spiritual annihilation and absorption in the Divine. For devotees of Kali, the Divine Mother is not simply an external deity to be worshipped among other deities, but a manifestation of the Divine Essence, as well as the creative energy that generates and destroys forms. Kali is often depicted as black, which symbolizes the mystery and blinding luminosity of the Divine Essence. Ramakrishna states,

> Brahman alone is addressed as the Mother. This is because a mother is an object of great love. One is able to realize God just through love. Ecstasy of feeling, devotion, love, and faith—these are the means.[8]

6. Alf Hiltebeitel and Kathleen M. Erndl, eds, *Is the Goddess a Feminist?* (Sheffield, England: Sheffield Academic Press, 2000), p. 11.
7. *Sufism and Bhakti*, pp. 70–71.
8. *The Gospel of Sri Ramakrishna*, p. 108. See also, *Ibid.*, pp. 134–136.

The devotees of the Goddess often see Her as transcending other deities, such as Shiva and Vishnu in power and beauty. It becomes clear from Ramakrishna's life and teachings, however, that each Divine manifestation is a unique expression of the same Reality, as well as a state of being which corresponds to a level of realization in the sage.[9] This was true for Ramakrishna when he was contemplating Hindu deities and avatars, as well as Divine theophanies and prophets from other religions. Ramakrishna's devotion to each of these particular forms are all expressions of his unitive vision of God.[10] The forms and substance of the numerous deities in Hinduism are comparable, in certain respects, to the Ninety-Nine Names of God in the Islamic tradition. In Islam, all of these Names are aspects of the Supreme Name and Reality Allah, just as Hindu deities are manifestations of the Supreme Principle Brahman. Kali is in some ways analogous to the Divine Name *al-Raḥmān* or the Infinitely Good in Islam, although She also has a fierce and majestic side. Kali also manifests in the world through a variety of forms, especially women of great sanctity. If Hinduism appears to be more explicit about the immanence of the Divine and the manifestation of God through the human form, we discover below that this aspect and understanding of God is by no means absent in Islam.

Ramakrishna saw many women in his life, including children, complete strangers, and even prostitutes, as manifestations of the Goddess Kali or another feminine deity. This form of adoration of

9. René Guénon, *The Multiple States of the Being*, trans. Henry D. Fohr (Hillsdale, New York: Sophia Perennis, 2004).

10. Ramakrishna states, "A single sense perception of Brahman, no less than a beatific vision of the Divine Face. The opening of a single flower is Brahman, no less than the unfolding of the constellations. Boundless Consciousness, without separate subjects or objects, miraculously manifests as materiality. You may wonder how Ātman—sheer awareness and transparency—can appear as what one senses to be impenetrable earth and stone. To clear this and every doubt, simply remember that Divine Presence is capable of any manifestation whatsoever. God will never be limited by what people perceive as the bounds of possibility, no matter how expanded their relative knowledge may become." Lex Hixon, *Great Swan: Meetings with Ramakrishna* (Boston: Shambhala Publications, 1992), p. 180.

women is called *shorashi pujā* in Tantra.[11] Regarding his marriage to the famous female Hindu saint Sarada Devi (1853–1920), Ramakrishna relates:

> After several years of ecstasy, when I was twenty-three, my beloved earthly mother arranged my marriage to Sarada in order to shock this mind into some worldly responsibility, but I experienced the five-year old bride as a complete manifestation of the Universal Mother in Her delicate wisdom-aspect as Goddess Sarasvatī.[12]

Ramakrishna was concerned how his young bride could "survive the painful social pressures of being married to a homeless *paramahamsa* with no worldly sensibility whatsoever."[13] He goes on to say:

> When Sarada finally came to visit me here at the Temple Garden—sixteen years of age and beautiful with a transcendent Divine Beauty—I no longer worried. Why? Because I perceived that she is a full conscious manifestation of the Goddess.... Such power to assimilate Divine Ecstasy—and to conceal from others her constant ecstatic experience—I have never encountered in any practitioner, before or since.[14]

Ramakrishna's primary and central form of devotion was to the Goddess and Her various manifestations, yet in a manner similar to Ibn 'Arabī, Ramakrishna did not see the feminine theophany as a form that excluded other forms. Rather, he saw the Divine Mother as a symbol or manifestation of the Divine Essence and the creative aspect of God. For Ramakrishna the Divine feminine is the Infinite fount of all Divine Self-disclosures, as well as his own celestial spiritual guide. According to I. H. Azad Faruqi,

> To the question whether Srī Ramakrishna wanted to be guided on this path [of Advaita Vedānta] Srī Ramakrishna replied that this

11. *The Gospel of Sri Ramakrishna*, p. 37. It should be noted that Ramakrishna appears to venerate all women in his life, including his wife, in a Platonic manner and according to his monastic vow of celibacy. Likewise, his practice of Tantra was purely symbolic and contemplative without the concomitant sexual dimensions. *God of All*, pp. 42–51, 112–122

12. *Great Swan*, p. 85.

13. Ibid., pp. 85–86.

14. Ibid., p. 86.

depended on the will of Mother Kali. As he received permission from Her he was all set for his new experiment in spirituality.[15]

From Kali, Ramakrishna was given unique permission to practice various Hindu forms and many of the world's great religions that he encountered, including Advaita Vedānta, Tantra, Vaishnavism, Christianity and Islam. Moreover, he was responsible for asserting the essential unity of the supreme mystical experience in these religions, which he became aware of through reaching the end of each path he embarked on.[16] If Srī Ramana Maharshi (d. 1950) was providentially chosen to bear witness to the primacy of the Self in contemporary India, Ramakrishna's unique function was to practice various traditional forms and remind us that they each lead to realization of the same Divine Reality. Ramakrishna states,

> I have always considered religious one-sidedness to be the major obstacle to such awakening [in Ātman or Brahman]. Therefore, I

15. *Sufism and Bhakti*, p. 78. "At their first meeting, when Tota Puri inquired of Srī Ramakrishna if he wished to practice the Advaita Vedānta *sadhana*, for he seemed well qualified to the wandering monk, Srī Ramakrishna replied, 'Wait, I'll ask my Mother. It all depends on her.' He returned a little later in a semiconscious state and beaming with joy. He told Tota Puri that Divine Mother has instructed him, 'Go and learn—it was to teach you that the monk came here.'" *God of All*, p. 62. After practicing Advaita Vedānta for six months and attaining the highest level of realization, Kali intervenes and tells Ramakrishna, "Remain on the threshold of relative consciousness for the sake of humanity." Ibid., p. 66. See also, Ibid., pp. 45, 100.

16. Christopher Isherwood writes, "One result of experiencing *nivikalpa samadhi* [non-dual realization] was that Ramakrishna became even more catholic in his views and felt keen sympathy for any and every sect which sincerely struggled to know God. At this time, a certain Govinda Rai came to Dakshineshwar; he was a Hindu of the kshatriya caste by birth, but, as a seeker after truth, he had studied many religions and had finally embraced Islam.... Ramakrishna happened to talk with him and was charmed by his faith and love of God. 'This also is a path to God-realization,' Ramakrishna said to himself. 'The Mother has shown herself to many people through this *sadhana* also. I must practice it'.... Saradananda finds great significance in Ramakrishna's practice of Islam. He believers that Ramakrishna wished to demonstrate by it that non-dualistic Vedanta is the only valid link between the many dualistic religions. It is certainly idle to pretend, as some well-intentioned liberals do, that there is very little difference between religions, or races. There is a very big difference—on the surface. Unity can only be found by going deep, to the underlying, all-projecting Brahman." *Ramakrishna and His Disciples* (New York: Simon and Schuster, 1965), pp. 124–125.

> have sought and received countless sacred teachings. In the holy Vṛindāvan I was initiated as a Vaishnava monk, wearing traditional robes, imbibing and entirely assimilating that particular mystic atmosphere. At the Temple Golden in Dakshineswar I was initiated into the mystery of Rama worship, painting my forehead with sandalwood paste and wearing a diamond amulet around my neck. In both instances, after three days these outer expressions no longer seemed appropriate, as the inner power of the initiation had fully blossomed. With the same wholehearted spirit, I practiced the ways of Christianity and Islam, each for a period of three days of total intensity, during which these particular mystic ideals came to full and permanent fruition in my being. No genuine initiation ever disappears. But now I have become a vat that can dye cloth whatever primary color or subtle hue anyone may desire. All the most advanced spiritual experiences from human history are contained in the form now before you, as in a transparent case. I swear to you that I know nothing but God![17]

After traveling through several different traditions, Ramakrishna was able to know—through direct experience—that all paths lead to the same Divine summit.[18] In a lecture entitled "Sri Ramakrishna and Religious Tolerance" Ananda K. Coomaraswamy remarks, "Such an understanding may be rare, but is absolutely normal in the East. . . ."[19] Ramakrishna states, "The Reality is one and the same; the difference is in name and form . . . some address the Reality as 'Allah', some as 'God', some as 'Brahman', some as 'Kali', and others by such names as 'Rama', 'Jesus', 'Durga', 'Hari'."[20] Ramakrishna was also sensitive to religious differences, and was careful to only practice one traditional form at a time. He states in his own words, "A man can reach God if he follows one path rightly. Then he can learn about all the other paths. . . ."[21]

17. *Great Swan*, p. 289.

18. Ananda K. Coomaraswamy, "Paths that Lead to the Same Summit," *The Bugbear of Literacy*, pp. 50–67.

19. Ananda K. Coomaraswamy, "Sri Ramakrishna and Religious Tolerance," *Prabuddha Bharata* XLI (1936); and *Vincit Omnia Veritas* II, no. 2 (June 2006).

20. *The Gospel of Sri Ramakrishna*, p. 135.

21. Ibid., p. 374.

Due to the fact that we are comparing Ramakrishna to Ibn ʿArabī, it is important to more closely examine Ramakrishna's brief but profound experience as a Muslim and his initiation at the hands of a Sufi shaykh in 1866. Ramakrishna states:

> I received initiation and instruction from the Sufi Master Govinda Rai. He transmitted to my heart the beautiful Divine Name Allah, which I then repeated with every breath. I visited the small mosque behind the Temple Garden, learning to make the call to prayer and to perform *namāz*, the graceful cycles of prostration and praise offered by devout Muslims five times every day. My practice of Islam was crowned by a vision of the noble Prophet Muḥammad—a robed, dignified, bearded figure of supreme sanctity—who merged intimately with my being, pervading my body with rose fragrance and lifting my awareness into union with him and then into mystic union with Allah Most High. It was precisely the same profound *samādhi* attained along the paths of Veda and Tantra. Muslims call it *fanā'*. During this brief but intense period of Islamic *sadhana*, I enjoyed Muslim dishes and wore Muslim clothes. I removed the pictures of Hindu deities from my room and constantly chanted verses in Arabic from the Holy Quran. . . .[22]

What is interesting about his practice of Islam and other traditions is that he completely dedicated himself to each tradition that he set his heart and mind to until he reached its highest level of realization. He did not practice the rites or features of one tradition alongside those of another, but fully lived and worshipped within each religion that he practiced. Moreover, he did not allow all of his disciples to practices all of the traditions that he did.[23] According to Faruqi, "There is no doubt however that whatever discipline he practiced he always returned to the Mother Goddess as

22. *Great Swan*, pp. 255–256. Ramakrishna also states, "Do you know what the truth is? God made different religions to suit different aspirants, times, and countries. All doctrines are only so many paths; but a path is by no means God Himself. Indeed, one can reach God if one follows any of the paths with whole-hearted devotion." *Ibid.*, p. 559.

23. *Sufism and Bhakti*, pp. 77–78.

his beloved ideal."[24] Moreover, Kali directed Ramakrishna to practice the various forms he dedicated himself to and consecrated his efforts. He states, "When I took up a particular *sadhana* and asked Divine Mother importunately with a glowing eagerness of heart for the realization of its result, She benignly crowned me with success in three days only."[25] Ramakrishna demonstrates that the bhaktic or devotional way in Hinduism contains an opening to gnosis.[26] His devotion to the Divine Mother and Her various manifestations opened him to the highest level of realization in Hinduism, Christianity, and Islam.

Muḥyī al-Dīn ibn 'Arabī

Muḥyī al-Dīn ibn 'Arabī (1165–1240), known as the Greatest Master (al-Shaykh al-Akbar) in many Sufi circles, was born in Murcia during Muslim rule of the Iberian Peninsula. He is best known for his treatises *The Ringstones of Wisdom* (*Fuṣūṣ al-ḥikam*) and *The Meccan Openings* (*al-Futūḥāt al-makkiyyah*), and the famous poem *The Interpreter of Desires* (*Tarjumān al-ashwāq*), which is central to this discussion due to the young Persian woman Niẓām who inspired the work. Ibn 'Arabī's theophanic vision of Niẓām helped to catalyze his universal vision of Divine Unity and religious diversity. His understanding of love and devotion (*maḥabbah*) was not separate from gnosis or illumination (*ma'rifah*). If the paths of action, love, and gnosis are more strictly differentiated in Hinduism, they are generally seen as complementary in Islamic esoterism. While Ibn 'Arabī was first and foremost a gnostic, his poem the *Tarjumān al-ashwāq* demonstrates that his contemplative vision of Reality was based on love. Conversely, if Rūmī is often seen as the supreme expositor of love in Islam, his *Mathnawī* demonstrates that Divine love is actually a form of gnosis. In both cases one can assert that either love or gnosis is the dominant theme, but that neither are absent. As such, Ibn 'Arabī's perspective on love and devotion is highlighted with the

24. Ibid., p. 79.
25. *God of All*, p. 47.
26. Frithjof Schuon, *The Transcendent Unity of Religions*, pp. 139–140.

understanding that this love is inseparable from the knowledge of God.

Before examining the role of Niẓām in the life of Ibn ʿArabī it is necessary to say a few words about love and devotion in Islam in general. According to the Islamic tradition God has Ninety-Nine Names, which are either Names of Majesty (*Jalāl*), Beauty (*Jamāl*), or Perfection (*Kamāl*). These Names are the quintessence of the Quranic revelation, the invocation of which leads to the recollection of the Named. The first category includes Names such as the Just (*al-ʿAdl*), the All-Powerful (*al-Qādir*), and the Avenger (*al-Muntaqim*), the second refers to Names such as the Infinitely Good (*al-Raḥmān*), the Peace (*al-Salām*), and the Loving (*al-Wadūd*), while the third includes the Truth (*al-Ḥaqq*), the Light (*al-Nūr*), and the One (*al-Aḥad*), which are beyond every duality.[27] In the context of this chapter, knowledge of the second category of Divine Names represents the pinnacle of Divine love in Islam, with the understanding that the Names of Majesty and Perfection are also inseparable from the Names of Beauty and ultimately the Divine Essence.[28] In Islam, the Names of Beauty have a certain primacy over the Names of Majesty, which is indicated by the sacred formula that begins all but one of the chapters of the Quran, "In the Name of God—the Infinitely Good, the All-Merciful" (*Bismi'Llāh al-Raḥ-*

27. Seyyed Hossein Nasr, *The Heart of Islam*, pp. 4–5.

28. Claude Addas writes, "Ibn ʿArabī concludes the scriptural argumentation of this introductory paragraph by mentioning a series of *akhbār*, "traditions" attributed to the Prophet. I shall only reiterate one, due to the great significance it has within the Akbarian doctrine of love, "God is beautiful," the Envoy of God declared, "and He loves beauty." This *ḥadīth* is in fact ubiquitous in Ibn ʿArabī's writings on love (including this chapter [178] of the *Futūhāt*)—whether he refers to it explicitly, or discreetly alludes to it—so indissociable are these two notions of love and beauty for him. It is true that Imam Ghazzālī accords equally great importance to this subject in the long chapter of the *Iḥyāʾ ʿulūm al-dīn* entitled *Kitāb al-maḥabbah*. However, for him beauty is only one cause (*sahab*) of love among others; for Ibn ʿArabī it is the primary and inexhaustible source. Therefore, he replies without a hint of hesitation to Tirmidhī's one hundred and eighteenth question: "Where does love come from?" by saying, "From his epiphany in the Name *al-Jamīl*." "The Experience and Doctrone of Love in Ibn ʿArabī," trans. Cecilia Twinch, *Journal of the Muhyiddin Ibn ʿArabi Society* XXXII (Autumn 2002).

mān al-Raḥīm), the verse, "He has prescribed Mercy for Himself" (6:12), and the *ḥadīth qudsī* that is written on the Divine Throne, "Verily My Mercy precedeth My Wrath." It is also necessary to state that Ibn 'Arabī was devoted to the One alone and identified the Divine Essence with the name *al-Raḥmān*—a name etymologically related to the Arabic word for womb (*raḥim*).[29] His primary forms of devotion were the same forms that all Muslims use to worship and know the ineffable and ubiquitous Divine Reality—Allah—such as the five daily prayers, fasting, and the recitation of the Quran, including the revealed Names of God in Arabic. Through the intimacy with God that he gained through following the Law (*Sharī'ah*) and the spiritual path (*ṭarīqah*) of Islam, he was able to recognize the Names and signs of God in and beyond creation.

In Ibn 'Arabī's sacred cosmology and anthropology, all of creation is a reflection of one or more of the Divine Names, while the One who is Named transcends the cosmos and the human being. It is therefore possible and even necessary to see reflections of Divine majesty and beauty in creation, which indicate the One who is reflected. There are many symbols or theophanies of God in Islamic esoterism, including the Quran, the Ka'bah, nature, sacred art, and especially the Universal or Perfect Man (*al-insān al-kāmil*). The Arabic word *insān* means man and woman, so while this term is generally translated as man, it applies to all human beings. This becomes more obvious when one examines Ibn 'Arabī's devotion to Niẓām, as well as the treasury of Persian Sufi poetry devoted to women as a symbol of the Divine Essence. The doctrine of the Universal Man was given fuller doctrinal expression by one of Ibn 'Arabī's successors 'Abd al-Karīm Jīlī in his treatise *al-Insān al-*

29. The Infinite also corresponds to the Name *al-Raḥmān* or "the Infinitely Good," as the Good must radiate outwardly to communicate Itself through so many veils or garments composed of relative degrees of goodness and evil. Thus creation, emanation, multiplicity or the world, has as its principle the "feminine" Nature of God, while the singularity and uniqueness of God—before which all things are effaced—can be said to correspond to His "masculine" Nature. Of course these dualities are perfectly reconciled and united in the Divine Reality and Essence, which as the Absolute and the Infinite contains the principles of both masculinity and femininity, unity and multiplicity.

kāmil.[30] Along with the Quran or the Word of God, the Universal Man is the central theophany of God in Islam. The Prophet of Islam (as well as the other prophets) is the Universal Man *par excellence*, who reflects the Names of Majesty, Beauty, and Perfection in the center of the cosmos. While other created beings reflect particular combinations of the Names of God, only the Universal Man reflects all of the Names or the comprehensive Name Allah.

Referring to the reflection of the Divine Names in the human microcosm, Seyyed Hossein Nasr writes:

> The difference between the sexes cannot be reduced to anatomy and biological function. There are also differences of psychology and temperament, of spiritual types and even principles within the Divine Nature which are the sources *in divinis* of the duality represented on the microcosmic level as male and female. God is both Absolute and Infinite. Absoluteness—and Majesty, which is inseparable from it—are manifested most directly in the masculine state; Infinity and Beauty in the feminine state. The male body itself reflects majesty, power, absoluteness; and the female body reflects beauty, beatitude, and infinity.... But since God is one and man, that is, the human being of whichever sex it might be, a theomorphic being who reflects God's Names and Qualities, each human being also reflects the One and seeks to return to the One.[31]

30. 'Abd al-Karīm Jīlī, Universal Man (*al-Insān al-kāmil*), trans. Titus Burckhardt and Angela Culme-Seymour (Roxburgh, Scotland: Beshara Publications, 1995). For women's approaches to God in Islam and Sufism, see Sachiko Murata, *The Tao of Islam* (Albany, NY: State University of New York Press, 1992); Maria Massi Dakake, "'Walking upon the Path of God like Men'? Women and the Feminine in the Islamic Mystical Tradition," in Jean-Louis Michon and Roger Gaetani, eds., *Sufism: Love & Wisdom* (Bloomington, Indiana: World Wisdom, Inc., 2006), pp. 131–151; Camille Adams Helminski, *Women of Sufism: A Hidden Treasure* (Boston: Shambhala Publications, Inc., 2003); and Annemarie Schimmel, *My Soul Is a Woman: The Feminine in Islam* (New York, Continuum, 1999).

31. Seyyed Hossein Nasr, *Traditional Islam in the Modern World*, p. 49. These metaphysical and cosmological principles do not always manifest in the same way here below. This is illustrated by, for example, intersex or third gender individuals who in our view reflect something of the celestial prelapsarian androgyne here on earth by already possessing masculine and feminine qualities and attributes. While

It is helpful to understand the complementarity of the "masculine" and "feminine" Divine Names in Islam because it directly relates to our discussion of Ibn 'Arabī and his devotion to Niẓām, for she manifested Divine wisdom and beauty for him and enabled the Shaykh to contemplate and apprehend the various manifestations of truth and beauty in the world.[32] Moreover, we would suggest that the Absolute or "masculine" Nature of God determines a Muslim's understanding of orthodoxy and the exoteric aspects of tradition, while the Infinite or "feminine" Nature of God enables a Muslim to grasp the universality of Divine Self-disclosures in the various religions and esoterism in general.[33] It is not an accident that most of the messengers and prophets in the Abrahamic religions have been men, establishing particular laws and spiritual paths, while women have so often embodied the universal or inner wisdom of religion.[34] The creative aspect of the womb itself leads to

---

traditional Muslim societies have tended to emphasize the masculinity of the man, the femininity of the woman, and their complementarity, other possibilities of course existed in premodern contexts, including the third gender, effeminate men, masculine women, platonic lovers, homosexuals, celibates, and many other types of human beings. In our view, every human being is called to realize and return to the Unity and Perfection of the One.

32. "Masculine" and "feminine" are used with quotation marks because strictly speaking God is neither male nor female in Islamic theology and metaphysics, but rather *Dhu'l-Jalāl wa'l-Ikrām* or "the Possessor of Majesty and Generosity."

33. Frithjof Schuon writes, "...*Dhāt*, the divine "Essence," is a feminine word which—like the word *ḥaqīqah*—can refer to the superior aspect of femininity: according to this way of seeing things, which is precisely that of Hindu shaktism, femininity is what surpasses the formal, the finite, the outward; it is synonymous with indetermination, illimitation, mystery, and thus evokes the "Spirit which giveth life" in relation to the "letter which killeth." That is to say that femininity in the superior sense comprises a liquefying, interiorizing, liberating power: it liberates from sterile hardnesses, from the dispersing outwardness of limiting and compressing forms. Frithjof Schuon, "*Mahāshakti*," *Roots of the Human Condition* (Bloomington, IN: World Wisdom, 2002), pp. 40–41.

34. This situation is of course often reversed, depending upon the individual in question. Be that as it may, our perspective here is that of metaphysical and cosmological principles. Moreover, just as the Tai Chi symbol in the Chinese tradition contains an element of *Yin* within the *Yang* and *Yang* within the *Yin*, the particular aspects of a religion—taken in sufficient depth—lead to the Universal, and the Universal has no locus of manifestation save through the particular. In the words of Ibn

the plurality of human beings and consequently different perspectives. The Universal Human in Islam, whatever sex or gender they may be, is able to know and reflect something of the Absolute and Infinite Nature of God—symbolized by the Name Allah—and is therefore completely orthodox while understanding and appreciating the universality of Divine manifestations in the various religions, nature, and the heart.

Women played a central role in the life of Ibn 'Arabī in many ways. Not only did he love and appreciate the beauty of the feminine form, but two women also guided him on the spiritual path, Fāṭimah bint al-Muthannā and Shams Umm al-Fuqarā'.[35] He therefore acknowledged the wisdom of both men and women, who served as his guides upon the spiritual path at different times in his life. Regarding his understanding of the feminine theophany of God, Ibn 'Arabī writes,

> When man contemplates God in woman, his contemplation rests on that which is passive; if he contemplates Him in himself, seeing that woman comes from man, he contemplates Him in that which is active; and when he contemplates Him alone, without the presence of any form whatsoever issued from Him, his contemplation corresponds to a state of passivity with regard to God, without intermediary. Consequently his contemplation of God in woman is the most perfect, for it is then God, in so far as He is at once active and passive, that he contemplates, whereas in the pure interior contemplation, he contemplates Him only in a passive way. So that the Prophet—Benediction and Peace be upon him—was to love women because of the perfect contemplation of God in them. One would never be able to contemplate God directly in absence of all (sensible or spiritual) support, for God, in his Absolute Essence, is independent of all worlds. But, as the (Divine) Reality is inaccessible in respect (of the Essence), and there is contemplation (*sha-*

Arabī, "Whoever universalizes Him specifies Him, and whoever specifies Him universalizes Him. No identity is outside another, light shares identity with darkness. Whoever overlooks this will find sorrow in himself. . . ." Muḥyī al-Dīn ibn 'Arabī, *The Ringstones of Wisdom* (*Fuṣūṣ al-ḥikam*), trans. Caner K. Dagli (Chicago: Great Books of the Islamic World, 2004), p. 130.

35. Claude Addas, *Quest for the Red Sulphur*, trans. Peter Kingsley (Cambridge: Islamic Texts Society, 1993), pp. 87–88.

> *hādah*) only in a substance, the contemplation of God in women is the most intense and the most perfect; and the union which is the most intense (in the sensible order, which serves as support for this contemplation) is the conjugal act.[36]

Here Ibn 'Arabī argues that the contemplation of God in the feminine form is the most perfect form of contemplation. Moreover, this contemplation does not exclude, but rather is enhanced by physical union with the earthly beloved. It is of course true that the Shaykh al-Akbar was a man and that this, in addition to other factors, determined his vision of things. Other points of view can of course also be considered, without denying the significance of the one in question. In Ibn 'Arabī's writings we observe the foundations and exposition of a contemplative form of spirituality analogous to Tantra in Islam. This theoretical discussion of the Shaykh's embodied metaphysics and cosmology—which is arguably representative of Islamic spirituality in general—sets the stage for Ibn 'Arabī's providential meeting with Niẓām.

At the beginning of the thirteenth century on a pilgrimage to Mecca, Ibn 'Arabī had a glimpse of a young Persian maiden that would change his life and inspire his exquisite Arabic poem the *Tarjumān al-ashwāq*.[37] Sayyidah Niẓām was the daughter of an eminent scholar from Isfahan, and at only fourteen she is said to have possessed great wisdom, as well as inward and outward beauty.[38]In this regard Martin Lings writes,

> In [Ibn 'Arabī's] commentary he stresses that fourteen, the number of the full moon, indicates the 'perfect soul'; and in connection with her name Niẓām, which he considers to be eloquently expressive of her incomparability, I feel that he would have applauded the following quotation which I venture to make from a great Sufi of the last century . . . 'Īsā Nūr al-Dīn, though he is known to us, from his remarkable books, as Frithjof Schuon. In one of his yet unpublished texts, written especially for his disciples, he affirms

36. *Traditional Islam in the Modern World*, p. 51.

37. Muḥyī al-Dīn ibn 'Arabī, *The Interpreter of Desires* (*Tarjumān al-ashwāq*), trans. Reynold A. Nicholson (London: Theosophical Publishing House LTD, 1978).

38. Seyyed Hossein Nasr, *Three Muslim Sages*, p. 96

> that the perfection of human virtue is 'to be in harmonious confrontation with God'. Now can it not be said that the most eloquent worldly symbol of the relationship between God and man is the relationship between the two luminaries, the sun and the moon? The words 'moon' and 'man' are even etymologically connected; and it is on its fourteenth night, when it is full, and only then, that the moon is in harmonious confrontation with the sun. The name Niẓām, Harmony thus enables the maiden of fourteen to personify most marvelously perfection of virtue.[39]

In the poetry and prose of the great Sufi masters, as well as in the Quran itself, an understanding of sacred symbols is necessary to know God and our position in the cosmos in relation to the Divine Principle. Ibn 'Arabī was able to read the cosmic book and relate the meaning of certain symbols in his writings. For Ibn 'Arabī, Niẓām becomes a symbol of the Beloved and a theophany of Divine beauty and wisdom. S. H. Nasr writes, "He met a young girl of great devoutness and beauty who henceforth became the embodiment of the eternal *sophia* for him and fulfilled a role in his life which resembles that of Beatrice in the life of Dante."[40] In Ibn 'Arabī's own words he writes,

> There rose for me twixt Adhri'at and Busrā
> A maiden of fourteen like a full moon.
> Higher than time she stood in majesty,
> Transcendent over it in pride and glory.
> Each moon when it hath reached its plentitude
> A waning suffereth to fulfill the month,
> Save this: no movements hath she through the Signs
> Nor maketh, being repeated, two of One.
> Treasury, thou, of blended fragrances,
> Meadow that putteth forth spring herbs and flowers,
> Beauty hath reached in thee her utmost end.
> For others like to thee there is no room
> In all scope of what is possible.[41]

39. *Sufi Poems*, pp. 60–61.

40. *Three Muslim Sages*, p. 96 See also, Henry Corbin's *Alone with the Alone: Creative Imagination in the Sūfism of Ibn 'Arabī* (Princeton, NJ: Princeton University Press, 1998), pp. 136–175.

41. *Sufi Poems*, p. 62.

It was through contemplating the Divine Reality in the feminine form that Ibn 'Arabī was able to write the above verses and his most famous lines of poetry, lines which illustrate Niẓām's importance not only as a particular form for contemplation, but also as an opening for Ibn 'Arabī to approach God through the *religio cordis* or religion of the heart:

Receptive now my heart is for each form;
For gazelles pasture, for monks a monastery,
Temple for idols, Ka'bah to be rounded,
Tables of Torah and script of Quran.
My religion is love's religion: where'er turn
Her camels, that religion my religion is, my faith.
An example is set us by Bishr, lover
Of Hind and her sister, and likewise the loves
Of Qays and Laylā, of Mayya and Ghaylān.[42]

In Ibn 'Arabī's commentary to the verse, "My religion is love's religion," he explicitly connects the religion of love (*dīn al-ḥubb*) with the inner and outer reality of the Quran and *Sunnah* of the Prophet of Islam. He writes, "'My religion is love's religion,' [is] in reference to the verse, 'Say [Muḥammad], If you love God, follow me, and God will love you and forgive you your sins. . . .'" (Quran 3:31) He goes on to state that, "This is a peculiar prerogative of Muslims, for the station of perfect love is appropriated to Muḥammad beyond any other prophet, since God took him as His beloved."[43] Thus, Ibn 'Arabī connects his universal vision of Reality—one which embraces the Self-disclosures of the Real in Judaism, Christianity, Islam, idolatry, nature and women—to the very particularity of the Prophet Muḥammad and his spiritual station. It would be easy to dismiss these references as pious exaggerations, however, for the Shaykh al-Akbar, the Prophet of Islam encompasses all prophetic inheritances as the Seal of the prophets. Moreover, he is the prophetic reviver of Abrahamic monotheism, which while negating the divinity of all that is other than God, allows us to see the signs and Names of God—the traces and very Face of the Beloved—wherever we turn. For Mus-

42. Ibid., p. 62.
43. *The Interpreter of Desires* (*Tarjumān al-ashwāq*), p. 69.

lims, the prototypical romance is the meeting between God and His Prophet. We participate in this love by following the *Sunnah* of the Prophet through which God loves us. Thus, the religion of love is not primarily a capacity to appreciate various religions, but God's Love for us, which we attract by following in the footsteps of one of His prophets, which in turn allows us to love and recognize Him in the diverse theophanies in creation. While each revelation and prophetic pattern has the capacity to open us to the religion of love, it is important for contemporary spiritual seekers and scholars to take note of the particular religious paths that sages such as Ibn 'Arabī and Ramakrishna took to arrive at their universal visions of Reality.

Ibn 'Arabī's recognition of the veracity of religions other than his own is strikingly similar to Ramakrishna's, especially because in both cases their understanding of the unity and diversity of religions was catalyzed by a feminine theophany of the Divine. However, unlike Ramakrishna, Ibn 'Arabī only practiced one religion. He certainly appreciated other forms of worship inwardly and demonstrates a profound intellectual understanding of these forms, but he did not try to practice these religions as we see in the life of Ramakrishna. In a manner similar to Ramakrishna, however, Ibn 'Arabī's devotion to a particular form provided an opening for him to appreciate the transcendent unity of religions, expressed here below as the terrestrial harmony (*niẓām*) of religions. For scholars who followed Ibn 'Arabī, this metaphysical unity and cosmological harmony is best expressed in the famous doctrine *waḥdat al-wujūd* or the transcendent Unity of Being, for the religions only truly meet in the Divine Principle. While Sri Ramakrishna was able to express his understanding of religious unity by participating in various religions, Ibn 'Arabī's universalism was experienced in the heart, which is the locus of the Divine Being and Presence according to the *ḥadīth*, "The heart of the believer is the throne of the All-Merciful." From this perspective it may be asserted that the religions do in fact meet in the heart of the Muslim gnostic.[44] Only from this point of view can one speak

44. Seyyed Hossein Nasr, "The Heart of the Faithful is the Throne of the All-Merciful" in James Custinger, ed., *Paths to the Heart: Sufism and the Christian East*, pp. 32–45.

of an immanent unity of religions in Islam, if one keeps in mind that this unity still transcends the formal level through its immanence.

There are numerous examples in the writings of Ibn 'Arabī of his sympathy for and understanding of other religious forms, some of which are cited in chapter one. One, therefore, cannot dismiss his poetic expressions as simply allegorical given that he makes the same observations in his treatises. In these selections it is clear that Ibn 'Arabī understood that the diverse religious forms are based on the infinite possibilities that issue from the Divine Names and Nature. It follows that his metaphysics and cosmology were based on knowledge of the Divine Reality and not only on devotion to a particular form or manifestation of Reality such as Niẓām, who nevertheless served as a support for and an expression of love and gnosis in the life and teachings of the Shaykh.

Some Conclusions

It is necessary to stress that while both Srī Ramakrishna and Muḥyī al-Dīn ibn 'Arabī saw the Divine Reality in various forms and in the feminine form in particular, their understanding of Divine Self-disclosures was not limited by any one form. Ramakrishna states:

> *Sat-cit-ānanda* (being-consciousness-bliss) is like an infinite ocean. Intense cold freezes the water into ice, which floats on the ocean in blocks of various forms. Likewise, through the cooling influence of *bhakti*, one sees forms of God in the Ocean of the Absolute. These forms are meant for bhaktas, the lovers of God. But when the Sun of Knowledge rises, the ice melts; it becomes the same water it was before. Water above and water below, everywhere nothing but water.[45]

This statement mirrors the words of Ibn 'Arabī:

> None but God is loved in the existent things. It is He who is manifest within every beloved to the eye of every lover—and there is no existent thing that is not a lover. So the cosmos is all lover and beloved, and all of it goes back to Him. . . . Though no lover loves any but his own Creator, he is veiled from Him by the love for

45. *The Gospel of Sri Ramakrishna*, p. 191.

> Zaynab, Suʿād, Hind, Laylā, this world, money, position, and everything loved in the world. Poets exhaust their words in writing about all of these existent things without knowing, but the gnostics never hear a verse, a riddle, a panegyric, or a love poem that is not about Him, hidden beyond the veil of forms.[46]

Ultimately, both sages worshipped the Supreme Reality and taught that one of the greatest symbols or manifestations of that Reality is the feminine form. While there are marked differences in Ramakrishna's and Ibn 'Arabī's visions and expressions of pluralism, both men believed that all revealed religions issue from and lead to the same Divine source. Moreover, their understanding of this truth came as a result of their love and devotion to a feminine theophany, whose beauty, strength, and wisdom enabled them to see these attributes in other religions.

While Ramakrishna and Ibn 'Arabī are exceptional examples in their respective traditions, there are other moments in the history of Hinduism, Islam, and other traditions, where sages were expanded and illuminated through an encounter with a feminine theophany. According to tradition, the first wife of the Prophet Muḥammad and the first Muslim believer, Khadījah, consulted her cousin Waraqah—a learned Christian—to verify her husband's encounter with the Angel Gabriel after he received the first verses of the Quran.[47] The Prophet of Islam also married a Jewish woman, Ṣafiyyah, and another who was a Coptic Christian, Māriyah, who were not compelled to accept Islam, although they both eventually embraced the faith and were known as "Mothers of the believers" along with the Prophet's other wives.[48] Martin Lings states, "On one occasion [Ṣafiyyah] came to the Prophet in tears because one of her new companions had tried to make her feel inferior. He said: 'Say unto them: my father is Aaron, and mine uncle is Moses.'"[49]

46. William Chittick, "Ibn al-'Arabi as Lover," *Sufi* 75 (Summer 2008), p. 63.

47. Martin Lings, *Muhammad: His Life Based on the Earliest Sources*, pp. 44.

48. Ibid., pp. 268–271, 277.

49. Ibid., pp. 270–271. The Prophet's love for women in general is a leitmotif of his life and teachings and is expressed through his chivalrous qualities recorded in the *Sīrah* and numerous *Ḥadīth*, including, for example, "Three things of this

Fāṭimah, the daughter of Muḥammad and Khadījah and the husband of 'Alī, is among the most saintly women in Islam and frequently compared to the Virgin Mary. In both Shī'ism and Sunnism, the biological and spiritual descendents of the Prophet issue from Fāṭimah and 'Alī. According to Henry Corbin, "The First Imam and Fāṭimah are related to each other in the same reciprocal way as the two first hypostases, *'aql* and *nafs*, Intelligence and Soul, or in terms more familiar to us . . . *Logos* and *Sophia*."[50] Also noteworthy are the mothers of the Fourth and Twelfth Shī'ite Imams, Shahrbānū and Narjis, who according to some traditions were originally a Zoroastrian Sassanid princess and a Christian Byzantine princess, and

world of yours were made lovable to me: women, perfume—and the coolness of my eye was placed in the ritual prayer," "The whole of this world is an object of delight and the best object of delight in this world is a devout woman," "Marriage is half of religion," and "Heaven lies at the feet of mothers." On the symbolism of the first *ḥadīth* and its significance in Islam and Sufism, see Muḥyī al-Dīn ibn 'Arabī, *The Ringstones of Wisdom* (*Fuṣūṣ al-ḥikam*), pp. 277–294.

50. Henry Corbin, *Spiritual Body and Celestial Earth*, trans. Nancy Pearson (Princeton, New Jersey: Princeton University Press, 1977), p. 64. See also, Henry Corbin, *Alone with the Alone*, p. 160; and Henry Corbin, *The Voyage and the Messenger: Iran and Philosophy*, trans. Joseph Rowe (Berkeley, CA: North Atlantic Books, 1998), pp. 217–230. Patrick Laude also writes that Louis Massignon, "perceives of Fāṭimah as the only member of the *Ummah* who, at the time of Muḥammad's death, conceived of the mission of her father as incomplete. This incompleteness is particularly connected to the status of non-Arab converts in the community: While Fāṭimah has been the host par excellence of this category of companions, the advent of Abū Bakr and 'Umar represented the crystallization of an Arab, purely agnatic, identity of Islam that the cognatic mode of adoption, exemplified by the relationship between the *Ahl al-Bayt* and the Persian Salmān Pāk, called into question. What is at stake, in a sense, is nothing less than the universality of Islam, and it is no coincidence that a woman be the guarantor of this ideal. It bears mentioning that, in his study on "The Umma and its Synonyms," Massignon noted that the term *Ummah*, which refers to the Islamic community of the faithful, is etymologically akin to *Umm*, the mother, and by extension, to the cognatic family, its domestic household, and those placed under its protection, in opposition to the agnatic clan, *sha'b*, the ethnic and nationalist character of which relates to male leadership. The spiritual affinities of the *Ummah* with the inclusion and protection of non-Arabs in Islam are in perfect consonance with Fāṭimah's function vis-à-vis the *Bayt* (the Household) and its "clients" (*māwāli*)." *Pathways to an Inner Islam: Massignon, Corbin, Guénon, and Schuon* (Albany, NY: State University of New York Press, 2010), pp. 106–107.

therefore integrated their heritages and blood with those of the family of the Prophet.[51] There is also a wealth of Arabic and especially Persian Sufi poetry on this subject, among the most striking examples being the story of Shaykh-i Ṣan'ān and the Christian girl in Farīd al-Dīn 'Aṭṭār's *Conference of the Birds* mentioned in chapter one.[52] Also significant is Sayyid 'Alī Hamadānī and his encounter with and respect for the dancing Shaivite, Lalla Yogīshwarī.[53]

To this list may be added the believing women of the Bible who are also a part of the Islamic tradition and represent the universality of Islam and Abrahamic monotheism in general in diverse ways, including, for example, the wives of Abraham and matriarchs of the Judeo-Christian and Islamic traditions, Sarah and Hagar, the wife of Pharaoh, Āsiyah, and the Queen of Sheba, Bilqīs, whose stories are also related throughout the Quran. Foremost among these women is the Virgin Mary, who was a Jewish woman from the line of David, the mother of Jesus the Messiah, *Sedes Sapientiae* or "Throne of Wisdom," and according to the Quran, "chosen . . . above the women of the worlds." (3:42)[54] Frithjof Schuon saw the Virgin Mary (Maryam al-Batūl) as the celestial patroness of his Sufi order the Shādhiliyyah Maryamiyyah and esoterically as "Mother of all the prophets."[55] He writes,

51. M.A. Amir-Moezzi, *The Spirituality of Shi'i Islam*, trans. David Streight, David Bachrach, Amy Jacobs, and Hafiz Karmali (London: I.B. Tauris Publishers, 2011), pp. 45–100; and M.A. Amir-Moezzi, *The Divine Guide in Early Shi'ism*, trans. David Streight (Albany: NY: State University of New York Press, 1994), pp. 108–109.

52. Farīd al-Dīn 'Aṭṭār, *Conference of the Birds* (*Manṭiq al-ṭayr*), trans. Afkham Darbandi and Dick Davis, pp. 57–75. See also, Seyyed Hossein Nasr, *Islamic Art and Spirituality*, pp. 105–107.

53. Frithjof Schuon, *Islam and the Perennial Philosophy*, pp. 17, 32.

54. Schuon writes, "Divine *Māyā*—Femininity *in divinis*—is not only that which projects and creates; it is also that which attracts and liberates. The Blessed Virgin as *Sedes Sapientaie* personifies this merciful wisdom which descends towards us and which we too, whether we know it or not, carry in our very essence; and it is precisely by virtue of this potentiality or virtuality that Wisdom comes down upon us. The immanent seat of Wisdom is the heart of man." Frithjof Schuon, "Sedes Sapientiae," *Studies in Comparative Religion* (Summer–Autumn 1980), p. 179.

55. Schuon writes, "There are Sufis who claim a mystical connection with a particular prophet: they are *Ibrāhīmī*, *Mūsawī*, *'Isawī*, as may be seen from the *Fuṣūṣ al-ḥikam* of Ibn 'Arabī. It is thus that the Shaykh of our *ṭarīqah* is *Maryamī*

> The Virgin Mary, who—according to a symbolism common to Christianity and Islam—has suckled her children, the prophets and sages, from the beginning and outside of time...Mother of all the prophets and matrix of all the sacred forms, she has her place of honor within Islam even while belonging *a priori* to Christianity; for this reason she constitutes a kind of link between these two religions, whose common purpose is universalizing the monotheism of Israel. The Virgin Mary is not merely the embodiment of a particular mode of sanctity; she embodies sanctity as such. She is not one particular color or one particular perfume; she is colorless light and pure air. In her essence she is identified with merciful Infinitude, which—preceding all forms—overflows upon them all, embraces them all, and reintegrates them all.[56]

Schuon also states,

> Muḥyī al-Dīn ibn ʿArabī, after declaring that his heart 'has opened itself to all forms', that it is 'a cloister for monks, a temple of idols, the Kaʿbah', adds: 'I practice the religion of Love'; now it is over this informal religion that—Semitically speaking—Sayyidatnā Maryam presides. She is thus to be identified with the supreme *Shakti* or with the heavenly *Prajnāpāramitā* [transcendent Wisdom] of the Asiatic traditions.[57]

Also relevant to Muslims are the references to wisdom through-

---

[i.e., Schuon]—the Shaykh al-ʿAlawī having been unquestionably *ʿĪsawī*, whence his stress on inwardness and his detachment with respect to forms. The *ḥikmah Maryamiyyah* coincides quite obviously with the *ḥikmah ʿĪsawiyyah*, while adding to the latter an element of femininity, beauty, virginity, and maternity—an accentuation of sanctifying receptivity, adamantine purity, and appeasing and salvific goodness. Every *ṭarīqah* is by definition *Muḥammadiyyah*; to say Islam is to say Muḥammad." Frithjof Schuon, *Christianity/Islam*, p. 205.

56. Ibid., p. 88. It would be a worthwhile endeavor to compare Ibn ʿArabī's understanding of Muḥammadan sanctity to Schuon's understanding of Marian sanctity. They are essentially equivalent, with only an outward accentuation on either the masculine or feminine dimensions of the highest degree of sanctity—since this degree necessarily contains the perfection of both the masculine and feminine dimensions implied by the term *al-insān al-kāmil*. In any case, Schuon understood that Marian or *Maryamī* sanctity in Islam was encompassed by, like all other prophetic inheritances, Muḥammadan sanctity.

57. Frithjof Schuon, "The Wisdom of Sayyidatnā Maryam," *Dimensions of Islam* (Lahore: Suhail Academy, 1999), pp. 95. See also, Frithjof Schuon, "The Religion of

out the Bible and especially "Lady Wisdom" in Solomon's Book of Proverbs.[58] We read, "Blessed is the man who has found wisdom. . . . Her ways are good ways, and all her paths are peaceful. She is a tree of life to all that lay hold upon her." (Proverbs 3:13, 17–18) Like the Hebrew word *ḥokmah*, the Arabic word *ḥikmah* is feminine—both meaning wisdom—and thus directly related to our understanding of *sophia*. Not unrelated are the Hebrew term *shekinah* and its Arabic equivalent *sakīnah*, also feminine, meaning Divine peace, tranquility and the immanent presence of God in the heart and the world. We read in an initiatic verse of the Quran, "He it is Who sends down the Divine peace (*al-sakīnah*) into the hearts of the believers, that they might add faith unto their faith. . . ." (48:4)[59] The Hebrew word *barak* also corresponds to the Arabic *barakah*—again feminine—and means blessing, grace and the radiation of the Divine presence through prayer, holy books, the prophets, saints, sacred and traditional art, sacred sites such as Mecca, Medina, and Jerusalem, and virgin nature. All of these terms are grammatically feminine and intuitively associated by Muslims with the feminine or beautiful aspect of God, and also with women in general, who are often named Sakīnah or Barakah, for example.[60] Moreover, the Arabic word for mother, *umm*, can be translated as archetype and finds expression in such terms as "the Mother of the

the Heart," *Esoterism as Principle and as Way*, trans. William Stoddart (Bedfont, Middlesex: Perennial Books, 1990), pp. 229–234.

58. See, for example, the Book of Proverbs 1:20–33; 3:13–18; 4:5–9; 8:1–36.

59. Ibn 'Aṭā' Allāh al-Iskandarī writes in his *Miftāḥ al-falāḥ*, " It is said that peace (*al-sakīnah*) is a mystery like the wind, or was created with a face like that of a human being, or that it is a spirit from God which speaks to men and guides them when they differ on a matter, and so on. From what we have already mentioned, peace is probably something similar to that which descends on whoever recites the Quran or gathers to invoke, because it belongs to the Spirit and the angels. God knows best!" *The Key to Salvation: A Sufi Manual of Invocation* (*Miftāḥ al-falāḥ wa miṣbāḥ al-arwāḥ*), trans. Mary Ann Koury Danner (Cambridge, UK: The Islamic Texts Society, 1996), p. 55.

60. At the highest level, all feminine qualities—as well as all masculine qualities—have their principle in the Divine Essence (*al-Dhāt*), a feminine word that is symbolized for the Sufis by Laylā, a name that means night and refers to the hidden and veiled nature of the Divine Ipseity.

Book" (*Umm al-kitāb*), which refers to the common transcendent archetype and essence of all Divine revelations, as well as the particular form and essence of the Quran.[61] It is also helpful to recall the primacy of the Divine Names of Beauty (*Jamāl*) over those of Majesty (*Jalāl*) in Islam, which relates to the Nature and very Essence of God as envisaged by the Sufis.

Devotion to the feminine is so ubiquitous in Hinduism that it is not possible for us to due justice to the rich tradition devoted to the Goddess and Her various manifestations in this chapter. All of the examples mentioned above, as well as Kali in the life of Ramakrishna and Niẓām in the life of Ibn 'Arabī, are so many manifestations of the celestial and eternal Sophia, which is the shared wisdom at the heart of all religions. According to Ananda K. Coomaraswamy:

> The beauty of the Beloved *there* is no longer as it is here contingent and merely a participation or reflection, but that of Supernal Wisdom, that of the One Madonna, that of the intrinsic being of the Bride, which "rains down flames of fire" (*Convivio*) and as claritas illuminates and guides the pure intellect.[62]

This understanding of wisdom compels us to correct our modern understanding of religion and philosophy, which is the love of Divine Wisdom or Sophia as *She* manifests in the feminine form and in the heart of every man and woman.[63] Today, if one accepts that anything can be known at all, philosophy is generally associated with reason, analysis and the bifurcation of subject and object, whereas ancient sages saw wisdom as essentially intuition, synthesis

61. Samuel Zinner, "The Semiotics of Inliteration of the *Umm al-Kitab* and Sacred Time Dilation," *Christianity and Islam: Essays on Ontology and Archetype* (London: Matheson Trust, 2010), pp. 11–17.

62. Ananda K. Coomaraswamy, "On the Pertinence of Philosophy" in Rama Coomaraswamy, ed., *The Essential Ananda K. Coomaraswamy* (Bloomington, IN: World Wisdom, 2004), p. 81.

63. Seyyed Hossein Nasr writes, "The person often called the "father" of Western logic and philosophy was Parmenides, who is usually presented as a rationalist who happened to have written a poem of mediocre quality. But as the recent brilliant studies of Peter Kingsley have clearly demonstrated, far from being a rationalist in the modern sense, he was deeply immersed in the world of prophecy in its Greek religious sense and was a seer and visionary. In his poem, which contains his

and unification. The feminine theophany is the objective manifestation and mirror of our own inner wisdom, both of which have their roots in the Supreme Wisdom of God and even the hidden Divine Essence.[64] In the lives of Ramakrishna, Ibn 'Arabī and a number of the greatest luminaries of Hinduism, Islam, and other traditions, devotion to the feminine symbol of the Divine plays a central role. What is remarkable about these figures is that they came to a similar understanding of the transcendent unity of religions through their relationship to a feminine theophany of the One Absolute and Infinite Reality. Ultimately, love is able to break down barriers and transport us beyond the confines and limitations of the ego through the beatific vision of and ultimate union with the Beloved.

philosophical message, Parmenides is led to the other world by the Daughters of the Sun who came from the Mansion of Light situated at the farthest degree of existence.... Thus Parmenides undertakes the inner journey until he meets the goddess who teaches him everything of importance, that is, teaches him what is considered to be the origin of Greek philosophical speculation...." *Islamic Philosophy from its Origin to the Present*, p. 2.

64. Sachiko Murata writes, "My 'feminist agenda' is to help those Muslims who are so inclined to reestablish the vision of the Divine Feminine, which is the Essence of God. The sapiential perspective allows people to see feminine qualities situated at the peak of reality. The Real in Itself is receptive to every entification, every thing. It gives birth to the bipolar God who is both merciful and wrathful, yin and yang, mother and father. The mercy of this bipolar God precedes Her wrath, which is to say that Her femininity is more real and fundamental than Her masculinity." *The Tao of Islam*, p. 324. Seyyed Hossein Nasr also states, "the word *al-dhāt* itself is feminine in Arabic reflecting the metaphysical truth that the internal dimension of the Divinity which is identified with Beauty and Infinity is the prototype of femininity and is 'feminine' in the highest sense of this reality." *Islamic Art and Spirituality*, p. 112.

3

Thou art Dhāt

I am the Self residing in the hearts of all beings. . . .
—Bhagavad Gita[1]

The heavens and the earth do not contain Me,
but the heart of My faithful servant contains Me.
—*Ḥadīth qudsī*

Beyond our devotion to the personal God is an awareness of the impersonal Essence of God that transcends all limitations, descriptions and dualities. In the Upanishads we are told *Tat tvam asi* or "Thou art That," which as an initiatic suggestion means that you are the Divine Essence or Self. One of the words most commonly used for the Divine Essence in Sufism is *al-Dhāt*, which refers to the ineffable and apophatic Source or Possessor of the Divine Names and Attributes that is Itself beyond all qualifications and the ultimate root of our own existence and consciousness.[2] In this chapter we compare Islamic metaphysical expressions to teachings of Advaita

1. *Bhagavadgītā: With the commentary of Sankarācārya*, trans. Swāmī Gambhīrānanda (Calcutta: Advaita Ashrama, 2003), p. 413. We also read in the Upanishads, "In this seat of Brahma (*Brahma-pura*) [i.e., the heart] . . . there is a small lotus, a place in which is a small cavity (*dahara*) occupied by Ether (*Ākāsha*); we must seek That which is in this place, and we shall know It." (Chhāndogya Upanishad VIII.1.1) Quoted from René Guénon, "The Vital Center of the Human Being: Seat of Brahma," *Man & His Becoming According to the Vedānta*, trans. Richard C. Nicholson (Hillsdale, New York: Sophia Perennis, 2004), p. 33.

2. *Dhāt* is the grammatically feminine form of *Dhū* or "Possessor." *Dhū* in the Divine Name *Dhu'l-Jalāl wa'l-Ikrām* or "the Possessor of Majesty and Generosity" expresses the Divine Essence or Self that possesses all masculine and feminine Divine qualities or those of Majesty and Beauty. God in His Essence is beyond this and all duality, while containing the perfection of both in His Nature before their bifurcation.

Vedānta, which posit that the innermost essence of man, in Sanskrit Ātman, is not other than the transcendent Divine Reality or Brahman. This Unity or non-duality is also the secret (*sirr*) of the purified heart of the Sufis, which is none other than Union or an awareness of the Divine Reality or Self underlying and animating our being and consciousness. There is One Absolute and Infinite Principle that transcends the cosmic order and at the same time resides in the heart of man as the immanent Self. The metaphysics of non-duality is especially associated with the Vedānta, but is also related to the nature of things. Therefore, all metaphysical doctrines, both in the East and the West, are necessary variations and partial descriptions of the same Divine Reality or Self. Advaita Vedānta as expounded in the Upanishads, Bhagavad Gita, Brahmasūtras, and the writings of sages—especially Srī Ādi Samkarācārya or Shankara—offers a particularly direct expression of this doctrine. However, the metaphysical doctrine of non-duality expounded in Advaita Vedānta is also present in Islam—and in fact all revealed religions—and made accessible through the faculty of the Intellect in all men and women.

The formal expression of metaphysics or gnosis differs from one religion to another. Even within a particular religion such as Hinduism or Islam one finds a diverse spectrum of metaphysical, symbolic and artistic expressions. Therefore, it is not possible to find the exact formal equivalent to Advaita Vedānta anywhere in the world, including outside the school of Advaita Vedānta in India.[3] Yet in its essence Advaita Vedānta or non-dual metaphysics according to Vedānta is nothing other than *tawḥīd* or Divine Unity according to its inner meaning in the Quran.[4] In this chapter we survey various metaphysical doctrines in Islam that closely correspond to Advaita

3. It would be fruitful to also compare Advaita Vedānta and Islamic metaphysics with Kashmir Shaivism, although such a comparison is not possible here. Suffice it to say, the metaphysics and cosmology of Kashmir Shaivism also closely resemble those of the Islamic tradition.

4. We are concerned with both metaphysics and ontology in Hinduism and Islam with the understanding that the first determination of the Absolute for Hindu and Muslim sages does not exclude, but rather opens onto and is prefigured in the Divine Essence or God as Beyond Being.

Vedānta. These include esoteric commentaries on the *shahādah* (testimony of faith) and the Supreme Name Allah, verses from the Quran, and the *Sunnah* of the Prophet Muhammad, which includes his sayings or *Ḥadīth*. In addition to examining the primary Islamic sources, we also look at the sayings of the Shī'ite Imams, the theophanic locutions (*shaṭḥiyyāt*) of Sufis such as Bāyazīd Basṭāmī and Manṣūr Ḥallāj, Arabic and Persian Sufi poetry, especially the poetry of Farīd al-Dīn 'Aṭṭār and Jalāl al-Dīn Rūmī, and the school of theoretical gnosis (*'irfān-i naẓarī*) associated with figures such as Muḥyī al-Dīn ibn 'Arabī, 'Abd al-Karīm Jīlī, and Mullā Ṣadrā.[5] Through these sources, as well as the writings and commentaries of those men who revived the traditional understanding of the perennial philosophy, such as René Guénon and Frithjof Schuon, we hope to demonstrate that the identity of the Divine Reality and Self to which explicit reference is made in the teachings of Advaita Vedānta is also present and accessible through the esoteric, philosophical, and artistic dimensions of the Islamic tradition.

Advaita Vedānta in Light of the Perennial Philosophy

Advaita Vedānta refers to the metaphysical doctrine of non-duality according to the Vedānta, or the conclusion of and commentaries upon the Vedas. The primary sources of Advaita Vedānta are the Upanishads,[6] Brahmasūtras,[7] and Bhagavad Gita. Advaita (non-dual) Vedānta denies that there is a distinction between the Supreme Object (Brahman) and Supreme Subject (Ātman). Brahman—the Divine Reality—is unqualified (*neti neti*, "not this, not

5. For a definition and summary of the history of theoretical gnosis in Islam see Seyyed Hossein Nasr, "The Tradition of Theoretical Sufism and Gnosis" in *The Garden of Truth*, pp. 209–234.

6. Seyyed Hossein Nasr writes that the Qādirī Sufi Dārā Shikūh, who translated the Upanishads, Bhagavad Gita, and *Yoga Vasishtha* into Persian, "believed the Upanishads to be the 'Hidden Books' to which the Quran refers (lvi. 77–80) and wrote that: 'They contain the essence of unity and they are secrets which have to be kept hidden!' His *Majma' al-baḥrayn* is an attempt to show the identity of the Muslim and Hindu doctrines of unity." *Sufi Essays*, pp. 140–141.

7. Eliot Deutsch and Rohit Dalvi, *The Essential Vedānta* (Bloomington, Indiana: World Wisdom, Inc., 2004), pp. 3–92.

that") and beyond all limitations, yet is often referred to by the ternary *sat* (being), *cit* (consciousness), and *ānanda* (bliss).[8] The Upanishads state, "*Om*! He who knows Brahman attains to the Most High. On this there is the verse: Brahman is truth, knowledge and endless (*satyam jñānam anantam brahma*)."[9] Ātman as the Self, the Source of consciousness or Brahman envisaged as the Subject, is also unqualified and beyond limitations. In the Upanishads we read:

> Finer than the finest, larger than the largest, is the Self (Ātman) that lies here hidden in the heart of a living being. Without desires and free from sorrow, a man perceives by the Creator's grace the grandeur of the Self. (*Kaṭha Upanishad*)[10]

The doctrine of Advaita Vedānta is also summarized in what are considered by many the four great statements (*mahāvākyas*) of the Upanishads:

> "Consciousness is Brahman" (*prajñānam Brahma*);
> "This Self (Ātman) is Brahman" (*ayam Ātmā Brahma*);
> "Thou art That" (*Tat tvam asi*); and
> "I am Brahman" (*aham Brahmāsmi*).[11]

It is not possible to examine all of the diverse meanings contained in these expressions here, which are in any case apparent, but only fully realized and actualized by a sage or saint.[12] It can be related, however, that Advaita Vedānta conveys a metaphysical doctrine which states that Brahman, the Infinite Reality as such, and Ātman, the Infinite Reality within man, are non-dual.[13] In other words, the Supreme Subject or Source of individual consciousness is not other than God as Ultimate Reality or Beyond Being. Advaita

8. Ibid., p. 393.

9. Ibid., p. 20.

10. Ibid., 30.

11. Julia Leslie, *Authority and Meaning in Indian Religions: Hinduism and the Case of Vālmīki* (Burlington, VT: Ashgate Publishing Company, 2003), p. 185.

12. For an illuminating exposition of these statements and others see *Shankara's Crest-Jewel of Discrimination* (*Viveka-Chudamani*), trans. Swami Prabhavananda and Christopher Isherwood (Hollywood, CA: Vedanta Press, 1975), pp. 67–76.

13. *The Essential Vedānta*, p. 395.

Vedānta is a clear and superlative answer to the age-old question, "Who I am?" that was posed by the contemporary Indian saint Srī Ramana Maharshi.

As a gnostic jewel within the epic poem the Mahābhārata, the Bhagavad Gita also offers us an abundance of sacred knowledge that points to the unity of Ātman and Brahman through the discourses of Krishna to the warrior Arjuna on the battlefield. While the Upanishads and the Vedas as a whole are considered *shruti* or Revelation in a manner similar to the Quran in Islam, the Bhagavad Gita is considered *smrti* or Divine inspiration (literally recollection), which is comparable to the traditions or *Ḥadīth* of the Prophet Muḥammad, especially the *ḥadīth qudsī* or sacred traditions where God speaks through the Prophet in the first person.[14] The Bhagavad Gita is an ocean of Divine inspiration from Krishna—an incarnation of Vishnu—to Arjuna. Krishna can in fact be seen as a manifestation of the Self, transmitting metaphysical knowledge and the ways to its realization. The Bhagavad Gita contains the distilled wisdom of the Vedas, including in-depth discussions of *karma*, *bhakti*, and *jñāna* yoga or the paths to union through action, love, and gnosis.[15] While all of these ways offer important and indispensable insights into the nature of Advaita Vedānta, the way of gnosis or *jñāna* yoga, most clearly contains the metaphysical doctrine of non-duality. In the Bhagavad Gita it is stated:

> He whose heart is steadfastly engaged in yoga, looks everywhere with the eyes of equality, seeing the Self in all beings and all beings in the Self. He who sees Me in all and all in Me, from him I vanish not, nor does he vanish from Me.[16]

Brahman is that which is immutable, and independent of any cause but Itself. When we consider Brahman as lodged within the

14. Ibid., p. 59.

15. This ternary corresponds to *makhāfah*, *maḥabbah*, and *ma'rifah* in Islamic esoterism. Quintessential Sufism is nothing other than *ma'rifah/'irfān* or knowledge of the Divine Reality, although fear, love, and knowledge of God are never absent in any authentic expression of Sufism.

16. Whitall N. Perry, *A Treasury of Traditional Wisdom* (Louisville, KY: Fons Vitae, 2000), p. 887.

individual being, we call Him the Ātman. The creative energy of Brahman is that which causes all existences to come into being.[17]

Many important sages have expounded the perspective of Advaita Vedānta throughout history. Foremost among them is Shankara who was born into the brahmin caste in the year 788.[18] At a young age Shankara renounced the world at the feet of his master Govinda—a student of Gauḍapāda, the first person to express the teachings of Advaita Vedānta in a treatise.[19] According to Eliot Deutsch, Shankara's expression of the doctrine,

> [I]nsists upon *nirguṇa* Brahman—Brahman without qualities—as the sole reality, upon the absolute identity of man with this distinctionless Reality, and upon the relativity, if not falsity, of all empirical experience. And this philosophy, which is obviously meaningful to only an intellectual-spiritual elite, soon became the dominant philosophical system in the whole of India.[20]

Shankara's exposition of the Vedānta is perhaps best summarized in the following formulation: "God is real, the world is appearance; the soul is like unto God" (*Brahma satyam; jagan mithyā; jīvo Brahmaiva nā'paraḥ*).[21] Discerning between the Real and the illusory or the Absolute and the relative is also the liberating function of the *shahādah* in Islam. What must be emphasized—especially for a western audience—is that Shankara's intellectual understanding and masterful articulation of metaphysics took place in a particular context. As a Hindu brahmin, Shankara had access to a living tradition that included a doctrine and a method for its realization, which are rooted in the substance, indeed the very soil of India. Moreover, before one can realize the nature of the Self or the Absolute, one has to renounce the false and illusory nature of the ego and the world. It is common for many western students of Shankara, Plato, or Ibn 'Arabī to study their metaphysical doctrines outside of an orthodox

17. *Bhagavad-Gita: The Song of God*, trans. Swami Prabhavanand and Christopher Isherwood (New York, NY: Penguin Books Ltd., 2002), p. 74.

18. *The Essential Vedānta*, p. 161.

19. Ibid., p. 157.

20. Ibid., p. 162.

21. *Shankara's Crest-Jewel of Discrimination* (*Viveka-Chudamani*), p. 7.

religion that can provide a practical method for their realization. This problem is exacerbated when the student mistakes his theoretical knowledge—which was the fruit of realized knowledge for the sage—for gnosis or direct knowledge of the Principle. In Shankara's own words,

> To know the real Self to be one's own is the greatest attainment according to the scriptures and reasoning. To know wrongly the non-self such as the ego to be the Self is no attainment at all. One, therefore, should renounce this misconception of taking the non-self for the Self.[22]

With the help of a revealed tradition, one must strive to unveil the immanent Intellect, which is capable of discerning between the Real and the illusory nature of the ego and the world. There is nothing more dangerous than confusing the lower self with the Supreme Self. Before one can assert that "I am Brahman" or "*māyā* is Ātman" one must perceive the relative and non-existent nature the ego and the world in light of the Absolute. Moreover this realization is inaccessible without possessing the necessary moral qualifications and receiving spiritual guidance from a realized sage.

Several key Muslim scholars in the premodern period studied and appreciated Hinduism and were in fact pioneers of comparative religious studies.[23] Abū Rayḥān Bīrūnī (d. 1048) translated the *Patañjali Yoga* into Arabic and also wrote an important work on Hinduism entitled *Taḥqīq mā li'l-hind,* where he compares the doctrine of Patañjali to the *fanā'* (annihilation in God) and *baqā'* (subsistence through God) of the Sufis.[24] In his seminal *al-Insān al-*

22. *A Thousand Teachings*, trans. Swāmi Jagadānanda (Mylapore, Madras: Sri Ramakrishna Math, 1949). In this regard, someone came to Ramakrishna and said, "Virtue and vice are both unreal, for the universe is unreal; and I am the Ātman. Nothing can touch me." Ramakrishna said, "If this is your Vedānta, I spit on Vedānta." *A Treasury of Traditional Wisdom*, p. 430.

23. One could also cite those important figures such as Kabīr, Sāī Bābā, or the Sikhs who display both Muslim and Hindu characteristics, and demonstrate the unique and providential meeting of these two traditions in India.

24. *Sufi Essays*, p. 138–139; and Abū Rayḥān Bīrūnī, "The Belief of the Hindus in God from *Taḥqīq mā li'l-Hind* (India)", trans. E.C. Sachau in S.H. Nasr & M. Aminrazavi, eds., *An Anthology of Philosophy in Persia*, vol. I, p. 452.

kāmil, 'Abd al-Karīm Jīlī (d. 1428) states that the Hindu brahmin "testify to His Oneness of Being" and also compares them to "the prophets before their prophetic mission."[25] Mīr Findiriskī (d. 1640–1) wrote a commentary on the *Yoga Vasíshtha* in Arabic, and an anthology and commentary on this work in Persian.[26] 'Abd al-Raḥmān Chishtī (d. 1683) states in his *Mir'āt al-ḥaqā'iq*, "Krishna explained to Arjuna by analogy the secrets of *tawḥīd*."[27] The great Mogul prince Dārā Shikūh (d. 1659) translated the Upanishads, Bhagavad Gita, and *Yoga Vasíshtha* into Persian, and wrote an important treatise comparing Islamic and Hindu metaphysics and cosmology entitled *Majma' al-baḥrayn* (*The Confluence of the Two Seas*).[28] Dārā Shikūh writes,

> After knowing the Truth of truths and ascertaining the secrets and subtleties of the true religion of the Sufis.... I thirsted to know the tenets of the religion of Indian monotheists; and, having had repeated interactions and discussions with the seekers and perfect sages of this religion who had attained the highest level of perfection in religious exercises, comprehension [of God], intelligence and insight, I did not find any difference, except verbal, in the way in which they sought and comprehended Truth.[29]

Dārā Shikūh also states, "There are many secrets concealed in the Holy Quran . . . whose interpreter it was difficult to find. So I desired to read all the revealed Books, for the utterances of God elucidate and explain one another."[30] After reading the Bible and other scriptures, the Prince finally discovered the secrets of *tawḥīd* in the

25. *Sufi Essays*, p. 139.

26. Seyyed Hossein Nasr, *Islamic Philosophy from its Origin to the Present*, p. 216.

27. Roderic Vassie, "'Abd al-Raḥman Chishtī & the Bhagavadgita: 'Unity of Religion' Theory in Practice" in Leonard Lewisohn, ed., *The Heritage of Sufism: The Legacy of Medieval Persian Sufism (1150–1500)*, vol. II (Oxford: Oneworld Publications, 1999), p. 369. 'Abd al-Raḥmān also translates various words for God in the Bhagavad Gita as *Khudā* or "God," *Ḥaqq* or "Truth," and *ān-dhāt* or "That Essence." Ibid., p. 370.

28. *Sufi Essays*, p. 140–141.

29. Slightly revised translation based on *Majma'-ul-Baḥrain or The Mingling of the Two Oceans by Prince Muhammad Dārā Shikūh*, trans. M. Mahfuz-ul-Haq (Kolkata, The Asiatic Society, 2007), p. 38.

30. Ibid., p. 13.

Upanishads. He states,

> Any difficult problem or sublime idea that came to my mind and was not solved in spite of my best efforts, becomes clear and solved with the help of this ancient work, which is undoubtedly the first heavenly Book and the fountain-head of the ocean of monotheism, and, in accordance with or rather an elucidation of the Quran.[31]

The Prince harmonizes the metaphysical perspectives of Islam and Hinduism in his description of the doctrine of Self in his *Risāla-i Ḥaqq-Numā* (*The Compass of the Truth*):

> You should realize that "All is He" (*hamah u-ast*). Then ask who are you? You will be forced to admit that your very self is indeed the divine essence and can be nothing else! . . . This is the truth of divine unity (*haqīqat-i tawḥīd*) and the self-disclosure of the essence (*tajall-i dhāti*) "in their selves if only you would see." [Quran 41:53][32]

In light of the contributions and appraisals of the aforementioned Muslims scholars and others, we should not be surprised that some contemporary Muslim sages were also drawn to the study and appreciation of Hindu texts and doctrines. René Guénon or Shaykh 'Abd al-Wāḥid Yaḥyā and Frithjof Schuon or Shaykh 'Īsā Nūr al-Dīn Aḥmad considered the teachings of Advaita Vedānta to be among the most sublime and direct metaphysical doctrines that the world has ever known and devoted important studies to Hindu metaphysics including Guénon's *Introduction to the Study of Hindu Doctrines* and *Man & His Becoming according to the Vedānta* and Schuon's *Language of the Self.*[33] Because of this fact some contemporary interpreters of Guénon and Schuon have marginalized other religions and their metaphysical doctrines. We maintain that this is

31. Ibid., p. 13.

32. Dara Shikuh, *Risāla-i Ḥaqq-Numā* (*The Compass of the Truth*), trans. Scott Kugle, *Sufi Meditation and Contemplation: Timeless Wisdom from Mughal India*, Scott Kugle, ed. (New Lebanon, NY: Omega Publications, 2012), p. 156.

33. One could also cite Guénon's *The Mutiple States of Being* and *Studies in Hinduism*, and all of Schuon's books, which contain copious references to Hinduism to elucidate the perennial philosophy.

partly due to the writings of Guénon and Schuon, which do privilege the use of Indian metaphysics and terms.[34] However, Guénon and Schuon were both clear about the essential unity of all metaphysical doctrines and in particular highlighted the unanimity of Hindu and Islamic metaphysics, despite their unique modes of expression. According to Guénon,

> Where metaphysics is concerned, all that can alter with time and place is, on the one hand, the manner of expression, that is to say the more or less external forms which metaphysics can assume and which may be varied indefinitely, and on the other hand, the degree of knowledge or ignorance of it to be found among men; but metaphysics in itself always remains fundamentally and unalterably the same, for its object is one in its essence, or to be more exact 'without duality', as the Hindus put it, and that object, again by the very fact that it lies 'beyond nature', is also beyond all change: the Arabs express this by saying that 'the doctrine of Oneness is one'.[35]

He also writes,

> The 'Self' . . . must not be regarded as distinct from Ātman, and, moreover, Ātman is identical with Brahman itself. This is what may be called the 'Supreme Identity', according to an expression borrowed from Islamic esoterism, where the doctrine on this and on many other points is fundamentally the same as in the Hindu tradition, in spite of great differences of form.[36]

As surveyed above in chapter one, Guénon practiced the Islamic tradition to know the Supreme Principle in not only a theoretical, but also a practical manner. He also wrote a number of important essays on Islamic metaphysics, initiation, symbolism, and the significance of the inner and outer dimensions of his traditional form.

34. In addition to the books of Schuon, the works of traditionalist scholars such as Titus Burckhardt, Martin Lings, Seyyed Hossein Nasr and Reza Shah-Kazemi clearly emphasize the importance of Islamic metaphysics as an important expression of the *sophia perennis*.

35. René Guénon, *Introduction to the Study of Hindu Doctrines*, trans. Marco Pallis (Hillsdale, NY: Sophia Perennis, 2004), p. 73. See also, René Guénon, *Insights into Islamic Esoterism and Taoism*, p. 14–15.

36. *Man & His Becoming According to the Vedānta*, p. 31.

Similarly, Schuon entered Islam, received a Sufi initiation, and unveiled the metaphysical doctrine of Islam in his books *Understanding Islam, Dimensions of Islam, Islam and the Perennial Philosophy, Sufism: Veil and Quintessence*, and other unpublished manuscripts. Schuon states in *Sufism: Veil and Quintessence*:

> The Doctrine (and the Way) of Unity is unique" (*al-tawḥīdu wāḥidun*): this classical formula expresses in a concise manner the essentiality, primordiality and universality of Islamic esoterism as well as of esoterism as such; and we might even say that all wisdom or gnosis—all *Advaita Vedānta*, if one prefers—is for Islam, contained within the *shahādah* alone, the two fold Testimony of faith.[37]

Schuon writes elsewhere,

> The Islamic formula *Lā ilāha illa'Llāh* means, according to gnosis, that "there is no 'me' except it be 'I'"—therefore no real or positive ego except the Self—a meaning which also springs from expressions such as the *Ana'l-Ḥaqq* ("I am the Truth") of al-Ḥallāj or the *Subḥānī* ("Glory to Me") of Bāyazīd. The Prophet himself enunciated the same mystery in the following terms: "He who has seen me, has seen the Truth (God)."[38]

These expressions and numerous others cited below demonstrate that the doctrine of Unity or the Oneness of God as envisaged in Islam is also a doctrine of the Supreme Self. However, it is important to reiterate that certain formal differences exist between Islamic metaphysics and Advaita Vedānta, which cannot simply be dismissed or circumvented in these respective paths towards liberation. Islamic metaphysical expressions usually emphasize the reality of the transcendent objective Principle. Consequently, the Muslim negates the dream of his relative ego and the world to gain an awareness of the everlasting Reality or Self of God. Conversely, sages from the school of Advaita Vedānta emphasize the identity of the Self with the transcendent objective Principle. Despite their different emphases, languages, and modes of expression—which are necessarily

37. Frithjof Schuon, *Sufism: Veil and Quintessence*, p. 132.
38. *Language of the Self*, p. 206. See also, ibid., pp. 19–22.

unique and diverse—both metaphysical traditions issue from and arrive at the one and only Reality or Self.[39] The eminent Hindu metaphysician and art historian Ananda K. Coomaraswamy states,

> We shall also deny in Hinduism the existence of anything unique and peculiar to itself, apart from the local coloring and social adaptations that must be expected under the sun where nothing can be known except in the mode of the knower. The Indian tradition is one of the forms of the *philosophia perennis*, and as such, embodies those universal truths to which no one people or age can make exclusive claim. The Hindu is therefore perfectly willing to have his own scriptures made use of by others as "extrinsic and probable proofs" of the truth as *they* also know it. The Hindu would argue, moreover, that it is upon these heights alone that any true agreement of differing cultures can be effected.[40]

The purpose of this chapter is to highlight the universality of the Self and its accessibility through the esoteric dimensions of Islam in particular—the awareness of which has been eclipsed in modern man, Muslim and non-Muslim alike, who has been reduced to his most outward aspects alone and is ignorant of his Divine Center.

39. Schuon states, "It is not other than the Truth, in which subject and object coincide, and in which the essential takes precedence over the accidental—or in which the principle takes precedence over its manifestation – either by extinguishing it, or by reintegrating it, depending on the various aspects of relativity itself." *Esoterism as Principle and as Way*, p. 15.

40. Ananda K. Coomaraswamy, *Hinduism and Buddhism* (New Delhi: Munshiram Manoharlal Publishers Pvt. Ltd., 1996), p. 4. It should be noted that Coomaraswamy approved of and praised Guénon and Schuon's efforts in particular: "There exists, then, in this commonly accepted axiology or body of first principles a common universe of discourse; and this provides us with the necessary basis for communication, understanding, and agreement, and so for effective co-operation in the application of commonly recognized spiritual values to the solution of contingent problems of organization and conduct. It is clear, however, that all this understanding and agreement can be reached and verified only by philosophers or scholars, if such are to be found, who are more than philologues and to whom their knowledge of the great tradition has been a vital and transforming experience; of such is the leaven or ferment by which the epigonous and decaying civilizations of today might be 'renewed in knowledge.' I quote St Paul's 'in knowledge' not with reference to a knowledge of the 'facts of science' or any power to 'conquer nature,' but as referring to the knowledge of the Self which the true philosophers of East and

The various metaphysical expressions in the Islamic tradition reveal that the doctrine of Unity in Islam is an expression—like Advaita Vedānta—that points to the Absolute and Infinite Reality that is beyond the subject-object dichotomy.

Non-Dual Metaphysics in the Islamic Tradition

In the Islamic tradition non-dual metaphysics is seen from two complementary vantage points: the infinite and ineffable nature of Ultimate Reality and the manifestation of the Real in the heart of the Muslim gnostic. Central to everything Islamic, including law, theology, philosophy, mysticism and art, is the *shahādah* or testimony of faith, *Lā ilāha illa'Llāh* or "There is no god but God," followed by *Muḥammadun rasūl Allāh* or "Muhammad is the Messenger of God." Uttering these two succinct Arabic phrases with faith, which are the essence of the Quran and the *Sunnah* of the Prophet, is what makes one a Muslim. These phrases are not, however, exhausted by their outward or apparent meaning. Many Sufis, philosophers, and artists throughout the ages have expounded the inner or esoteric meaning of the *shahādah* through prose, poetry, symbolism, and more importantly by living as veritable theophanies of the Divine Reality here on earth. Ultimately, duality is only reconciled at the level of the Divine Essence or Beyond Being. When Muslim sages affirm that "There is no reality but the Reality" or "There is no self

West alike have always considered the *sine qua non* of wisdom; and because this is not a matter of anyone's 'illiteracy' or ignorance of 'facts,' but one of the restoration of meaning or value to a world or 'impoverished reality.' East and West are at cross purposes only because the West is *determined*, i.e. at once resolved and economically 'determined,' to keep on going it knows not where, and call this rudderless voyage…'progress.' It is far more, of course, by what our ideal philosophers and scholars, functioning as mediators, might *be*, far more by the simple fact of their presence, as a catalyst, than any kind of intervention in political or economic activities that they could operate effectively; they would have no use for votes or wish to 'represent' their several nations at Geneva; and remaining unseen, they could arouse no opposition. At the present moment I can think of only two or three of this kind: René Guénon, Frithjof Schuon, Marco Pallis; one cannot consider from this point of view those who know only the West or only the East, however, well." *The Bugbear of Literacy* (Bedfont, Middlesex: Perennial Books Ltd., 1979), pp. 80–81.

but the Self"—based on the *shahādah*, the Supreme Name of God and other Names that designate that which is beyond all definitions and limitations—they always assert the relative reality of the servant and the Lord, as well as the world, Satan, and man's egocentric self.[41] Therefore, the doctrines and commentaries that follow should not lead one to the conclusion that one has realized their truth simply because one is in agreement with their meaning. One must also realize the illusory or perishing nature of the world and struggle against Satan and egocentricity of the lower self if one is to know Ultimate Reality or the Supreme Self. For the Divine Presence in the heart to radiate outwardly, care must be taken to purify the soul and make it a suitable locus of manifestation or reflection. This is accomplished through the doctrines and rites of religion, the intermediaries of objective Revelation and prophecy, as well as the faculty of the Intellect or Spirit, which reconnect man to his transcendent Center. The Self is eternally present, but we cannot sustain an awareness of it without engaging our relative faculties in the pursuit of sacred knowledge through revealed religion.

Frithjof Schuon provided some of the most clear and powerful elucidations of the esoteric meaning of the *shahādah* in any European language. He states in one passage:

> All metaphysical truths are comprised in the first of these testimonies and all eschatological truths in the second. But it could also be said that the first *shahādah* is the formula of discernment or "abstraction" (*tanzīh*) while the second is the formula of integration or "analogy" (*tashbīh*): in the first *shahādah* the word "divinity" (*ilāha*)—taken here in its ordinary current sense—designates the world inasmuch as it is unreal because God alone is real, while the name of the Prophet (*Muḥammad*) in the second *shahādah* designates the world inasmuch as it is real because nothing can be outside God; in certain respects all is He. Realizing the first *shahādah* means first of all becoming fully conscious that the Principle alone is real and that the world, though on its own level "exists," "is not"; in one sense it therefore means realizing the universal void.

41. Frithjof Schuon, *Dimensions of Islam*, pp. 46–53.

> Realizing the second *shahādah* means first of all becoming fully conscious that the world—or manifestation—is "not other" than God or the Principle, since to the degree that it has reality it can only be that which alone "is," or in other words it can only be divine; realizing this *shahādah* thus means seeing God everywhere and everything in Him. "He who has seen me," said the Prophet, "has seen God"; now everything is the "Prophet," on the one hand in respect of the perfection of existence and on the other in respect of the perfections of mode or expression. If Islam merely sought to teach that there is only one God and not two or more, it would have no persuasive force.[42]

The primary metaphysical meaning of the *shahādah* is thus equivalent to Shankara's saying "God is real, the world is appearance; the soul is like unto God" (*Brahma satyam; jagan mithyā; jīvo Brahmaiva nā'paraḥ*).[43] In Islamic esoterism, the world and the soul are simultaneously God and other than God (*Huwa lā Huwa*). To the extent that the world and the soul are Real and eternal their reality is not other than God; to the extent that the world and the soul are illusory and perishing they are other than God. What does indeed exist and endure in the world and the soul—indicated by the Divine Names and Qualities—is nothing other than God, while the illusory and perishing aspects of the world and the soul are ultimately non-existent.[44] The *shahādah* reminds us that God alone truly is behind the veils that make up the cosmos and the soul through so many signs *(āyāt Allāh)* that reveal His Being. In the end, "There is no reality but the Divine Reality" because He is the

42. Frithjof Schuon, *Understanding Islam* (Bloomington, Indiana: World Wisdom Inc., 1998), pp. 6–7. See also, *Sufism: Veil and Quintessence*, pp. 133–138.

43. Among the extended forms of the *shahādah* is *Lā ilāha illa'Llāhu waḥdahu lā sharīka laHu* or "There is no god but God alone, He who has no associate." William Stoddart writes, The term "non-dualism" [*advaita*] is, so to speak, a double negative, and has parallels in the other Vedāntic phrase "the One without a second" and in the Islamic expression "He who has no associate" (*lā sharīka laHu*)." *Hinduism and Its Spiritual Masters* (Louisville, KY: Fons Vitae), p. 85.

44. The beauty of a sunset, the love of a mother for her child, the consciousness of man, are nothing other than the Beauty, Love and Consciousness of God. *Lā ilāha illa'Llāh*, therefore means "There is no beauty but God," "There is no love but

Absolute and Necessary Being before which the relative and contingent beings are entirely dependent and ultimately subsumed.

If in Islam God appears primarily as Reality or Being (*wujūd*), He is also Consciousness (*wijdān*) and Bliss (*wajd*) or in Sanskrit *sat, cit* and *ānanda*.[45] While the most well known exposition of the metaphysical doctrine in Islam is *waḥdat al-wujūd* or the transcendent Unity of Being, the doctrine of Unity (*al-tawḥīd*) can also be interpreted to support the transcendent Unity of Consciousness and Bliss. Indeed, all of the Ninety-Nine Names of God, including, for example, the Witness (*al-Shahīd*) or the Infinitely Good (*al-Raḥmān*) indicate the nature of the One Reality or Self that alone truly is and knows. Therefore, the *shahādah* may also be read as "There is no self but the Self," which denies the independent existence of the relative self except as a ray from the Divine Self or Sun. However, to affirm the absolute existence of God alone or to know God as the Supreme Object is to also know God as the Supreme Subject, for there is no duality or partition in the Unity of God. The essence of the *shahādah*, as of the Quran, is the Supreme Name Allah. In Islam, the Name refers to both the Supreme Object and the Supreme Subject or Self. The metaphysics of Islam does not posit a duality to begin with except on lower levels of existence that necessitate duality, such as that between the servant and the Lord, which is in any case reconciled by the effacement of the servant before the Lord. If the doctrine of Advaita Vedānta refers to the poles of absolute Consciousness and Being as Ātman and Brahman and simultaneously denies their duality, the Oneness of Consciousness and Being is affirmed in Islam through the Name Allah and not by equating the soul (*nafs*) or even the Spirit (*al-rūḥ*) with Ātman, which are nevertheless relative gradations or reflections of the Supreme Self in the cosmic order. Beyond the levels of the soul and

God," and "There is no consciousness but God." Every positive attribute in the world and the soul is Real to the extent that it is or is from God, and illusory or nonexistent to the extent that we perceive these gradations as separative. Clearly the manifestation of a Divine Quality is relative in this world, but nonetheless an extension of and an opening to the Divine Reality as such.

45. William Chittick, ed., *The Essential Seyyed Hossein Nasr*, p. 121.

the Spirit, it is the Muslim's realization of Allah in the innermost heart—often referred to as the *sirr* or secret of the Sufis—that is analogous to a Hindu's realization of Ātman. Regarding the Name Allah, Schuon writes,

> The first syllable of the Name refers, according to a self-evident interpretation, to the world and to life inasmuch as they are divine manifestations, and the second to God and to the beyond or to immortality. While the Name begins with a sort of hiatus between silence and utterance (the *hamzah*) like a *creatio ex nihilo*, it ends in an unlimited breathing out which symbolically opens into the Infinite—that is, the final *hā* marks the supraontological Non-Duality—and this indicates that there is no symmetry between the initial nothingness of things and the transcendent Non-Being. Thus the Name Allah embraces all that is, from the Absolute down to the tiniest speck of dust, whereas the Name *Huwa*, "He," which personifies the final *hā*, indicates the Absolute as such in Its ineffable transcendence and Its inviolable mystery.[46]

Elsewhere Schuon states, "The Sufic formula *Lā anā wa lā anta: Huwa* (Neither I nor thou: He) is thus equivalent to the formula of the Upanishads *Tat tvam asi* (Thou art That)."[47] Therefore, the final consonant in the Name Allah or *hā* and the name He or *Huwa* designate the Supreme Principle or Self in Islam that is at once transcendent and immanent and beyond all limitations and descriptions. However, God also refers to Himself as "I" or *Anā* throughout the Quran, which is the basis for our own consciousness and even the initial "I bear witness" (*ashhadu*) of the *shahādah*.[48] Ultimately, it is God alone that knows Himself through us. God alone is truly I and the Sufis such as Ḥallāj who assert that

46. *Understanding Islam*, p. 150. See also, Leo Schaya, "On the Name Allāh", *Sufism: Love & Wisdom*, pp. 207–216.

47. *Language of the Self*, p. 21.

48. Martin Lings also writes, "the certitude that each one of us has of being "myself", of being "I", is just such a loan from *Anā* (the Arabic word *anā* denotes the first personal pronoun). In the Quran God not only says "No god but God" and "no god but He" but also "no god but I." This brings us back to the Sanskrit word Ātman, the One and Only Self of Hindu doctrine." *A Return to the Spirit*, p. 25.

"I am the Truth" (*Ana'l-Ḥaqq*) are absent before the Divine I within them.[49] Among the other central terms used in Islam to refer to the Divine Essence is *al-Dhāt* or the Possessor or Source of the Divine Names and Attributes that is Itself beyond all qualifications and limitations. The Arabic word *dhāt* is in fact feminine, which implicitly refers to the hidden nature of the Divine Ipseity or Beyond Being that is complemented by the first determination of God as Light or Being. When Sufi poets refer to the Beloved as Laylā—a name that means night—they are in fact alluding to the Supreme Principle or *al-Dhāt* that precedes and is the Source of all manifestation. The title of the present chapter links this Arabic word for the Divine Essence to the Vedantic expression "Thou art That" (*Tat tvam asi*) and reminds us of the ultimate unanimity of traditional metaphysics, despite necessary differences in expression. The Arabic *Dhāt* and the Sanskrit *Tat* both refer to That which alone is—the Divine Reality or Self that is beyond the cosmos and at the center of the human heart. The expression "Thou art *Dhāt*" may appear bold to a Muslim at first glance, but it must be remembered that God is referred to throughout the Quran as "Thou" or *Anta* and is moreover the ultimate and innermost Thou of every thou. Others Names of God from the Quran that refer to the Divine Essence are the One (*al-Aḥad*), the Self-Sufficient (*al-Ṣamad*), the Absolute Reality (*al-Ḥaqq*), and the Infinitely Good (*al-Raḥmān*). Ultimately, all Divine Names are contained in the Essence in an undifferentiated state and only appear as multiple from the point of view of the world.

Metaphysical realization in Islam is closely linked to the invocation or remembrance (*dhikr*) of the *shahādah* and the Supreme

49. Seyyed Hossein Nasr writes, "To know the Truth with one's whole being is ultimately to "become the Truth," to realize that the root of our "I" is the Divine Self Itself, who alone can ultimately utter "I." It was not the individual ego of al-Ḥallāj who uttered *anā'l-Ḥaqq*. That would be blasphemy, and that is how those ignorant around him who did not understand interpreted it. In reality, one who does not utter *anā'l-Ḥaqq* is still living as a polytheist and idol worshipper positing his or her own ego as a reality separate from God as *al-Ḥaqq* and idolizing that ever-changing and evanescent ego as well as the world as a divinity." *The Garden of Truth*, p. 32.

Name of God. All of the Names of Allah taken from the Quran are quintessential manifestations of the Logos or Word of God, which mysteriously unite the invoker (*dhākir*) with the One Reality that is invoked (*madhkūr*). In the same way that the Prophet of Islam was blessed through the descent of the Quran on the Night of Power (*laylat al-qadr*) and eventually raised to the Divine Presence during the Night of Ascent (*laylat al-miʿrāj*), the aspirant on the Sufi path is given a Name of God from the Quran to invoke that makes his or her journey to God possible. Therefore, theoretical gnosis in Islam is connected to a method, which allows the wayfarer to concentrate on the Supreme Principle. The profundity of remembrance is exemplified by the saying "the Name is the Named" and also a reading of the *shahādah* that suggests that "there is no name but the Name"—all other Divine and human appellations being ultimately extinguished and subsumed in the Supreme Name. This Name is the true identity behind the Ninety-Nine Names, as well as the relative "I" and "thou" that we normally identify ourselves with. Through remembrance and exclusive concentration on the Name the seeker becomes aware of the only Name or Named that truly is. The Name, as the quintessence of the Revelation, is an objective power and grace (*barakah*), a sacred vibration like to monosyllable *Om* in Hinduism that sanctifies and deifies the heart that receives it. The invocation and remembrance of the Word of God simply reveals and makes one aware of the Divine Reality that is already within us and all around us, but is veiled by forgetfulness and neglect. Moreover, the methods associated with Islamic esoterism are only effective when practiced alongside the exoteric dimension of the tradition and with the initiation and guidance of a living master. In this regard, both Sufism and Advaita Vedānta have certain necessary preconditions and concomitants that facilitate the realization of the Supreme Identity.

As the central theophany in Islam, the Quran contains numerous verses that pertain directly to pure metaphysics, the transcendent unity of Being and Consciousness or non-duality. It would be impossible for us to cite every verse related to our subject or for that matter to exhaust the meaning of any one verse. However, a few highly representative examples of sapiential esoterism from the

Quran may be given. According to Seyyed Hossein Nasr:

> The metaphysical doctrine of God as absolute and infinite is contained in an explicit fashion in the Quranic chapter called Unity or Sincerity, *al-Tawḥīd*, or *al-Ikhlāṣ* (CXII), which according to Muslims summarizes the Islamic doctrine of God:
>
> In the Name of God—Most Merciful, Most Compassionate
> Say: He is God, the One (*al-Aḥad*)!
> God, the eternal cause of all beings (*al-Ṣamad*)!
> He begetteth not nor was He begotten.
> And there is none like unto Him.
>
> The "Say" (*qul*) already refers to the source of manifestation in the Divine Principle, to the Logos which is at once the Divine Instrument of Manifestation and the source of manifestation in the Divine Order. He (*huwa*) is the Divine Essence, God in Himself, God as such or in His suchness. *Al-Aḥad* attests not only to God's oneness but also to his absoluteness. God is one because He is absolute and absolute because He is one, *al-aḥadiyyah* or quality of oneness implying both meanings in Arabic. *Al-Ṣamad*, a most difficult term to render in English, implies eternal fullness or richness which is the source of everything; it refers to the Divine Infinity, to God being the All-Possibility. The last two verses emphasize the truth that God in His Essence is both above all relations and all comparisons. The chapter as a whole is therefore the revealed and scriptural counterpart of the metaphysical doctrine of the Divine Nature as absolute and infinite, this knowledge also being "revealed" in the sense that it issues from that inner revelation which is the intellect.[50]

In a manner similar to the *shahādah*, the chapter of Unity or Sincerity in the Quran is an affirmation of the absolute oneness and infinite plentitude of the Divine. It reveals that God's Oneness (*al-Aḥad*) alone is and that God is the Source (*al-Ṣamad*) of our own being and consciousness. The verses, "He begetteth not nor was He begotten. And there is none like unto Him" not only mean that God does not have a son or a father, but also that God alone is, having no

50. Seyyed Hossein Nasr, *The Need for a Sacred Science* (Albany, NY: State University of New York Press, 1993), p. 10.

before nor after.[51] Everything that appears in creation, including the prophets and saints, are not so many partners or children of God, but theophanies of God Himself. To the *ḥadīth* "In the beginning was God and beside Him there was nothing," the Sufis add, "and He remains as He was."[52] To this can be added the saying "The Sufi is not created" (*al-Ṣūfī lam yukhlaq*), referring to the transpersonal Intellect—*increatum et increabile*—and by extension the man who has reached and abides in this Center. Here it is not a question of man becoming God, but of realizing the Divine spark of intelligence within the heart, which is like a ray of light from the Sun.

When the Quran says, "God is the Rich, and you are the poor," (47:38) it means that only God possesses Being, Consciousness, and Bliss, and that His creation has absolutely nothing, except that which issues from Him. The ontologically impoverished slave (*'abd*) realizes that he has always been nothing before God and that his existence is simply a reflection of the One Supreme Self as It radiates and is known through the mirror of multiplicity. According to a famous *ḥadīth qudsī* where God speaks through the Prophet in the first person, "I was a Hidden Treasure and I loved to be known, and so I created the world." The cosmos and the Universal Man (*al-insān al-kāmil*) in Islamic esoterism are simply theophanies of the Divine Names and Attributes. According to Abū Ḥāmid Ghazzālī (d. 1111), the famous Sufi scholar who formally reintegrated the exoteric and esoteric dimensions of Islam through his *The Revival of the Religious Sciences* (*Iḥyā' 'ulūm al-dīn*) and other texts:

> Each thing hath two faces, a face of its own, and a face of its Lord; in respect of its own face it is nothingness, and in respect of the Face of God it is Being. Thus there is nothing in existence save only God and His Face, for *everything perisheth but His Face,* always and forever. (Quran 28:88)[53]

51. We do not deny that God has spoken and revealed Himself through His Word or Logos, which includes the Quran and Jesus, for example. When Muslims, following the Quran, state that God has no son or is not a father, they simply deny the literal meaning of these terms in relation to Jesus and Allāh or the Christian Father. The Quran affirms that Jesus is the Logos or Word and Spirit of God.

52. *A Treasury of Traditional Wisdom*, p. 804.

53. Martin Lings, *A Sufi Saints of the Twentieth Century*, p. 123.

The Face (*wajh*) of God in the Quran refers to the Divine Essence, as well as the particular qualities that God reveals Himself as and turns towards man and the world. The doctrine of *māyā* is also present in Islam through the veils (*ḥujub*, pl. of *ḥijāb*) of light and darkness in the cosmos and man that conceal and reveal the Face of the Beloved.[54] While relativity is real on it own level, according to the Quran, as well as Ghazzālī's esoteric commentary, the only abiding Reality is the Face of God.

Regarding the Quranic verse, "He is the First and the Last and the Outwardly Manifest and the Inwardly Hidden," (57:3) Shaykh al-Darqāwī (d. 1823) wrote,

> I was in a state of remembrance and my eyes were lowered and I heard a voice say: *He is the First and the Last and the Outwardly Manifest and the Inwardly Hidden*. I remained silent, and the voice repeated it a second time, and then a third, whereupon I said: 'As to the First, I understand, and as to the Last, I understand, and as to the Inwardly Hidden, I understand, but as to the Outwardly Manifest, I see nothing but created things.' Then the voice said: 'If there were any outwardly manifest other than Himself I should have told thee.' In that moment I realized the whole hierarchy of Absolute Being.[55]

The unveiling of the above verse brings into sharp relief and clarity the significance of the Divine Name and Reality the Outwardly Manifest (*al-Ẓāhir*). In Arabic, a locus of Divine manifestation is often referred to as a *maẓhar* (pl. *maẓāhir*), which has the same root (*ẓ-h-r*) as the Name *al-Ẓāhir*. Sufis also often use the term *tajallī* (pl. *tajalliyyāt*) to refer to the Self-disclosure of God either objectively as a theophany in the cosmos or subjectively as an epiphany of the soul. All existents are so many mirrors that reflect the Divine Names and Attributes and ultimately the One Supreme Self. We read in the Quran, "To God belong the East and the West. Wheresoever you turn, there is the Face of God. God is All-Encompassing, Knowing." (2:115) Everything in creation is an aspect of the Face of God or the particular Divine Names that He manifests Himself as. If God is the

54. *Esoterism as Principle and as Way*, pp. 47–64.
55. *A Sufi Saints of the Twentieth Century*, p. 131.

Outwardly Manifest in relation to us, He is also the Inwardly Hidden (*al-Bāṭin*) in relation to us as well. While *al-Bāṭin* is generally assumed to refer to the Divine Reality that is hidden above and beyond forms, the Name also points to the Presence of the Real within the heart that is only veiled by its immanence.

The Quran also states, "Sight comprehends Him not, but He comprehends all sight. And He is the Subtle, the Aware." (6:103) While particular forms can never exhaust the Divine Reality, the eye of the heart is the inner Witness through which God sees all things. Moreover, this Divine consciousness or the Unity of Consciousness can be seen as the principle of the Unity of Existence or Being. The Divine manifestations or Self-disclosures that we see all around us are in reality projections of the Supreme Self that resides in the heart—Itself unseen—which is like the Sun in relation to the Moon of existence. We can know our true Self through a process of interiorization that unveils the true Reality and Principle of all things. Just as we cannot see our own face without a mirror, which while being a faithful reflection is not the face itself, God as the Self looks through our eyes to see His reflection in the creations that mirror the Supreme Identity. To become aware of God's knowledge of Himself in and through us is to perceive the Divine Vision and Awareness itself as the source of our own consciousness. By moving inward towards the Divine Light in our own being, the luminous source of all things becomes intelligible. God is certainly everywhere and beyond His creation, but we can only truly know Him through our own Center. By approaching and abiding in this Center, which underlies all things, we can recognize it as the principle of the periphery.

There are numerous other verses from the Quran that draw our attention to the non-differentiated Unity of God or the doctrine of non-duality. The Quran describes the turning point at the Battle of Badr when the outnumbered Muslim community defeated the Meccan army under the leadership of the Prophet: "Thou [Muḥammad] threwest not when thou threwest, but God threw. . . ." (8:17) Similarly, the Quran refers to the Prophet and the believer's pact at Ḥudaybiyyah as follows, "Truly those who pledge allegiance unto thee [Muḥammad], pledge allegiance only unto God. The Hand of God is over their hands. . . ." (48:10) Some exoteric Muslim scholars are forced to circumvent the literal meaning of these verses to preserve a theological position that categorically separates God from His Prophet and creation, which is classical dualism. The Quran also refers to the Prophet Muḥammad as "a mercy unto the worlds" (*raḥmatan lil-ʿālamīn*) (21:107) and "a luminous lamp" (*sirājun munīr*) (33:46). When we read these verses alongside others such as "My Mercy encompasses all things" (7:156) and "God is the Light of the heavens and the earth. The likeness of His Light is as a niche wherein is a lamp. . . . " (24:35), it becomes clear that the mercy of the Prophet and the light that radiates from his heart and manifests upon his blessed face is none other than the Mercy and Light of God. For all Divine Names and Qualities are God's alone and to suggest that any prophet, saint or believer manifests mercy or light of his or her own is, from the Islamic perspective, a form of polytheism or *shirk*. To see the positive qualities of the Prophet and by extension all of creation as the Qualities of God is to understand the true meaning of *tawḥīd*. However, no creation can exhaust, in its formal manifestation, the fullness of the Divine Qualities that nonetheless manifest in creation through so many gradations.[56] If this were possible, the manifestation of the unmitigated Mercy and Light of God would extinguish all hatred and darkness on earth and therefore all separation, free-will and ultimately a possible and therefore necessary expression of the Infinite. In any case, wherever they are found and in whatever measure "unto Him belong the most beautiful Names." (20:8)

Turning to the *Ḥadīth*, the Prophet said, "Whoever has seen me has seen the Truth," which affirms that the Messenger of God, and by extension all messengers and prophets, are always manifesting the Real. The inner reality of the Prophet Muḥammad is the Divine Truth. Unlike other religions which lay emphasis on the incarnation of God as this or that prophet or avatar, the Prophet of Islam is absent

56. The heart of man nevertheless exists as a door opening inwardly onto the Infinite, and therefore Allah or Ātman who alone knows and is the Absolute or the plenitude of the Divine Names and Qualities and That which is beyond them. The body, soul and Spirit of man reflect a limited measure of these Qualities, while the heart mysteriously encompasses the Divine, as we read in a *ḥadīth qudsī*: "The heavens and the earth do not contain Me, but the heart of My faithful servant contains Me."

or annihilated before God. Thus his humility as the perfect servant of God is elevated to effacement and transparency before the Divine Reality. In a manner similar to the founders of other religions, despite certain theological and semantic differences, God communicates something of His Reality and Presence to humanity through the Prophet Muḥammad. The Prophet conveys the doctrine of and way to Unity and Union, which are the essence of the Quran and *Sunnah*. For the essence of the Quran, or the Message that the Messenger conveys, is God Himself. Moreover, it is through the spiritual light and substance of the Prophet—who is according to the Quran "closer to the believers than are they to themselves" (33:6)—that we can encounter God or the Self within. Islamic spirituality is a timeless romance between the Prophet and God or lover and Beloved. The Muslim who follows his inner and outer *Sunnah* and is thus illuminated by the Prophetic light, station, and virtues, may also realize the Supreme Union that is reserved for the Universal or Perfect Man.

The Prophet also said, "He who knoweth himself knoweth his Lord." This saying has inspired numerous Muslim philosophers and Sufis throughout history and is the basis for Islamic autology. In another *ḥadīth* God states through the Prophet, "I am Aḥmad without the *mīm*; I am an Arab with out the *'ayn*." The saying reveals that *al-Aḥad* or "the One" is the essence of Aḥmad, and that *al-Rabb* or "the Lord" is the archetype of the Arab—Aḥmad and Arab both referring to the Prophet Muḥammad and by extension all of human and cosmic manifestation. Non-dual realization is extended to all servants of God in the famous *ḥadīth qudsī* where God states through the Prophet:

> Whosoever shows enmity to someone devoted to Me, I shall be at war with him. My servant draws not near to Me with anything more loved by Me than the religious duties I have enjoined upon him, and My servant continues to draw near to me with supererogatory works so that I shall love him. When I love him I am his hearing with which he hears, his seeing with which he sees, his hand with which he strikes and his foot with which he walks. . . .[57]

57. *Forty Hadith Qudsi*, trans. Ezzeddin Ibrahim and Denys Johnson-Davies (Cambridge: The Islamic Texts Society, 1997), p. 104.

According to another famous *ḥadīth* of the Prophet, "The heart of the faithful is the throne of the All-Merciful (*al-Raḥmān*)." In Islam, the heart is the locus of the Divine Reality—the inner Ka'bah where the Presence of the Real resides. The above *ḥadīth* directly corresponds to an illuminating article by René Guénon's entitled "The Vital Centre of the Human Being, Seat of *Brahma*."[58] In Seyyed Hossein Nasr's essay, "The Heart of the Faithful is the Throne of the All-Merciful," which is an esoteric commentary on the *ḥadīth* of the Prophet, he speaks of the heart or Intellect as a vessel for all of the Divine Self-disclosures.[59] The heart is like the Moon that, from the point of view of the earth, alternates in its receptivity to the Light of the Sun. The heart is so central in Islam that God said through the Prophet in another *hadīth qudsī*, "The heavens and the earth do not contain Me, but the heart of My faithful servant contains Me." Both of these sayings can be read as commentaries on the Quranic verse, "We are nearer to [man] than his jugular vein." (50:16)

After the Quran and the *Ḥadīth* of the Prophet Muḥammad, the sayings of the Imams among the family of the Prophet are among the most direct expressions of metaphysics in the Islamic tradition. While the majority of these sayings are preserved among Ithnā 'asharī, Ismā'īlī, and Zaydī Shī'ites, many are also recorded in classical Sunni sources. In must not be forgotten that as many as eight of the Ithnā 'asharī Imams are poles (*aqṭāb*) in certain Sunni Sufi

58. *Man & His Becoming according to the Vedānta*, pp. 31–38. In this article Guénon writes, "The vital center is considered as corresponding analogically with the smaller ventricle (*guhā*) of the heart (*hridaya*); but it must not be confused with the heart in the ordinary sense of the word, that is to say with the physiological organ bearing that name, since it is in reality the center not only of the corporeal individuality, but of the integral individuality, capable of indefinite extension in its own sphere.... The heart is regarded as the center of life, and in fact, from the physiological point of view, it is so by reason of its connection with the circulation of the blood, with which vitality itself is essentially linked in a very special way, as all traditions are unanimous in recognizing; but it is further considered as a center on a higher plane and in a more symbolic sense, through its connection with the universal Intelligence (in the sense of the Arabic term *al-'aqlu*) as related to the individual." Ibid., p. 32.

59. Seyyed Hossein Nasr, "The Heart of the Faithful is the Throne of the All-Merciful," in James Cutsinger, ed., *Paths to the Heart*, pp. 32–45.

orders, such as the Qādiriyyah and Shādhiliyyah. Indeed, there is no legitimate Sufi order in the Shī'ite or Sunni world that does not have the name of Imam 'Alī on it chain of transmission (*silsilah*).[60] Therefore, as we present some of the gnostic sayings of the Imams one must be keep in mind that they have influenced the transmission and trajectory of esoterism in the Sunni world as much as they have in the Shī'ite world.[61] In response to a question at the Battle of the Camel, 'Alī paused to give discourse on the meaning of the Unity of God.[62] According to Reza Shah-Kazemi,

> This evokes the discourse of Krishna, whose revelation of the Bhagavad Gita to Arjuna was given on the battlefield of Kurukshetra just before the battle between the Pandavas and the Kauravas. The Imam combines in fact both roles: Krishna, as divinely inspired sage, and Arjuna, as invincible warrior.[63]

'Alī was careful to put first things first and in fact states in the opening sermon of the *Nahj al-balāghah*: "Foremost in religion is

60. Reza Shah-Kazemi writes, "It is often said that the Naqshabandī *ṭarīqah* is the exception to this rule, tracing its decent from the Prophet through the first caliph, Abū Bakr, rather than through 'Alī. But it should be noted that this affiliation with Abū Bakr pertains only to one of its three principal *silsilahs*. In his work, *al-Ḥadā'iq al-wardiyyah fī ḥaqā'iq ajilla al-Naqshabandiyyah*, (Damascus, 1306/1889), p. 6, 'Abd al-Majīd b. Muḥammad al-Khānī, himself a Naqshabandī-Khālidī shaykh, refers to the first *silsilah* (*al-silsilat al-ūlā*) as the 'golden chain', and this begins with 'Alī, proceeding through the Shi'i Imams until 'Alī b. Mūsā, then to Ma'rūf al-Karkhī and the other masters. The second *silsilah* (*al-silsilatu'l-thāniya*) likewise begins with 'Alī and proceeds through Ḥasan al-Baṣrī. It is only the third *silsilah*, which is called *al-silsilat al-ṣiddīqiyya* which proceeds from the Prophet to Abū Bakr (*al-ṣiddīq*)." *Justice and Remembrance: Introducing the Spirituality of Imam 'Alī* (London: I.B. Tauris Publishers, 2006), p. 190.

61. According to both Frithjof Schuon and Seyyed Hossein Nasr, after the Prophet, 'Alī ibn Abī Ṭālib (d. 661) is the representative *par excellence* of Islamic esoterism. Therefore, not only has he had the most profound influence on Sunni and Shī'ite Muslims in general, but more specifically on traditionalist Muslims who have rearticulated Islamic metaphysics and the *sophia perennis* in the twentieth century. See, Frithjof Schuon, *The Transcendent Unity of Religions*, pp. 44–45; and Seyyed Hossein Nasr, *Ideals and Realities of Islam*, p. 121. We are grateful to Reza Shah-Kazemi for this observation.

62. 'Allāmah Ṭabātabā'ī, *A Shī'ite Anthology*, trans. William C. Chittick (Albany, New York: State University of New York Press, 1981), pp. 37–38.

63. *Justice and Remembrance*, p. 65.

knowledge of Him" (*Awwal al-dīn ma'rifatuhu*).[64] The sage who puts contemplation before action is able to reflect a measure of the Divine Names here below as virtues. It was Imam 'Alī's metaphysical vision that led to his heroic and chivalrous deeds. Anyone can fight in the name of this or that cause, including mercenaries, but only a sage does so in the service of the True, the Good and the Beautiful, and as a consequence possesses the discernment and self-retraint that all men and women must cultivate, especially those charged with the responsibility to make political and military decisions that involve matters of life and death. It is striking that the greatest warrior of Islam was first and foremost a contemplative. Concerning his vision of the Real through the eye of the heart, 'Alī was asked,

> "O Commander of the Faithful! Hast thou seen thy Lord?" ['Alī] said, "Woe unto thee, O Dhi'lib! I would not be worshipping a Lord whom I have not seen." He said, "O Commander of the Faithful! How didst thou see Him?" ['Alī] answered, "O Dhi'lib! Eyes see Him not through sight's observation, but hearts see Him through the verities of faith (*ḥaqā'iq al-īmān*). Woe to thee, O Dhi'lib! Verily my Lord is subtle in subtlety (*laṭif al-laṭāfah*), but He is not described by subtleness (*luṭf*); tremendous in tremendousness (*'azīm al-'azamah*), but not described by tremendousness (*'izam*); grand in grandeur (*kabīr al-kibriyā'*), but not described by grandness (*kibr*); and majestic in majesty (*jalīl al-jalālah*), but not described by greatness (*ghilaz*).... He is in all things, but not mixed (*mutamāzij*) with them, nor separate (*bā'in*) from them. He is Outward (*ẓāhir*), not according to the explanation of being immediate (to the senses: *mubāsharah*); Manifest (*mutajallin*), not through the appearance of a vision (of Him: *istihlāl ru'yah*); Separate, not through distance (*masāfah*); Near (*qarīb*), not through approach (*mudānāh*); Subtle, not through corporealization (*tajassum*); Existent (*mawjūd*), not after nonexistence (*'adam*)...."[65]

This description of the Divine by 'Alī parallels the Vedic description of Brahman as "not this, not that" (*neti, neti*). In both traditions, God has attributes, but He cannot be reduced or confined to

64. Ibid., p. 208.
65. *A Shī'ite Anthology*, pp. 38–39.

these attributes. The above passage highlights the ineffable and infinite nature of God, which ʿAlī beheld with the eye of the heart or the Intellect, which is capable of perceiving the One True Reality. While the transcendence of God stands out in most of the sayings of Imam ʿAlī, he is recorded to have said in his famous *Khuṭbat al-bayān*:

> I am the Sign of the All-Powerful. I am the gnosis of the mysteries. I am the Threshold of Thresholds. I am the companion of the radiance of the divine Mystery. I am the First and the Last, the Manifest and the Hidden. I am the Face of God. I am the mirror of God, the supreme Pen, the *Tabula secreta*. I am he who in the Gospel is called Elias. I am he who is in possession of the secret of God's Messenger.[66]

The Prophet himself remarked, "Gazing upon ʿAlī is an act of worship."[67] While the Quran rejects anthropomorphism and the exclusive localization of God and constantly reminds Muslims of both the immanence and transcendence of the Divine Reality, the perfect servant of God reflects the Divine Names and Attributes of God here on earth and exists as the most complete sign of God. Therefore, the Imams and the saints—like the prophets before them—manifest the Divine Reality at the center of the cosmos. While some Muslims are wary of any suggestion that ʿAlī was a manifestation of God because of certain esoteric currents in Shīʿism that appear to limit God to the Imam, all men and women are capable of the same Self-realization. For those with knowledge and spiritual sobriety, ʿAlī does not become an object of devotion, but a superlative symbol of what all human beings are capable of—a mirror and anticipation of our own inner sanctity. In Islam, each Muslim approaches God directly as the transcendent Reality, who then reveals His Presence in the immanent abode of the heart.

According to Imam Jaʿfar al-Ṣādiq (d. 765), who is both the Sixth Imam in Shīʿism and an early Pole in most Sufi orders, "We are the

66. Henry Corbin, *History of Islamic Philosophy*, trans. by Liadain Sherrard and Philip Sherrard (London: Kegan Paul International, 1993), p. 49. For a valuable commentary of this passage, see *Justice and Remembrance*, pp. 187–188.

67. Ibid., p. 19.

Names of God."[68] Sayings such as these are not limited to the Imams, but were also uttered by the Prophet before them and certain Sufis after them. We also read in a series of questions posed to Imam al-Ṣādiq by a disciple Abū Baṣīr:

> Abū Baṣīr has related that he said to Abū 'Abdallāh [Imām al-Ṣādiq]—upon whom be peace—"Tell me about God, the Mighty and Majestic. Will believers see Him on the Day of Resurrection?" He answered, "Yes, and they have already seen Him before the Day of Resurrection." Abū Baṣīr asked, "When?" The Imam answered, "When He said to them, 'Am I not your Lord?' They said 'Yea, verily' (Quran 7:172)." Then he was quiet for a time. Then he said, "Truly the believers see Him in this world before the Day of Resurrection. Doest thou not see Him now?" Abū Baṣīr then said to him, "That I might be made thy sacrifice! Shall I relate this (to others) from thee?" He answered, "No, for if thou relatest it, a denier ignorant of the meaning of what thou sayest will deny it. They will suppose that it is comparision and unbelief (*kufr*). But seeing with the heart (*al-ru'yah bi'l-qalb*) is not like seeing with the eyes (*al-ru'yah bi'l-'ayn*). High be God exalted above what the comparers (*mushabbihūn*) and heretics (*mulḥidūn*) describe![69]

The esoteric teachings of the Imams—which are based on the Quran and *Sunnah*—are an important impetus for the later manifestation of theoretical and practical Sufism or *'irfān*. Bāyazīd Basṭāmī (d. 874), remembered by tradition as a disciple of Imam al-Ṣādiq, is known for saying "Glory be unto Me! How great is My majesty" (*Subḥānī mā 'aẓama Sha'anī*), "I am He" (*Anā Huwa*) and "Thou art That" (*Takūnu Anta Dhāka*).[70] In a vision attributed to Basṭāmī, he saw the Throne of God and found it empty and

68. Sayyid Muḥammad Ḥusayn Ṭabāṭabā'ī, *Kernel of the Kernel: Concerning the Wayfaring and Spiritual Journey of the People of Intellect* (*Risāla-yi Lubb al-Lubāb dar Sayr wa Sulūk-i Ulu'l Albāb*), Sayyid Muḥammad Ḥusayn Ḥusaynī Tihrānī, ed., trans. Mohammad H. Faghfoory (Albany, NY, State University of New York Press, 2003), p. 19. See also, M.A. Amir-Moezzi, *The Spirituality of Shi'i Islam*, pp. 103–132.

69. *A Shī'ite Anthology*, p. 42.

70. Gerhard Böwering, "Ideas of Time in Persian Sufism," *The Heritage of Sufism,* vol. I, p. 218. Seyyed Hossein Nasr states, "The similarity between some of the locutions (*shaṭḥīyāt*) of Basṭāmī . . . and certain Vedantic formulations have led

proceeded to seat himself upon it saying: "I am I and thus am 'I.'"[71] He also states:

> Once He raised me up and stationed men before Him, and said to me, 'O Abū Yazīd, truly My creation desire to see thee.' I said, 'Adorn me in Thy Unity, and clothe me in Thy Selfhood, and raise me up to Thy Oneness, so that when Thy creation sees me they will say, We have seen Thee: and Thou wilt be That, and I shall not be there at all.'[72]

The famous Sufi Manṣūr Ḥallāj (d. 922), who is compared to Christ in Louis Massignon's seminal study, was executed for his theophanic locution (*shaṭḥ*), "I am the Truth" (*Ana'l-Ḥaqq*). Interestingly, Ḥallāj states that this knowledge was possessed and transmitted by 'Alī, Ḥasan, and Ḥusayn, who concealed it from the community at large.[73] Martin Lings begins his collection *Sufi Poems* with the following statement:

> *Thou art That*—This Hindu expression of what is often called the Supreme Identity has necessarily its equivalent in all other religions. In Islam, of which Sufism is the innermost aspect, the truth in question is expressed by the Quran in the words: 'We [God] are nearer to him [man] than his jugular vein;'...[74]

Lings then goes on to quote a poem by Ḥallāj: "I saw my Lord with the eye of the Heart. I said: 'Who art Thou?' He answered: 'Thou.'"[75] The sayings and poems of Ḥallāj unveil the secret of the doctrine of

---

R.C. Zaehner to posit a Hindu origin for the school of Sufism propagated by Basṭāmī.... But such formulations as "that art thou" (*takūnu anta dhāka*) of Basṭāmi, or the Sanskrit *tat tvam asi*, are so universal and so deeply rooted in the texture of reality that they do not need to point to any historical borrowing whatsoever." *Three Muslim Sages*, p. 158.

71. "Ideas of Time in Persian Sufism," p. 218.

72. *A Treasury of Traditional Wisdom*, p. 894.

73. Ḥallāj states, "Of course, I conceal the jewels of my knowledge, lest the ignorant, beholding it, should be tempted. Abū'l-Ḥasan ['Alī] did the same before me, and he transmitted it to Ḥusayn and Ḥasan...." Louis Massignon, *The Passion of al-Ḥallāj*, vol. II, trans. Herbert Mason (Princeton, New Jersey: Princeton University Press, 1982), p. 169.

74. Martin Lings, *Sufi Poems*, p. vii.

75. Ibid.

Unity or non-duality in perhaps the most explicit manner possible. It was his function to disclose the secret of the heart, which more sober Sufis—like the Prophet before them—had kept hidden. Ḥallāj states:

> One with Thee make me, O my One, through Oneness
> Faithed in sincerity no path can reach.
> I am the Truth, and Truth, for Truth, is Truth,
> Robed in Its Essence, thus beyond separation. . . .[76]

Ḥallāj also states,

> Is it I or Thou? These twain! Two gods!
> Far be it, far be it from me to affirm two!
> Selfhood is Thine in my nothingness forever:
> Mine all, over all, casts illusion twofold:
> For where is Thine Essence, where from me, for me to see,
> When mine hath no where, as already plain?
> And Thy Countenance, where with my two sights may I seek it,
> In the seeing of my heart, or the seeing of mine eye?
> Twixt Thee and me an 'I am' is, o'ercrowding me:
> Take, be Thine own 'I am', mine from between us.[77]

In a manner similar to Shankara, Ḥallāj affirms the absolute existence of the transcendent Self alone. For Ḥallāj, duality is overcome when we realize our own non-existence in light of the One. He begins by asserting the Reality of the One alone, but unlike many theologians and jurists, Ḥallāj sees no room in the doctrine of Unity for anything other than God. What remains is therefore nothing other than the Real.

Among the most striking examples of the doctrine of non-duality in the annals of Sufism is found in the *Mawāqif* (*The Book of Spiritual Stayings*) and the *Mukhāṭabāt* (*The Book of Spiritual Addresses*) of Muḥammad ibn 'Abd al-Jabbār Niffarī (d. 965). In these works, God speaks to and through Niffarī in a consistent manner and not only in intermittent ecstatic locutions. Niffarī's teachings primarily focus on the Self, who in fact speaks in the first person, while also

76. Ibid., p. 28.
77. Ibid.

taking into account the relative aspects of man that must be effaced on the contemplative path, which is the perpetual remembrance or awareness of God. Indeed, the quality of a gnostic or *'ārif* is the degree to which he or she, through wayfaring and the grace of God, sustains an awareness of the Supreme Identity as opposed to the lower self, including its apparently praiseworthy attributes such as knowledge and gnosis inasmuch as these are envisaged as other than God. Niffarī transmits a measure of the unparalleled Divine wisdom and inspiration he received from God in his *Mawāqif*:

> Where is he that makes My gnoses a means of coming to Me? If I had shown him the tongue of sovereignty, his gnosis would have been changed to agnosia, and he would have been shaken, as the heavens are shaken on the day of their shaking.
> If I do not cause thee to witness my Glory in that which I cause thee to witness, then I have set thee in abasement in it.
> The party of the people of heaven and earth are in the abasement of circumscription. But I have servants, whom heaven cannot contain with all its tiers, and whose hearts the sides of earth cannot support. I have caused the eyes of their hearts to witness my Glory's lights, which fall not on anything but they destroy it. Their hearts behold nothing in the heavens, that they should affirm it, and they have no place of return in the earth, that they should dwell in it.
> Take that which thou needest to concentrate thee upon Me, or I will restore thee unto thy need and separate thee from Me.
> When My gnosis is present, there is no need: while My gnosis is coming, take what thou needest.[78]

An outstanding example of a Sufi sage who left vestiges of his transpersonal realization in Arabic poetry is Abu'l-Ḥasan Shushtarī (d. 1269). He states:

> Truly I am a wondrous thing for him who sees Me:
> Lover and Beloved, both am I, there is no second.
> O seeker of the essential Truth, thine eye's film hides it.

78. Muḥammad ibn 'Abd al-Jabbār Niffarī, *The Mawáqif and Mukháṭabát of Muḥammad Ibn 'Abdi'L-Jabbār Al-Niffarī*, trans. Arthur John Arberry (Cambridge: E. J. W. Gibb Memorial Trust, 1987), p. 27.

Return unto thyself, take note: none is but Thee.
All good, all knowledge springs from Thee;
In Thee's the Secret. Thou the mirror art for gazing,
Pole of the times...
My self's sun setteth ne'er from vision Face to face.
Behold My beauty, witness of Me in every man,
Like the water flowing through the sap of branches...[79]

Pure metaphysics or gnosis is also expressed in Persian Sufi poetry. These expressions were influenced by the Quran, the Prophet, and the wealth of grace (*barakah*) that issue from these sources and make the journey to the One possible. Like the previous selections from Arabic sources of Islamic esoterism, only a few passages from this genre that are highly representative of the subject are cited here. Farīd al-Dīn 'Aṭṭār (d. 1220) is famous for his poem *The Conference of the Birds* (*Manṭiq al-ṭayr*), where the soul's journey on the spiritual path to realization is represented by thirty birds' journey and ascent through valleys and mountains to the eternal Sīmurgh—a giant mythical bird similar to a phoenix or griffin who comes to symbolize the Supreme Self. Through a brilliant play on words 'Aṭṭār demonstrates that the thirty birds or *sī murgh* are simply a reflection of the Sīmurgh or Supreme Self. At the summit of the celestial Mt. Qāf the birds are transfigured by a beatific vision of the Sīmurgh. 'Aṭṭār writes,

> At that moment, in the reflection of their countenance, the Sī-murgh (*thirty birds*) saw the face of the eternal Sīmurgh. They looked: it was veritably that Sīmurgh, without any doubt, *that* Sīmurgh was veritably *these* Sī-murgh. Then amazement struck them into a daze. They saw themselves Sī-murgh in all; and Sīmurgh was in all Sī-murgh. When they turned their eyes to the Sīmurgh, it was veritably *that* Sīmurgh which was there in that place. When they looked at themselves, here too it was Sī-murgh. And when they looked both ways at once, Sīmurgh and Sī-murgh were one and the same Sīmurgh. There was Simurgh twice, and yet there was only one; yes, one alone, and yet many. This one was that one; that one was this one. In the whole universe none under-

79. *Sufi Poems*, p. 86.

stood such a thing. All were sunk in amazement; they remained in a state of meditation outside of meditation.[80]

'Aṭṭār's Persian masterpiece can be seen as a commentary on the Prophetic *ḥadīth*, "He who knoweth himself, knoweth the Lord."[81] Seyyed Hossein Nasr states, "In gaining a vision of the Sīmurgh, the birds not only encounter the beauty of Her Presence, but also see themselves as they really are, mirrored in the Self which is the Self of every self."[82] 'Aṭṭār states,

To be consumed by the light of the presence of the
Sīmurgh is to realize that,
I know not whether I am Thee or Thou art I;
I have disappeared in Thee and duality hath perished.[83]

Other examples of the inner meaning of the doctrine of Unity or non-duality are found in the poetry of Jalāl al-Dīn Rūmī (d. 1273), who was inspired by his beloved friend and spiritual companion Shams al-Dīn Tabrīzī and other souls he met on the spiritual path. What is intriguing about Rūmī's poems in praise of Shams al-Dīn (the Sun of religion) is that it is difficult or impossible to tell if they are referring to Shams the man as a Divine theophany, Shams as a manifestation of Rūmī's own Intellect, the Divine Principle Itself, or all three of these possibilities simultaneously. Shams appears in the life and poetry of Rūmī as an enigma manifesting the Divine Mystery or Supreme Identity for Rūmī and all seekers who have been nourished by the traces of gnostic love that they left. Rūmī states: "Shams al-Ḥaqq (Sun of the Divine Truth), if I see in your clear mirror aught but God, I am worse than an infidel!"[84] Mawlānā Rūmī also states: "Whether it be infidelity or Islam, listen: You are either the light of God or God, Khudā!"[85] Beyond the manifestation of the Self in a particular form, Rūmī also makes direct references to the doctrine of non-duality:

80. Seyyed Hossein Nasr, *Islamic Art and Spirituality*, pp. 109–110.
81. Ibid., p. 100.
82. Ibid.
83. Ibid.
84. Annemarie Schimmel, *Rumi's World*, p. 21.
85. Ibid., p. 21.

A man knocked at the door of his beloved.
'Who are you, trusted one?' thus asked the friend.
He answered: 'I' The friend said: 'Go away,
Here is no place for people raw and crude!'
What, then, could cook the raw and rescue him
But separation's fire and exile's flame?
The poor man went to travel a whole year
And burned in separation from his friend,
And he matured, was cooked and burnt, returned
And carefully approached the friend's abode.
He walked around it now in cautious fear
Lest from his lips unfitting words appear.
His friend called out: 'Who is there at my door?'
The answer: 'You, dear, you are at the door!'
He said: 'Come in, now that you are all I—
There is no room in this house for two 'I's!'[86]

In the mystical verse of Rūmī, the lover is like a moth who must be annihilated and consumed by the flame of the candle—the presence of the Beloved. The above poem illustrates that in Islamic spirituality God is first approached as the absolute Other or Object, Rūmī's "You," and then reveals Himself as the exclusive Subject or "I." The seeker's primary concern must be for the Divine Reality that transcends the lower self. When this Reality is known the seeker realizes that God alone is. This Divine ubiquity encompasses the seeker's consciousness, which is in fact the Self's locus of manifestation. Elsewhere Rūmī states: "I have put duality away. I have seen that the two worlds are one; One I seek, One I know, One I see, One I call."[87] Rūmī clarifies the nature of the Real when he writes, "It is neither inside of this world nor outside; neither beneath it nor above it; neither joined with it nor separate from it; it is devoid of quality and relation."[88]

Closely related to the Persian Sufi poets are the great expositors of

86. Ibid., p. 112.

87. Jalāl al-Dīn Rūmī, *Selected Poems From the Dīvāni Shamsi Tabrīz*, trans. R.A. Nicholson (Padstow, Cornwall: Curzon Press, 1999), p. 127.

88. Jalāl al-Dīn Rūmī, *The Mathnawī of Jalālūddīn Rūmī*, vol. II, p. 167.

theoretical gnosis (*'irfān-i naẓarī*) in Islam.[89] There are numerous currents of wisdom within the Islamic intellectual tradition that deserve closer attention, such as Ibn Sīnā and the Muslim peripatetics, the Brethren of Purity (Ikhwān al-Ṣafā'), and Suhrawardī and the school of *Ishrāq*, to name only a few. Within this vast intellectual heritage the present study is limited to the metaphysics and ontology of Ibn 'Arabī's *Akbarī* school because its expressions most closely resemble the doctrine of Advaita Vedānta.[90] In this section are examined Ibn 'Arabī's own writings on the doctrine of Unity or what later became known as *waḥdat al-wujūd* (the transcendent Unity of Being), as well as the writings of 'Abd al-Karīm Jīlī and Mullā Ṣadrā. This particular intellectual tradition merits greater attention because Ibn 'Arabī's vision, reflected in diverse ways in later generations, became the dominant sapiential perspective in the Islamic world. S.H. Nasr writes,

> Many different views on the transcendent unity of Being have been expounded by various philosophers and Sufis over the ages with different degrees of profundity, some revealing the Unity of the Godhead in its full splendour and others veiling this Unity by emphasizing the Divine immanence and the theophany of the One in the mirror of the many.[91]

Muḥyī al-Dīn ibn 'Arabī (d. 1240) laid the groundwork for such key doctrines as the transcendent Unity of Being and the Universal Man, which are the central esoteric interpretations of the first and

89. Maḥmūd Shabistarī's *Gulshan-i rāz* is one example of the nexus between the traditions of Persian Sufi poetry and theoretical and practical gnosis in Islam. See S.H. Nasr's "Metaphysics, Logic and Poetry in the Orient" in *Islamic Art and Spirituality*, pp. 87–97.

90. S.H. Nasr writes, "The Advaita Vedānta school of Sankara can obviously be best understood by a Muslim by comparing it with the doctrine of *waḥdat al-wujūd* (unity of being) of Ibn 'Arabī and his followers; for a Muslim who cannot understand the doctrine of *waḥdat al-wujūd* is unlikely to comprehend the Advaita doctrine, which is like the reflection of the former doctrine in another spiritual universe." *Islam and the Plight of Modern Man* (Lahore: Suhail Academy, 1988), p. 42.

91. Seyyed Hossein Nasr, *Islamic Life and Thought*, p. 175.

second *shahādah* in Sufism.[92] Even though Ibn 'Arabī did not establish a formal *ṭarīqah* or Sufi order, almost all Muslim sages after him were directly or indirectly influenced by his intellectual vision and corpus. Ibn 'Arabī states in his *Fuṣūṣ al-ḥikam*:

> The Oneness of God from the point of view of the Names that lay claim to us is the Oneness of Multiplicity (*aḥadiyyah al-kathra*); but the Oneness of God in the sense that He has no need either of us or of the Names is the Oneness of Essence (*aḥadiyyah al-'ayn*).[93]

Ibn 'Arabī's understanding of *tawḥīd* embraces and explains multiplicity. For the Shaykh al-Akbar, the cosmos and man are nothing but so many theophanies or reflections of the Divine Names.[94] Each created being is determined by a particular Divine Name that governors it. Man is quintessentially a servant (*'abd*) before the Name that God epiphanizes Himself through, which is his Lord (*Rabb*). The multiplicity of Names—the origin of apparent multiplicity in the cosmos—does not affect the Unity of Being or the Oneness of the Divine Essence, which is the Source of the Names that transcend the created order. Moreover, the servant does not introduce duality or negate the Unity of God because creation's existence is nothing before the Divine Names, which are the abiding realities or Reality of the world.[95] According to Ibn 'Arabī, the goal of life is to reach the station of servitude (*'ubūdiyyah*) or perfect sanctity, where man realizes his nonexistence before the Name of God that governs

92. For a discussion of Ibn 'Arabī's relation to the term and doctrine of *waḥdat al-wujūd*, which he never actually uses, but nonetheless approximates and implies, see William Chittick, "Oneness of Being" in *Imaginal Worlds*, pp. 15–29.

93. Claude Addas, *Quest for the Red Sulphur*, p. 279.

94. For in-depth studies of Ibn 'Arabī's metaphysics see William Chittick, *The Sufi Path of Knowledge* (Albany, NY: State University of New York Press, 1989); and Toshihiko Izutsu, *Sufism and Taoism* (Berkeley, CA: University of California Press, 1983).

95. In the words of Ibn 'Arabī, "It is impossible for the things other than God to come out of the grasp of the Real, for He brings them into existence, or rather, He is their existence and from Him they acquire (*istifāda*) existence. And existence/Being is nothing other than the Real, nor is it something outside of Him from which He gives to them.... On the contrary He is Being, and through Him the entities become manifest." *The Sufi Path of Knowledge*, p. 94.

him.[96] One of the Prophet of Islam's names 'Abd Allāh or "servant of God" is indicative of this supreme station. However, beyond the station of servitude is the station of no station (*maqām lā maqām*), which is also attributed to the Prophet Muḥammad. According to Ibn 'Arabī, "The people of perfection have realized all stations and states and passed beyond these to the station above both majesty and beauty, so they have no attribute and no description."[97] Chodkiewicz writes, "Taken to its farthest degree, *'ubūdiyyah* is cancelled out, is reabsorbed in *'ubūdah*, which is pure presence in God, with no trace of duality."[98] Ibn 'Arabī quotes Anṣārī to describe his own understanding of this annihilation (*fanā'*) and subsistence (*baqā'*) through God: "then what has never been disappears, and what has never ceased to be remains."[99] In other words, man was never an independent existent to be annihilated. He must simply realize—through the spiritual methods of Islam and practical Sufism—the perpetual non-existence of his lower self in light of the abiding Reality or Self that alone is. In Ibn 'Arabī, one begins to sense the spiritual elevation that can be attained through servitude, humility or spiritual poverty. It may seem counter-intuitive, but it is precisely through abasing our ego and surrendering our will to God—even

96. *Quest for the Red Sulphur*, pp. 40–41, 120; Michel Chodkiewicz, *An Ocean Without Shore: Ibn Arabi, The Book, and the Law*, trans. David Streight (Albany, NY: State University of New York Press, 1993), pp. 125–126. According to Ibn 'Arabī, the friend of God must realize, to the extent possible, his ontological poverty in a concrete manner by observing the principal dimension of the *Sharī'ah*—*'ibādāt* or the acts of worship—which he most clearly manifests through observing the ritual prayer (*ṣalāh*). *An Ocean Without Shore*, p. 120.

97. *The Sufi Path of Knowledge*, p. 376.

98. *An Ocean Without Shore*, p. 127.

99. Ibid., p. 127. This is echoed is the *Risālat al-aḥadiyyah* (*Treatise on Unity*), attributed to Ibn 'Arabī but most likely by Awḥad al-Dīn Balyānī: "And most of those who know God make a ceasing of existence and the ceasing of that ceasing a condition of attaining the knowledge of God, and that is an error and a clear oversight. For the knowledge of God does not presuppose the ceasing of existence nor the ceasing of that ceasing. For things have no existence, and what does not exist cannot cease to exist. For the ceasing to be implies the positing of existence, and that is polytheism. Then if thou know thyself without existence or ceasing to be, thou knowest God; and if not, then not." "Whoso Knoweth Himself," trans. T.H. Weir (Abingdon, Oxon: Beshara Publications, 1988), p. 114.

through the most basic yet central rite of prostration—that we can realize our nonexistence before Ultimate Reality and reflect a measure of those universal and Divine Qualities that alone ennoble man. This secret of Islam was concisely expressed by the Prophet Muḥammad when he said, "Spiritual poverty is my pride."

While Ibn 'Arabī generally avoided using the more bold theophanic locutions that are attributed to Ḥallāj and Basṭāmī, he writes in the chapter on Jesus in his *Fuṣūṣ al-ḥikam*:

> If not for Him, and if not for us
> What is would not yet be
> We worship truly
> And indeed God is our Master
> And we are identical with Him
> So know, when you say 'man'
> Do not veil using 'man'
> For He hath given thee a proof
> Be thou the Real or be thou creation
> Thou wilt be, through God, All-Merciful. . . .[100]

To assert the independent existence of man is from the Sufi point of view a form of idolatry, for man is only real to the extent that he is a theophany of God. Ibn 'Arabī attests to numerous visionary encounters with various Divine theophanies, prophets and saints through the imaginal faculty and world—the isthmus between the physical and intelligible worlds where spiritual realities take subtle forms. Among these include a meeting at the Ka'bah with an enigmatic Youth (*fatā*) who identifies himself as the Quran and the Divine Names.[101] In this mysterious Youth, the Shaykh al-Akbar reads the essential content of his thirty-seven-part magnum opus *al-Futūḥāt al-makkiyyah*, which Ibn 'Arabī finished composing in

100. *The Ringstones of Wisdom* (*Fuṣūṣ al-ḥikam*), trans. Caner K. Dagli, pp. 164–165.

101. Ibid., p. 79, *Quest for the Red Sulphur*, p. 202. Chodkiewicz writes, "The first, several years before the event that constitutes the birth of the *Futūḥāt al-makkiyyah*, is an account of the first encounter with the young man (*fatā*) 'whose essence is spiritual and whose attributes are lordly' and before whom Ibn 'Arabī prostrates himself." *An Ocean Without Shore*, p. 79.

1238.[102] On another occasion the Youth tells Ibn ʿArabī, "You are yourself the cloud veiling your own Sun! So recognize the essential Reality of your being!"[103] This sublime symbolism indicates that the soul that has not become a perfect servant veils the Supreme Self that resides in the heart, while the soul that has realized the station of servitude is like a thin cloud that evaporates before the light of the Sun.[104] The Youth also instructs, "O you who seek the path leading to the secret. Turn back, for it is in you that the entire secret is found."[105]

Ibn ʿArabī and countless other Muslim gnostics affirmed the Unity of the Divine Reality in the most complete and uncompromising manner and took the *shahādah* to its intellectual and ontological conclusions by affirming the reality of the Absolute alone and rejecting the existence of man and the cosmos except in as much as they reflect the Divine Names and Attributes. In an important passage often attributed to Ibn ʿArabī from the *Treatise on Unity* (*Risālat al-aḥadiyyah*), but most likely by Awḥad al-Dīn Balyānī, we read:

> He is, and there is with Him no after nor before, nor above nor below, nor far nor near, nor union nor division, nor how nor where nor when, nor time nor moment nor age, nor being nor place. And He is now as He was. He is the One without oneness and the Single without singleness. He is not composed of name and named, for his name is He and His named is He...Understand therefore.... He is not in a thing nor a thing in Him, whether entering in or proceeding forth. It is necessary that thou know Him after this fashion, not by knowledge, nor by intellect, nor by understanding, nor by imagination, nor by sense, nor by perception. There does not see Him, save Himself; nor perceive Him,

102. *Quest for the Red Sulphur*, pp. 202–203, 206.

103. Ibid., p. 202.

104. For an illuminating discussion of Ibn ʿArabī and his meeting with this Youth, see Seyyed Hossein Nasr, "Spiritual Chivalry" in Seyyed Hossein Nasr, ed., *Encyclopaedia of Islamic Spirituality*, vol. II, pp. 312–314.

105. Muḥyī al-Dīn ibn al-ʿArabī, *The Meccan Revelations* (*al-Futūḥāt al-makkiyyah*), vol. II, Michel Chodkiewicz, ed., trans. Cyrille Chodkiewicz & Denis Gril (Oxford: Pir Press, 2004), p. 43.

> save Himself. By Himself He sees Himself, and by Himself He knows Himself. None sees Him other than He. His veil is [only] the concealment of His existence in His oneness, without any quality. None sees Him other than He—no sent prophet, nor saint made perfect, nor angel brought nigh know Him. His Prophet is He, and His sending is He, and His Word is He. He sent Himself with Himself to Himself.[106]

Ultimately all that exists, including Revelation, the prophets, the world and the soul, are all manifestations of the One God. The above passage, like so many others in the *Akbarī* corpus, reminds one of the *ḥadīth qudsī*, "I was a hidden treasure; I wanted to be known, so I created the world." In other words, God is known and manifests through His creation. The purpose of creation is the perpetual dawning of Self-consciousness in men or God knowing Himself anew through His variegated creations or theophanies. Depending on the point of view, God is known through creation either as the Supreme Subject that knows or the Supreme Object that is reflected in the cosmos. From either perspective, man and the world are both mirrors that enable the contemplation and reflection of the One in the many. While we cannot attribute the above passage to Ibn 'Arabī, it exemplifies the metaphysical perspective of Islam, which is closely mirrored by Advaita Vedānta. Despite certain theological perspectives in Islam that sometimes veil the universal and sapiential understanding of *tawḥīd*, the unmitigated understanding of Divine Unity has always been preserved among Muslims with the necessary aptitude for theoretical and practical gnosis.

'Abd al-Karīm Jīlī (d. 1428) is among the most influential Sufi sages and scholars after Ibn 'Arabī and is famous for the text *The Universal Man* (*al-Insān al-kāmil*). Within Jīlī's writings are to be found an astonishing abundance of passages dealing with pure metaphysics. He writes:

> Know that the Essence (*al-Dhāt*) signifies Absolute Being in its state of being stripped of all connection, relation, assignation and aspect. It is not that all these are situated outside the Absolute Being, on the contrary, all these aspects and all that they imply are

106. *Three Muslim Sages*, p. 107; "*Whoso Knoweth Himself*", pp. 3–4.

> contained in It. They are found there neither individually nor as connections, but they are essentially the Absolute Being. This is the pure Essence in which are manifested neither Names nor Attributes nor relations nor connections nor anything else. As soon as something is manifested there, the aspect in question is attributed to that which supports the manifestation and not to the pure Essence, since the principle of the Essence is precisely the synthesis of the Universal and individual realities. . . .[107]

In this passage, Jīlī refuses the confine or limit the Divine Essence. The nature of the Real is beyond or above all qualities and relations, while encompassing the qualities and attributes that pertain to the first determination of the Absolute and the various levels of existence. While Jīlī attests to the incomparable and infinite nature of Divine Reality, he also discusses how this Reality manifests in the world:

> The word 'Unity' (*al-aḥadiyyah*) designates the revelation of the Essence in which appear neither the Names nor the Qualities nor any trace of their effects; it is then a Name of the Essence in so far as this is beyond all Divine and created comparisons. Now, there does not exist for Unity, in all the cosmos, a single place of manifestation (*maẓhar*) more perfect than thyself, when thou dost plunge thyself into thine own essence in forgetting all relationship, and when thou seizest thyself in thine own essence, forgetting all relation, and thou dost seize thyself by thyself, stripped of all thy appearances, so that thou art thyself in thyself and that all the Divine Qualities or the created attributes...no longer relate to thee. It is this state of man that is the most perfect place of manifestation of Unity in all existence.[108]

Jīlī also writes, "By 'those who have realized the Essence' (*al-dhātiyyūn*), one means the men in whom lives the Divine Subtle Reality. . . ."[109] Following Ibn 'Arabī and other Sufis, Jīlī affirms that the individual must be annihilated before he can act as a locus for

107. 'Abd al-Karīm al-Jīlī, *Universal Man* (*al-Insān al-kāmil*), trans. by Titus Burckhardt and Angela Culme-Seymour (Roxburgh, Scotland: Beshara Publications, 1995), pp. 56–57.

108. Ibid., p. 23.

109. Ibid., p. 58.

the manifestation of the Essence and become, like the prophets, a true vicegerent (*khalīfah*) of God on earth.[110] Jīlī identifies himself with this class of men when he writes in a poem, "My essence is His Essence, and my name is His Name. My relation towards It is that I am engulfed in Union. In Reality we are not two essences in a single being, but the lover is himself the Beloved."[111] The negation "not two" used by Jīlī is reminiscent of the term *advaita* or non-dual. Here the unqualified Essence of man and God is but one Reality.

What is particularly interesting about Jīlī, as far as the present study is concerned, is that he knew and respected Hindus (whom he identifies with the brahmin caste) and the Vedas. He considered them to be among the "People of the Book" or those who have received Divine revelation and writes that "they testify to His Oneness of Being."[112] It is not a coincidence that an eminent Sufi metaphysician such as Jīlī saw in Hinduism and the Vedas the doctrine of

110. Ibid.

111. Ibid., p. 43.

112. According to Seyyed Hossein Nasr, "The Sufi master 'Abd al-Karīm al-Jīlī writes in his *al-Insān al-kāmil*: 'The people of the book are divided into many groups. As for the *barāhimah* [Hindus] they claim that they belong to the religion of Abraham and that they are of his progeny and possess special acts of worship.... The *barāhimah* worship God absolutely without [recourse to] prophet or messenger. In fact, they say there is nothing in the world of existence except that it be the created of God. They testify to His Oneness of Being, but deny the prophets and messengers completely. Their worship of the Truth is like that of the prophets before their prophetic mission. They claim to be the children of Abraham—upon whom be peace—and say that they possess a book written for them by Abraham—upon whom be peace—himself, except that they say that it came from His Lord. In it the truth of things is mentioned and it has five parts. As for the four parts they permit their reading to everyone. But as for the fifth part they do not allow its reading except to a few among them, because of its depth and unfathomableness. It is well known among them that whoever reads the fifth part of their book will of necessity come into the fold of Islam and enter into the religion of Muḥammad—upon whom be peace.' Al-Jīlī distinguishes between Hindu metaphysics and the daily practice of the Hindus and identifies especially their metaphysical doctrine with the doctrine of Divine Unity in Islam. His reference to the 'Fifth Veda' signifies precisely the inner identity of the esoteric and metaphysical doctrines of the two traditions. He, like other Sufis, sought to approach Hinduism through a metaphysical penetration into its mythological structure to reveal the presence of the One behind the many." *Sufi Essays*, pp. 139–140.

Unity because all Muslims believe that Heaven sent messengers and prophets to all nations. A Muslim sage well versed in the Islamic intellectual and spiritual tradition who has encountered authentic representatives of Hinduism or read their sacred and inspired texts, cannot but see in their vision of the Absolute some of the most sublime expressions of *tawḥīd* revealed to humanity.

Another Muslim sage who wrote extensively about the doctrine of Unity and was able to synthesize Islamic peripatetic philosophy, *Ishrāqī* philosophy and *Akbarī* gnosis, was Ṣadr al-Dīn Shīrāzī (d. 1571–1572) or Mullā Ṣadrā. He revived the idea of the unity of the knower, knowledge, and that which is Known, where the illuminated Intellect of the sage is mysteriously united with the Supreme Object. Mullā Ṣadrā also dealt extensively with *waḥdat al-wujūd*, as well as the gradation and principiality of Being. He writes,

> The first degree [of existence] is Pure Being which is without limit. This the gnostics call the Hidden Ipseity (*al-huwiyyat al-ghaybiyyah*), the absolutely Hidden (*al-ghayb al-muṭlaq*), and the Essence of Unity (*al-dhāt al-aḥadiyyah*). It is this being which has no name and no quality and which discursive knowledge and perception cannot reach, for everything that possesses name and description is a concept among others and is found in the mind or in apprehension. And all that which can be attained by knowledge and perception possesses a relation with that which is other than itself and is attached to that which is different than itself. Whereas It (Pure Being) is not like that, for it comes before all things and It is in itself without change or transformation. It is pure Hiddenness and Mystery and the absolutely unknowable except by means of its concomitants and effects. And as far as its sacred Essence is concerned, It cannot be limited or determined by any determination, even that of absoluteness, for this would place Its Being under the conditions of restrictions and particularizations such as particular differences and individuating characteristics. The concomitants of His Essence are conditions for Its manifestation and not the causes of Its existence, for were such to be the case it would cause imperfection in His Essence. This absoluteness is therefore negative, requiring the negation of all qualities and attributes from the root of His Essence, and the negation of relativity and change with respect to quality, name, determination or anything else, and

even the negation of these negations, since all these are concepts deduced by the mind. . . .[113]

Mullā Ṣadrā goes on to describe the relativity and deployment of Being in the temporal realm. It is clear from the above passage that one cannot confine or limit the Divine Essence. What is striking in the above passage is the insistence that the Essence "cannot be limited or determined by any determination, even that of absoluteness..." This unique insight reveals that being unlimited is itself a limitation that does not apply to the Supreme Principle. There are many implications that one can draw from this, including, for example, that God can "limit" Himself in the human heart or the world or appear as the Divine Word. Moreover, man, the world, and Revelation reside, prior to their existentiation, in an undifferentiated state *in divinis* or in the Mind of God, and thereafter manifest the infinitude of the Divine Reality. It is therefore a mistake to identify and reduce all sages who approach the Essence or Self through a particular Divine manifestation or Quality, including Being, as mere qualified non-dualists, since the unqualified and unlimited Essence can and indeed must manifest and reveal Itself through apparent limitations and qualifications. Mullā Ṣadrā, Ibn 'Arabī, Jīlī and other Muslims sages, dealt extensively with sacred cosmology and anthropology, or the gradation of Being in the various levels of existence because the Divine Reality or Essence does not exclude manifestation. If one fails to take into account the relative, its non-existent and existent aspects, one has not fully understood and appreciated the plenitude and infinitude of the Absolute. In Vedantic terms this means that one must see Ātman in *māyā* and *māyā* in Ātman. The world is not only an opaque or impenetrable veil that obscures our vision and obstructs our access to the Divine, but also a thin and transparent veil that reveals the Face of God and can lead to intimacy and union, ultimately to the knowledge that the world and the soul are in the final analysis nothing but God. The relative can only be known in light of the Absolute, however, which means that the world and the soul become intelligible through the

113. Seyyed Hossein Nasr, *Islamic Life and Thought*, pp. 177–178.

supreme knowledge of the Sacred and not as independent existents.[114]

The few passages cited in this chapter do not even begin to exhaust the diverse metaphysical expressions in the Islamic tradition that resemble Advaita Vedānta. They are but a few drops from the ocean of Divine wisdom. Moreover, the expressions themselves necessarily betray that ineffable and infinite Reality or Self that each of these sages approached through prayer, invocation, and contemplation of God in the inward depths of the heart. While one can only be grateful to those who articulated their knowledge of the Supreme Principle in poetry and prose, a perhaps greater number of Muslims sages realized the same inner meaning of *tawḥīd*, yet remained silent or only taught this sacred knowledge to their qualified disciples. Be that as it may, the vestiges of realization that have survived in oral or written form bear witness to that fact that ultimately the *shahādah* means, "There is no reality but the Reality" and "There is no self but the Self."

Some Conclusions

Jalāl al-Dīn Rūmī cautions in his *Mathnawī*:

> Pharaoh said, "I am God," and became despicable. Ḥallāj said, "I am God," and was saved. That "I" brought with it God's curse, but this "I" brought His Mercy, oh friend! . . . To say "I" at the wrong time is a curse, but to say it at the right time is a mercy. Without doubt Ḥallāj's "I" was a mercy, but that of Pharaoh became a curse. Note this![115]

True Self-realization requires that we first surrender our limited ego to God through the doctrines and rites of a revealed religion. For Muslims, this means that we must become a servant before the Lord and realize our existential poverty before the transcendent Reality or Self that alone is. This is possible through remaining faithful to God through following the conditions of the Sacred Law,

114. "But seek first His kingdom and His righteousness, and all these things will be added to you." (Matthew 6:33)

115. William C. Chittick, *The Sufi Path of Love: The Spiritual Teachings of Rumi* (Albany, NY: State University of New York Press, 1983), p. 193.

including the obligatory acts of worship, cultivating virtue and embarking on the spiritual path through the guidance of a living master. In Islam, both salvation and sanctification are made possible through the inner reality and grace of the Quran and the Prophet Muḥammad. God communicates His Reality and Presence to Muslims through the Book, which makes the realization of Unity and Union possible through the sacraments of the *shahādah* and the Supreme Name—both of which were revealed and fully realized through the Prophet or the Universal Man. Moreover, one must turn towards all of the Names and Qualities that God reveals Himself as in the Quran—especially the Names of Mercy—if one is to be delivered from the ego and the centrifugal forces of the world. In the path of knowledge there is nothing more essential than Divine Love, which is like the warmth of the Sun that indicates the direction and source of Light. When we remember God through the inner and outer dimensions of religion, the presence of the Beloved in the heart can be perceived. If we are persistent, God may unveil the secret that His Identity, the Supreme Identity, is our own true Identity. Then the soul and its longings and the mind and its distractions will be seen as peripheral in relation to the Divine Center in the heart. Through a process of reintegration, all of our faculties can harmoniously reflect and radiate the Divine Reality or Self in the world, despite the necessary limitations or gradations associated with manifestation. The Unity or non-duality of the Self is the ultimate meaning of the *shahādah* and its realization remains accessible through Islam and Sufism.

Following the Quran and the *Sunnah*, countless Muslim sages and saints have disclosed the inner meaning of the doctrine of *tawḥīd* through their teachings and presence. Among contemporary Muslim sages, René Guénon and Frithjof Schuon benefited from the wisdom of both Sufism and Advaita Vedānta and unveiled the metaphysical doctrines of Islam and Hinduism, as well as the sapiential doctrines of other traditions. One might conclude that these sages have done for the Islamic tradition, the Quran and its quintessence the *shahādah*, what Shankara did for Hinduism, the Vedas and the *mahāvākyas*, by exposing in explicit fashion the doctrine of and way to the Self. They maintain that there is only one true

Reality, one Self in the heart of every man and woman, whether from the East or the West. True charity and the peace we seek with our neighbors, including other religions and cultures, is ultimately based on the inner realization that there is One Universal Self underlying our outward diversity. Thus we should love our neighbor as ourself because our neighbor is also our true Self. Through an initiatic and contemplative discipline—in the context of an orthodox religion—we can begin to realize the heights and depths of Divinity, which is the realization of God as such and an awareness of God in the heart.

4

Christic Sanctity in Islam

> Everything that the Holy Scriptures say about Christ is equally true of every good and divine man.[1]
>
> —Meister Eckhart

> The learned are the heirs of the prophets.
>
> —The Prophet of Islam

Few contemporary Christian or Muslim scholars have taken note of the special role that Jesus ('Īsā in Arabic) plays in the Quran, *Ḥadīth*, Sufism, and in the lives of certain Muslim saints or friends of God throughout Islamic history.[2] We read in the Quran: "Verily the Mes-

1. Frithjof Schuon, *The Transcendent Unity of Religions*, p. 119.

2. For a fine summary of Jesus in the Islamic tradition as a whole, see Neal Robinson's *Christ in Islam and Christianity* (Albany, New York: State University of New York Press, 1991). Other notable exceptions are cited throughout this chapter. It must be stressed at the outset that Sufism is based primarily on the inner teachings and presence of the Quran and soul of the Prophet Muḥammad. Therefore, the teachings and presence of Jesus or any of the pre-Islamic prophets in Sufism must be seen as one element within the basic structure of the Islamic tradition and not an optional prophet or path that excludes the authority and teachings of the Quran, the Prophet Muḥammad, or the essential aspects of the Islamic Law. If from the Islamic perspective the Prophet of Islam came to revive humanity's awareness of the totality of religion, Jesus can be said to represent the quintessential aspects of the Quran and the teachings of the Prophet Muḥammad that are associated with the spiritual path (*ṭarīqah*), God consciousness (*iḥsān*) or Sufism. However, the Quran and the Prophet of Islam also instituted a Divine Law or *Sharī'ah* for Muslims, which is comparable to the teachings of Moses or the *Halakhah* in Judaism. Islam is in fact based on the harmony between the Divine Law and spiritual path, and can be said to strike a balance between the teachings of Moses and Jesus and how these messages have crystallized in Judaism and Christianity.

siah, Jesus son of Mary, was only a messenger of God, and His Word, that He committed to Mary, and a Spirit from Him. . . ." (4:171) The Arabic revelation also states: "O Mary, truly God gives thee glad tidings of a Word from Him, whose name is the Messiah, Jesus son of Mary, high honored in this world and the Hereafter, and one of those brought nigh [unto God]." (3:45) While Jesus is a prophet and messenger of God in Islam and not a Divine incarnation, it is highly significant that the Quran refers to Jesus as the "Word of God" (*kalimat Allāh*), the "Spirit of God" (*rūḥ Allāh*), and the "Messiah" (*al-Masīḥ*). Jesus as the Word or Logos in Christianity and Islam is analogous to the Quran in Islam, while the Virgin Mary and Muḥammad the unlettered Prophet (*al-nabī al-ummī*) both received their respective Divine revelations from the Angel Gabriel. Therefore, in Islam the Quran itself is the closest reality to Jesus—each being the central Divine theophany and a unique manifestation of the uncreated Logos for a particular human collectivity. Jesus is also an objective manifestation of the Divine Spirit or Breath that God blew into Adam and his progeny. In the human microcosm the Spirit (*al-rūḥ*) is a higher faculty that must be employed through spiritual poverty and the sacrament of prayer to restrain the lower self (*al-nafs*). Through spiritual practice man begins to identify himself with the Spirit. From a certain point of view the Spirit is the Jesus of one's being, which is mysteriously connected to God like a ray from the Sun. It is worth highlighting the fact that Jesus is also referred to as the Messiah (*al-Masīḥ*) in the Quran and Muslims expect his Second Coming after the appearance of the Mahdī, who is discussed in detail in the following chapter. It is from this standpoint that Jesus is envisaged as the "Universal Seal of Sanctity" by Ibn 'Arabī, bestowing wisdom and guidance not only in the past and present, but also in the future before the Day of Judgment.

The Quran also recalls the preeminent status of the Virgin Mary: "O Mary, truly God has chosen thee and purified thee, and has chosen thee above the women of the worlds." (3:42)[3] In *sūrat Maryam* or the Chapter of Mary in the Quran we also read,

3. Frithjof Schuon remarks, "A striking characteristic of the 'Isan message is its Marian or Maryaman dimension: in the Quran, Jesus and Mary are in fact closely

> She [Mary] said: "How should I have a boy when no man has touched me, nor have I been unchaste?" He [the Angel Gabriel] said, "Thus has thy Lord decreed, 'It is easy for Me. And [it is thus] that We might make him a sign unto mankind, and a mercy from Us. And it is a matter decreed.'" (19:20–21)

While the Virgin Birth is maintained in the Quran, the *Ḥadīth* also support the Immaculate Conception. According to the Prophet Muḥammad, "Hardly a single descendent of Adam is born without Satan touching him at the moment of his birth. . . . The only exceptions are Mary and her son." The Prophet is also reported to have said,

> If anyone testifies that there is no god but the One God who has no associates; that Muḥammad is His servant and His Messenger; that Jesus is God's servant and Messenger, His Word addressed to Mary and a Spirit from God; that Paradise really exists and that Hell really exists, God will cause him to enter Paradise regardless of his actions.[4]

While there are marked differences between Islam and Christianity—which in fact enable these two great religions to remain distinct—such as their theological and soteriological doctrines and understanding of the Crucifixion, Jesus has an esteemed and pivotal position in Islam and Sufism that is wed to the Quran and the spiritual substance of the Prophet Muḥammad. Many Sufis have spoken about the spiritual function of Jesus in Islam as the prophet of inwardness, such as Abū Ḥāmid Ghazzālī and Jalāl al-Dīn Rūmī, while a number of the friends of God throughout Islamic history have manifested an unmistakable resemblance to Jesus, including Ḥusayn ibn 'Alī and Manṣūr Ḥallāj, who are discussed in detail

linked, to the point of appearing almost as a unique and indivisible manifestation. Christ is 'Jesus son of Mary'—'Īsā ibn Maryam—and the Quran expresses this unity 'Jesus-Mary' in these terms: 'And We (Allah) made the son of Mary and his Mother to be a (miraculous) sign, and We gave them refuge on a height offering tranquility (and safety) and watered with springs.' (23:50)." *Dimensions of Islam*, pp. 82–83.

4. *The Sayings of Muhammad*, trans. by Neal Robinson, p. 35.

below.[5] In the words of Frithjof Schuon,

> The Quran repeatedly quotes the names of earlier prophets and relates their stories; this must have a meaning for our spiritual life, as the Quran itself attests. It can happen indeed that a Sufi is attached—within the very framework of the Muḥammadan Way, which is his by definition—to some pre-Islamic prophet; in other words the Sufi places himself under the symbol, influence, affective direction of a prophet who personifies a congenial vocation. Islam sees in Christ—Sayyidnā ʿĪsā—the personification of renunciation, interiorization, contemplative and solitary sanctity, Union; and more than one Sufi has claimed this spiritual filiation.[6]

Christic Sanctity According to Ibn ʿArabī

Among the clearest proofs of the influence of Jesus and the presence of Christic sanctity in the Islamic tradition is found in the life and writings of Muḥyī al-Dīn ibn ʿArabī. It would be impossible for us to exhaust the understanding and significance of Jesus in the writings of Ibn ʿArabī, which includes a penetrating Quranic based Christology in his *Fuṣūṣ al-ḥikam* and references to Jesus as "the Universal Seal of Sanctity."[7] Our intended purpose here is to examine the references to Jesus in the writings of the Shaykh that help to define a

5. Jalāl al-Dīn Rūmī states in his *Dīwān-i Shams*: "Only when the 'Jesus of the soul' turns away from the world may one soar in spiritual flight beyond the azure vault of the skies." Javad Nurbakhsh, *Jesus in the Eyes of the Sufis*, trans. Terry Graham, Leonard Lewisohn, and Hamid Mashkuri (London: Khaniqahi Nimatullahi Publications, 1992), p. 56. According to Tarif Khalidi, "[Abū Ḥāmid] Ghazzālī had a particular and pronounced interest in Jesus, whom he designated 'prophet of the heart,' enshrining him as one of the central figures of Sufi spirituality." *The Muslim Jesus* (Cambridge, Massachusetts: Harvard University Press, 2003), p. 164.

6. Frithjof Schuon, *Sufism: Veil and Quintessence*, p. 122. Seyyed Hossein Nasr also writes, "There is in fact a special type of 'Christic' wisdom (*ḥikmah ʿīsawiyyah*) within Islam, consisting of elements of inwardness, anteriority and a kind of Divine elixir or nectar which can be seen in certain forms of Sufism." *Islamic Life and Thought*, p. 211.

7. *The Ringstones of Wisdom* (*Fuṣūṣ al-ḥikam*), trans. by Caner K. Dagli, pp. 157–175; Michel Chodkiewicz, *Seal of the Saints: Prophethood and Sainthood in the Doctrine of Ibn ʿArabī*, trans. by Liadain Sherrard (Cambridge: The Islamic Texts Society, 1993), pp. 116–127.

theoretical framework for the manifestation of Christic sanctity in the lives of certain Muslim saints, and Imam Ḥusayn and Manṣūr Ḥallāj in particular.

In Ibn 'Arabī's perspective, each saint or friend (*walī*) of God takes his station from a particular prophet, including, for example, Adam, Enoch, Noah, Abraham, Moses, David, Jesus, and Muḥammad.[8] In the writings of the Shaykh, one finds references to *Idrīsī* (Enoch-like), *Ibrāhīmī* (Abraham-like), *Mūsawī* (Moses-like), *'Īsawī* (Jesus-like or Christic), and of course Muḥammadan saints, who as Muslims inherit their sanctity from a particular prophet through the intermediary of the Prophet of Islam.[9] William Chittick writes concerning this doctrine,

> In [Ibn 'Arabī's] view, every age must have at least 124,000 friends of God, one heir for each prophet. The prophetic inheritances delineate the possible modes of authentic experience and correct knowledge of God, the universe, and the human soul. In other words, to attain true knowledge, one must know and act in accordance with a paradigm of human perfection embodied in a prophet. No one comes to know things as they are without these divinely appointed intermediaries.[10]

While the mark of a particular prophet is seen in the knowledge, station, qualities, and/or miracles that the saint displays, he follows the Law and spiritual path according to the Quran and *Sunnah* of the Prophet Muḥammad. Further, for Ibn 'Arabī all of the 124,000

8. It is important to note that Ibn 'Arabī's hagiology is primarily based upon a saint's nearness to God. An inheritance is thus bestowed through a Divine Name and secondarily or concomitantly through a particular prophet via the Prophet of Islam. For Ibn 'Arabī, each created being is determined by a particular Divine Name that governors it. Claude Addas states, "every being is the servant (*'abd*) of a Name which is its lord (*rabb*), and its knowledge of God will never go beyond the Name that governs it." *Quest for the Red Sulphur*, p. 281. Only the saint is completely effaced before his Divine Name and therefore reflects—to an eminent degree in creation—that Name and Quality in the cosmos.

9. *Seal of the Saints*, pp. 77, 106, 170.

10. William Chittick, *Ibn 'Arabi: Heir to the Prophets* (Oxford: Oneworld Publications, 2005), p. 14.

prophets are envisaged as aspects of the Prophet of Islam, and the highest level of sanctity is Muḥammadan sanctity or a saint who takes his station from the Prophet. Therefore, *'Īsawī* saints in Sufism derive their sanctity from Jesus and Muḥammad. Ibn 'Arabī states,

> Sometimes, as death approaches, the prophet from whom the person has inherited will be disclosed to him, for [as the Prophet said], "The possessors of knowledge are the heirs to the prophets." Hence as death approaches, he will see Jesus, Moses, Abraham, Muḥammad, or some other prophet. Some of them may pronounce the name of the prophet from whom they have inherited in joy when he comes to them, for the messengers are all among the felicitous. While dying, such a person will say "Jesus," or he will call him "Messiah," as God himself has done—this is what usually happens. Those present will hear the friend of God speak words of this sort and become suspicious, saying that at death he became a Christian and Islam was negated from him. Or he will name Moses or one of the Israelite prophets, and they will say that he became a Jew. But this person is one of the greatest possessors of felicity in God's eyes, for the common people never know this locus of witnessing, only the Folk of God, the possessors of unveilings.[11]

It is clear from the above passage that the Sufis who take their sanctity from Jesus, Moses or another prophet do not leave the religion of Islam. We do not mean to imply that a Christian or Jew cannot attain sanctity through Christianity or Judaism, for example, only that the Sufis reach this nearness to God through the Islamic tradition, within which the prophets and luminaries of the Bible remain spiritually alive and accessible.

Ibn 'Arabī states regarding Jesus, "He was my first teacher, the master through whom I returned to God."[12] Running parallel with and even initially preceding his study of Sufism in texts and with living teachers were his visions and dreams of the prophets and

11. William Chittick, *Imaginal Worlds*, p. 100.
12. *Quest for the Red Sulphur*, p. 39.

saints in the imaginal world (*ʿālam al-khayāl*).[13] The Shaykh also writes,

> It was at his [Jesus'] hands that I was converted (i.e. turned towards God and the spiritual path); he prayed for me that I should persist in religion (*dīn*) in this low world and in the other, and he called me his beloved. He ordered me to practice renunciation (*zuhd*) and self-denial (*tajrīd*).[14]

As a result of the spiritual influence of Jesus, Ibn ʿArabī renounced the world, including women for his first eighteen years of wayfaring. Ibn ʿArabī states of himself, "I am—without any doubt—the Seal of [Muḥammadan] Sainthood, in my capacity as heir to the Hashimite [Muḥammad] and the Messiah."[15] While Ibn ʿArabī eventually realized that he was the heir of the Prophet of Islam and all of the prophets, he entered the spiritual path as an *ʿĪsawī* or Christic saint. Likewise, is several places Ibn ʿArabī identifies other saints as *ʿĪsawī* or those who "walk in the footsteps of Jesus" (*ʿalā qadam ʿĪsā*), such as the disciples and apostles of Christ, Ibn ʿArabī's first living master Abu'l-ʿAbbās ʿUryabī, Bāyazīd Basṭāmī and Manṣūr Ḥallāj.[16] In Ibn ʿArabī's poem the *Tarjumān al-ashwāq*, the Shaykh writes of the female saint Niẓām, "Her speech

13. Michel Chodkiewicz states, "For Ibn ʿArabī, the most perfect illuminating knowledge first takes place in the sphere of intelligibles, of pure spirits free of matter and of form. It is in a second stage, and only then, that it "takes a body" in the *ʿālam al-khayāl*, and it is then that it takes on words and images that will allow its transmission to those who do not have access to this universe of pure light." *An Ocean Without Shore*, p. 83.

14. *Quest for the Red Sulphur*, p. 39.

15. Ibid., p. 79. In Ibn ʿArabī's hagiology, Jesus is "the Universal Seal of Sanctity" because of his function at the end of time, which corresponds to the closing of an eminent degree of sanctity associated with the *afrād* or solitary saints, while Ibn ʿArabī himself is—despite reservations even from other Sufis—"the Seal of Muḥammadan Sanctity" or the last friend of God to inherit the fullness of Muḥammadan sanctity, which is the sum and synthesis of prophetic inheritances and sanctity. On this delicate question, see M. Chodkiewicz "The Three Seals," in *Seal of the Saints*, pp. 116–127.

16. *Seal of the Saints*, pp. 17, 75, 81; *The Ringstones of Wisdom (Fuṣūṣ al-ḥikam)*, p. 164.

restores to life, as tho' she, in giving life thereby, were Jesus."[17] Other prominent Sufis who have been identified as *'Īsawī* throughout Islamic history include 'Ayn al-Quḍāt Hamadānī, who was martyred as a heretic at the age of thirty-three, 'Ubayd Allāh Aḥrār, Siti Jenar from Java, and the Algerian Shaykh Aḥmad al-'Alawī.[18] Concerning the particular qualities of Christic saints, Michel Chodhiewicz states:

> The *'Īsawī* saint sees the best in all things. This is also true of Muḥammad, inasmuch as he is the sum of all the prophetic types and consequently integrates within himself the particular virtues of each: on passing by a decaying carcass, his companions said: 'How it stinks!', but the Prophet said: 'How white are its teeth!' But in the case of the Muḥammad-type of saint, the universal compassion that results from this perception of the positive quality of created beings, of the beauty or perfection which is inherent in them, is not made nakedly manifest as in the case of the Christ-like saint. God is compassion; but He is also Rigour, and the latter aspect may at times veil the former in the behavior of the Prophet of Islam or of his heirs.[19]

One should note that there is precedence for this doctrine in the traditions of the Prophet of Islam regarding his family and close companions. We read in an important *ḥadīth*, "The learned (*al-'ulamā'*) are the heirs of the prophets."[20] In another *ḥadīth* the Prophet tells his son-in-law 'Alī, "Are you not pleased that your position in relation to me is that of Aaron in relation to Moses?"[21] The Prophet also said of a close companion of his, "The sky has not cast shade, nor the earth raised up green plants growing luxuriantly, for anyone who more resembles Jesus son of Mary in truthfulness and trustworthiness than Abū Dharr."[22]

What is clear from the writings of Ibn 'Arabī and alluded to in the

17. Muḥyī al-Dīn ibn 'Arabī, *The Interpreter of Desires* (*Tarjumān al-ashwāq*), pp. 49; see also, ibid., pp. 51, 52, 56, 123.

18. *Seal of the Saints*, pp. 82–83.

19. Ibid., p. 80.

20. Ibid., p. 51.

21. *The Sayings of Muhammad*, p. 38.

22. Ibid.

Ḥadīth is that certain Muslim saints inherit a mode of sanctity from a particular prophet. What is of utmost importance for this study and which may illuminate a point of convergence between Islam and Christianity are those Muslim saints whose lives, sayings, and legacies bear traces of Christic sanctity. While it is impossible to document all of the *'Īsawī* saints throughout Islamic history, we have chosen two additional figures—Ḥusayn ibn 'Alī and Manṣūr Ḥallāj—who closely resemble Jesus and who manifest a type of sanctity in the early centuries of Islam that was only written about and analyzed in detail later. Moreover, Ḥusayn and Ḥallāj also inherited their sanctity from the Prophet of Islam, which demonstrates that the great exemplars of Islamic spirituality—like Ibn 'Arabī himself—are intimately connected to the souls of both the Prophet and the Messiah.

Ḥusayn ibn 'Alī

Ḥusayn ibn 'Alī (d. 680), also known as Sayyid al-shuhadā' or "lord among the martyrs," was the grandson of the Prophet, the Third Shī'ite Imam, and a Pole (*quṭb*) in many Sufi orders such as the Qādiriyyah and Shādhiliyyah. He was the son of Fāṭimah, the daughter of the Prophet, and 'Alī ibn Abī Ṭālib (d. 661), the Fourth Caliph and First Shī'ite Imam. His body is buried in Karbalā' in present day Iraq, while his head rests at the center of Cairo in Egypt. He is honored, revered, and mourned by Shī'ites and many Sunnis across the Muslim world, despite their differences. It must be stressed at the outset that Ḥusayn is also revered by classical and contemporary Sufis (who are either Shī'ite or Sunni). In a poem of Jalāl al-Dīn Rūmī we read,

> In the fire of its yearning, my heart keeps up its cries,
> Hoping that a welcoming call will come to it from the direction of union
> My heart is Ḥusayn and separation Yazīd—
> My heart has been martyred two hundred times
> In the desert of torment and affliction (*karb-o-balā*)...[23]

23. Trans. William C. Chittick, "Rūmī's view of the Imam Ḥusayn," *Al-Serat: A Journal of Islamic Studies* XII (Spring and Autumn 1986), p. 11.

Annemarie Schimmel cites the words by 'Aṭṭār, "Be either a Ḥusayn or a Manṣūr," and goes on to write:

> That is, Ḥusayn b. Manṣūr al-Ḥallāj, the arch-martyr of mystical Islam, who was cruelly executed in Baghdad in 922. He, like his namesake Ḥusayn b. 'Alī, becomes a model for the Sufi; he is the suffering lover, and in quite a number of Sufi poems his name appears alongside that of Ḥusayn: both were enamoured by God, both sacrificed themselves on the Path of divine love, both are therefore the ideal lovers of God whom the pious should strive to emulate.[24]

While one cannot exclusively interpret Imam Ḥusayn's life and teachings in light of Sufism, Sunni and Shī'ite Sufis remember Ḥusayn as a proto-Sufi master or gnostic (*'ārif*) who—along with the Prophet and the other Imams—transmitted what became known as Sufism or *'irfān* to later generations. Therefore, Ḥusayn's legacy relates to the inner dimensions of both Shī'ite and Sunni Islam.[25]

Before examining the close resemblance between Ḥusayn and Jesus, it is necessary to look at the similarities that exist between Ḥusayn's mother Fāṭimah and the Virgin Mary. According to the Prophet's wife 'Ā'ishah, "I have never come across a greater personality than that of Fāṭimah except that of her father, the Prophet of

24. Annemarie Schimmel, "Karbala and the Imam Husayn in Persian and Indo-Muslim literature," *Al-Serat* XII, p. 31. M.A. Amir-Moezzi go so far as to claim: "As far as al-Ḥusayn's case is concerned, to our knowledge none of his successors interpreted his presence in Karbalā' as being a "political" act aimed at upsetting the powers that be. According to his own successors, the act of the Imam was of a friend of God (*walī*) fulfilling his destiny according to the will of the Beloved (*mawlā*)." *The Divine Guide in Early Shi'ism*, p. 66.

25. Some might raise the objection that including Ḥusayn or Ḥallāj in this study is anachronistic by applying a doctrine expressed by a scholar in the thirteenth century to figures who lived hundreds of years before him. One must keep in mind that other central doctrines associated with Ibn 'Arabī and his school, such as *waḥdat al-wujūd* (the transcendent Unity of Being) and *al-insān al-kāmil* (the Universal Man), are essentially esoteric commentaries on the first and second *shahādah* (the Islamic testimony of faith) which were revealed during the lifetime of the Prophet. We do not claim that Ibn 'Arabī's writings or those of any sage fully exhaust the inner meaning of Divine Unity, prophecy or sanctity, but simply that they begin to illuminate and make explicit doctrines and realities that were present before their appearance in his writings.

Islam."[26] Fāṭimah (d. 633) has frequently been likened to the Virgin, both of whom are seen as the most saintly women in Islam, along with the Prophet's first wife Khadījah and Āsiyah the wife of Pharaoh.[27] Like Mary, Fāṭimah was given the epithet al-Batūl or "the Virgin", which remained even after her marriage to 'Alī because of her inward purity and asceticism.[28] It is thus fitting to describe Fāṭimah as the first *Maryamī* or Marian saint in Islam, a term that was used by Frithjof Schuon following the hagiology of Ibn 'Arabī.[29]

Both Fāṭimah in Islam and the Virgin Mary in Christianity suffered the loss of their sons, in the case of Fāṭimah her three sons: Ḥasan, Ḥusayn, and Muḥsin. When Shī'ites imagine and reenact the tragedy of Karbalā' they frequently remember and offer prayers of sympathy for the mother of the Imams and her grief.[30] James Bill and John Williams observe,

26. Robert Frager, *The Wisdom of Islam* (Hauppauge, New York: Barron's Educational Series, Inc., 2002), p. 117.

27. Camille Adams Helminski observes, "It is interesting to note that one of the most important appearances of the Virgin Mary in recent times is 'Our Lady of Fatima.' Mary appeared to three young children in Portugal in 1917, near the small village of Fatima, named after the Prophet Muḥammad's daughter, and was subsequently witnessed there by tens of thousands of people. Since that event, numerous Christians worldwide address the Virgin Mary in prayer as 'Our Lady of Fatima'. . ." *Women of Sufism*, p. 9.

28. Ibid., p. 9.

29. Frithjof Schuon, *Christianity/Islam: Perspectives on Esoteric Ecumenism*, p. 204. Schuon's chapter "The Wisdom of Sayyidatnā Maryam" in his book *Dimensions of Islam* also seems to follow the model of Ibn 'Arabī's *Fuṣūṣ al-ḥikam* and can perhaps be seen as an addendum. *Dimensions of Islam*, pp. 88–101. One must add that according to the Quran, the prophet Zachariah followed the Way of the Virgin during her own life and is thus the first Marian or *Maryamī* saint, while of course also being a prophet. Fāṭimah is the first *Maryamī* saint after the descent of the Quran to the Prophet of Islam, while the Prophet Muḥammad's own sanctity contains all of the modalities of sanctity attributed to the pre-Islamic prophets, including the Virgin. It would, however, be misleading to suggest that he was an *'Īsawī* or *Maryamī* to the exclusion of other modes of sanctity and the universal reality of sanctity which, at least for Muslims, he defines and embodies most perfectly.

30. It is true that Fāṭimah died well before the events at Karbalā' took place. Her posthumous grief is however honored. Moreover, she is seen by the faithful as possessing knowledge of future events and therefore knew that her sons would be martyred during her lifetime.

Suffering is a central element in the comparative study of Mary and Fāṭimah. Whereas Mary suffered at the foot of the cross upon which her son was crucified, Fāṭimah's image is bracketed by the traumatic deaths of her father, her husband, and her son.[31]

Fāṭimah is venerated across the Muslim world as al-Zahrā' or "the Resplendent," al-Ṭāhirah or "the Pure," al-Muḥaddithah or "the One Spoken to by Angels," and Umm Abī-hā or "Mother of her Father," because she cared for the Prophet after the death of her mother Khadījah.[32] If the cycle of prophecy was closed with the death of the Prophet Muḥammad, the cycle of sanctity in Islam was opened by him and continued through his enduring Light as it manifests through his daughter Fāṭimah and her descendents, both biological and spiritual.[33] In a manner similar to the Virgin Mary, Fāṭimah is often seen as a manifestation of Divine wisdom or *sophia* (*ḥikmah*) and a symbol for the universal soul (*al-nafs al-kulliyyah*) and the archetypal guarded tablet (*lawḥ al-maḥfūẓ*), which receives its words from Heaven.[34] According to Bill and Williams,

> Both Fāṭimah and the Virgin Mary stand as female members of a central holy family; both are considered immaculate and impeccable; both are extensions of their fathers and sons; both are mothers of sorrows. Whereas Mary links her son Jesus with the human race, Fāṭimah is linked in the minds of Shī'ī believers with her father Muḥammad, her husband 'Alī, and her sons Ḥasan and Ḥusayn. In Shī'ī legend, the figures of Mary and Fāṭimah and Jesus and Ḥusayn become curiously intertwined. Fāṭimah is sometimes referred to by Shī'īs as al-Maryam al-kubrā (the Greater Mary),

31. James A. Bill and John Alden Williams, *Roman Catholics and Shi'i Muslims: Prayer, Passion, and Politics* (Chapel Hill, North Carolina: The University of North Carolina Press, 2002), p. 53.

32. This last name also suggests a close spiritual connection between Fāṭimah's sons and the Prophet of Islam.

33. S.H. Nasr observes, "According to the famous *Ḥadīth-i kisā'* (the tradition of the garment) the Prophet called Fāṭimah along with 'Alī, Ḥasan, and Ḥusayn and placed a cloak upon them in such a manner that it covered them. The cloak symbolizes the transmission of the universal *walāyah* of the Prophet in the form of partial *walāyah* (*walāyat-i fāṭimiyyah*) to Fāṭimah and through her to the Imāms who were her descendents." *Sufi Essays*, p. 109.

34. Henry Corbin, *Spiritual Body and Celestial Earth*, p. 64.

and Jesus is thought of as "in some sense, the brother of Ḥusayn."[35]

In Shīʿism, Ḥusayn's martyrdom is seen as a tragic, yet providential act to awaken and revive the Muslim community. Initially one of the Prophet Muḥammad's chief adversaries was the Meccan aristocrat Abū Sufyān, who formally accepted Islam in the year 630 when Mecca was captured by the Prophet and his army. Abū Sufyān's son Muʿāwiyah would later fight ʿAlī in 657 for the Caliphate, which Muʿāwiyah eventually gained after the martyrdom of ʿAlī in 661. Muʿāwiyah then promised to hand over the Caliphate to ʿAlī's first son Ḥasan, but instead gave it to his own son Yazīd. Interestingly, the grandson of Abū Sufyān and the son of Muʿāwiyah—Yazīd—would become the central antagonist in the life of Ḥusayn.

While Sunnis believe that both Abū Sufyān and Muʿāwiyah died as Muslims, Yazīd's status is often questioned. In Shīʿism, Muʿāwiyah and Yazīd are seen as usurpers whose political ambitions blinded them to the pure Imam of their time. This is especially true of Yazīd, who can be likened to Pontius Pilate who asks Jesus in the Gospel, "Art thou the King of the Jews?" (John 18:33) In other words, "Are you a threat to my power?" In the Gospel of John, Jesus replies, "Thou sayest that I am a king. To this end was I born, and for this cause came I into the world, that I should bear witness unto the Truth. Every one that is of the truth heareth my voice." To which Pilate replied, "What is truth?" (John 18:37–38) In a similar manner, Yazīd was threatened by Ḥusayn and demanded that the grandson of the Prophet swear allegiance to him. Ḥusayn's subsequent resistance and martyrdom is seen as an act of submission to the Truth. Yazīd is remembered by Shīʿites as a drunken leader, prone to concupiscence and vice, who came to power because of nepotism and political ambition. Yazīd and his army can also be interpreted symbolically as the lower self or *nafs* in man, which the Spirit or Intellect—outwardly represented by Ḥusayn—must battle in the greater *jihād* (*al-jihād al-akbar*). In the words of Jalāl al-Dīn Rūmī,

35. *Roman Catholics and Shīʿi Muslims*, p. 53.

Religion is your Ḥusayn,
While desires and hopes are pigs and dogs—
Yet you kill the first through thirst and feed these two.
How can you keep on cursing the wicked Yazīd and Shimr?
You are a Shimr and a Yazīd for your own Ḥusayn.[36]

In Shīʿite traditions, Ḥusayn is seen as possessing knowledge of the events to come at Karbalāʾ, yet accepts his fate as the will of Heaven, because according to the Quran to accept injustice is a greater evil than slaughter. (2:191)[37] He could not swear allegiance and acquiesce to the illegitimate rule of Yazīd when he felt the weight of responsibility before God and the Prophet to live according to the Quran, *Sunnah*, and the Divine principles of Truth and Justice. Thus the stage was set for a confrontation whose consequences still reverberate to this day. Below ʿAllāmah Ṭabāṭabāʾī summarizes the events at Karbalāʾ:

> On the tenth day of Muḥarram of the year 61/680 the Imam lined up before the enemy with his small band of followers, less than ninety persons consisting of forty of his companions, thirty some members of the army of the enemy that joined him during the night and day of war, and his Hashimite family of children, brothers, nephews, nieces, and cousins. That day they all fought from morning until their final breath, and the Imam, the young Hashimites and the companions were all martyred. Among those killed were two children of Imam Ḥasan, who were only thirteen and eleven years old; and a five year old child and a suckling baby of Imam Ḥusayn.
>
> The army of the enemy, after ending the war, plundered the *ḥaram* of the Imam and burned his tents. They decapitated the bodies of the martyrs, denuded them and threw them to the ground without burial. Then they moved the members of the *ḥaram*, all of whom were helpless women and girls, along with the heads of the

36. "Rūmī's view of the Imam Ḥusayn," *Al-Serat* XII, p. 5. Shimr is the commander of the army of Yazīd who personally beheaded the Imam, killed most of his male relatives and companions, and forced the bound survivors, mostly women and children, to cross the desert from Iraq to Syria on foot.

37. ʿAllāmah Ṭabāṭabāʾī, *Shiʿite Islam*, trans. Seyyed Hossein Nasr (Albany, New York: State University of New York Press, 1977), p. 197–198.

martyrs, to Kūfa. Among the prisoners there were three male members: a twenty-two year old son of Imam Ḥusayn who was very ill and unable to move, namely 'Alī ibn Ḥusayn, the forth Imam; his four year old son, Muḥammad ibn 'Alī, who became the fifth Imam; and finally Ḥasan Muthannā, the son of the second Imam who was also the son-in-law of Imam Ḥusayn and who, having been wounded during the war, lay among the dead. They found him near death and through the intercession of one of the generals did not cut off his head. Rather, they took him with the prisoners to Kūfa and from there to Damascus before Yazīd.[38]

The historical events and circumstances leading up to 'Āshūrā' (the tenth day of the first Islamic month Muḥarram) have also been meticulously documented in S.M.H. Jafri's study *The Origins and Early Development of Shi'a Islam*, where the author demonstrates that Ḥusayn accepted his fate to awaken the Muslim community during the decadent Umayyad period. Concerning Ḥusayn, Jafri writes,

> He realized that mere force of arms would not have saved Islamic action and consciousness. To him it needed a shaking and jolting of hearts and feelings. This, he decided could only be achieved through sacrifice and sufferings. This should not be difficult to understand, especially for those who fully appreciate the heroic deeds and sacrifices of, for example, Socrates and Joan of Arc, both of whom embraced death for their ideals, and above all of the great sacrifice of Jesus Christ for the redemptive suffering of mankind.[39]

Regarding the martyrs the Quran states, "And deem not those slain in the way of God to be dead. Rather, they are alive with their Lord, provided for. . . ." (3:169) The memory of Karbalā' is etched in the hearts and minds of Shī'ites and many Sunnis. The events at Karbalā' were first narrated by the sister of Ḥusayn—Zaynab—in the very court of Yazīd, where she courageously confronted the Caliph for the massacre that was carried out against her family in

38. *Shi'ite Islam*, pp. 199–200.

39. S.H.M. Jafri, *The Origins and Early Development of Shi'a Islam* (Oxford: Oxford University Press, 2006), pp. 203–204.

Yazīd's name. The Prophet of Islam, the grandfather of Zaynab in fact said, "The best *jihād* is to speak a true word to a tyrannical ruler."[40]

During the month of Muḥarram the events at Karbalā' are dramatically retold by preachers, remembered by the faithful in processions, and reenacted in passion plays (*ta'ziyah*) by actors, all of which have remarkable parallels in the Christian world. The month of Muḥarram, culminating on the tenth day of 'Āshūrā', is one of the most widely observed days for Shī'ites on the Islamic calendar and is comparable to Good Friday and Easter among Christians.[41] Through their mourning, remembrance, and devotion, pious Shī'ites mystically participate in the martyrdom of Ḥusayn, which is seen as a meta-historical event on trans-national ground. According to a famous saying, "Every day is 'Āshūrā'; every land is Karbalā'." Ḥusayn's martyrdom at Karbalā' is a crystallized moment in time that reveals the nature of truth and falsehood, justice and injustice, and light and darkness in the daily lives of all Shī'ites. While the idea of redemptive suffering is foreign to Islam, the Shī'ite is strengthened in his faith by remembering the sacrifice, character and mission of the pure and holy martyr. According to Frithjof Schuon,

> After a certain fashion—and as an approximation only—Shī'ism is an "Islamic Christianity"; its fundamental theme is the "divine humanity" of its great saints, then the martyrdom of the uncomprehended light, and finally the sacramental presence of this light in the form of the Imamate.[42]

Schuon also observes,

> Shī'ism is a mysticism based upon the necessary defeat—changed ultimately into victory—of the earthly manifestation of the Logos,

40. *The Sayings of Muhammad*, p. 61.

41. Ramaḍān, the month in which the Quran was first revealed to the Prophet in 610 and which was consecrated in the Quran as the month of fasting for Muslims, is comparable to the celebration of Christmas for Christians.

42. Frithjof Schuon, *Islam and the Perennial Philosophy*, trans. J. Peter Hobson, p. 103. Schuon goes on to state, "Shī'ism is to Islam what Arianism is to Christianity, but in an inverted sense, since it accentuates the human Manifestation of God, whereas Arianism accentuates Transcendence." Ibid., p. 108

> and it is thereby linked to the mystery enunciated by the Gospel according to St. John: "And the light shineth in darkness and the darkness comprehended it not."[43]

While Islam, including Shīʿism, is opposed to the exclusive localization of the Divine Reality and emphasizes both the immanence and the transcendence of God, the Imam—like the Prophet before him—is seen as the Universal or Perfect Man (*al-insān al-kāmil*). He harmoniously reflects the Names and Attributes of the Divine Reality here on earth. If in Christianity God is anthropomorphic, in Islam—especially Shīʿism and Sufism—man is theomorphic. Moreover, the Light of the Imam is primarily seen as the Light of the Prophet Muḥammad. Therefore, neither Ḥusayn nor any of the Imams eclipse the Light of the Prophet but rather they reflect it as the Moon does the Sun in the night that follows the cycle of prophecy.

Some Shīʿite gnostics have also spoken of the "Imam of one's being."[44] The Imam is the objectification or personification of the Intellect and the Intellect or eye of the heart is the subjective Imam of the believer. The idea of the "Imam of one's being" closely corresponds to the image of Christ held in Orthodox Christianity, as well as in certain mystical currents of Catholicism and Protestantism, where Christ prays to the Father in the heart of the deified Christian. Ḥusayn and the Imams in general represent the highest faculty of intelligence or consciousness within man that is capable of discerning truth from falsehood, light from darkness, and directly knowing Ultimate Reality. In the words of M.A. Amir-Moezzi,

> What is seen with the "eye of the heart" is a light (*nūr*), or more precisely several modalities of light (*anwār*). It is located at the center of the heart and is sometimes identified with Hiero-Intelligence (*al-ʿaql*): "Hiero-Intelligence in the heart is like a lamp in the center of the house." *ʿAql* is the means of vision with the heart and in this case it is a synonym of *īmān*, faith, but at the same time its reality (*ḥaqīqah*) constitutes the object of vision. It is known

43. Ibid., p. 98.
44. Seyyed Hossein Nasr, *Sufi Essays*, pp. 66, 111.

that the reality of *'aql* is identical to the Imam: *'aql* is the interior Imam of the believer. . . .[45]

Amir-Moezzi goes on to quote the grandson of Ḥusayn, Muḥammad Bāqir, "The light of the Imam in the hearts of the faithful is more brilliant than that of the brilliant day star."[46] It is this spiritual archetype that summons man to his higher nature and is in fact identical to it. The Imam helps to orient man's gaze inward towards his heart and the angelic world, which is the locus of the Divine Presence, inspiration (*ilhām*) and sacred knowledge (*'irfān/ma'rifah*). In *'irfānī* Shī'ite epistemology, it is through the Intellect or the "Imam of one's being" that one is guided and oriented towards the Divine Reality.

The life, spiritual function and teachings of Ḥusayn, as well as Fāṭimah and the rest of the Imams, possess striking similarities to the life and message of Jesus, the Virgin, and the whole of Christianity. Nevertheless, there are also certain important differences between Shī'ism and Christianity. While the Imam is central in Shī'ism, he is not seen as the Son of God, but rather the spiritual, intellectual, and political leader of the Muslim *ummah* or community. Moreover, while Shī'ism emphasizes the martyrdom of Ḥusayn, Islam is not based on redemptive suffering, but on faith and submission to the will of God, and correct action that issues from that faith and submission. Furthermore, Ḥusayn's struggle with the sword does not outwardly correspond to the non-violence espoused and practiced by Christ. Despite these differences and many others, the Imam and the Messiah share a common archetype, which is uniquely reflected in their respective religious universes. Ḥusayn and Jesus were born from the most saintly women, bore witness to the Truth with their lives, suffered persecution and

45. *The Divine Guide in Early Shi'ism*, p. 48.

46. Ibid., p. 49. These teachings are also found in Sufism. We read in a poem by Manṣūr Ḥallāj: "For the Lights of religion's Light are Lights in men, for the Secret, Secrets in secret depths of souls, and for Being, in beings, is a Being that saith 'Be'. Reserved for it my heart is, guided, and chosen. O ponder what I say with the Intellect's eye. Keen is the Intellect of hearing and of insight." Trans. Martin Lings, *Sufi Poems*, p. 30.

martyrdom, and are remembered and mourned by faithful Muslims and Christians to this day. Therefore, Ḥusayn, while primarily reflecting the light of the Prophet Muḥammad, can also be thought of as a Christic or *'Īsawī* saint from the first Islamic century.

Manṣūr Ḥallāj

Al-Ḥusayn ibn Manṣūr al-Ḥallāj (d. 922) was born in the province of Fars in Iran, and is among the most studied and celebrated Sufis in the Islamic world and the West. The name Ḥallāj refers to his father's occupation as a carder of wool.[47] This name is highly symbolic because the Arabic word *ṣūf* means "wool", and was most likely used to refer to the early Sufis as ascetics and wearers of woolen garments. Hence, Ḥallāj revealed the doctrine of Sufism and his own inner secret in the most explicit manner possible by discarding the garment that concealed his inner reality. Ḥallāj was a disciple of Sahl Tustarī and Abu'l-Qāsim Junayd, and is one of the central figures associated with the formative period of Sufism and the school of Baghdad.

His life and teachings have been extensively studied by the French scholar Louis Massignon in his seminal four-volume work, *La Passion de Ḥusayn ibn Manṣūr Ḥallāj* that was later translated into English by Herbert Mason as *The Passion of al-Ḥallāj.*[48] Seyyed Hossein Nasr calls Massignon, "Perhaps the greatest academic scholar of Islam that the West has ever produced."[49] Massignon was a Catholic scholar of Islam, Shī'ism and Sufism, who had a deep understanding of and sympathy for Islamic spirituality. Concerning Massignon's own mystical connection to Ḥallāj, Nasr writes,

> The fact that Ḥallāj in a sense 'visited' Massignon inwardly is not at all an academic question; rather, it is a providential event. Ḥallāj

47. *Roman Catholics and Shi'i Muslims*, p. 88.

48. Louis Massignon, *La Passion de Ḥusayn ibn Manṣūr Ḥallāj: martyr mystique de l'Islam exécuté à Baghdad le 26 mars 922; etude d'histoire religieuse* (Paris: Gallimard, 1975); and *The Passion of al-Ḥallāj: Mystic and Martyr of Islam*, trans. Herbert Mason (Princeton, NJ: Princeton University Press, 1982). See also, Mason's abridged translation, *Ḥallāj: Mystic and Martyr* (Princeton, NJ: Princeton University Press, 1994).

49. Seyyed Hossein Nasr, *Traditional Islam in the Modern World*, p. 254.

> represents within Sufism the special grace of Christ as it manifests itself in the Islamic universe. He is a Christic Sufi, if we can use such a term; that is, he manifests *al-barakat al-ʿīsawiyyah* (to use the Arabic term) within himself. It is not that he was influenced by Christianity in a historical sense. This type of manifestation has nothing to do with the presence of Christianity as another religion. Rather, the structure of Islam is such that, within the Islamic tradition there is a possibility of the 'shining forth of the ray' of the founders of other religions, especially of Judaism and Christianity. . . . In the case of Ḥallāj, he represents a Christic embodiment within the Muḥammadan universe of spirituality.[50]

Ḥallāj is perhaps the clearest example of Christic sanctity in Islamic history. He was crucified and martyred for uttering the theophanic locution (*shaṭḥ*), *Ana'l-Ḥaqq* or "I am the Truth," as well as for other theological positions and associations.[51] These statements scandalized the more conservative jurists and theologians of his day and had grave political consequences. It is far from a coincidence that Ḥallāj is among the most widely studied and celebrated Muslims in the West. Nasr writes,

> [T]he Ḥallājian perspective represents in fact the most accessible opening towards Sufism for the West, which is fundamentally Christian in its spiritual attitudes. Even if it tries to leave its traditional religion behind, it has nevertheless for the most part a Christian perspective upon the reality of Sufism in general and, of course, that of Islam, of which Sufism is the heart. Therefore the choice of Ḥallāj for Massignon or of Massignon for Ḥallāj, far from being an accident, represents in fact a providential event in the encounter between Islam and Christianity in the modern world.[52]

Furthermore, while the Catholic tradition inevitably colored Massignon's vision of Islam, Sufism, and Ḥallāj, he was among the first orientalists to recognize the Quranic and Muḥammadan origins of

50. *Traditional Islam in the Modern World*, pp. 254–255.

51. Kathryn Babayan, *Mystics, Monarchs, and Messiahs* (Cambridge: Center for Middle East Studies, 2003), pp. 414–416.

52. *Traditional Islam in the Modern World*, p. 255.

Sufism.[53] Indeed, we maintain that Massignon was more faithful to traditional Islam and Sufism in his studies than many modernists and fundamentalists in the Islamic world.[54] Far from a digression, it is crucial to understand the magnitude and precision of Massignon's work in light of much of the polemical material on Islam and Sufism that passes for scholarship in the West, as well as the

53. Ibid., pp. 259–260. Seyyed Hossein Nasr writes, "Through the study of Ḥallāj, he demonstrated that Sufism has its roots in the Quran. Far from being a heretic, Ḥallāj was the epitome of orthodoxy, for only the saint is orthodox in the most universal sense of the term. He stands at the Center and, from the traditional perspective, everyone else is located at a point which is peripheral *vis-à-vis* that Center. Massignon realized that meditation upon the verses of the Quran, emulation of the Prophet and the grace issuing from the Quranic revelation constituted the origin and substance of Sufism." Ibid., pp. 259–260. Nasr also writes, "Père Charles de Foucault and Louis Massignon, took important steps in laying the foundation upon which an authentic understanding can be achieved between the followers of Christ and followers of the Prophet and the Quranic revelation, which created a world in whose Islamic firmament the light of Christ as Sayyidnā 'Īsā (Jesus)—upon whom be peace—continues nevertheless to shine." Rob Baker and Gray Henry, eds., *Merton and Sufism: The Untold Story* (Louisville, KY: Fons Vitae, 1999), p. 13.

54. Seyyed Hossein Nasr reminds his readers that, "some of the best known intellectual figures in the Arab world were either directly his students or were influenced by him. I need mention only two names: 'Abd al-Raḥmān Badawī, perhaps the most famous Egyptian scholar of Islamic philosophy, and the late 'Abd al-Ḥalīm Maḥmūd, the Grand Shaykh of al-Azhar University...." *Traditional Islam in the Modern World*, p. 266. James Bill and John Williams also write, "Although he was not a Roman Catholic cleric but a married priest of the Melkite (Syro-Byzantine) Catholic Church, his great service was to persuade high circles in French and Roman Catholicism that Islam is a revealed religion." *Roman Catholics and Shi'i Muslims*, p. 88. Thomas Merton states, "He was a man of great comprehension and I was happy to have been numbered among his friends, for this meant entering into an almost prophetic world, in which he habitually moved. It seems to me that mutual comprehension between Christians and Muslims is something of very vital importance today, and unfortunately it is rare and uncertain, or else subjected to the vagaries of politics. I am touched at the deep respect and understanding which so many Muslims had for him, indeed they understood him better than many Christians." Ibid., p. 92. Finally, Martin Lings writes concerning one of Massignon's students, "'Uthmān Yaḥyā, a Muslim of Syrian origin who had settled in France, told me that he had felt so drawn towards his teacher that he had almost decided to become a Christian. But Massignon dissuaded him: 'You will find nothing,' he said, 'in Christianity that you cannot find in Sufism.'" *Sufi Poems*, p. 94.

relative decline and suppression of the Islamic intellectual and spiritual tradition in many parts of the Muslim world.[55]

In a manner similar to Jesus in Christianity, Ḥallāj was tried for heresy, lashed, crucified, and eventually martyred. Ḥallāj is remembered in hagiographies for performing Christic miracles, living a life of asceticism and interiority, and teaching the most esoteric truths to his disciples and companions. Moreover, his life resembles Jesus as he is envisaged in both the Gospels and the Quran. Massignon observes,

> This typical effigy of the Quranic Jesus struck by legendary history, this ideal symbol of martyrdom consistent with the Christology of Sufism—Ḥallāj appears before the observer as a strangely living image of the real Christ as we know him, an original image, certainly, with his marriage, his secession from other mystics, his apostleship among Qaramathian Shīʿites and among the infidels, his long and so hypocritically legal trial. It is an image powerfully modeled on the surface, in the concerted dramatization of his life, and the exquisite figuration that surrounds his death: brutal politicians, remaining undecided or skeptical; corrupt doctors of the Law, implacable or indifferent; powerless disciples, either timorous or sold out; observers touched with emotion, compassionate women, faithful hearts. Their simple grouping, the correlation of their gestures, reveal the secret intentions of these onlookers who become gripped, enlightened, and searched, to the depths of their souls, by the flame of this central light which they observe, and which judges them.[56]

55. A clear example of this is cited by Nasr, "The tomb [of al-Ḥallāj] had been among a cluster of beautiful tombs of Sufis of the third and fourth Islamic centuries, situated in an old cemetery that was becoming part of an ugly urban development. Because of the pressure that Massignon had put upon Iraqi authorities, although that whole area had been taken over for construction of a new quarter, one small room was built on to the tomb of Ḥallāj to protect it. Although a pathetic sight, the fact that the tomb is still there is nevertheless proof of the efforts that Massignon made and of his success in turning the attention of authorities in Baghdad towards its preservation. Without his efforts, the very site of the tomb might have been lost or covered by an unmarked structure, as has happened in so many places in the Islamic world." *Traditional Islam in the Modern World*, p. 259.

56. *The Passion of al-Ḥallāj*, vol. III, p. 221.

Ḥallāj spoke extensively about the return of the Messiah, and saw the friends of God as being mystically united with the Mahdī and Jesus. There are even reports that someone else may have been executed in Ḥallāj's place and that like Christ people saw him after his apparent martyrdom.[57] Ḥallāj's teachings concerning the Messiah, as well as his own life and death, all bring the spirit of Jesus to the center of Muslim consciousness. Indeed, the many differences between Christianity and Islam seem minor in light of Ḥallāj's legacy.

Of central importance are Ḥallāj's ecstatic locutions, for which he was tried, persecuted, and martyred. Martin Lings writes,

> His death at the age of sixty-five was the result of his being accused of heresy for having said: 'I am the Truth.' These words occur in one of his poems, but it is not known whether the accusation resulted from the poem or from one of his spontaneous ejaculations. However that may be, after a trial that lasted for seven months, he was found guilty and put to death, in 309 AH/922 AD, with monstrous cruelty. But the verdict against him, which was final for his life on earth, has proved anything but final in other respects. His case has been retried by every succeeding generation of Muslims down to the present day, nor did it take long for the verdict 'no man has the right to speak these words' to be annulled in favour of the appeal 'man was not in this case the speaker.'[58]

Farīd al-Dīn 'Aṭṭār also remarks,

> It seems strange to me that someone should consider it proper for the voice of "Verily, I am God" [Quran 28:30] to come from a bush, without the bush intervening—Why then isn't it proper for "I am the Truth" to come from Ḥusayn [Ḥallāj], without Ḥusayn intervening?[59]

'Aṭṭār reminds us that Ḥallāj was far from incarnationism or pantheism, but also refused to obstruct the Self-disclosure of the Real in the heart, which according to a Prophetic *ḥadīth* is the "Throne of

57. Ibid., vol. I, pp. 590, 636–637; vol. II, pp. 98–99.

58. *Sufi Poems*, p. 26.

59. Farīd al-Dīn 'Aṭṭār, *Farid ad-Din 'Attar's Memorial of God's Friends* (*Tadhkirat al-awliyā'*), trans. by Paul Losensky (New York: Paulist Press, 2009), p. 395

the All-Merciful." An uncompromising understanding of Divine Unity demands an awareness of the ubiquitous Presence and Reality of God. God is not limited to any one form in Islam, but there is no place in existence that the Infinite does not extend to. As we explored in chapter three, the ultimate source of consciousness is God, who alone has the right to say "I." The Prophet himself said, "He who has seen me, has seen the Truth." This state of mystical union—or annihilation (*fanā'*) in and subsistence (*baqā'*) through God—is extended to the elect among the faithful in a *ḥadīth qudsī*, where God speaks through the Prophet in the first person:

> Whosoever shows enmity to someone devoted to Me, I shall be at war with him. My servant draws not near to Me with anything more loved by Me than the religious duties I have enjoined upon him, and My servant continues to draw near to Me with supererogatory works so that I shall love him. When I love him I am his hearing with which he hears, his seeing with which he sees, his hand with which he strikes and his foot with which he walks. . . .[60]

From a Sufi perspective, Christ's saying, "I am the Way, the Truth, and the Life..." (John 14:6) is a reference to the inner reality of prophecy in particular and the station of the sanctified soul in general, although Ḥallāj and the Sufis never claimed to be prophets with a new religious dispensation. Many Muslims unfamiliar with the mysteries of Sufism were alarmed or put off by the assertions of Ḥallāj. Massignon remarks, "Ḥallāj . . . was only uttering aloud what Sufism, ever since Ḥasan Baṣrī, Ma'rūf, and Muḥāsibī, was effecting in silence; but he felt compelled to say it, and the time for it to be said had come. . . ."[61] We may recall here a saying of a close companion of the Prophet Muḥammad, Abū Hurayrah, "I have memorized two kinds of knowledge from the Messenger of God, peace and blessings be upon him. I have divulged one of them to you and if I divulged the second, my throat would be cut."[62] Ḥallāj

60. *Forty Hadith Qudsi*, trans. Ezzeddin Ibrahim and Denys Johnson-Davies, p. 104.

61. *The Passion of al-Ḥallāj*, vol. II, p. 90.

62. *Ṣaḥīḥ al-Bukhārī*, book 3, *ḥadīth* 121. Trans. by Tayeb Chourief, *Spiritual Teachings of the Prophet*, trans. by Edin Q. Lohja (Louisville, KY: Fons Vitae, forthcoming). 'Alī is also reported to have said, "By God, if Abū Dharr had known what

himself is quoted to have said, "Of course, I conceal the jewels of my knowledge, lest the ignorant, beholding it, should be tempted. Abū'l-Ḥasan ['Alī] did the same before me, and he transmitted it to Ḥusayn and Ḥasan. And the devout should approve my execution. . . ."[63] Ḥallāj's own poetry can be read as an exposition and defense of his understanding of the doctrine of Unity (*tawḥīd*), selections of which are cited above in chapter three.[64] However, in a number of sources he accepts and even embraces his fate:

> Kill me now, my faithful friends,
> For in my death is my life.
> My death would be to go on living
> And my life would be to die.
> To me removal of my self
> Would be the noblest gift to give
> And my survival in my flesh
> The ugliest offense, because
> My life has tired out my soul
> Among its fading artifacts.
> So kill me, set aflame
> My dried out bones
> And when you pass by my remains
> In their deserted grave,
> You will perceive the secret of my Friend
> In the inmost folds of what survives.[65]

Many Muslims from the time of Ḥallāj to the present have presented different views concerning his mystical utterances and subsequent execution and martyrdom. Among the Sufis he was supported by his contemporary Abū Bakr Shiblī (d. 945), Abū Ḥāmid Ghazzālī (d. 1111), Shihāb al-Dīn Suhrawardī (d. 1191), Farīd al-Dīn 'Aṭṭār (d. 1220), Abu'l-Ḥasan Shādhilī (d. 1258), Jalāl al-Dīn Rūmī (d. 1273), Yūnus Emre (d. 1321), 'Abd al-Raḥmān Jāmī (d. 1492), 'Abd

was in the heart of Salmān, he would have killed him. . . ." M.A. Amir-Moezzi, *The Spirituality of Shi'i Islam*, pp. 294–295.

63. *The Passion of al-Ḥallāj*, vol. II, p. 169

64. *Sufi Poems*, pp. 26–39.

65. Slightly revised translation from Herbert Mason, *The Death of al-Hallaj* (Notre Dame, IN: University of Notre Dame Press, 2005), pp. xiv-xv.

al-Qādir Jazā'irī (d. 1883), and many others up to our own day.[66] He also found favor among certain Shī'ite philosophers and Sufis, including Naṣīr al-Dīn Ṭūsī (d. 1274), Ibn Abī Jumhūr (d. 1499), and Mullā Ṣadrā (d. 1640).[67] Not every Sufi, however, agreed with Ḥallāj, especially Ibn Taymiyyah (d. 1328), who stated that his sentence was just and anyone who defended Ḥallāj should also be put to death.[68] Other Sufis who disagreed with Ḥallāj were more measured in their criticism, suggesting that what Ḥallāj said was true, but that it should not have been disclosed to the public.

Shiblī is recorded to have said, "I said the same thing he did, but my madness was certified, and his sanity killed him."[69] Initiates of the Shādhiliyyah order are famous for their defense of Ḥallāj. The founder of the order, Abu'l-Ḥasan Shādhilī said, "I hate two things about the jurisprudents (*fuqahā'*): they deny that Khiḍr may be alive, and they excommunicate Ḥallāj!"[70] Jalāl al-Dīn Rūmī states, "As for me, I am the servant of those who say '*Ana'l-Ḥaqq*' and who keep their hearts free of any fault; they have written a book on their essence and their attributes, and they called its index '*Ana'l-Ḥaqq*.'"[71] Seyyed Hossein Nasr states,

> In reality, one who does not utter *Ana'l-Ḥaqq* is still living as a polytheist and idol worshipper, positing his or her own ego as a reality separate from God as *al-Ḥaqq* and idolizing that ever-changing and evanescent ego as well as the world as a divinity.[72]

66. *The Passion of al-Ḥallāj*, vol. II, p. 106.
67. Ibid., pp. 19, 46.
68. Ibid., pp. 45–50.
69. Ibid., vol. I, p. 612.
70. Ibid., vol. II, pp. 330–331.
71. Ibid., p. 267.
72. Seyyed Hossein Nasr, *The Garden of Truth*, p. 32. This is clarified in an earlier passage where Nasr writes, "The highest meaning of servanthood is in fact the realization of our 'nothingness' before God. It is only by passing through this gate of 'annihilation,' or what the Sufis call *fanā'*, that we are able to gain subsistence, *baqā'*, in God and to reach the root of our 'I' and also therefore the Divine. Human beings qua human beings cannot enter the Divine sanctuary, but there is within us a reality that is already Divine. To be fully human is to realize our perfect servitude and to remove the veil of separative existence through spiritual practice so that God, transcendent and immanent within us, can utter 'I.'" Ibid., p. 13.

Throughout the centuries Ḥallāj's influence has traveled across the Muslim world, and is well documented in Massignon's study. Not only did Ḥallāj have supporters in Arabia, Persia, Africa, Anatolia, India, and the Malay world, but certain "Ḥallājian" Sufis also suffered the same fate of Ḥallāj, such as 'Ayn al-Quḍāt Hamadānī (d. 1131) and Siti Jenar (d. 1488) from Java, for claiming that they too were plunged into the depths of the Divine Being.[73] In later Islamic history, Hallāj—like Imam Ḥusayn—takes on archetypal importance as the sanctified martyr.

Ḥallāj is also recorded to have said, "It is in the religion of the cross that I will die."[74] A literal interpretation of this saying contradicts Ḥallāj's life, as well as his death, which was punctuated by the daily prayers, fasting, alms, the pilgrimage to Mecca, as well as the recitation of the Quran and other Sufi practices. All of Ḥallāj's Sufi supporters affirm that he was a Muslim. Even the Catholic scholar Massignon writes, "The last utterance attributed to the dying al-Ḥallāj was a verse from the Quran (42:18) taken from a *Ḥāmīm*, therefore a Muḥammadan *Sūrah*, signifying his vocation as the heir of the Prophet. . . ."[75] Therefore, like Ibn 'Arabī and Ḥusayn, Ḥallāj's connection to the sanctity of Jesus issued from the *barakah* or grace of the Quran and the soul of the Prophet. Chodkiewicz remarks,

> [Ḥallāj] is mentioned several times in Chapter Twenty of the *Futūḥāt* where Shaykh al-akbar discusses 'the knowledge of Jesus', and where he actually says, 'This knowledge was possessed by Ḥusayn ibn Manṣūr'—a remark which has particular reference to Ḥallāj's doctrine of *ṭūl* and *'arḍ* ('height' and 'breadth'), terms which are plainly related to the symbolism of the cross. The miracles traditionally associated with Ḥallāj, the sayings attributed to him, especially the famous verse: 'I will die in the religion of the cross' (*fa-fī dīn al-ṣalīb yakūnu mawtī*), even his 'passion'—all these are powerful confirmation of his connection with the Christ-like type of saint, which should be seen simply as the manifestation of one

73. *The Passion of al-Ḥallāj*, vol. II, pp. 166–169, 290–291.

74. Ibid., p. 221.

75. "Those who do not believe in it would hasten it, and those who believe are wary of it and know that it is the truth. Are not those who dispute the Hour far astray?" (Quran 42:18) Ibid., vol. I, p. 642.

of the possibilities included in the sphere of Muḥammadan *walāyah*.[76]

René Guénon has indicated in his book *The Symbolism of the Cross* that the cross can be seen as a symbol of the Universal or Perfect Man (*al-insān al-kāmil*), which is so central in Sufism.[77] The Universal Man has ascended the vertical axis of his being to reach the spiritual world and the Transcendent, while his sanctified presence radiates horizontally to humanity and the natural world. The two axes meet in the heart of the gnostic. Guénon remarks:

> 'If Christians have the sign of the cross, Muslims have the doctrine of it.' We would add that, in the esoteric order, the relationship between 'Universal Man' and the Word on the one hand, and the Prophet on the other, leaves no room, as regards the actual basis of the doctrine, for any real divergence between Christianity and Islam.[78]

Likewise, the contemporary Catholic scholar Stratford Caldecott wrote,

> In Islamic terms, Jesus perhaps corresponds most closely to the Sufi idea of the Universal Man, through whom alone union with God may be realized, even if the Incarnation as such is necessarily veiled to Muslims.[79]

If most exoteric Christians would not accept another Divine manifestation or theophany such as Jesus, a number of Christian mystics from the Eastern and Western Churches have spoken of the deification of man. Meister Eckhart in fact states, "Everything that

76. *Seal of the Saints*, pp. 80–81. Michel Chodkiewicz writes elsewhere, "According to Ibn 'Arabī . . . , who points out that this technical use of the words *ṭūl* and *'arḍ* was instituted by Ḥallāj . . . 'the height (*ṭūl*) of the universe designates the spiritual world, that is to say the world of pure ideas and of the divine Commandment' and 'the width (*'arḍ*) of the universe designates the world of creation, of nature and of bodies.'" *The Spiritual Writings of Amir 'Abd al-Kader*, p. 197.

77. René Guénon, *The Symbolism of the Cross*, trans. by Angus Macnab (Hillsdale, New York: Sophia Perennis, 2004), pp. 12–15.

78. Ibid., p. 17.

79. Stratford Caldecott, "Beyond 'Unity': An Approach to Inter-Spiritual Dialogue," *Communio: International Catholic Review* (Spring 2006).

the Holy Scriptures say about Christ is equally true of every good and divine man."[80] The Sufi—like the Prophet and Jesus before him—has reached the heights of Divine knowledge and Selfhood, and sees the One Divine Self in his heart and the heart of his neighbor. Ḥallāj, as the *'Īsawī* Sufi *par excellence*, possessed intimate knowledge of the Divine Reality and an awareness of his own extinction in and subsistence through the Divine Self. Moreover, he suffered persecution and martyrdom, and left an influential legacy that has been debated and defended by both Muslim and Christian mystics to the present day.[81]

Some Conclusions

Ibn 'Arabī's paradigm of prophetic-sanctity depicts a rich history of *'Īsawī* saints in Islam and Sufism, whose lives parallel those of the great saints of Christendom such as Francis of Assisi, Joan of Arc and Padre Pio of Pietrelcina. Imam Ḥusayn's struggle for truth and justice on 'Āshūrā' and Manṣūr Ḥallāj's theophanic locutions and Union remarkably reflect the Christic archetype in the Islamic tradition. We have sought to present the lives of these Muslim saints and sages without ignoring the influence that the Quran and the grace of the Prophet Muḥammad had on them. By attaching themselves to the heart of the Quran and *Sunnah* of the Prophet, an unexpected *imitatio Christi* emerges in the lives of a number of the

80. Frithjof Schuon, *The Transcendent Unity of Religions*, p. 119.

81. *The Passion of al-Ḥallāj*, vol. II, p. 645. In addition to Massignon, the Catholic Trappist monk Thomas Merton also described Ḥallāj as a "great saint and mystic, martyr of truth and love." According to James A. Bill and John Alden Williams, "As Catholics, Massignon and Merton were profoundly struck by al-Ḥallāj's discussion of the innermost secret heart (*sirr*) of every person—which Massignon called *le point vierge*, 'the virgin point'—in a passage that Massignon translated as follows: 'Our hearts, in their secrecy, are a virgin alone, where no dreamer's dream penetrates . . . the heart where the presence of the Lord alone penetrates, there to be conceived.' At this 'primordial point' (*nuqṭah aṣliyyah*), present in the heart of every human, the reality of God can bring to reality the full latent personality of each human being. Merton later wrote: 'This little point . . . is the pure glory of God in us . . . like a pure diamond, blazing with the invisible light of heaven.' Catholic faith and Islamic mysticism flow together through the extraordinary story of the tenth-century mystic al-Ḥallāj." *Roman Catholics and Shi'i Muslims*, p. 92.

most eminent Muslim saints, precisely because the inner reality of the Quran and the spirituality of the Prophet contain Christic elements and openings to the direct guidance and Spirit of Jesus. According to Frithjof Schuon,

> Another objection might be made by some, who would say that Christian and Muslim mysticism, far from being opposed types, on the contrary present such striking analogies that one is felt bound to conclude that there have been either unilateral or reciprocal borrowings. To this the answer is that, if we suppose the starting of Sufis to have been the same as the Christian mystics, the question arises why they should have remained Muslims and how they were able to stand being Muslims; in reality they were saints not in spite of their religion but through their religion. Far from having been Christians in disguise, men like al-Ḥallāj and Ibn 'Arabī on the contrary did no more than carry the possibilities of Islam to their highest point, as their great forerunners had done. Despite certain appearances, such as the absence of monasticism as a social institution, Islam, which extols poverty, fasting, solitude and silence, includes all the premises of a contemplative asceticism.[82]

In a time when the clash of civilizations thesis is promoted and used for exclusivist religious and political objectives by some Christians, Muslims, and secularists, it is urgent to study those dimensions—usually associated with esoterism—where these two great Abrahamic traditions meet. While open and fruitful dialogue between Christians and Muslims at the theological, social, and political levels may contribute to greater understanding and social harmony, true ecumenism is only possible through the esoteric and gnostic dimensions of religion. By following the spiritual path based upon the Quran and the *Sunnah* of the Prophet of Islam, Imam Ḥusayn, Manṣūr Ḥallāj and Ibn 'Arabī attained eminent degrees of nearness to the Divine Reality, the center and summit from which Islam, Christianity and all revealed religions issue and to which they ultimately lead. Through the heart of the saint may be

82. Frithjof Schuon, *Understanding Islam* (Bloomington, Indiana: World Wisdom Inc., 1998), pp. 8–9.

seen intimations of the vertical and inward nexus between religions, precisely because he has approached the Divine Reality and reflects a measure of those universal possibilities and Divine Qualities that constitute the human state. For Muslims, Jesus is not only an object of veneration, but like all of the prophets, an indication of our highest potential and nature—for every man and woman can attain a measure of sanctity or nearness to God that some Christians reserve for Jesus alone.

5

The Eliatic Function in Islam

> And he shall go before him in the spirit and power of Elias, to turn the hearts of the fathers to the children, and the disobedient to the wisdom of the just; to make ready a people prepared for the Lord.
> (Luke 1:17)

> "Peace be upon Elias (*'Ilyāsīn*)." Thus indeed do We recompense the virtuous... (Quran 37:130–131)[1]

This chapter takes as its starting point Leo Schaya's seminal article "The Eliatic Function,"[2] where the author sheds light on the esoteric and universal function of Elijah or Elias ('Ilyās in Arabic),[3] mentioned in the Hebrew Bible, Gospel, and Quran and revered as a prophet by Jews, Christians and Muslims. Concerning Elias and the Eliatic function, Schaya writes,

1. In this instance, the Quran refers to Elijah/Elias ('Ilyās) in the plural form 'Ilyāsīn, which literally means "Elijahs" or "Eliases" and suggests to most commentators an association of Elias with his immediate community of believers, including the prophet Elisha (Alyasaʿ), his immediate successor. However, it seems plausible to us to extend the usage of 'Ilyāsīn to include all prophets who accentuate the esoteric dimension of religion, such as Khiḍr, as well as the Mahdī and other friends of God who fulfill the "Eliatic function" as described below. I wish to thank Aasim Hasany for bringing this verse and its significance to my attention.

2. Leo Schaya, "The Eliatic Functon," *Studies in Comparative Religion* 13, no. 1 and 2 (1979), pp. 31–40. This article was also published in a slightly revised form as "The Mission of Elias," *Studies in Comparative Religion* 14, no. 3 and 4 (1980), pp. 159–167.

3. For the sake of continuity we will use Elias for all further references to Elijah/Elias.

> Through the words of Elisha, the Scripture (II Kings 2:1–18) shows that Elias could not be found because he had truly been raised to heaven. Now according to Judeo-Christian tradition the prophet Elias not only ascended alive to heaven, but has, since his ascension, descended many times in secret and continues mysteriously to make himself known on earth. And thus, in Judaism, he is invisibly present at every circumcision of a male infant on the eighth day after his birth, and also at every Passover meal celebrated by families; in addition, he reveals himself to certain spiritual persons in order to initiate them into the Mysteries of the Scripture. To the majority of Israel his presence signifies the blessing which descends directly from heaven, and to the elect more particularly he represents the illuminating influence. The Eliatic manifestation is destined, in a world which is moving towards its end, to revive the study and observance of the Law of Moses and, in particular, the spiritual realization of his Mysteries.[4]

It is recorded in the Gospel that John the Baptist (Yaḥyā) is asked, "'Art thou Elias?' And he saith, 'I am not...'" (John 1:21), while Jesus the Messiah ('Īsā al-Masīḥ) proclaims: "And if ye will receive it, [John] is Elias, which was for to come." (Matthew 11:14) These apparently contradictory statements do not imply the literal transmigration or reincarnation of the soul of Elias—which John categorically denied—but John's association by Jesus with the spiritual archetype and function of Elias.[5] The Eliatic function is invested in particular chosen souls, either prophets (*anbiyā'*) or friends (*awliyā'*) of God who often live miraculously long lives, traversing and connecting the Divine, angelic and corporeal worlds and even human epochs to initiate and guide men and women in dreams, visions, and encounters in the flesh, reviving both the exoteric and esoteric dimensions of religion, which are characterized by Schaya

4. "The Eliatic Function," p. 32.

5. *The Holy Bible*, King James version. Frithjof Schuon states, "'Elias is come,' said Christ, thinking of Saint John the Baptist, even though John had denied he was Elias; it is true that Christ was referring only to the function and not the person whereas the Forerunner was speaking of his own person and not the function; but Jesus' indirect and elliptical expression nonetheless illustrates the liberty that prophetic language may take with the facts when a principial truth is at stake." *Christianity/Islam; Perspectives on Esoteric Ecumenism*, p. 132. See also, "The Eliatic Function," pp. 35–36.

as the Law of Moses and the Mysteries. These highly exceptional figures also often demonstrate the relativity of exoteric forms in light of their esoteric knowledge. Although they are each situated in a particular orthodox tradition and do not contradict the principles or exoteric forms of the Law, they manifest the inner meanings thereof through direct Divine inspiration as opposed to imitation. In addition to John and Jesus, Schaya associates a number of Biblical and Quranic prophets, friends of God and the hidden men (*rijāl al-ghayb*) of Islamic esoterism with the Eliatic function, including Khiḍr and the Mahdī.[6] Regarding Khiḍr and the Eliatic function, Leo Schaya states,

> The Muslim tradition also has a spiritual function which corresponds to that of Elias, and affirms that it is exercised by two people in particular, each of whom has his own field of activity. We do not mean Elias himself, who is mentioned in the Koran along with Jesus (VI, 85) and also in his battle against the worshippers of Baal (XXXVII, 123–132); firstly, it is al-Khiḍr or al-Khaḍir, the "Green" or "Verdant", who, in the esoteric tradition of Islam, is invested with the same fundamental characteristics as Elias, or at least with those of his function as spiritual Master, "ever-living" and descending suddenly from a supra-terrestrial world to manifest himself in secret to anyone eager for the Absolute. He is, above all, Master of the spiritual solitaries, of those elect beings to whom he reveals himself as an ocean of initiating and universal wisdom, an inexhaustible source of enlightenment, a withholder and giver of the "water of life".[7]

According to the eschatological teachings of Judaism, Christianity, and Islam, at the end of this cycle of cosmic existence a number

6. Seyyed Hossein Nasr states, "The word *rijāl* carries a masculine gender, but lest one think it refers simply to the male gender, it is important to recount the famous Sufi tradition according to which on the Day of Judgment when all human beings are standing before God, He will say, 'The *rijāl* [in the spiritual sense] step forward.' And the first person to step forward will be the Virgin Mary." *The Garden of Truth*, p. 24. For more on the *rijāl al-ghayb* see William Chittick, *Science of the Cosmos, Science of the Soul: the Pertinence of Islamic Cosmology in the Modern World* (Oxford: Oneworld Publications, 2009), pp. 75–108.

7. "The Eliatic Function," p. 36.

of these messianic figures and revivers of tradition will openly manifest their initiatic function and authority and disclose the metaphysical knowledge at the heart of the revealed religions among the faithful. While the religions remain distinct, their followers are brought into peace and harmony through the guidance and authority of these figures and the sacred knowledge that they convey, which, among other things, reveals the transcendent unity of the revealed religions. According to Schaya when Elias returns he will also bring a heavenly scripture:

> The "Book" of Elias is the integral Wisdom of the unanimous Tradition and the eschatological Manifestation of the unique Principle. Elias represents to the Jews the passage from their traditional exclusivism to the universality that they too possess, since they affirm that the Tishbite [Elias] will raise his voice so loud to announce spiritual peace that it will be heard from one end of the world to another; and the Doctors of the Law teach that "the just of all nations have their part in the future life", and moreover that all "the men, who are not idolaters can be considered as Israelites."[8]

While it is not advisable to speculate on the exact point at which this cosmic cycle will end, and the signs that will immediately precede it, including the return of the Mahdī and Jesus the Messiah, the exclusivism that permeates religious communities can be partially assuaged by coming to terms with these figures' universal function. The traditional sources highlight that these luminaries will not simply save those in one particular religion alone and oppose or "leave

8. Ibid., p. 38. Schaya notes elsewhere, "This 'exclusivism', which denies the other religions and could not have any valid reason other than the protection of Israel's traditional form, was ruptured from time to time, even on the exoteric plane of Judaism, by 'universalist' affirmations on the part of certain of its great representatives. Such as Saadya (tenth century), Maimonides (twelfth century), or Yehudah Halevy; on this subject one need only quote the following remark made by the latter in his dialogue *Al-Khazarī*, written about 1140: 'Christianity and Islam are the precursors and the initiators of the messianic era; they too serve to prepare men for the reign of truth and justice....'" *The Universal Meaning of the Kabbalah*, trans. Nancy Pearson (Baltimore: Penguin Books Inc., 1973) p. 11. See also, Leo Schaya, "Some Universal Aspects of Judaism" in Ranjit Fernando, ed., *The Unanimous Tradition* (Colombo: The Sri Lankan Institute of Traditional Studies, 1999), pp. 57–75.

behind" the vast majority of humanity who providentially practice another religion, an idea that is often proposed to justify the hostility that some religious groups have towards one another. Rather, those invested with the Eliatic function will restore the original forms of all orthodox religions and inculcate peace and harmony among the faithful through a revival of metaphysical knowledge (*'irfān/ma'rifah*)—the common esoteric teachings at the heart of each religion—through which the Unity of the Supreme Principle as the transcendent source of our diverse religions will be perceived. Foremost among these figures whose reign is expected by Muslims before the Second Coming of Christ is the Mahdī. Schaya writes,

> As for the other person who reflects Elias in Islam, he is the one who will come at the end to establish what the Judeo-Christian tradition calls the "Glorious Reign of the Messiah," he is Al-Mahdī, the one "Guided" by God. Shī'ite Islam identifies him with the Twelfth Imam, living hidden for centuries and due to re-appear to fulfill his eschatological work. . . .[9]

Islamic sources and the writings of classical and contemporary sages bring to light the significance of Khiḍr and the Mahdī. The Eliatic function in Islam is by no means limited to these two eminent individuals, but they are the chief exemplars of it next to Elias, Enoch (Idrīs), John, Jesus, the Virgin, and the Prophet of Islam himself, whose esoteric teachings and immediate light and presence continue to guide Muslim seekers.[10] At a time when Islam is more often than not misunderstood and attacked by outsiders and even

9. "The Eliatic Function," p. 36. See also, René Guénon, *Perspectives on Initiation*, trans. Henry D. Fohr (Hillsdale, NY: Sophia Perennis, 2004) p. 254.

10. Ivan Aguéli or 'Abd al-Hādī in fact calls this type of initiation a "Marian initiation": "The two initiatic chains: One is historical, the other spontaneous. The first is spread in known and established Sanctuaries under the direction of a living authorized Shaykh (Guru), who possesses the keys to the mystery. Such is the *al-Ta'līmur-rijāl* or instruction of men. The other is *al-Ta'līmur-rabbānī* or dominical or lordly instruction, which I venture to call 'Marian initiation' since it is that received by the Holy Virgin, mother of Jesus, son of Mary. There is always a master, but he can be absent, unknown, even dead for several centuries. In this initiation you draw from the present the same spiritual substance that others draw from antiquity. . . ." quoted from René Guénon, *Initiation and Spiritual Realization*, p. 180.

parodied and betrayed by some Muslims, those who manifest the Eliatic function in Islam convey to us the most essential and universal elements of the religion, which have close analogies with the esoteric currents of Judaism, Christianity and other religions.

Khiḍr

The Shādhilī Shaykh Ibn 'Aṭā' Allāh al-Iskandarī (d. 1309) writes in his *Laṭā'if al-Minan*, "Know that Khiḍr's continued existence [in this world] is a matter of unanimous agreement among the members of the community, while saints of every age recount having met him and received teaching on his authority."[11] Along with Elias, Khiḍr drank from the fountain of eternal life gaining direct Divine knowledge (*al-'ilm al-ladunī*) and remains present on earth to guide qualified seekers on the spiritual path and instruct them in the Divine mysteries.[12] He is regarded by Muslims as an enigmatic prophet or friend of God and a *uwaysī* guide that instructs the solitary saints (*afrād*) in dreams and visions and even through brief encounters on earth.[13] Named by tradition Khiḍr or al-Khaḍir, which means the "Green" or "Verdant One" and Mu'allim al-anbiyā' or "Teacher of the prophets," he is not mentioned by name in the Quran, but is identified in several sayings of the Prophet as the

11. Ibn 'Aṭā' Allāh al-Iskandarī, *The Subtle Blessings in the Saintly Lives of Abū al-'Abbās al-Mursī and his master Abū al-Ḥasan al-Shādhilī* (*Kitāb Laṭā'if al-Minan fī Manāqib Abī al-'Abbās al-Mursī wa Shaykhihi Abī al-Ḥasan*), trans. Nancy Roberts (Louisville, KY: Fons Vitae, 2005), p. 101.

12. Éric Geoffroy writes, "*Taṣawwuf* has also been defined notably by Ibn Khaldūn, as 'the knowledge that comes directly from God' (*al-'ilm al-ladunī*), in reference to verse 18:65: 'We taught him a knowledge [emanating] from Us.'" "Approaching Sufism" in Jean-Louis Michon and Roger Gaetani, eds., *Sufism: Love & Wisdom*, p. 51. See also, A.K. Coomaraswamy, "Khwāja Khaḍir and the Fountain of Life, in the Tradition of Persian and Mughal Art," *Studies in Comparative Religion* 4, no. 4 (1970).

13. The term "*uwaysī*" derives from a name of a contemporary of the Prophet of Islam, Uways al-Qaranī (d. 657), who was guided by the Prophet Muḥammad spiritually while residing in Yemen without having ever met the Prophet in the flesh. Uways was recognized as among the most eminent disciples of the Prophet and later joined Imam 'Alī and was martyred in battle. Sufis who receive guidance from Khiḍr, the Hidden Imam, and other guides among the *rijāl al-ghayb* are considered to have a *uwaysī* guide and initiation.

enigmatic guide of the prophet Moses referred to in *sūrat al-Kahf* as "a servant among Our servants whom We had granted a mercy from Us and whom We had taught knowledge from Our Presence." (Quran 18:65)[14]

The way to Khiḍr is indicated to Moses by the disappearance of a fish in his possession at "the junction of the two seas" (*majmāʿ al-baḥrayn*). Khiḍr represents the isthmus or *barzakh* in Arabic that connects and also separates these two bodies of water, the nexus and barrier between esoteric knowledge (*ʿilm al-bāṭin*) and exoteric knowledge (*ʿilm al-ẓāhir*), as well as the Divine and corporeal worlds. The *barzakh* symbolizes the abode of the macrocosmic Pole (*quṭb*) and also our own spiritual center—the heart (*qalb*)—where Heaven and earth meet.[15] Moses' initial encounter with Khiḍr is related in the Quran as follows:

> Moses said unto him, "Shall I follow thee, that thou mightest teach me some of that which thou has been taught of sound judgment?" He said, "Truly thou wilt not be able to bear patiently with me. And how canst thou bear patiently that which thine awareness encompasses not?" He said, "Thou wilt find me patient, if God wills, and I shall not disobey thee in any matter." He said, "If thou wouldst follow me, then question me not about anything, till I make mention of it to thee." (18:66–70)

The Quran proceeds to describe three apparently antinomian acts that Khiḍr performs which draw the objection of Moses. The mysterious sage makes a hole in a vessel that had carried the two, then he kills a young man, and finally he rebuilds a wall in a town that had been inhospitable to them. Each time Moses breaks his

14. On Khiḍr's association with Moses' guide in *sūrat al-Kahf*, see Ibn Kathīr, *Qiṣaṣ al-anbiyāʾ* (*Stories of the Prophets*), trans. by Muhammad Mustafa Gemeiah (Mansoura, Egypt: El Nour Publishing, 1997), pp. 257–264. The Prophet of Islam states, "Al-Khaḍir was named so because he sat over a barren white land, [and] it turned green with plantation thereafter." *Ṣaḥīḥ al-Bukhārī*, book 55, *ḥadīth* 614. According to traditional Muslim commentators, Khiḍr's full name is Abu'l-ʿAbbās al-Khaḍir Balyā ibn Malikān.

15. Titus Burckhardt, "Concerning the 'Barzakh'", *Studies in Comparative Religion* 13, no. 1 and 2 (1979), pp. 24–30; and Martin Lings, *What is Sufism?*, pp. 50–51.

oath of silence and objects to the actions of Khiḍr on the basis of his knowledge of the revealed Law. The Quran states:

> He said, "This is the parting between thee and me. I shall inform thee of the meaning of that which thou couldst not bear patiently: As for the ship, it belonged to indigent people who worked the sea. I desired to damage it, for behind them was a king who was seizing every ship by force. And as for the young boy, his parents were believers and we feared that he would make them suffer much through rebellion and disbelief. So we desired that their Lord give them in exchange one who is better than him in purity, and nearer to mercy. And as for the wall, it belonged to two orphan boys in the city, and beneath it was a treasure belonging to them. Their father was righteous, and thy Lord desired that they should reach their maturity and extract their treasure, as a mercy from thy Lord. And I did not do this upon my own command. This is the meaning of that which thou couldst not bear patiently." (18:78–82)

Here Moses accentuates the exoteric dimension of religion, horizontal knowledge, and the Mosaic Law in Judaism and the *Sharīʿah* in Islam, while Khiḍr represents esoterism, vertical knowledge, and the Eliatic function, as well as the Kabbalah in Judaism and Sufism in Islam. The Quranic account demonstrates the relativity of outward or exoteric forms in light of direct Divine inspiration and guidance that unveils the hidden and underlying meaning of forms from the world of the unseen (*ʿālam al-ghayb*), to which only the elect among the friends of God have access. Farīd al-Dīn ʿAṭṭār (d. 1220) remarks,

> There are things on the path that do not appear to square with the externals of the religious law. . . . And thus too when Khiḍr killed the young boy. . . . But anyone who has not reached this rank and sets foot here is an atheist and heretic unless he follows the dictates of religious law.[16]

In the annals of the Islamic tradition there are certain sages and servants of God whose actions and purpose cannot be easily under-

16. Farīd al-Dīn ʿAṭṭār, *Farid ad-Din ʿAṭṭār's Memorial of God's Friends (Tadhkirat al-awliyāʾ)*, trans. Paul Losensky, pp. 172–173.

stood by the outward dimension of the Law alone and who accentuate and exemplify the quintessential dimensions of religion in their lives and teachings, although as the story of Moses and Khiḍr demonstrates, the latter's actions were in accord with the Divine command, the principles of the Law, and ultimately worked towards the greater good.[17]

The Quran and *Sunnah* of the Prophet of Islam bring the Law of Moses and the Way of Khiḍr into an equilibrium and symbiosis for Muslims as the straight or middle path *(al-ṣirāṭ al-mustaqīm)*, which also became normative for orthodox Sufis.[18] The Sacred Law (*Sharīʿah*) is a path to salvation and a necessary source of protection and grace (*barakah*) for those on the spiritual path (*ṭarīqah*). Islamic esoterism or Sufism (*taṣawwuf*) can be described as the spiritual path to the Truth (*al-Ḥaqq*) to be followed in this life on the basis of the practice of the Sacred Law, along with the attainment of metaphysical knowledge (*maʿrifah*), which also reveals the true meaning of forms in this world. Avoiding extremes, the significance of the Sacred Law should not be denied, nor should Islam be reduced to its exoteric dimensions alone. Muslims who inherit the fullness of the Quranic and Prophetic teaching, to the extent possible, integrate within themselves knowledge of both the Law and the Way. In Muḥyī al-Dīn ibn ʿArabī's (d. 1240) chapter on Moses in the *Fuṣūṣ al-ḥikam,* Khiḍr in fact tells Moses before they part ways, "I have knowledge God hath taught me and which ye know not, and thou hast knowledge God hath taught thee, which I know not."[19] As

17. This story is also an Islamic answer to the question of theodicy if we extend Khiḍr's apparently unjust actions to the evil that exists in this world. In both cases what appears as evil works towards a greater good if we have enough patience or foresight. This does not imply, however, that we should accept relative evil from our own souls or those of others. Only someone at Khiḍr's station has the Divine permission and knowledge to preempt greater evils through acts, which at first glance appear to be in themselves evil, but are ultimately good and in accordance with the Divine Will.

18. The Way of Khiḍr might also be described as the Way of Elias, Jesus or Muḥammad, for example.

19. On the respect (*adab*) that Khiḍr shows to the prophet Moses, to whom God spoke, see Ibn ʿArabī, *The Ringstones of Wisdom (Fuṣūṣ al-ḥikam)*, trans. Caner Dagli, pp. 260, 264–265.

recipients of this most fascinating exchange and dialectic through the Divine Word, Muslims, including jurists and aspirants on the Sufi path, can reflect upon a sacred historical and trans-historical prophetic encounter that providentially unites them and helps to explain the nature of their differences.[20]

It is said that Khiḍr was present at the Prophet Muḥammad's funeral in 632 and recognized by Abū Bakr al-Ṣiddīq (d. 634) and 'Alī ibn Abī Ṭālib (d. 661):

> A powerful-looking, fine-featured, handsome man with a white beard came leaping over the backs of the people till he reached where the sacred body . . . lay. Weeping bitterly, he turned toward the Companions and paid his condolences. Abū Bakr and 'Alī said that he was Khiḍr.[21]

Tradition states that he joins Elias in the holy city of Jerusalem every year during the month of Ramaḍān. Shī'ites believe that Khiḍr accompanied the Twelfth Imam to the outskirts of the city of Qom in 964 to instruct Shaykh Ḥasan ibn Muthlih to build a mosque known as Masjid Jamkarān.[22] Encounters with Khiḍr are also replete throughout the history of Sufism, who, both perplexing and illuminating, descends upon seekers and wayfarers like a Zen koan incarnate. In Islamic hagiographies and other classical Sufi literature Ibrāhīm ibn Adham (d. 790), Sahl Tustarī (d. 896), Ḥakīm Tirmidhī (d. 932), Rūzbihān Baqlī (d. 1209), Muḥyī al-Dīn ibn 'Arabī, and Abu'l-Ḥasan Shādhilī (d. 1258) all meet and receive

20. This sacred story of course has significance for exoterists and esoterists from all religions.

21. Shawkat M. Toorawa, "Khidr: The History of a Ubiquitous Master" *Sufi* 30 (1996), pp. 45–49. Toorawa states: "That Abū Bakr and 'Alī are the ones to identify him is noteworthy. They are the only two Companions of Muhammad to whom are ascribed esoteric (*bāṭinī*) knowledge. This is why all Sufi *silsilas* (spiritual chains of investiture) derive from them and them alone. This hidden knowledge is not learned, it must be bestowed by God." Ibid.

22. Vali Nasr, *The Shia Revival: How Conflicts within Islam Will Shape the Future* (New York: W.W. Norton & Company, Inc., 2006), pp. 220–221.

23. In India and Sri Lanka, Khiḍr is venerated and recognized as a guide by some Muslims, Hindus, Buddhists, and others and is known as Khwājā Khiḍr, Pīr Badar, and Rājā Kidār. He is also associated with the Green Knight at King Arthur's

instruction from the solitary guide.[23] The Sufi saint Ibrāhīm ibn Adham, whose life resembles that of the Buddha, appears in Farīd al-Dīn 'Aṭṭār's *Tadhkirat al-awliyā'* as the king of Balkh immersed in a life of luxury and opulence. A visitor appears in Ibrāhīm's court searching for a camel on the roof. 'Aṭṭār relates the words of Ibrāhīm: "You ignorant man, why are you looking for a camel on the roof? What would a camel be doing on the roof?" To which the visitor replies, "You heedless man, are you looking for the Lord while you sit on a golden throne and wear satin clothes?"[24] Then the visitor approaches the king's throne:

> Ibrāhīm said, "What do you want?" "I'm stopping over at this inn," the man said. "This is no inn. This is my palace." "Who did this palace belong to before this?" "It belonged to my father," "Who did it belong to before him?" "It belonged to somebody or other." "Who did it belong to before him?" "It belonged to his father." "Where have they all gone?" "They have all died." "But isn't an inn a place where people come and go" He said this and quickly left the palace. Ibrāhīm went running after him shouting, "Stop, so I can have a word with you!" The man stopped, "Who are you?" Ibrāhīm asked. "Where do you come from? You have kindled a fire in my soul.""I am a land and a sea, an earth and a sky. I am best known as Khiḍr."[25]

Khiḍr's words imparted on Ibrāhīm the fear of God and a yearning for spiritual guidance. Ibrāhīm then tells the Green One, "'Wait here, while I go home and come back.' 'The matter is more pressing than that,' [Khiḍr] said and disappeared."[26] Ibrāhīm turns to God in repentance, embraces a life of spiritual poverty (*faqr*), and eventually meets Khiḍr again. In 'Alī Hujwīrī's (d. 1070) *Kashf al-maḥjūb*, Ibrāhīm states, "During that time Khiḍr consorted with me

Round Table in the story *Sir Gawain and the Green Knight*, a figure in Chaucer's *Canterbury Tales*, and appears in the *Alexander Romance*. See A.K. Coomaraswamy, "Khwāja Khaḍir and the Fountain of Life, in the Tradition of Persian and Mughal Art."

24. *Farid ad-Din 'Aṭṭār's Memorial of God's Friends*, p. 128.

25. Ibid., pp. 128–129.

26. Ibid., p. 129.

and taught me the Great Name of God. Then my heart became wholly empty of 'other' [than God and His Name]."[27]

According to Ibn 'Arabī, along with the Pole (*quṭb*) Enoch, Jesus, and Elias, Khiḍr is one of the four spiritual pillars (*awtād*) who remain perpetually alive at the head of the celestial hierarchy of the Sufis.[28] Michel Chodkiewicz states,

> Even though it is generally held in Islam that the four people mentioned by Ibn 'Arabī belong forever to the world of the living (two of them [Enoch] and Jesus, dwell in the celestial spheres, and the other two, Elias and Khaḍir, dwell on this earth unseen by most mortals), this is the first time that they have been assigned the supreme offices in the esoteric hierarchy.[29]

Ibn 'Arabī also met the enigmatic Khiḍr several times and received the *khirqah khaḍiriyyah* or the initiatic mantle of Khiḍr in 1196 in Seville and in 1205 in Mosul.[30] On one occasion Khiḍr tells the Shaykh al-Akbar to submit to his master, Abu'l-'Abbās al-'Uryabī, regarding a particular matter upon which they disagreed.[31] Henry Corbin relates that Khiḍr came to Ibn 'Arabī without revealing his identity and said:

27. 'Alī Hujwīrī, *Revelation of the Mystery* (*Kashf al-maḥjūb*), trans. R.A. Nicholson (Accord, NY: Pir Publications, 1999), p. 105.

28. According to the Shaykh al-Akbar, each of the four pillars has an earthly representative who fulfills this function as a deputy or representative. On the question of the Pole and the pillars in the vision of Ibn 'Arabī, see Michel Chodkiewicz, *Seal of the Saints, Prophethood and Sainthood in the Doctrine of Ibn 'Arabī*, pp. 89–102. Chodkiewicz also states, "[the four pillars] are also called 'mountains' (*jibāl*) on account of Allāh's words (Qur'ān 78:6–7): 'Have we not made the earth into a cradle and the mountains into pillars (*awtādan*)?' For He stabilized the movement of the earth by means of the mountains, and the authority (*ḥukm*) of those of whom we are speaking (over the world) is analogous to the authority of the mountains over the earth." Ibid., p. 97. Khiḍr is also often described as among the *afrād* or solitary saints who are not under the jurisdiction of the Pole. See René Guénon, *Initiation and Spiritual Realization*, pp. 181–182.

29. *Seal of the Saints*, pp. 93–94.

30. Ibid., p. 62. Ibn 'Arabī's initiatic influences were by no means limited to Khiḍr. He also took the Way from his living masters, Jesus, other prophets, and the especially the Prophet of Islam.

31. Claude Addas, *Quest for the Red Sulphur*, pp. 63–64.

> "O Muḥammad [Ibn 'Arabī]! Trust your master". . . . The young man retraced his steps, meaning to inform his master that he had changed his mind, but upon seeing him [Abu'l-'Abbās] stopped him with these words: "Must Khiḍr appear to you before you trust your master's words?"[32]

Khiḍr appears to the Shaykh al-Akbar to stress the importance of his own master's guidance. Similarly, the esoteric rites and practices of Sufism are also a method of gaining the same Divine knowledge that God imparted to Khiḍr. Ibn 'Arabī relates in his introduction to *al-Futūḥāt al-makkiyyah,*

> [I]f the properly prepared person persists in *dhikr* ('remembering' God) and spiritual retreat, emptying the place (of the heart) from thinking, and sitting like a poor beggar who has nothing at the doorstep of their Lord—then God will bestow upon them and give them some of that knowing of Him, of those divine secrets and supernal understandings, which He granted to his servant Khiḍr.[33]

Dhikr Allāh, the remembrance or invocation of God and His Names, is the central practice of Sufism which communicates the knowledge and presence of the One who is invoked. *Dhikr* is not only the repetition of the most beautiful Names of God *(asmā' al-ḥusnā*), but the immediate recollection and awareness of these realities, and ultimately Reality as such, in the heart of the invoker.

In a manner similar to Khiḍr, Jalāl al-Dīn Rūmī (d. 1273) explained the meaning (*ma'nā*) behind every form (*ṣūrat*) through an encompassing vision of reality that was unlocked by his beloved friend Shams al-Dīn Tabrīzī (d. 1248), who Rūmī's son Sulṭān Valad (d. 1312) compares to Khiḍr.[34] The Green One also appears in Rūmī's *Mathnawī* (d. 1273):

32. Henry Corbin, *Alone with the Alone*, p. 63.

33. Muḥyī al-Dīn ibn al-'Arabī, *The Meccan Revelations* (*al-Futūḥāt al-makkiyyah*), vol. I, Michel Chodkiewicz, ed., trans. James W. Morris (Oxford: Pir Press, 2005), p. 14.

34. Franklin D. Lewis, *Rumi: Past and Present, East and West* (Oxford: Oneworld Publications, 2000), p. 34.

> One night a certain man was crying "Allah!" till his lips were growing sweet with praise of Him.
>
> The Devil said, "Prithee, O garrulous one, where is the (response) 'Here am I' to all this 'Allah'?
>
> Not a single response is coming from the Throne: how long will you cry 'Allah' with grim face?"
>
> He became broken-hearted and laid down his head (to sleep): in a dream he saw Khiḍr amidst the vendure.
>
> He (Khiḍr) said, "Hark, you have held back from praising God: how is it that you repent of having called unto Him?"
>
> He said, "No 'Here am I' is coming to me in response, hence I fear that I may be (a reprobate who is) driven away from the Door."
>
> He (Khiḍr) said, "(God saith), That 'Allah' of thine is My 'Here am I,' and the supplication and grief and ardour of thine is My messenger (to thee).
>
> Thy shifts and attempts to find a means (of gaining access to Me) were (in reality) My drawing (thee towards Me), and released thy feet (from the bonds of worldliness).
>
> Thy fear and love are the noose to catch My favor: beneath every 'O Lord' (of thine) is many a 'Here am I' (from Me)...."[35]

Here Khiḍr serves to remind the reader that prayer itself is a Divine response to man, an *oratio infusa* or Divine Act within the heart of man that in reality proceeds from above. In a prayer for his companion Ḥusām al-Dīn Çelebī (d. 1284), Rūmī states in his *Mathnawī*, "May thy life in the world be like (that of) Khiḍr, soul-increasing and help-giving and perpetual! Like Khiḍr and Elias, mayst thou remain in the world (forever), that by thy grace earth may become heaven!"[36]

The contemporary Sufi sage Frithjof Schuon or 'Īsā Nūr al-Dīn Aḥmad (d. 1998) inspired Leo Schaya's essay and designation "The

35. Jalāl al-Dīn Rūmī, *The Mathnawī of Jalālu'ddīn Rūmī*, vol. IV, pp. 14–15.
36. Ibid., vol. VI, p. 268.

Eliatic Function."[37] In a letter to Leo Schaya written in 1973—which predates the publication of Schaya's "The Eliatic Function" (1979)—Schuon sheds light on the archetype and spiritual function of Khiḍr:

> Al-Khiḍr is really the Holy Spirit; in this sense he is Mary's spouse; he is also the human form of Metatron, and the Intellect that lives within us is his microcosmic manifestation. Elias is a historical manifestation—but also suprahistoric—of this principle.[38]

Here the *uwaysī* guide reflects and reveals the Intellect—the "Khiḍr" or "Imam of one's being" to use the language of Shīʿite *ʿirfān*—the inner faculty of perception or eye of the heart (*ʿayn al-qalb*) through which man sees and encounters God directly.[39] In a man-

37. Schaya also explicitly connects Schuon's corpus with the "Eliatic flow": "This spirituality appears, despite the contrary currents launched by the "Adversary", to be making headway; one notes at the outward level, among other things, the growing interest in comparative religion, in the metaphysics of East and West and the various authentic paths leading man to the absolute. But it is important, as far as contemporary literature on this unanimous spirituality is concerned, to distinguish very carefully between what really expresses the truth revealed by the traditions—such as the works of Frithjof Schuon—and what is only a very inadequate, or even completely false, approach to it. The true "Eliatic flow" will grow stronger, according to the Scriptures, as the world's darkness grows deeper. . . ."The Mission of Elias," p. 167.

38. *Frithjof Schuon: Life and Teachings*, p. 162. Schuon also states, "We can compare the particular mode of inspiration and orthodoxy that is esoterism to the rain which falls vertically from the sky, whereas the river—the outward tradition—flows horizontally, and in a continuous movement; in other words, tradition gushes forth from a spring, it is identified with a given founder of religion, whereas esoterism refers, above all and a priori, to an invisible filiation, represented in the Bible by Melchizedech, Solomon, and Elias, and associated in Sufism with al-Khiḍr, the mysterious immortal." *In the Face of the Absolute* (Bloomington, IN: World Wisdom, Inc., 1994), p. 234. It should be noted that in a letter to Schuon in 1946, Guénon refers to the connection between Elias, Khiḍr, and other figures: "Regarding what you say in your reply about St John, there might be only this to add: many Muslims also consider St John to be a Prophet, belonging to the spiritual family of al-Khiḍr, Sayyidnā Idrīs, and Sayyidna 'Ilyās, but in any case, it is understood that he would only be a *nabī* and not *rasūl*." Frithjof Schuon, *René Guénon: Some Observations*, p. 61.

39. This association has also been made by Sufis with the Prophet of Islam, other prophets, the angels, and the Imam in Shīʿism. See Henry Corbin, *The Man of Light in Iranian Sufism*, Nancy Pearson (New Lebanon, NY: Omega Publications, 1994) pp. 121–144.

ner similar to the Angel Gabriel, the Prophet of Islam and the founders of the great religions, Khiḍr is a manifestation of the Universal Spirit (*al-rūḥ*) who helps us recall our own primordial nature and spirit that receives knowledge and guidance from God directly. Seyyed Hossein Nasr writes that man must,

> Seek the fountain of life, led in this quest by the figure whom Islamic esoterism calls Khiḍr, the guide upon the spiritual path, the representative and symbol of the Eliatic function which cannot but be always present. Having drunk of the water of immortality, which is also the elixir of Divine knowledge, man regains his original consciousness and primordial abode. His wandering ceases and he arrives after his long cosmic journey at that from which his true self never departed.[40]

The disciples of Khiḍr become transfigured and consequently reflect his function and guidance, in varying degrees, in their own lives and work. Although Khiḍr and other *uwaysī* masters cannot be chosen as guides, they can appear providentially to those in need of guidance. However, the attempt to circumvent the regular channels of guidance and initiation offered by Heaven through the Sufi orders or other orthodox esoteric paths in hope of encountering Elias, Khiḍr or the Mahdī indicates an unwillingness on the part of the "seeker" to submit to esoteric guidance, and would in any case also make one unqualified for *uwaysī* guidance.[41] For the teachings of the authentic living Sufi masters are in complete harmony and accord with those of a Khiḍr. Seyyed Hossein Nasr writes,

> This story [Quran 18:60–85] is the prototype of the function of the spiritual master to instruct disciples and to reveal to them when they are ripe for the understanding of the inner significance of

40. Seyyed Hossein Nasr, *Knowledge and the Sacred*, p. 323.

41. René Guénon writes, "Recently, another question concerning initiatic affiliation has been raised, but to correctly assess its scope we should first of all say that it particularly concerns cases where initiation is obtained outside the ordinary and normal channels, and it must be clearly understood above all that such cases are never anything but exceptional, and that they occur when certain circumstances render normal transmission impossible, since their raison d'être is precisely to substitute in some measure for that transmission. We say 'in some measure' because such a thing can only happen with individuals possessing qualifications far beyond

things. In Sufi literature, in fact, the spiritual master, who is usually called *shaykh*, *pīr* (both meaning elder), *murshid* (the guide), and *murād* (the person sought by the will of the disciple), is also called the Khiḍr of the spiritual path (*khiḍr-i rāh* in Persian).[42]

One should not wait for an encounter with the *rijāl al-ghayb* to gain metaphysical knowledge. The Divine Reality remains accessible through the revealed religions and the esoteric paths contained therein. The teachings and mysteries that Elias, Khiḍr, the Mahdī and other Eliatic figures convey are accessible through authentic spiritual guides here on earth, who direct serious seekers towards inner and outer equilibrium and a vertical ascension to the One.

the ordinary and aspirations strong enough to in a way attract to themselves the spiritual influence that they would not find if left to their own devices, and also because for such individuals it is even rarer still—for lack of the assistance provided by constant contact with a traditional organization—that the results obtained through such an initiation are anything but fragmentary and incomplete. This cannot be insisted on too much, and yet to speak of such a possibility is nevertheless perhaps still not entirely without danger, if only because too many people have a tendency to entertain illusions in this regard; let an event occur in their lives that is a little extraordinary—or so it seems to them—but that is really rather commonplace, and they interpret it as a sign that they have received this exceptional initiation; and present-day Westerners in particular are all too easily tempted to seize upon the flimsiest pretext of this kind in order to dispense with a regular affiliation, which is why it is quite justified in insisting that as long as this latter is not in fact impossible to obtain one should not expect to receive any other kind of initiation apart from it." *Initiation and Spiritual Realization*, pp. 29–30. See also, Ibid., pp. 180–182; and Seyyed Hossein Nasr, *Islam and the Plight of Modern Man*, p. 59.

42. *The Garden of Truth*, p. 108. Regarding spiritual wayfaring and ascension, Nasr also states "Some have achieved the climb successfully without a human guide, through agencies of what Sufism calls "absent" or invisible guides (*rijāl al-ghayb*), such as Khiḍr, or the Hidden Imam. But they are the exceptions and not the rule. In Sufism the duties laid upon the shoulders of the disciples require their being active and not only in a passive state waiting for graces to descend from Heaven, although he or she must possess both active and passive perfection. That is why the disciple is called *murīd*, that is, the person who exercises his or her will, or *sālik*, which means traveler. It is as a traveler seeking to reach the peaks [of the spiritual path] that the disciple has need of a guide, who is none other than the spiritual master." Ibid., p. 112.

The Mahdī

In a manner similar to Elias, who both Jews and Christians expect before the coming of the Messiah, Muslims expect the coming of a descendent of the Prophet Muḥammad known as the Mahdī who will restore peace and justice on earth and directly precede the Second Coming of Jesus.[43] Traditions concerning this figure are recorded in the books of *Ḥadīth*, but Sunnis and Shī'ites do not agree on his exact identity. Most Sunnis believe that the prophesied Mahdī, which means "the Guide" or "the Rightly-Guided One," has not been born, while Ithnā 'asharī or Twelver Shī'ites believe that the Twelfth Imam is the expected Mahdī foretold by the Prophet of Islam. Despite their points of divergence, both Sunni and Shī'ite sources shed important light on the identity and function of this figure.

In the Sunni books of *Ḥadīth* a number of companions narrate sayings of the Prophet concerning the Mahdī, including 'Umar ibn al-Khaṭṭāb (d. 644), 'Abd al-Raḥmān ibn 'Awf (d. 652), 'Uthmān ibn 'Affān (d. 656), Ṭalḥah ibn 'Ubayd Allāh (d. 656), 'Alī ibn Abī Ṭālib (d. 661), Umm Salamah bint Abī Umayyah (d. 680), Abū Hurayrah 'Abd al-Raḥmān (d. 681), and Anas ibn Mālik (d. 709).[44] It is recorded in the *Kitāb al-Mahdī* in *Sunan Abū Dā'ūd* that the Prophet of Islam said,

> The Mahdī will be of my stock and he will be broad of forehead and aquiline of nose. He will fill the earth with right and with justice even as it hath been filled with wrong and oppression. Seven years will he reign.[45]

43. It seems likely to us that prophecies concerning the return of Elias before the end of time recorded in the Bible are references to none other than the Mahdī. This can be explained in light of John's association by Jesus with Elias, which indicates that more than one person may fulfill the Eliatic function described in this chapter. While signs and indications of the Mahdī's return are replete throughout the Islamic sources, we are told, "those who state a time [for the Return] are liars." Mohammad Ali Amir-Moezzi, *The Divine Guide in Early Shi'ism*, p. 123.

44. Jassim M. Hussain, *The Occultation of the Twelfth Imam* (London: Muhammadi Trust, 1982), p. 19.

45. Martin Lings, *Muhammad*, p. 330; *Sunan Abū Dā'ūd al-Sijistānī*, book 36 *ḥadīth* 4272.

> If only one day of this time remained [in this world], God would raise up a man from my family who would fill this earth with justice as it has been filled with oppression.[46]

> The Mahdī will be of my family, of the descendents of Fāṭimah.[47]

As noted above, the exact identity of the Mahdī is unclear from Sunni sources. The majority community does however agree on his eventual appearance and general function. In a tradition of the Prophet recorded in Shīʿite sources we read:

> Al-Mahdī is from my progeny. His name is similar to mine and his epithet is similar to mine. In his physique and character he looks exactly like me. He will be in a state of occultation and there will be confusion in which people will wander about. Then he will come forth like a sharp, shooting star to fill the earth with justice and equity as it was filled before with injustice and inequity.[48]

In Ithnā ʿasharī Shīʿism, the Twelfth Imam (868–present)—the son of the Eleventh Imam Ḥasan al-ʿAskarī (d. 872) and a Byzantine princess Narjis—is the Mahdī and the Imam al-Zamān or "Imam of the Age."[49] The Twelfth Imam went into the lesser occultation (*al-ghaybat al-ṣughrā*) in the year 872 and was represented by four

46. Ibid., *ḥadīth* 4270.

47. Ibid., *ḥadīth* 4271.

48. *The Occultation of the Twelfth Imam*, p. 17.

49. The Twelve Imams are by no means exclusively Shīʿite, as the first eight are considered early poles of Sufism in both Sunni and Shīʿite orders. Moreover, more than one Sunni Sufi order, especially those in Central Asia, venerate all Twelve Imams and consider the Twelfth Imam to be the Mahdī. From our point of view the Twelve Imams can be considered as leaders of the Muslim *ummah*, Sunnis and Shīʿites alike, despite their differences. There seems to be no sufficient reason for Sunnis to dismiss the Twelve Imams other than an aversion to Shīʿism. However, once one grasps the trans-denominational function of the Prophet and the Imams one can accept their teachings and remain faithful to the Sunni or the Shīʿite perspective. One can simply cite the facts that the Prophet Muḥammad taught both his family and his companions; Imam ʿAlī is remembered to have taught his sons Ḥasan and Ḥusayn as well as the proto-Sunni theologian and Sufi Ḥasan al-Baṣrī; Imam Jaʿfar al-Ṣādiq taught his sons Imam Mūsā al-Kāẓim and Imam Ismāʿīl, who became the respective heads of the Ithnā ʿasharī and Ismāʿīlī Shīʿism, as well as the Sunni jurists Imam Abū Ḥanīfah and Imam Mālik and a number of early Sufis;

deputies (*abwāb*) during that period.[50] At the time of the death of the last of these deputies in 939, the Imam entered what is known as the greater occultation (*al-ghaybat al-kubrā*) in Medina or Sāmarrā', and ascended from earth to the imaginal world (*'ālam al-mithāl*), where he remains miraculously alive until the present and occasionally reappears to the faithful in dreams, visions, and even in the flesh.[51] His continuous presence and function in Shī'ism is analogous to the Pole or *quṭb* in Sufism, to whom can be applied the saying, "The earth shall never be empty of the witness of God (*ḥujjat Allāh*)."[52] The Hidden Imam's occultation is indicative of the Supreme Center being concealed during the Kali Yuga.[53] Henry Corbin writes,

> For [Twelver] Shī'ites, the Imam of our period, the *twelfth Imam* is in occultation (*ghaybah*), having been raised from this world as Enoch and Elias were ravished. . . . In his absence, no simple officiants assume this role, but persons who have been put to the test

and Imam 'Alī Riḍā taught his son Imam Muḥammad Taqī, as well as the famous Sufi Ma'rūf al-Karkhī. We can therefore affirm that the Imams are envisaged by both Sunnis and Shī'ites as their leaders, despite the much more theologically and politically pronounced function of the Imam in Shī'ism. In light of Sufism or *'irfān*, as well as the fact that most Shī'ites were resigned to accept their frustrated political ambitions after the martyrdom of Imam Ḥusayn, there is very little that separates Sunnis and Shī'ites, except what might naturally distinguish a Mālikī from a Shāfi'ī, for example. It seems that the Twelfth Imam can be accepted by both Sunnis and Shī'ites as the Mahdī without exclusively placing him in one of these two branches alone to the exclusion of the other, but while simultaneously allowing Sunnis and Shī'ites to preserve their own understanding of him and themselves. Only a truly Muḥammadan saint, such as 'Alī, the Mahdī, Ibn 'Arabī or Rūmī, could manifest a presence and teaching that resonate and are indispensable to Sunni and Shī'ite sages alike.

50. 'Allāmah Ṭabāṭabā'ī, *Shi'ite Islam*, pp. 210–211.

51. Ibid., pp. 210–211. The abode of the Hidden Imam in the imaginal world (*'ālam al-mithāl*) or the eighth clime is sometimes identified as a celestial green island (*al-jazīrah al-khaḍrah*) or the land of Hūrqalyā. Henry Corbin, *History of Islamic Philosophy*, trans. by Liadain Sherrard and Philip Sherrard (London: Kegan Paul International, 1993), p. 70.

52. Seyyed Hossein Nasr, *Sufi Essays*, p. 28.

53. René Guénon, *The King of the World*, trans. Henry D. Fohr (Hillsdale, NY: Sophia Perennis, 2004) pp. 49–53. Shī'ite sources give several reasons for the greater

> and are known for their high spiritual quality; they are not appointed like functionaries, but are gradually recognized and promoted by the community.[54]

After a series of cosmological signs, the Hidden Imam will return to restore peace and justice on earth for a number of years, which will manifest through his sacerdotal and royal initiatic function. First and foremost, the Imam revives the doctrine of Unity (*al-tawḥīd*) through a restoration of the esoteric and exoteric dimensions of the Islamic tradition, including gnosis (*maʿrifah/ʿirfān*), wisdom (*ḥikmah*), esoteric scriptural exegesis (*taʾwīl*),[55] a direct interpretation of Islamic Law (*Sharīʿah*), and a just and peaceful social order that extends to Muslims and people of all faiths under his domain. According to Saʿd al-Dīn Ḥamūyah (d. 1252), "'The Hidden Imam will not appear before the time when people are able to understand, even from the very thongs of his sandals, the secrets of *tawḥīd*'—that is to say, the esoteric meaning of Divine Unity."[56] His outward reappearance will correspond to and catalyze an awakening of hearts among the faithful, the faculty of discernment capable of knowing the Absolute and Infinite Reality and its essential attributes: Truth, Goodness and Beauty. In his treatise *al-Insān al-kāmil*, ʿAbd al-Karīm Jīlī writes,

> By 'those who have realized the Essence' (*al-dhātiyyūn*), one means the men in whom lives the Divine Subtle Reality, in the sense where we were saying that God, when He reveals Himself to His servant and He extinguishes the individuality, establishes in

---

and lesser occultations, including safeguarding the Imam, avoiding political entanglements, and testing the believers. To these can be added the fact that the providential cyclical decline of humanity would not have been possible if the *axis mundi* of the age held temporal power as well. According to Imam al-Ṣādiq, however, "The deep reason [for the occultation] will not be unveiled until after [the Mahdī's] manifestation, exactly in the same way that the deep reason for the sabotage of the ship, for the murder of the young man, and for the construction of the wall by al-Khiḍr was not revealed to Moses until later. . . ." *The Divine Guide in Early Shiʿism*, p. 114.

54. *Alone With the Alone*, p. 258.

55. "The Eliatic Function," pp. 36–37.

56. *History of Islamic Philosophy*, pp. 71–72.

> him a Divine Subtle Reality which may be of the nature of the Essence or of the nature of the Divine Qualities. When it is of the nature of the Essence, the human constitution (*haykal*) (where it lives) will be the Unique Perfect Being, the Universal Support, the pole around which existence turns.... Through him God safeguards the world. He is the Mahdī, the Seal of the Sainthood and the representative (*al-khalīfah*) of God on earth.... He influences the realities of existence like the magnet draws iron. He tames the world by his grandeur, and by his power he does that which he wishes....[57]

Like the Prophet of Islam before him, the Mahdī's will, actions, qualities and very existence are extinguished in and subsist through God's Will, Actions, Qualities, and the Divine Essence or Self (*al-Dhāt*). He conveys to humanity the supreme metaphysical knowledge of both Unity and Union. While the Mahdī acts according to the inner and outer teachings of the Quran and *Sunnah* of the Prophet, he also derives his knowledge directly from God, and is therefore able to interpret the Islamic sources through this realization as opposed to imitation. Imam Ja'far al-Ṣādiq (d. 757) states,

> When the [Mahdī] of the family of Muḥammad, may God bless him and his family, comes he will judge among the people with the judgment of David, peace be upon him. Through the inspiration of God, the Exalted, he will not need evidence. He will judge through his knowledge and he will inform each people about what is their innermost secret. He will know his friend from his enemy by a process of immediate recognition....[58]

The Imam al-Mahdī will return and reestablish peace and justice on earth through the sword, understood as worldly power and as a symbol for spiritual warfare, the *jihād al-akbar* or greater struggle against the lower self that reigns supreme over most men in our

57. 'Abd al-Karīm al-Jīlī, *Universal Man* (*al-Insān al-kāmil*), p. 58. Burckhardt then adds the following commentary: "One must not lose sight of the fact that the essence of this Unique Being is identical to the Divine Essence, so that there cannot be divergence between him and God. One may say that he does not do what God would not have done, or that God acts through him." Ibid., p. 58.

58. Shaykh al-Mufīd, *The Book of Guidance* (*Kitāb al-irshād*), trans. by I.K.A. Howard (Qum: Anṣariyan Publications), p. 554.

age.[59] Just as Imam ʿAlī ibn Abī Ṭālib inaugurated the cycle of *futuwwah* (spiritual chivalry) in Islam, the Mahdī is the Seal of *futuwwah* (*khātam al-futuwwah*).[60] With his companions, he will fight oppression and tyranny and establish peace, justice, virtue, and order, both macrocosmically and in the inner beings of the faithful. Imam al-Ṣādiq states, "After receiving permission [to manifest himself], the [Hidden] Imam will pronounce the Hebrew name of God; then his companions, 313 in all, will gather around him in Mecca, in the same way that small clouds come together in autumn."[61] It is fascinating to note the Mahdī's invocation of the Hebrew name of God, presumably the tetragrammaton YHVH as it is written without vocalization in the Jewish tradition—the invocation of which is not permissible in Judaism until the coming of the messianic age.[62]

According to Muḥyī al-Dīn ibn ʿArabī, the ministers of the Mahdī followed by the multitudes of believers will pledge allegiance to the Imam in the same way that the family and companions of the Prophet Muḥammad swore an oath of allegiance to him at Ḥudaybiyyah.[63] In his *An Ocean Without Shore* Michel Chodkiewicz has demonstrated that chapter 366 of Ibn ʿArabī's *al-Futūḥāt al-makkiyyah* on the ministers of the Mahdī and their pact with him (*mubāyaʿat al-quṭb*) directly corresponds to *sūrat al-Fatḥ* or chapter 48 in the Quran where the pact at Ḥudaybiyyah is discussed and God tells the Prophet and the believers, "Truly those who pledge allegiance unto thee [Muḥammad], pledge allegiance only unto God. The Hand of God is over their hands. . . ." (48:10)[64]

59. On the symbolism of the sword in Islam, see René Guénon, *Symbols of Sacred Science*, pp. 179–184.

60. Seyyed Hossein Nasr, "Spiritual Chivalry" in Seyyed Hossein Nasr, ed., *Encyclopaedia of Islamic Spirituality*, vol. II, pp. 304–315.

61. *The Divine Guide in Early Shiʿism*, pp. 121–122.

62. On the esoteric significance on the Supreme Name in the Jewish tradition, see Leo Schaya, "The Great Name of God," in *The Universal Meaning of the Kabbalah*, pp. 145–165.

63. *Muḥammad*, pp. 252–256. This oath of allegiance to the Prophet of Islam became the prototype for the initiatic pact made with the Shaykh in Sufism.

64. Michel Chodkiewicz, *An Ocean Without Shore*, trans. by David Streight, p. 68. Ibn ʿArabī also states, "God will appoint as His ministers a group [of spiritual

With his companions, the Imam will then wage battles to confront tyranny, oppression, and false messiahs, and redress historical and current grievances and injustices. According to one tradition attributed to Imam al-Ṣādiq, "When [the Mahdī] rises he will deal with the Arabs and Quraysh only by the sword."[65] Ibn 'Arabī (d. 1240) also states in his *al-Futūḥāt al-makkiyyah*:

> [The Mahdī] will manifest religion as it [really] is in itself, the religion by which the Messenger of God would judge and rule if he were there. He will eliminate the different schools of [religious law] so that only the pure religion (Quran 39:3) remains, and his enemies will be those who follow blindly the *'ulamā'*, the people of *ijtihād*, because they will see the Mahdī judging differently from the way followed by their imams [i.e., the historical founders of the schools of Islamic law]. So they will only accept the Mahdī's authority grudgingly and against their will, because of their fear of his sword and his strength, and because they covet [the power and wealth] that he possesses. But the common people of the Muslims and the greater part of the elite among them will rejoice in him, while the true knowers of God among the People of [spiritual] Realities will pledge allegiance to him because of God's directly informing them [of the Mahdī's true nature and mission], through [inner] unveiling and immediate witnessing.[66]

While the Mahdī's mission will be fulfilled through outward and inward battles that reestablish justice and order in this world, his being and function are also embodiments of Divine Hope, Light,

men] whom He has kept hidden for him in the secret recesses of His Unseen [i.e., the spiritual world]. God has acquainted [these Helpers], through unveiling and immediate witnessing, with the [Divine] Realities and the contents of God's Command concerning His servants. So the Mahdī makes his decisions and judgments on the basis of consultation with them, since they are the true knowers, who really know what is There [in the Divine Reality]. . . ." "The Mahdī's Helpers~Chapter 366," trans. James W. Morris in *The Meccan Revelations* (*al-Futūḥāt al-makkiyyah*), vol. I, p. 70.

65. *The Occultation of the Twelfth Imam*, p. 25.

66. *The Meccan Revelations* (*al-Futūḥāt al-makkiyyah*), vol. I, p. 69. It is necessary to state that nowhere, to our knowledge, does Ibn 'Arabī identify the Mahdī as the Twelfth Imam, although some Shī'ites have read in his writings on the Mahdī references to the Twelfth Imam.

and Mercy.[67] The Mahdī's mission will be marked by the manifestation of Mercy, which is an essential Quality of God and of the Prophet Muḥammad, who according to the Quran is "a mercy unto the worlds." (21:107) Ibn 'Arabī writes,

> For if a human being gets angry of his own accord, his anger does not contain mercy in any respect; but if he becomes angry for God's sake [i.e., in fulfilling the divine commandments], then his anger is God's Anger and God's Anger is never free from being mixed with Divine Mercy. . . . Because (God's) Mercy, since it preceded [His] Anger, entirely covers all engendered being and extends to every thing (Quran 7:156). . . . Therefore this Mahdī does not become angry except for God's sake, so that his anger does not go beyond [what is required in] upholding God's limits that He has prescribed; this is just the opposite of the [ordinary] person who becomes angry because of his own desires for [something happening] contrary to his own personal aims. And likewise the person who becomes angry [only] for God's sake can only be just and equitable, not tyrannical and unjust."[68]

The Mahdī—who embodies the virtues of the Prophet, such as humility, magnanimity, and truthfulness—is a theophany of Divine Guidance and Mercy, a benevolent leader to the faithful and a guide for serious seekers. As the *insān al-kāmil* or Universal Man he will naturally reflect and bring into equilibrium the Divine Qualities of Mercy and Rigor here on earth. While he will be an insurmountable warrior and a just ruler, it must be remembered that mercy always

67. Henry Corbin writes concerning the color symbolism Shaykh Muḥammad Karīm-Khān Kirmānī associates with Imam al-Mahdī, "The pillar of white light is here the mystical figure of the Twelfth Imam, the Imam of our times, the 'Imam hidden from the senses but present to the hearts of those who believe in him.' He is never named without the interpolation, 'May God hasten our joy of him!' This joy is his future advent as the Imam of the Resurrection, Renewer of the world, he who will restore the world to the state of purity that it possessed originally, at its creation (restoration, *apokatastasis*). This no doubt accounts for his role as the keeper of the white light. He bears the forename of the Prophet; he is the secret of *walāyah*, which . . . is itself the secret or esoteric dimension of prophecy, of the prophetic vocation and message. . . ." *Temple and Contemplation*, trans. Liadain Sherrard and Philip Sherrard (London: Kegan Paul International, 1986) p. 42.

68. *The Meccan Revelations* (*al-Futūḥāt al-makkiyyah*), vol. I, p. 77.

takes precedence among the true *awliyā' al-Raḥmān*, or "friends of the Merciful" as they are known by tradition.

In a very important saying attributed to Imam Muḥammad al-Bāqir we read,

> He was named the Mahdī [the Guided One] as he will be guided to a hidden [*khafi*] matter: he will recover the Torah and other Books of God from a cave . . . then will he judge between the people of the Torah by the Torah, between the people of the Gospel by the Gospel . . . and between the people of the Quran [lit. *al-Furqān*] by the Quran. . . .[69]

Here the cave symbolizes the inner heart or initiatic center and esoteric knowledge that is mostly hidden from humanity during the occultation of the Imam.[70] When the Mahdī rises and emerges from his concealment he reveals the diversity and transcendent unity of the revealed religions to humanity. In the above account we see the concrete restoration of the revealed religions for the various orthodox religious communities and the Divinely mandated unveiling of their common metaphysical principles and unity. The Mahdī's Eliatic function makes humanity aware that these diverse religious paths lead to the same summit, where we find the transcendent unity of religions. Knowledge of this esoteric and transcendent unity will in fact lead to, through the wisdom and reign of the Mahdī and Jesus, eventual peace and harmony among the various religious communities.[71] According to Seyyed Hossein Nasr,

> According to Islam when the Mahdī appears before the end of time, not only will he reestablish peace but he will also uplift the

69. Trans. by Kareem Monib from Ibn Bābūyih al-Ṣadūq, *'Ilal al-sharā'i'* (Najaf, 1966), p. 161. Amir-Moezzi, also translates a section of this *ḥadīth* as follows, "He will take the Torah and the other holy Books from the cave and will judge the faithful of the Torah from the Torah, and the faithful of the Gospels from the Gospels . . . and the faithful of the Quran according to the Quran. . . ." *The Divine Guide in Early Shi'ism*, p. 225.

70. For more on the symbolism of the cave, see René Guénon, *Symbols of Sacred Science*, pp. 193–222.

71. The parody of this function and unity is the reign and system of the Anti-Christ. See René Guénon, *The Reign of Quantity & the Signs of the Times*, trans. Lord Northbourne (Hillsdale, NY: Sophia Perennis, 2001), pp. 267–274.

> outward religious forms to unveil their inner meaning and their essential unity. . . . Similar accounts are to be found in other traditions such as Hinduism. . . .[72]

In addition to Islam, the Imam affirms and restores all of the revealed religions for the various communities under his dominion. While guiding the Muslim community, the Mahdī does not simply universally implement the Islamic tradition, but also revives Judaism, Christianity and even the religions of the East. Through his wisdom and the Divine command he calls the faithful of all revealed religions to live according to their scriptures and traditions, establishes their terrestrial harmony, and demonstrates their celestial unity in God. By restoring and unveiling the inner content of the revealed religions, the Mahdī orients each religious community towards their common Source and prepares humanity for the Second Coming of Jesus the Messiah.[73] In the words of Henry Corbin,

> What the sages perceived is that the advent of the Imam would make manifest the hidden meaning of all the Revelations. The

72. *Knowledge and the Sacred*, p. 308. Nasr also writes, "Muslims have always had an innate feeling of possessing in their purest form the doctrines that all religions have come to proclaim before. In Islamic gnosis, or Sufism, this truth is *al-tawḥīd* in its metaphysical sense, the eternal wisdom, the *religio perennis*, which Islam has come to reveal in its fullness. For the Sharīʿite Muslim it is the doctrine of monotheism which he believes to have been revealed by every prophet. That is why at the end of the cycle the appearance of the Mahdī brings to light the common inner meaning of all religions." *Sufi Essays*, p. 132. Amir-Moezzi also states, "The Mahdī will also restore other religions, likewise abandoned and disfigured, to their original truth, in effect, it is said that he will take out of his cave, where they are hidden, all the holy Books of the earlier prophets, and that he will have their principles followed by their faithful." *The Divine Guide in Early Shiʿism*, p. 119. See also, *The Occultation of the Twelfth Imam*, p. 25.

73. Seyyed Hossein Nasr notes, "Ibn ʿArabī and following him Dāʾūd al-Qayṣarī consider Christ as the universal 'seal of sanctity', and Ibn ʿArabī refers indirectly to himself as the 'particular seal of sanctity' whereas most Shīʿite authors believe these titles belong to ʿAlī and the Mahdī respectively. In this delicate question the distinction between the 'universal seal of sanctity' and the 'particular or Muḥammadan seal of sanctity' must be kept especially in mind. . . ." *Sufi Essays*, p. 108. For the purpose of this subject the above passage highlights the more particular Islamic function of the Mahdī and the universal function of Jesus the Messiah, which certainly embraces Islam or submission to God and the Muslim community.

> *ta'wīl* will triumph, enabling the human race to discover its unity, just as, throughout the time of the *ghaybah*, the secret of the only true ecumenism will have been contained in esotericism.[74]

In addition to disclosing the inner content of the revealed books, the Mahdī also makes the signs of God upon the horizons and within us transparent phenomena by unveiling their archetypes, which are none other than the Divine Names and Attributes.[75] Imam al-Ṣādiq states: "[the companions of the Mahdī] are like sun worshippers and moon worshippers."[76] These two great celestial symbols can be interpreted in a variety of different ways. Suffice it to say, the signs of God on earth and upon the horizons will be read and understood by the Mahdī and his followers, catalyzing a recollection of their metaphysical archetypes and microcosmic analogies.[77] Indeed, the overemphasis on the transcendence of God has created an insurmountable barrier between God and His creation in the minds of some exoterists.[78] The Mahdī will affirm both the transcendence and the immanence of the Divine Reality, restoring Islam (submission to God) and the primordial tradition (*al-dīn al-ḥanīf*). Virgin nature will again be revered as a sacred book revealing the *vestigia Dei* or *āyāt Allāh* through an initiatic awakening of the Intellect (*al-'aql*) or eye of the heart (*'ayn al-qalb*) of men and women. The Mahdī's spiritual revival of man, his interior faculties and traditional modes of living, will have a restorative impact on the natural world and help to ameliorate the environmental crisis confronting humanity.

74. *History of Islamic Philosophy*, p. 71.

75. The Quran states, "We shall show them Our signs upon the horizons and within themselves till it becomes clear to them that it is the Truth. Does it not suffice that thy Lord is Witness over all things? Behold! They are in doubt regarding the meeting with their Lord. Behold! Truly He encompasses all things." (41:53–54)

76. *The Divine Guide in Early Shi'ism*, p. 121.

77. Here we have in mind the Supreme Knowledge of non-duality and *māyā* or the Unity and gradation of Light to use the language of Suhrawardī on the one hand, and the Intellect and the receptive rational and psychic faculties within man on the other.

78. Regarding the *fuqahā'*, Ibn 'Arabī states, "If the swords were not in [the Mahdī's] hands, they would give him the death sentence." *An Ocean Without Shore*, p. 21.

According to Islamic eschatological teachings the Mahdī's return will precede the Second Coming of Jesus the Messiah, the emergence of these two figures being the two great signs before the Day of Judgment.[79] Concerning Jesus or Sayyidnā 'Īsā, the Prophet Muḥammad stated: "God, the Exalted, will raise the Messiah, son of Mary, who will arrive close to the white minaret in the East of Damascus. . . . He will pursue the Anti-Christ (al-Dajjāl) and will encounter him at the gate of Lud and will slaughter him. . . ."[80] Eventually, the Mahdī will be accompanied by Jesus, whom the Mahdī will lead in prayer in the Masjid al-Aqṣā in Jerusalem.[81] Following 'Abd al-Karīm Jīlī (d. 1424), William Chittick sheds light on the inner significance of the Mahdī and Jesus, "The conflict between al-Dajjāl and Jesus refers to the battle between the ego and the Spirit, while the appearance of the Mahdī alludes to man's becoming 'the Possessor of Equilibrium at the pinnacle of every perfection.'"[82] Jesus the Spirit of God (*rūḥ Allāh*) must conquer the lower self (*nafs*). While the rebellious soul personified by the Anti-Christ is in perpetual conflict with the Spirit, the soul that has surrendered to God can be integrated into the Kingdom of Heaven within man through the guidance of the Spirit or the Intellect—the Imam of one's being.[83]

79. The Mahdī is not the Messiah himself, although part of the messianic function.

80. Imam Nawawī, *Gardens of the Righteous* (*Riyadh al-salihin*), trans. by Muhammad Zafrulla Khan (London: Islam International Publications Ltd., 1989), *ḥadīth* 1814, p. 305.

81. Moojan Momen, *An Introduction to Shi'i Islam* (New Haven: Yale University Press, 1985) p. 166. Imam Ja'far al-Ṣādiq also states, "There will come with the [Mahdī], peace be upon him, from the outskirts of Kūfa, twenty-seven men. Fifteen of the people of Moses who shed their blood for the truth and remained true to it, seven people from the cave, Joshua, Salmān, Abū Dujāna al-Anṣarī, al-Miqdād and Mālik al-Ashtar. They will act as helpers (*anṣār*) and judges in his presence." *The Book of Guidance*, p. 554.

82. William C. Chittick, "Eschatology," *Islamic Spirituality*, vol. I, p. 401.

83. Sufi psychology, based on the Quran and the soul of the Prophet, not only distinguishes between the body, soul and the Spirit, but also between the various levels of the soul. See Seyyed Hossein Nasr, *The Need for a Sacred Science*, pp. 15–23; and Mohammad Ajmal, "Sufi Science of the Soul," *Islamic Spirituality*, vol. I, pp. 294–307.

Not only are there future helpers of the Mahdī, but the past and present friends of God are said to be in communion with him throughout his occultation. Seyyed Hossein Nasr remarks,

> In speaking of the Sufi master in the Persian context one must remember the role of the Twelfth Imam, who is the Hidden Imam, both in Shīʿism and in Sufism as it exists in the Shīʿite world. Inasmuch as the Imam, although in concealment, is alive and is the spiritual axis of the world, he is the Pole (*quṭb*) with whom all Sufi masters are inwardly connected. He is to Shīʿism what the supreme pole is to Sufism in its Sunni context. In Shīʿism the Imams, especially ʿAlī, the first, and the Mahdī, the last, are the spiritual guides *par excellence*. The Hidden Imam, representing the whole chain of Imams, is the pole that attracts the hearts of the believers and it is to him that men turn for guidance.[84]

In a manner similar to Elias, the Hidden Imam plays not only an important function at the end of this cycle of human existence, but can also reveal himself to the elect among the faithful during his occultation. Nasr also writes that, "The Twelfth Imam is also the secret master of this world and can appear to those who are in the appropriate spiritual state to see him. . . ."[85] Nevertheless, Muslims who are searching for esoteric knowledge and guidance from the Mahdī or Khiḍr should first look to the authentic Sufi *shuyukh* and Shīʿite *ʿurafā'* or gnostics who reflect the light of the Prophet (*al-nūr al-muḥammadiyyah*) and the Pole (*quṭb*) in their lives and teachings. According to Amir-Moezzi:

> These believers are those that later sources called "men of the Invisible" (*rijāl al-ghayb*), and about whom it is said that their existence is indispensable to humanity, since they are the ones that will continue to transmit the Divine Science secretly until the Return of the Hidden Imam.[86]

The sources indicated are not referring to those who claim to represent the Mahdī politically or as authorities of the transmitted religious sciences alone. Better indications of such representatives

84. *Sufi Essays*, p. 66.
85. Seyyed Hossein Nasr, *The Heart of Islam*, p. 72.
86. *The Divine Guide in Early Shiʿism*, p. 137.

are the attainment of spiritual realization, the presence of sanctity, and virtue—all of which require, for Muslims, fidelity to the Sacred Law and theological doctrines of Islam. In a manner similar to the Christian world, where some ambitious religious and political leaders and groups claim to represent the Messiah, yet ignore the love and charity of Christ, not every charismatic leader in the Muslim world who claims to speak and act for the Mahdī actually does. More often than not, the initiates of the Hidden Imam among the *rijāl al-ghayb* perform their spiritual work in their own private and unassuming manner. Indeed, most of the spiritual luminaries who have written or spoken about their inward connection to the Mahdī only did so through enigmatic allusions and with the utmost discretion, while a great many others seemed to have remained silent on the matter.[87]

Some Conclusions

The Islamic sources provide us with abundant knowledge concerning the esoteric and Eliatic function of Khiḍr and the Mahdī, reminding Muslims of their shared heritage and destiny with their Jewish and Christian neighbors and believers from other traditions. Nevertheless, the function of the Universal Savior to appear in the Last Days—known alternatively as the expected Messiah in Judaism, Jesus in Christianity and Islam, the Kalki Avatar, Maitreya Buddha, and other designations—remains largely marginalized by adherents of the various traditions who believe that the Messiah will promote their religion alone and overwhelm or destroy all others.[88] By reflecting upon the sacred scriptures and traditional sources and realizing that there is only One Divine Reality who sent many prophets to establish the diverse revealed religions and who

87. On the relationship of the Shīʿite *ʿurafā'* and Sufis to the Hidden Imam during his occultation, see M.A. Amir Moezzi, *The Spirituality of Shiʿi Islam*, pp. 339–374, 418–485; Seyyed Hossein Nasr, *Ṣadr al-Dīn Shīrāzī and his Transcendent Theosophy*, pp. 36–37, 51; and Sayyid M.H. Ṭabāṭabā'ī, *Kernel of the Kernel* (*Risāla-yi Lubb al-lubāb*), pp. 121–122, 130.

88. For a comprehensive treatment of the subject of the Messiah in the world's religions, see Charles Upton, *Legends of the End* (Hillsdale, NY: Sophia Perennis, 2004). It is important to note that while the Mahdī and the Messiah are two distinct

will send the Mahdī and the Messiah to establish peace and justice among humanity during the messianic era, we can begin to acknowledge our shared heritage and destiny and perhaps live together—in the here and now—in greater peace and accord.

The Eliatic function in Islam is not limited to the figures mentioned here, but also manifests through authentic living spiritual guides among the Sufis and gnostics, as well as the lives and writings of those Muslim sages who have emphasized the inner nature and universality of Islam throughout history, including the Prophet of Islam and his family,[89] Uways al-Qaranī, Manṣūr Ḥallāj, Shihāb al-Dīn Suhrawardī, Farīd al-Dīn 'Aṭṭār, Jalāl al-Dīn Rūmī, Muḥyī al-Dīn ibn 'Arabī, Dārā Shikūh, and the Amīr 'Abd al-Qādir. In this regard, the works of René Guénon ('Abd al-Wāḥid Yaḥyā), Frithjof Schuon ('Īsā Nūr al-Dīn Aḥmad), Leo Schaya ('Abd al-Quddūs), Titus Burckhardt (Ibrāhīm 'Izz al-Dīn), Martin Lings (Abū Bakr Sirāj al-Dīn) and Seyyed Hossein Nasr are preeminent among Muslim scholars in the contemporary period and a saving barque for serious seekers because they emphasize the quintessential dimensions of religion, the transcendent unity of religions, and the need to practice one orthodox religion that God has revealed to humanity. In a symbolic sense, these Muslim sages inherited the "gift of tongues" and are therefore conversant in the various esoterisms that Heaven has given man access to, revealing the significance of Jewish, Christian and Islamic esoterism, Hinduism, Buddhism, Taoism, and the Shamanic traditions, and demonstrating their essential unity or the primordial "one language." We may conclude with these words of Leo Schaya:

figures, it seems likely to us that the Kalki Avatar and Maitreya Buddha are designations for Jesus the Messiah in Hinduism and Buddhism. Based upon our understanding there will not be several renewers, each in a different religion, but one primary restorer of Tradition or Messiah known by various appellations.

89. Imam 'Alī in fact said in his *Khuṭbat al-bayān*, "I am the Sign of the All-Powerful. I am the gnosis of the mysteries. I am the Threshold of Thresholds. I am the companion of the radiance of the divine Mystery. I am the First and the Last, the Manifest and the Hidden. I am the Face of God. I am the mirror of God, the supreme Pen, the *Tabula secreta*. I am he who in the Gospel is called Elias. I am he who is in possession of the secret of God's Messenger." *History of Islamic Philosophy*, p. 49.

The true "Eliatic flow" will grow stronger, according to the Scriptures, as the world's darkness grows deeper, until the final moment. Then, "your sons and your daughters shall prophecy, your old men shall dream dreams, your young men shall see visions. And also upon the servants and upon the handmaids in those days will I pour out my spirit. And will shew wonders in the heavens and the earth, blood and fire and pillars of smoke. The sun shall be turned to darkness and the moon into blood before the great and terrible day of YHVH come. And it shall come to pass that whosoever shall call on the name of YHVH shall be saved." (Joel 2:28–31)[90]

90. "The Eliatic Function," p. 40. On the universal significance of the invocation (*dhikr*) of the Name of God in various religions, especially as it relates to this epoch, see Frithjof Schuon, *The Transcendent Unity of Religions*, pp. 145–148, 163–166.

6

Hermetic Wisdom in Islam

> In truth, certainly and without doubt, whatever is below is like that which is above, and whatever is above is like that which is below, to accomplish the miracle of one thing. (*The Emerald Tablet*)[1]

> Naught is there, but that its treasuries (*khazā'in*) lie with Us, and We do not send it down, save in a known measure. (Quran 15:21)

Despite being a pivotal prophet in Islam and a seminal sage in the philosophical heritage of antiquity as a whole, an awareness of the significance of Hermes and the texts and wisdom attributed to him has been largely eclipsed in the Muslim world and the West, both of which inherited and cultivated the study of the philosophical and cosmological wisdom associated with this figure in the premodern period.[2] Classical Muslim sages frequently referred to Hermes as the "Father of the philosophers" (Abu'l-ḥukamā') and identified him with the antediluvian prophet Enoch (Ukhnūkh) in the Bible or Idrīs as he is known in the Quran, where we read: "And remember

1. Titus Burckhardt, *Alchemy: Science of the Cosmos, Science of the Soul*, trans. William Stoddart (Baltimore: Penguin Books Inc, 1974), p. 196.

2. After the Prophet of Islam, there are a few prophets who occupy a central position in the Quran and the Islamic tradition in general, including Adam, Abraham, Moses and Jesus. If each can be seen as an aspect of the Prophet of Islam and his teachings, Adam can be said to represent the primordial tradition (*al-dīn al-ḥanīf*), Abraham faith (*īmān/kalām*), Moses the law (*islām/Sharī'ah*), and Jesus the spiritual path (*iḥsān/ṭarīqah*). We would argue that the prophet Enoch or Idrīs deserves to be placed in their company because he stands at the origin of Islamic sapience (*ḥikmah*) or prophetic philosophy, including both its philosophical and mystical dimensions.

Idrīs in the Book. Lo! Verily he was truthful, a prophet. And We raised him to a high station." (19:56–57)[3] The fact that God "raised him to a high station" corresponds to the Biblical account of Enoch being taken alive to Heaven and also his transfiguration into the Metatron.[4]

Hermes is among the most universal figures of antiquity. In addition to being identified with Enoch or Idrīs, Hermes has also been associated with the Egyptian deity Thoth, Mercury of the Romans, and the Persian figure Hūshang. In ancient Greece, Hermes was seen as a deity, the son of Zeus and Maia, a messenger of the gods, and later as the son of Agathedemon and the teacher of Pythagoras.[5] He is thus one of the seminal figures of the Greek philosophical tradition, including Hermeticism, Pythagoreanism, Platonism and their diverse expressions in the Muslim world and the West. Among the writings attributed to Hermes are *The Hermetic Corpus*, *The Perfect Sermon*, Twenty-seven summaries of Stobaeus, twenty-five works found in Christian sources, and material in the writings of Zosimus, Fulgentius, Iamblichus, and Julian.[6] For the sake of clarity we will hereafter refer to the tradition based on Greek Hermetica and the Greco-Egyptian Hermes as Hermeticism and the

3. See also Quran 21:85. The earliest known recorded Muslim source that identifies Idrīs with Enoch is Wahb ibn Munabbih (d. c. 730) among the *tābi'ūn*. Kevin Van Bladel writes, "He is credited by early sources with the statement that Idrīs is Enoch and the Idrīs received thirty scrolls from God." *The Arabic Hermes: From Pagan Sage to Prophet of Science* (Oxford: Oxford University Press, 2009), pp. 156, 167.

4. On the Metatron, see René Guénon, *The King of the World*, pp. 13–19; and Andrei A. Orlov, *The Enoch-Metatron Tradition* (Tübingen, Germany: Mohr Siebeck, 2005). In Islam, the Metatron is synonymous with *al-Rūḥ* or the Spirit, who as the celestial or angelic Pole (*quṭb*) is identified with the archangels and reflected on earth by numerous prophets and saints, including the Prophet Muḥammad, Jesus, Elias, Enoch, Khiḍr, the Imam in Shī'ism and the Pole in Sufism, as well as the inner spiritual substance of each man and woman. The Metatron, like *al-Rūḥ* and *al-quṭb*, is more of a function and principle than a specific person, although specific angels, prophets and saints manifest this function, which in fact represents the highest cosmic reality of man, the lowest aspect of Divinity and the *barzakh* or isthmus between man and God.

5. Seyyed Hossein Nasr, *Islamic Life and Thought*, pp. 103–105.

6. Ibid., p. 104.

study and translation of these texts by Muslims and the philosophical and cosmological wisdom in their own tradition as the Hermetic wisdom (*ḥikmah idrīsiyyah*) of Islam.[7] The presence of Hermetic wisdom in Islam cannot properly be called Islamic Hermeticism, as Hermeticism is an integral tradition in its own right associated with the Greco-Egyptian religion that is no longer living. As an adjective, however, Hermetic can qualify Islam or Christianity because the cosmological vision associated with the figure Hermes is universal and to be found within each living religion.[8] Moreover, Muslims felt free to borrow from the arts and sciences of ancient prophets and sages and integrate these into their own civilization and worldview because most Muslim philosophers and scientists understood the wisdom of the Greeks and that of Hermes in particular to have been revealed by the One God.

The presence of Hermes and Hermetic wisdom in the Islamic tradition results from the study and transmission of Hermetic texts by Muslim philosophers and the reality and presence of analogous wisdom and cosmological doctrines within the Islamic sources themselves. Muslim sages and other scholars in the Abbasid period translated the writings attributed to Hermes from Greek and Middle Persian into Arabic and integrated these works and the cosmological sciences found therein into their own worldview.[9] Moreover,

7. Some scholars might object to our use of the term "Hermetic" to describe the cosmological doctrines of Islam itself. In the same way that we find traces of "Christic" and "Eliatic" wisdom in Islam without it being Christian or Jewish in origin, there is also a Hermetic wisdom in Islam which does not derive from Hermeticism, but from the Quran and *Sunnah*. However, in the case of this Hermetic wisdom, some Muslim sages did in fact also borrow from the pre-Islamic writings attributed to Hermes. This was possible because they were not borrowing a metaphysical or theological doctrine, nor the revealed rites of another tradition, but somewhat secondary cosmological doctrines, sciences, and symbols. In any case, it is also possible to translate the term Hermetic wisdom as *ḥikmah idrīsiyyah*. In the same way that Sachiko Murata observes a cosmological vision in Islam analogous to that of the Chinese tradition in her *The Tao of Islam* without it being Taoist in origin, we can speak of a Hermetic wisdom of Islam without it being necessarily derived from Greek, Middle Persian or even Arabic Hermetica.

8. René Guénon, *Traditional Forms & Cosmic Cycles*, trans. Henry D. Fohr (Hillsdale, NY: Sophia Perennis, 2004), pp. 74–76.

9. *The Arabic Hermes*, 23–63.

the presence of Hermetic wisdom is found in the Quranic revelation itself, as well as the *Ḥadīth* of the Prophet of Islam and the teachings of other early Muslim sages. Here it is not to be identified exclusively with Hermes, but the Divine Source of all Revelation that according to Muslim belief synthesized the wisdom of all pre-Islamic sacred books and prophets in the Quran as the sum of wisdom and "Mother of the book" (*Umm al-kitāb*) on the one hand, and the Prophet of Islam as the "Seal of the prophets" (*khātam al-anbiyā'*) on the other. Cosmology, symbolism and a hermeneutics of scripture, nature and the soul, which are necessarily rooted in metaphysical principles in every living religion, are in fact perennial forms of wisdom.[10] Moreover, the Greco-Egyptian teachings attributed to Hermes that were transmitted to Muslims and the Hermetic wisdom of the Islamic tradition itself interpenetrate throughout history. Discerning Muslim sages accepted Greek and Persian Hermetic writings as their own inheritance precisely because they recognized in the writings and sciences attributed to Hermes revealed wisdom in accord with the principle of Unity and originally issuing from the same Source of wisdom that revealed the Quran to the Prophet of Islam.

Those who cultivated the study of Hermetic wisdom in both the Islamic world and the West associated Hermes with the cosmological sciences, the original meaning of philosophy, symbolism, alchemy, astrology, geometry, architecture, and medicine. While the influence and function of Hermes and Hermetic wisdom varies considerably in the different streams of Islamic philosophy and Sufism, from those Muslims who translated and studied the writings attributed to Hermes to the more general employment of certain terms and symbols associated with alchemy or astrology to describe the purely Quranic and Muḥammadan spiritual path, it would not be an exaggeration to state that Hermes or Idrīs has a solar and axial function as the prophetic origin and pole of Islamic sapience (*ḥikmah*). He fulfills a cosmic intellectual function and influence in the Islamic tradition second only to the Quran and the Prophet of Islam.

10. See Titus Burckhardt, *Mirror of the Intellect*, pp. 17–26.

The diverse strands of the Hermetic heritage in the Islamic world envisaged Hermes differently. The Sabians of Ḥarrān claimed that Hermes was their prophet and for a time received protected legal status as People of the Book.[11] Through the influence and writings of Abū Yūsuf Ya'qūb al-Kindī (d. 866) and Abū Ma'shar al-Balkhī (d. 886), Muslims came to believe in three Hermeses: the antediluvian prophet Enoch or Idrīs (Hirmis al-harāmisah), the Babylonian Hermes and the Egyptian Hermes.[12] Despite the challenges that this doctrine raises, Muslims generally mean the prophet Idrīs when they refer to Hermes. The doctrine of the three Hermeses is seen as one of the meanings of the Greek epithet *trismegistus* or in Arabic *al-muthallath bi'l-ḥikmah* (triplicate in wisdom), but another interpretation is found in the *Tabula Smaragdina* (*The Emerald Tablet*). Titus Burckhardt relates,

> *Trismegistus* means 'thrice great' or 'thrice powerful.' The 'three parts of wisdom' correspond to the three great 'divisions' of the universe, namely, the spiritual, psychic, and corporeal realms, whose symbols are heaven, air, and earth.[13]

In his selection "Hermes and Hermetic Writings in the Islamic World," Seyyed Hossein Nasr identifies some of the writings attributed to Hermes in Arabic, including *Kitāb qarāṭīṣ al-ḥakīm*, *Kitāb al-ḥabīb*, *Kitāb tankalūsh* (also attributed to Ibn Waḥshiyyah), *Kitāb al-masmūmāt Shānāq*, the *Mu'āḍilat al-nafs* or *Zajr al-nafs* translated by Afḍal al-Dīn Kāshānī into Persian as *Yanbū' al-ḥayāt*, *Sirr al-khalīqah* (also attributed to Bālīnūs), *Qabas al-qābis fī tadbīr Hirmis al-Harāmis*, and also the *Ṣaḥā'if* or *Codices* of Idrīs cited in Majlisī's *Biḥār al-anwār*.[14] Special mention should also be made of *al-Fihrist* of Ibn al-Nadīm, which Nasr states is "the most important source of knowledge of Hermetic writings in Arabic."[15] Nasr also writes, "One might safely say that all those Muslim authors who

11. *The Arabic Hermes*, pp. 64–114.
12. Ibid., pp. 121–163; *Islamic Life and Thought*, pp. 105–106; and *Traditional Forms and Cosmic Cycles*, p. 91.
13. *Alchemy*, p. 201.
14. *Islamic Life and Thought*, pp. 106–107.
15. Ibid., p. 106.

were inclined towards a study of alchemy, astrology and other occult sciences were influenced to some degree by the Hermetic school."[16]

The seminal Muslim sage associated with the study of alchemy is Jābir ibn Ḥayyān (d. 815) or Geber in Latin, remembered by tradition as a disciple of the Sixth Shī'ite Imam Ja'far al-Ṣādiq and author of what has been termed the Jābirian corpus, which includes such foundational alchemical texts such as *Kitāb al-sab'īn* (*The Seventy Books*) and *Kitāb al-mīzān* (*The Book of the Balance*).[17] Another prominent Muslim alchemist is Ibn Umayl (d. c. 960), who is associated with the school of Jābir and penned the alchemical text the *Turba Philosophorum* wherein the origin of the science of alchemy is attributed to Hermes.[18] Other noteworthy alchemists in Islamic history include the Umayyad prince Khālid ibn Yazīd (d. 704), the early Egyptian Sufi Dhu'l-Nūn al-Miṣrī (d. 859), Muḥammad ibn Zakariyyā' al-Rāzī (d. 925), and Mīr Findiriskī (d. 1640–1), who was likely one of the teachers of Mullā Ṣadrā.[19] Mention must also be made of the anonymous alchemical text the *Ghāyat al-ḥakīm* or *Picatrix* in the West, and also the fact that alchemy is generally transmitted orally or through an apprenticeship.[20] The astrological works of Abū Ma'shar and 'Abd al-Jalīl al-Sijzī (d. c. 1020), as well as *al-Tafhīm* of Bīrūnī (d. 1048) also demonstrate the influence of Hermetic cosmology.[21] This brief survey of early Muslim sages associated with the Hermetic wisdom of Islam is not meant to be exhaustive. Rather, a few works and figures have been cited to demonstrate the presence of this wisdom during the period when the Islamic intellectual and spiritual tradition found expression in written form, which allows us to now examine in greater depth the

16. Ibid., p. 108.

17. Seyyed Hossein Nasr, *Islamic Science: An Illustrated Study* (Westerham, Kent: World of Islam Festival Publishing Company Ltd., 1976), p. 199.

18. *Islamic Life and Thought*, p. 107.

19. Ibid., pp. 108, 120–123. See also, John Eberly, *Al-Kimia: The Mystical Islamic Essence of the Sacred Art of Alchemy* (Hillsdale: NY: Sophia Perennis, 2004).

20. *Islamic Life and Thought*, p. 107.

21. Ibid., pp. 108, 111.

meaning that Muslims attached to the philosophical and cosmological wisdom associated with the prophet Idrīs.

Hermetic wisdom is essentially cosmological, although every true vision of the cosmic order sees its roots in metaphysical principles. By cosmological we mean a study of both the objective world of nature and the subjective soul and Spirit of man. Here the macrocosm and the microcosm are linked and can in fact be seen as mirror images of each other by virtue of being respective radiations of the single metaphysical Principle. This correspondence is expressed by the Ikhwān al-Ṣafā' in their *Rasā'il* by the saying "The world is a great man and man is a little world" (*al-'ālam insān kabīr wa'l-insān 'ālam ṣaghīr*).[22] The duality that we normally posit between subject and object or man and the world is reconciled by awakening the Intellect or the eye of the heart that sees things as they truly are. The analogy of the microcosm and the macrocosm is also expressed by the Sufi doctrine of the Universal Man (*al-insān al-kāmil*), where "man is a symbol of universal Existence" (*al-insān ramz al-wujūd*) because his own inner reality contains all of the possibilities and levels of Existence and ultimately Being, from the lowest to the highest.[23] Hermeticism or the analogous Hermetic wisdom of Islam employ various symbols derived from Revelation, the revealed sciences and the natural world that allow access to "the lesser mysteries" associated with knowledge of the various levels of the cosmos and the soul and prepare the soul and Spirit of man for knowledge of "the greater mysteries."[24] Sufis such as Ibn 'Arabī, Ṣadr al-Dīn Qūnawī and 'Abd al-Karīm Jīlī discovered this Hermetic wisdom

22. See *Traditional Forms & Cosmic Cycles*, p. 80; *Alchemy*, pp. 34–56; Seyyed Hossein Nasr, *An Introduction to Islamic Cosmological Doctrines*, pp. 66–74; *The Tao of Islam*, pp. 23–46; Anna-Teresa Tymieniecka, ed., *Islamic Philosophy and Occidental Phenomenology on the Perennial Issue of Microcosm and Macrocosm* (Dordrecht, The Netherlands: Springer, 2006); and William Chittick, *Science of the Cosmos, Science of the Soul.*

23. *Traditional Forms & Cosmic Cycles*, p. 78.

24. "The greater mysteries" are none other than metaphysics or the effacement of man before the One and knowledge of the Supreme Identity beyond the macrocosm and microcosm. In the school of Ibn 'Arabī this is often referred to as the doctrine of the transcendent Unity of Being (*waḥdat al-wujūd*). Cosmological wisdom

both through the Islamic sources and through their own vision of the cosmos and the soul.

Central to this affair is the sacred science of symbolism.[25] The English word symbol is derived from the Greek *sym+ballo*, which means "to throw together" and according to Adrian Snodgrass suggests "the way in which the symbol carries the mind to its referent."[26] Among the earliest recorded usages of the word symbol is in fact by Hermes in a Homeric hymn.[27] According to Henri Peyre, "In Greek the term meant a portion of an object (a piece of pottery, for example) broken in two. . . ."[28] A symbol is not simply an analogy or a sign as the terms are generally used and understood in modern parlance, but a natural or revealed phenomenon that represents and partially communicates a higher archetype from the noumemal or intelligible world. An analogy or sign in the ordinary sense of the words refer to a representation of something else in the physical world, whereas a symbol refers to and partially communicates and embodies an archetype from a higher level of existence. The first therefore represents a horizontal relationship between two things on one level of existence, while the second a vertical relationship between the symbol and its archetype on two or more levels of existence. Hermeticism and Hermetic wisdom is essentially synonymous with symbolism as the science of relating lower aspects of reality to the higher and ultimately the Most High. As we read in *The Emerald Tablet*, "In truth, certainly and without doubt, whatever is below is

---

describes the higher levels of man and the world, while metaphysics is the immediate knowledge of God alone. Because the roots of man and the world are in God, cosmology is necessarily linked to metaphysics.

25. See René Guénon, *Symbols of Sacred Science*; Martin Lings, *Symbol & Archetype: A Study on the Meaning of Existence* (Louisville: KY: Fons Vitae, 2006); and Samer Akkach, *Cosmology and Architecture in Premodern Islam: An Architectural Reading of Mystical Ideas* (Albany, NY: State University of New York Press, 2005), pp. 4–53.

26. Adrian Snodgrass, *The Symbolism of the Stupa* (Ithaca, NY: Cornell University Press, 1985) p. 3; *Cosmology and Architecture in Premodern Islam*, p. 28.

27. *The Homeric Hymns*, trans. Diane Rayor (Berkeley, CA: University of California Press, 2004), p. 56.

28. Henri Peyre, *What is Symbolism?*, trans. Emmet Parker (Tuscaloosa, AL: The University of Alabama Press, 1980), p. 6.

like that which is above, and whatever is above is like that which is below, to accomplish the miracle of one thing." Similarly we read in the Quran, "Naught is there, but that its treasuries (*khazāʾin*) lie with Us, and We do not send it down, save in a known measure." (15:21)

The most frequently used word in Islam for a symbol is *āyah* (pl. *āyāt*), which simultaneously refers to each verse of the Quran, the signs or symbols in nature and those in the soul. The worlds of nature and the soul are also revealed books and the Quran is a perfect reflection of these worlds. An *āyah* of the Quran, nature or the soul is in fact a sign or symbol of God or *āyat Allāh*. The Quran states, "We shall show them Our signs upon the horizons and within themselves till it becomes clear to them that it is the Truth. . . ." (41:53)[29] Sufi interpreters of the three grand books saw the process of esoteric hermeneutics or *taʾwīl* in Arabic as returning a thing to its origin.[30] Symbolism is thus moving from the outward appearance of a particular symbol to its inward essence or archetype in the Divine Reality or a particular aspect of the Divine expressed by one or more of the Names of God. The Sun, for example, is not only a source of physical light and warmth, but also a superlative and universal symbol for the Divine Light (*al-Nūr*) that illuminates all things in this world and the next. As a messenger of God (or gods in the Greek Pantheon) Hermes is naturally linked to the science of hermeneutics, interpreting symbols from the corporeal and psychic worlds and relating them back to the spiritual world and the Divine Reality.

The philosophical dimensions of Islam that closely reflect the wisdom of Hermes and the Greek philosophical heritage as a whole go back to the Prophet of Islam when he said, "He who knoweth himself, knoweth his Lord" (*Man ʿarafa nafsahu faqad ʿarafa Rabbahu*). Knowledge of the self has been cultivated and taught in different forms by some of the most eminent Muslim philosophers and

29. The Quran also states, "And upon the earth are signs for those possessing certitude, and within your souls. Do you not then behold?" (50:20–21)

30. If the world is the macrocosm and the soul the microcosm, the Quran and Divine revelation in general can be regarded as the bibliocosm, which as the Divine Logos contains the archetypes of all things.

Sufis. The Master of *Ishrāq*, Shihāb al-Dīn Suhrawardī (d. 1191), presented a vision of man and the cosmos based on a metaphysics, cosmology and angelology of Light. According to the Shaykh, each soul has a higher angelic double that it must rise to meet and know as its true identity. Following Ibn Sīnā and the Muslim peripatetics, Suhrawardī has several visionary recitals that depict this catharsis of the soul from the body and its encounter and wedding with its angelic theophany of Light.[31] Thus knowledge of the soul leads to knowledge of its angelic and quasi-divine archetype, which is synonymous with the Intellect, Spirit, the Angel Gabriel for the Prophet of Islam, and the Muḥammadan Spirit for Muslims. The visions of Suhrawardī closely parallel the revelations Hermes receives from the Nous or Intellect in *The Hermetic Corpus*.[32] This is not surprising, as Suhrawardī sees Hermes as the prophetic progenitor of the *Ishrāqī* school. Suhrawardī writes in his *al-Muṭāraḥāt*: "Hermes said I met a spiritual being who conveyed to me the science of things. I asked him who art thou? He said I am thy Perfect Nature."[33] As mentioned in chapter one, for Suhrawardī, Hermes stands at the origin of both the Greek and Persian philosophical lineages, which are perpetuated and revived in Islam by the Sufis of Egypt and Persia and finally meet in the person and teachings of Suhrawardī. Thus, the intellectual function and teachings of Hermes find expression and continuity in the school of *Ishrāq*, which is also based on the Quran and the wisdom and light of the Prophet of Islam. As one of the great expositors of the *sophia perennis* in Islamic history, Suhrawardī understood the essential unanimity of the world's great religious and philosophical traditions and found no tension between the Islamic

31. Shihāb al-Dīn Suhrawardī, *The Mystical and Visionary Treatises of Suhrawardi*, trans. W.M. Thackston, Jr. (London: The Octagon Press, 1982). See also, Henry Corbin, *Avicenna and the Visionary Recital*, trans. Willard R. Trask (Irving: TX: Spring Publications, 1980).

32. *The Way of Hermes: New Translations of The Corpus Hermeticum and The Definitions of Hermes Trismegistus to Asclepius*, trans. Clement Salaman, Dorine van Oyen, William D. Wharton, and Jean-Pierre Mahé (Rochester, VT: Inner Traditions, 2004). The meeting and union of Hermes with the Nous corresponds to the transfiguration of Enoch into the Metatron in Judaism.

33. *Islamic Life and Thought*, p. 109.

tradition and Greek and Persian philosophy.[34] Following Suhrawardī, other eminent Muslim sages in the school of *Ishrāq* inherited his veneration of Hermes and the cultivation of Hermetic wisdom, including Quṭb al-Dīn Shīrāzī, Jalāl al-Dīn Dawānī, and Mullā Ṣadrā. Mullā Ṣadrā (d. 1640), who created a grand synthesis of the Islamic sapiential tradition known as the transcendent theosophy (*al-ḥikmat al-muta'āliyah*), relates his understanding of the origin of philosophy in his *Risālah fi'l-ḥudūth*:

> Know that wisdom (*ḥikmah*) began originally with Adam and his progeny Seth and Hermes, i.e., Idrīs, and Noah because the world is never deprived of a person upon whom the science of Unity and eschatology rests. And it is the greatest Hermes who propagated it (*ḥikmah*) throughout the regions of the world and different countries and manifested it and made it emanate upon the true worshippers. He is the "Father of philosophers (*Abu'l-ḥukamā'*) and the master of those who are the masters of the sciences.[35]

Also significant is the lesser-known Persian Muslim philosopher Afḍal al-Dīn Kāshānī or Bābā Afḍal (d. 1213–14), who championed knowledge of the self as the most direct means of knowing the Unity of God and all things because of the unifying nature of the Intellect (*al-'aql*) with that which it knows. Kāshānī translated the aforementioned Arabic Hermetic text *Mu'āḍilat al-nafs* or *Zajr al-nafs* into Persian as *Yanbū' al-ḥayāt* (*The Fountain of Life*). The primacy and centrality of knowledge of the self is brought out in this remarkable text:

> O soul, you must become cognizant of the knowledge of your essence and the meanings and forms within it. Do not suppose that anything whose knowing is indispensable to you is outside your essence. Rather, all is with you and in you . . . all things that the soul must know are in the soul, and there is no otherness between them and the soul.[36]

34. Seyyed Hossein Nasr, *Three Muslim Sages*, pp. 60–62.

35. *Islamic Life and Thought*, p. 106.

36. William C. Chittick, *The Heart of Islamic Philosophy: The Quest for Self-Knowledge in the Teachings of Afḍal al-Dīn Kāshānī* (Oxford: Oxford University Press, 2001), pp. 110–111.

Bābā Afḍal also translated *The Treatise of the Apple* attributed to Aristotle from Arabic into Persian as *Risāla-yi tuffāḥa*. In this account of Aristotle with his students on his deathbed we read:

> Aristotle said: ...The first to whom this knowledge arrived by revelation [*waḥy*] in our land was Hermes.
>
> Diogenes said, From whence did it come to Hermes?
>
> Aristotle said: His spirit was taken to heaven, and it reached him from the Higher Plenum, who took it from the remembrance of the Wise. Through him it came to earth, and the knowers took it from him.[37]

Also noteworthy is Kāshānī's Persian treatise *The Book of the Everlasting* (*Jāvidān-nāma*) that was later translated by Mullā Ṣadrā into Arabic as *The Elixir of the Gnostics* (*Iksīr al-ʿārifīn*).[38] William Chittick writes that the general theme of Bābā Afḍal's work "is the necessity of reading the 'signs on the horizons and in the souls,' a Quranic expression that is commonly taken to refer to the macrocosm and the microcosm, that is, the universe and the human being."[39] Kāshānī also wrote an abridgement of the first part of al-Ghazzālī's Persian treatise *The Alchemy of Happiness* (*Kīmiyā-yi saʿādat*), which demonstrates the wedding of Hermetic symbolism, Islamic philosophy in general and Sufism in the teachings of Bābā Afḍal. The abridged work is entitled *The Four Headings of the Alchemy of Happiness* (*Chahār ʿunwān-i kīmiyā-yi saʿādat*), wherein Kāshānī writes a philosophical summary of his and al-Ghazzālī's views on "knowledge of self, of God, of this world, and of the next world."[40]

The twin traditional sciences closely associated with Hermetic

37. Ibid., p. 105. William Chittick comments that, "This can be taken as a gloss on one of the two Quranic passages in which Idrīs is mentioned: 'Mention in the Book Idrīs; he was a truthful man, a prophet. We raised him up to a high place' (19:56). The 'high place' can be the home of the angels, whom the Quran sometimes calls the 'Higher Plenum.'" Ibid., pp. 107–108.

38. Ibid., pp. 194–233; and Mullā Ṣadrā, *The Elixir of the Gnostics* (*Iksīr al-ʿārifīn*), trans. William C. Chittick (Provo: UT: Brigham Young University Press, 2003).

39. *The Heart of Islamic Philosophy*, p. 20.

40. Ibid., p. 22.

wisdom are astrology (*aḥkam al-nujūm*) and alchemy (*al-kīmiyā'*).[41] While it is not possible for us to provide an exhaustive account and history of these sciences here, below we attempt to bring out the basic principles and meaning that these symbolic sciences had and have among Muslim sages.[42] Astrology is seen as the heavenly or active counterpart to the earthly or passive science of alchemy. It is important to note that these traditional sciences differ from astronomy and chemistry, which in modern science are based on a purely quantitative and material understanding of the universe and its elements. It is also inaccurate and misleading to reduce astrology to divination and alchemy solely to the material process of turning lead or other metals into gold.[43] While these sciences have historically been cultivated for a number of reasons, including those mentioned above, the higher symbolic understanding was preserved among certain Muslim sages. The Ikhwān al-Ṣafā' write:

> Astrology does not pretend and has not the right to pretend to an anticipated knowledge of events. Many people believe that astrology proposes to study the science of the unseen (*ghayb*), but they are definitely wrong. What they call the science of the unseen is really the science of indetermination, the gratuitous pretension of anticipating the future without recourse to any symptom or reasoning, be it causal or deductive. In this sense the unknown is

41. Two of the best sources on these topics in western languages are Titus Burckhardt, *Mystical Astrology According to Ibn 'Arabi*, trans. Bulent Rauf (Louisville, KY: Fons Vitae, 2001); and Titus Burckhardt, *Alchemy*. See also Seyyed Hossein Nasr, *Islamic Science*, pp. 126–134, 193–206.

42. The most important of the arcane sciences in Islam is the science of letters (*'ilm al-ḥurūf*), which is directly related to the Quran and the Arabic language. See, for example, René Guénon, "The Science of Letters (*'Ilm al-ḥurūf*)," *Symbols of Sacred Science*, pp. 43–49; "Notes on Angelic Number Symbolism in the Arabic Alphabet," *Insights into Islamic Esoterism & Taoism*, pp. 29–32; Jean Canteins, "The Hidden Sciences in Islam," *Encyclopaedia of Islamic Spirituality*, vol. II, pp. 447–463; and Denis Gril, "The Science of Letters," Muḥyī al-Dīn ibn al-'Arabī, *The Meccan Revelations* (*al-Futūḥāt al-makkiyyah*), vol. II, pp. 105–219.

43. René Guénon, *The Crisis of the Modern World*, trans. Arthur Osborne, Marco Pallis, and Richard C. Nicholson (Ghent, NY: Sophia Perennis, 2001), pp. 48–49.

accessible neither to the astrologers, nor diviners, nor prophets, nor sages. It is the work of God only.[44]

According to Seyyed Hossein Nasr, what appears to be divination in traditional astrology is in reality the study of "the angelic aspect of cosmic reality in determining the course of events in the terrestrial domain. . . ."[45] This aspect of astrology degenerates into pure superstition once the angelic and higher metaphysical levels of reality are cut off from the lower. In other words, once the primary cause of events in the universe are lost sight of, namely God and the angels through which He acts, men believe that it is the position of material stars and constellations themselves that determine their destiny, as opposed to the metaphysical and angelic principles that determine the movement of the stars and all cosmic realities, including the earth. In the traditional Muslim world, as in the contemporary West, there existed a popular astrology concerned with predicting the future. However, this understanding of astrology was somewhat marginal among serious Muslim sages who brought out the higher meaning of this science.

The vault of the heavens is a theatre for the contemplation of the signs of God, the different levels corresponding to various Names of God, intellects, angels, prophets and saints, the essential realities of which also exist in the inner being of man. By heavens we mean both the physical planets, moons, stars, the signs of the Zodiac and all that is known and unknown in the material universe above the earth, as well as the spiritual heavens that correspond to higher and more subtle levels of existence that religious men and women envisage and hope for as their posthumous abode. When traditional men and women looked towards the night sky, they did not make a distinction between the corporeal and the celestial heavens and could still imagine the angels circling the Throne of God in Paradise above

44. *An Introduction to Islamic Cosmological Doctrines*, p. 82.

45. *Islamic Science*, p. 127. Nasr also writes, "In these [metaphysical] works astrology is revealed to be in its symbolic aspect a means whereby man rediscovers his own cosmic dimension and becomes aware of his own angelic and archetypal reality and the influence of this reality upon his terrestrial existence." Ibid., p. 131.

them. It is in fact the higher or subtle heavens and angelic beings that shine through and determine the influence and movement of the lower or material heavens and all that is beneath them. Through a chain of causality, which begins with and is ultimately subsumed in the omnipotence of the One, the spiritual heavens influence the earth and all life upon it—the material heavens being symbols for the spiritual heavens or the archetypes.[46] Seyyed Hossein Nasr writes,

> As traditionally considered, the metaphysical basis of astrology is the spontaneous identification of the rhythms of the heavens with the prototypes of the physical world, these prototypes existing in the heaven of the signs (*falak al-burūj*). The signs of the Zodiac in their indefinite variety hide and reveal Pure Being at the same time. They are at once a veil which covers the "face of the Beloved" and a prism which disperses the "light of Being" into its constituent colors which comprise the world of manifestation. The regular cycles of the heavens in their rhythms symbolize the "eternal essences" while their effects upon the Earth indicate the interrelatedness of the parts of the cosmos and the submission of the beings of the world to their heavenly prototypes. The basis of astrology is symbolically the indissoluble marriage between heaven and earth and the derivation of all things on earth from their celestial counterparts.[47]

Traditional astrology envisages the universe as hierarchically structured heavenly spheres that encompass the earth from a geo-

46. Titus Burckhardt writes, "Traditional cosmology does not make an explicit differentiation between the planetary skies in their corporeal and visible reality, and that which corresponds to them in the subtle order; because the symbol is essentially identified with the thing it symbolizes, and there is no reason for making a distinction between the one and the other, except where this distinction can be made practically, and finally that the derived aspect can be taken separately for the whole, as happens when the corporeal form of a living being is taken for the whole being; whereas in the case of the planetary rhythms—because it is these that constitute the different 'skies'—this distinction cannot be made except by the theoretical application of mechanical conceptions which are foreign to the contemplative mentality of traditional civilizations." *Mystical Astrology According to Ibn 'Arabi*, p. 15

47. *An Introduction to Islamic Cosmological Doctrines*, pp. 151–152.

centric perspective. While some traditional Muslim astronomers and ancient Greek and Indian sages may have been aware of the heliocentric model before its discovery in the West by Copernicus, traditional astrological symbolism requires that we envisage the heavens from where we are standing.[48] Even though the Sun is the gravitational center of the solar system, man does not stand on the Sun. He begins his own spiritual quest for transcendence from the earth. The Sun is nevertheless the symbolic center of the other heavenly spheres from the point of view of the earth. If we understand the heavenly spheres that are visible to the naked eye to include the Moon, Mercury, Venus, the Sun, Mars, Jupiter and Saturn, the Sun is at the center of these spheres when viewed from the earth outward.[49] Moreover, in Islam each heavenly sphere is linked to a particular prophet and the Sun itself is linked to Hermes or Idrīs.[50] Muḥyī al-Dīn ibn ʿArabī (d. 1240) in fact places Idrīs as the Pole (*quṭb*) at the head of the celestial hierarchy of the Sufis because he is perpetually alive and governs the heaven of the Sun and therefore the center of the known universe and all of the friends of God in the initiatic hierarchy.[51] It is only the representatives of Idrīs among each generation of Sufis who are known as the titular poles of their time.

48. *Islamic Science*, p. 133; Seyyed Hossein Nasr, *Knowledge and the Sacred*, p. 198; and Seyyed Hossein Nasr, *Religion and the Order of Nature* (Oxford: Oxford University Press, 1996), pp. 133–135.

49. Burckhardt states, "The astrological hierarchy of the planetary sky situates Mercury between Venus and the Earth since Mercury moves more rapidly than Venus, and this in spite of the fact that Venus is closer to the Earth, and Mercury closer to the Sun." *Mystical Astrology According to Ibn 'Arabi*, p. 16.

50. Burckhardt writes, "According to this order of correspondences, which however cannot be understood except within their spiritual perspective and in some way within the 'cyclic' of Islam, Abraham (Sayyidnā Ibrāhīm) resides in the sky of Saturn, Moses (Sayyidnā Mūsā) in that of Jupiter, Aaron (Sayyidnā Hārūn) in that of Mars, Enoch (Sayyidnā Idrīs) in that of the Sun, Joseph (Sayyidnā Yūsuf) in that of Venus, Jesus (Sayyidnā ʿĪsā) in that of Mercury and Adam (Sayyidnā Adam) in that of the Moon." *Mystical Astrology According to Ibn 'Arabi*, p. 31.

51. *Traditional Forms & Cosmic Cycles*, pp. 82–83. See also, Michel Chodkiewicz, *Seal of the Saints*, pp. 89–102; and Zachary Markwith, "The Imām and the *Quṭb*: The *Axis Mundi* in Shīʿism and Sufism," *Sophia Perennis* 1, no. 2 (Spring 2009), pp. 25–65.

The purpose of traditional astrology is to provide a contemplative and symbolic vision of the heavens and anticipate a spiritual ascension through the heavens to the Divine Presence, just as the Prophet of Islam was taken on his *mi'rāj* or ascension. The Prophet said, "The ritual prayer (*al-ṣalāh*) is the *mi'rāj* of the believer." It is recorded in the *Ḥadīth* that in his own ascension the Prophet in fact met Idrīs in the fourth heaven. While the Prophet of Islam made his *mi'rāj* in body and Spirit, the Muslim who follows this most elevated aspect of his *Sunnah* makes it in Spirit alone, allowing the Spirit to rise above the body. The Spirit (*al-rūḥ*) of man is his higher angelic-like reality that must be employed to take flight through the heavens to the Metacosmic Principle. In Ibn 'Arabī's own spiritual ascension he also meets Idrīs in the fourth heaven or the sphere of the Sun. The Shaykh al-Akbar asks Idrīs, "Where is your [spiritual] rank in relation to your place [at the center of the universe]?" To which Idrīs replies, "The outer is a sign of the inner."[52]

As previously stated, traditional astrology is not simply the popular belief that the stars influence man and his destiny, but an understanding of how God, the angels and prophets—all that are in the celestial heavens—influence the earth and are symbolized by the corporeal heavens. The direct correspondence between the macrocosm and the microcosm is also clearly demonstrated by mystical astrology. According to Sachiko Murata:

> For most Muslim thinkers, the object of this science was to bring out the manner in which heaven, along with the realities it contains, exercises specific influences on the earth. Astrological investigation takes the form of discovering the qualitative correspondences between things in the upper world and the lower world. For the more perspicacious, there is no question of any direct "influence" by the stars. Rather, the relationships among heavenly bodies and earth throw light on corresponding or analogical relationships found in this world and in the soul. The key here is analogy or correspondence. And this is established by the qualities that things manifest, all of which ultimately go back to the One. In other words, different things, at different levels of real-

52. *The Meccan Revelations* (*al-Futūḥāt al-makkiyyah*), vol. I, p. 221.

ity or in different times and places, manifest the same qualities of the Real (*al-Ḥaqq*).[53]

From this perspective, the heavens can be said to mirror the inner being of man and therefore manifest what is hidden within us because the primary cause of both the macrocosm and the microcosm is God. In the aforementioned Quranic verse we read, "We shall show them Our signs upon the horizons and within themselves till it becomes clear to them that it is the Truth. . . ." (41:53) While all of the different spheres are analogous to the inner faculties of man, the Sun—from a cosmological perspective—represents the Spirit or Intellect of man, while the moon represents the receptive psychic faculties associated with the soul and mind that receive illumination from the Intellect.[54] In Islamic cosmology, beyond the earth, the spheres of the elements, the planets, the fixed stars and the sky without stars, lies the Divine Pedestal and Throne that encompasses all of the spheres of universal Existence. Further demonstrating the correspondence between the inner and the outer, the Prophet Muḥammad said, "The heart of the believer is the Throne of the All-Merciful (*al-Raḥmān*)." As man moves from the periphery of his being to the Center, he is also taken in spiritual flight beyond the macrocosm to the Divine Presence and Reality that is beyond the subject-object distinction.

Following the Hermetic principle, "whatever is below is like that which is above, and whatever is above is like that which is below," each heavenly sphere is also linked to a particular metal or mineral associated with traditional alchemy.[55] It is worth noting here that

53. *The Tao of Islam*, p. 14.

54. From a metaphysical perspective the Sun also represents the Divine Self or Essence, while the Moon can be said to correspond to Universal Being and Existence. The Sun can also be said to represent God and the Moon the heart that alternates in its receptivity to the Divine theophanies it reflects. *Mystical Astrology According to Ibn 'Arabi*, p. 34.

55. The primary meaning of this saying is that the material universe—what is in the heavens and on the earth—are both influenced by higher levels of existence corresponding to the celestial heavens and the celestial earth or the archetypes of the material. Nevertheless, because a distinction between the corporeal and celestial was

the Sun is linked to gold and the Moon to silver.[56] While alchemy is generally understood as the material process of turning lead into gold, spiritually speaking it is the process of transmuting the base elements of the soul into the gold of the Spirit, of which material alchemy may or may not be a symbolic support. This work is always accomplished through the influence of a celestial element or Divine grace, represented in alchemy by the Philosopher's Stone (*ḥajarat al-falāsifah*) and the elixir (*al-iksīr*). In spiritual alchemy, it is a revealed prayer or specific Divine Name derived from Revelation that acts as the essential celestial catalyst to accomplish the great work of transfiguring the soul and wedding it to the Spirit. Those who cultivated the study of alchemy purely for material gain were known pejoratively as "charcoal burners." Moreover, in hagiographies a number of Sufis miraculously turn various metals or other substances into gold without the knowledge of material alchemy, but simply through the sanctity of their glance or breath.[57]

Be that as it may, the spiritual doctrine and methods of realization in Islam have been described by some Sufis using symbolism borrowed from alchemy, even though the doctrine and methods of Islam and Sufism derive exclusively from the Quran and *Sunnah*. As we discovered above, Abū Ḥāmid Ghazzālī (d. 1111) entitled one of his most famous treatises *The Alchemy of Happiness* (*Kīmiyā-yi sa'ādat*), while Ibn 'Arabī is known as the "red sulphur" (*al-kabrīt al-aḥmar*), which refers to the alchemical process of sulphur drawing gold out of lead and—in the case of the Shaykh al-Akbar—knowledge out of ignorance.[58] Not only did some of the most well-

never imposed upon the heavens by traditional peoples, they served to adequately represent the higher in traditional cosmologies.

56. The Moon is linked to silver, Mercury to quicksilver, Venus to copper, the Sun to gold, Mars to Iron, Jupiter to tin, and Saturn to lead. Titus Burckhardt writes, "The interpretation of the sign of Mercury as the key to the whole work is confirmed by the role of the God Mercury or Hermes in the Orphic mysteries. The messenger of the gods accompanied the soul after its death—bodily or mystical—through all the realms of the world of shadows, to its final place of rest." *Alchemy*, p. 185.

57. *Islamic Science*, pp. 203–204.

58. Cyril Glassé, ed., *The New Encyclopedia of Islam* (Walnut Creek, CA: AltaMira Press, 2002) p. 216

known Sufis in Islamic history make use of alchemical symbolism, but some even wrote treatises on the subject itself, including Dhu'l-Nūn Miṣrī, Junayd, and Ḥallāj.[59] Seyyed Hossein Nasr writes,

> Traditional alchemy is, in fact, a complete way of looking at things. It is at the same time a science of the cosmos and a science of the soul and is related to art and metallurgy on the one hand and spiritual psychology on the other. The alchemical point of view is based on the principle that 'everything is in everything', that everything penetrates everything (*tadākhul*), and that therefore the substance of things can be transmuted so that their nature can be changed rather than only their accidents as is taught in Aristotelian natural philosophy.[60]

In a manner similar to the study and making of other traditional arts and crafts, the outer substances that the alchemist seeks to transmute and perfect are supports for the inner work of the soul.[61] The alchemist looks at the qualitative and symbolic dimensions of the metals he works with. The principle qualities envisaged are the four natures, including heat, dryness, cold and humidity, and the four elements, namely fire, earth, water, and air. The combination of the

59. *Islamic Science*, pp. 199–200.

60. Ibid., p. 194.

61. In the contemporary world, this understanding of the higher meaning of art is preserved in a few circles in what remains of the traditional civilizations. The only place that it is widely acknowledged in the West is by those who study the martial arts, especially inward styles such as Tai Chi. Titus Burckhardt in fact ends his masterful treatise on alchemy with the following words: "The Japanese archer initiated into the mysteries of Zen may hit the target blindfold, given inner concentration and inward union with the timeless essence at the moment of the shot. In the same way the physical transmutation of metals was a sign which manifested outwardly the inward holiness both of gold and of man—of the man, that is, who had completed the inward work." *Alchemy*, p. 204. Also noteworthy in this regard is the Japanese Tea Ceremony. See Frithjof Schuon, "Diverse Aspects of Initiatory Alchemy" in *The Eye of the Heart: Metaphysics, Cosmology, Spiritual Life* (Bloomington, IN: World Wisdom, Inc., 1997), pp. 139–141. If done well and mindfully every type of honest work can be a spiritual support analogous to alchemy, including, for example, the making of or participation in sacred and traditional art, teaching, writing, farming, cooking and healing. To these can be added the conjugal act itself, which embodies all of the symbols of alchemy and is of course used as a means of spiritual realization in some traditions, most notably Tantra in Hinduism.

four natures yields the two philosophical substances or principles, mercury or quicksilver and sulphur, which are the feminine and masculine cosmic principles analogous to Yin and Yang in Chinese cosmology. The different metals naturally come into being through the wedding of mercury and sulphur under a particular celestial influence, which the alchemist seeks to quicken through his knowledge of alchemy and the inner composition of the metal in question, and with the aid of the Philosopher's Stone or elixir.[62] Nasr writes,

> According to Jābir, the key to the understanding of the structure of metals and, in fact, of all substances is the balance (*al-mizān*), which plays a crucial role in Islamic alchemy. The balance is not just a physical instrument to measure weights, and its presence in Jābirian alchemy is by no means the sign of the early appearance of quantitative analysis in the history of chemistry. Rather, the balance is the instrument which 'measures' the tendency of the World Soul towards a particular composition, the act of 'measurement' being meant here in its Pythagorean rather than modern sense. The balance is, therefore, concerned with inner and outer qualities and with numeral symbolism, as well as with the symbolic letters of the Arabic alphabet.[63]

The process of alchemy includes the blackening, bleaching and reddening of the stone or *materia*, as well as its dissolution and coagulation with the aid of the athanor.[64] In the human microcosm, blackening is the cognizance of one's imperfections, bleaching is the purification of the soul, and reddening is the attainment of spiritual perfection. Through the celestial influence of the heavenly spheres, the Philosopher's Stone, the elixir, and the alchemist's knowledge of

62. *Islamic Science*, pp. 194–195.

63. Ibid., p. 195.

64. It is interesting to recall that the Black Stone of the Ka'bah was originally white, but was blackened by the sins of man. Moreover, Ibn 'Arabī speaks of a celestial Ka'bah made of red gold or rubies that exists in the Land of Reality (*arḍ al-ḥaqīqah*) above our world. *Cosmology and Architecture in Premodern Islam*, pp. 177–179. Finally, an Arab poet remarked, "Muḥammad is a human being, but not like humankind; he is a precious ruby, while people are stones." In this context the ruby refers to the transparent nature of the Prophet or the Universal Man before the Divine Light that shines through him.

the science of inner and outer proportions and balance, the art and science of alchemy is meant to transmute base metals into pure gold, including and especially the base aspects of the soul into the incorruptible gold of the Spirit. The great work is to unite the soul with the Spirit, the feminine with the masculine, the queen with the king or the Moon with the Sun, which is symbolized in alchemy by the union of quicksilver and sulphur and also silver and gold.[65] In the words of Titus Burckhardt:

> On 'chemical marriage' quicksilver takes into itself sulphur, and sulphur, quicksilver. Both forces 'die', as foes and lovers. Then the changing and reflective moon of the soul unites with the immutable sun of the Spirit so that it is extinguished, and yet illumined, at one and the same time.[66]

As mentioned above, material or practical alchemy may or may not be a symbolic support for spiritual alchemy, which is essentially the alchemy of prayer.[67] In the alchemy of prayer, a formula or Name of God deriving from Revelation is the essential celestial element. Man cannot overcome the base elements of the soul and accomplish its wedding with the Spirit, except through employing the power and grace of the Word of God. In Islam, the Word or Logos is the Quran and the prayers and Divine Names throughout the Book are the efficacious means to accomplish the great work when accompanied by the guidance of a spiritual master. Frithjof Schuon writes,

> The sufficient reason for the invocation of the Name is the remembering of God; and this, in the final analysis, is not other than consciousness of the Absolute. The Name actualizes this consciousness and, in the end, perpetuates it in the soul and fixes it in the heart, so that it penetrates the whole being and at the same time transmutes and absorbs it.[68]

65. *Islamic Science*, pp. 196–197.

66. *Alchemy*, p. 156.

67. Ibid., pp. 157–160; Titus Burckhardt, *An Introduction to Sufi Doctrine*, trans. D.M. Matheson (Lahore: Suhail Academy Press, 1999) pp. 90–92.

68. Frithjof Schuon, *Stations of Wisdom* (Bloomington: IN: World Wisdom, Inc., 1995), p. 127

The adept's initiation at the hands of a shaykh connects him to the initiatic power (*walāyah*) of the Prophet, which is like the Philosopher's Stone that enables the transmutation of the soul through prayer. The perpetual invocation of any revealed formula or Name of God is a type of general spiritual alchemy that cleanses man of his faults, connects him to the Spirit of the Prophet and ultimately to God Himself who is beyond the cosmos and at the Center of the heart. There is also a more specific type of spiritual alchemy taught orally in many Sufi orders, where techniques of breathing and invoking are employed to connect certain Names of God, and consequently the Spirit, to both the soul and the body. Noteworthy in this context is the saying attributed to both the Fifth and Sixth Shī'ite Imams, the latter of which was a teacher of perhaps the greatest Muslim alchemist Jābir ibn Ḥayyān: "Our spirits are our bodies and our bodies are our spirits" (*Arwāḥunā ajsādunā wa ajsādunā arwāḥunā*). Nasr remarks that this saying "means, among other things, the alchemical transmutation which crystallizes and fixes the volatile Spirit and dissolves the coagulated and dense body."[69] It is also another example of the Hermetic maxim that summarizes the entire subject, "whatever is below is like that which is above, and whatever is above is like that which is below."

Some Conclusions

In this brief survey of the influence of Hermes and Hermetic writings in the Islamic world, and the Hermetic wisdom of Islam itself, it becomes clear that Hermes or Idrīs and the sciences associated with him were more central to traditional Muslims in the premodern period. Most traditional Muslim sages regarded Hermes as the first teacher of philosophy to humanity, and, after the Prophet of Islam, he continued to be regarded as the dominant prophetic influence in the most significant schools of Islamic sapience. He is considered by Suhrawardī as the prophetic founder of the school of *Ishrāq*, by Ibn 'Arabī as the chief Pole (*quṭb*) in the celestial

69. *Islamic Science*, p. 196. See also, Henry Corbin, *Spiritual Body and Celestial Earth*.

hierarchy of the Sufis, and by Mullā Ṣadrā and countless other Muslim sages throughout history as the "Father of the philosophers" (Abu'l-ḥukamā').[70] Of great relevance are the cosmological sciences and symbolic doctrines associated with Hermes, including astrology and alchemy, not to mention other arts and sciences not studied here but also linked by Muslims and others to Hermes, including medicine, geometry and architecture.

While the influence of Hermes or Idrīs on Muslims has taken diverse forms throughout Islamic history it would not be an exaggeration to state that he is the pivotal pre-Islamic prophet in the

70. It is also highly significant that one of the leading Muslim philosophers of the twentieth century, the Iranian scholar 'Allāmah Ṭabāṭabā'ī (d. 1981), also mentions in a private discussion on the theoretical and practical dimensions of *'irfān* an initiatic dream he had with the prophet Idrīs: "I remember that during the time that I was in Najaf Ashraf under the moral and spiritual guidance of the late Ḥājj Mīrzā 'Alī Qāḍī, may God be pleased with him, one day at dawn while I was sitting on the prayer mat on the veranda, I fell asleep for a short time and had a vision. I dreamt of two men sitting in front of me. One of them was the Prophet Ḥaḍrat Idrīs—may peace be upon him and upon our Prophet and his Progeny—and the other was my dear and honorable brother Ḥājj Sayyid Muḥammad Ḥasan Ṭabāṭabā'ī who resides in Tabriz at the present time. Ḥaḍrat Idrīs began a conversation with me in such a manner that he would converse and communicate his speech, but his utterances I heard from the tongue of my brother. Ḥaḍrat Idrīs said that 'terrible events and accidents occurred in my life and resolving them seemed impossible to me by natural course of events and by ordinary means. But they were all resolved unexpectedly. It became clear to me that a hand from the Invisible World and superior to ordinary means and causes was solving these problems and removing difficulties.'" 'Allāmah Ṭabāṭabā'ī then states, "This was the first transformation that connected the material world of nature to the supernatural for me. Our ties of connection [with Heaven] began from that point." Sayyid M.H. Ṭabāṭabā'ī, *Kernel of the Kernel* (*Risāla-yi Lubb al-Lubāb*), p. 72. Frithjof Schuon also remarks, "The great ambiguity of the human phenomenon resides in the fact that man is divine without being God: Koranically speaking, man gives all the creatures their names, and that is why the angels must prostrate before him—except for the supreme Angel, which indicates that man's divinity, and consequently his authority and autonomy, are relative, although 'relatively absolute'. Thus the fall of man as such could not be total, as is proven *a priori* by the natue and destiny of the patriarch Enoch, father of all 'pneumatics', so to speak. *The Fullness of God: Frithjof Schuon on Christianity*, James S. Cutsinger, ed. (Bloomington, IN: World Wisdom, 2004), p. 58.

Islamic sapiential tradition.[71] Muslim sages were able to integrate the figure and wisdom of Hermes into their own worldview because they understood him to be the prophet Enoch or Idrīs with revealed wisdom in complete harmony with the Quran, *Sunnah* and the doctrine of *tawḥīd*. The borrowing of Hermetic symbols and sciences by Muslims in the premodern period, as well as other teachings from the Greeks, Persians, Indians, and Chinese, is in keeping with the *ḥadīth* of the Prophet, "Seek knowledge even unto China." The Muslim secure in his faith and practice of Islam was not challenged by the existence of other forms of wisdom and what is essentially prophetic philosophy. Rather, he inherited and was enriched by the traditional wisdom of other civilizations and made it his own. Through his own discernment and that provided by the Quran and *Sunnah*, a contemporary Muslim can also approach the traditional sources of Hermeticism, and especially the Hermetic wisdom of Islam itself, for a more holistic and in fact Islamic science of nature than the modern world is able to offer. For the resuscitation of a sacred and symbolic science of nature, including the cosmos and the soul, nothing is more significant than the revival of the traditional wisdom and sciences cultivated in the bosom of the revealed religions. As humanity and the earth suffer from the spread of a totalitarian science synonymous with materialism and the exclusive study of the quantitative dimensions of nature, the Hermetic wisdom preserved in the Muslim world and to some extent in the West can help make us aware of the interdependence of humanity and the earth, and the dependence of both upon Heaven.

71. One can certainly argue that Jesus is more central in most branches of Sufism than Hermes or Idrīs, but the latter has a more central place in the philosophical dimensions of the Islamic sapiential tradition.

7

God's Vicegerent on Earth

Seyyed Hossein Nasr's Defense of Nature

> And when thy Lord said to the angels, "I am placing a vicegerent upon the earth," they said, "Wilt Thou place therein one who will work corruption therein, and shed blood, while we hymn Thy praise and call Thee Holy?" He said, "Truly I know what you know not." (Quran 2:30)

> God has opened a door in the middle of creation, and this open door of the world towards God is man; this opening is God's invitation to look towards Him, to tend towards Him, to persevere with regard to Him and to return to Him. . . .[1] (Frithjof Schuon)

Seyyed Hossein Nasr (1933–present) is among the most prolific contemporary Muslim scholars and a living representative of the Islamic sapiential tradition. Having written some of the most widely read and celebrated books in the twentieth century on subjects that include Islam, Islamic philosophy, science and art, Sufism, and the perennial philosophy or *sophia perennis*, his profound treatment of the environmental crisis has gone largely unnoticed among academics, scientists and environmentalists, for whom the secular paradigm dominates. Similarly, many contemporary religious men and women have ignored the teachings in their own traditions concerning the sacred character of the cosmos and have turned a blind eye to the destruction of the natural world, which threatens the very existence of humanity and the traditions and civilizations that we

1. Frithjof Schuon, *Echoes of Perennial Wisdom* (Bloomington, IN: World Wisdom Books, Inc., 1992), p. 56.

hold dear. Therefore, we felt it urgent to outline Nasr's defense of nature with the hope that more people will benefit from his intellectual and historical critique of modern philosophy and science, which enabled modern man to develop a technology capable of destroying the planet. Further, while documenting the trajectory of modern scientific and industrial "progress", Nasr has also helped to resuscitate traditional metaphysics, cosmology, and symbolism, which alone can awaken the intellectual and spiritual faculties in man and make it possible for him to live in harmony with the earth.

Not only has Nasr helped to revive the metaphysical and cosmological doctrines of the Islamic tradition, but he has also uniquely applied the principles of the *sophia perennis* to the environmental crisis. It was through his extensive academic training and most of all through recourse to his own tradition—Islam—including its exoteric and esoteric dimensions, that enabled Nasr to recognize in Islam, Christianity and other religions those latent doctrines and rites which reconnect the human being to the Metacosmic Reality. From Nasr's perspective, only when we are in harmony with Heaven will we be in harmony with the earth. Through an epistemology based on revelation, gnosis, and reason—not to be confused with rationalism—we can reorient our gaze towards the Transcendent and begin to recognize the signs of God in the immanent theophany that is nature.

While many academics, politicians, and activists with good intentions have promoted better environmental engineering, the paradigm shift that Nasr has suggested is the only solution that will actively engage our intelligence and will. To prevent the further destruction of the earth, men and women must see nature as sacred and have the moral discipline to act upon that vision. Only tradition can provide the necessary tools to aid in the resacralization of nature, and to remind men and women of their primordial nature as God's vicegerents on earth. The following chapter is a humble effort to bring more attention to one of Nasr's most important, yet often neglected contributions to this most urgent crisis of our time.

Life and Writings on Nature

Below we review those aspects of Seyyed Hossein Nasr's life and education that made him uniquely qualified to revive a traditional understanding of cosmology and his key works on the subject.[2] As a scientist, philosopher, and gnostic, Nasr has a unique background that enabled him to diagnose the philosophical and historical causes of the environmental crisis. As mentioned above in chapter one, Nasr earned a B.A. at M.I.T. in physics, an M.A. at Harvard in geology and geophysics, and a Ph.D. also at Harvard in the history of science, with an emphasis in Islamic science and philosophy. His dissertation was published as *An Introduction to Islamic Cosmological Doctrines: Conceptions of Nature and Methods Used for its Study by the Ikhwān al-Ṣafā', Al-Bīrūnī, and Ibn Sīnā* and remains one of the few books on the subject in European languages.[3] Nasr has written numerous other comprehensive studies on Islamic science and philosophy, and studied with some of the leading contemporary traditional Muslim philosophers in Iran. It is also relevant to recall his numerous contributions to the study of the Islamic tradition as a whole, such as *The Heart of Islam* and *Ideals and Realities of Islam*, because his solution to the environmental crisis comes precisely from religion, including its inner and outer dimensions, which can reorient man towards Heaven and allow man to become a channel of Divine grace here on earth. Unlike many works on Islam from an orientalist, modernist or postmodernist perspective, these books refuse to reduce Islam to political or socio-economic factors alone. Starting from the transcendent, intellectual, spiritual, and artistic dimensions of the religion, wherein the inner life of man and the cosmos are elucidated and reflected, he has with great erudition and insight lent expression to Islam's inner nature. Moreover, Nasr has dealt directly with Islamic esoterism or Sufism in several masterful volumes, including his recent *The Garden of Truth*. Along with his philosophical and scientific training, we would argue that Nasr's theoretical and practical understanding of Sufism is the most important feature of his life and vision that enabled him to resuscitate a sacred understanding of nature. It was

2. See chapter one of the present volume for a more in depth discussion of Nasr's life and writings.

3. Seyyed Hossein Nasr, *An Introduction to Islamic Cosmological Doctrines.*

through following a spiritual path within the context of a revealed religion that Nasr was able to move beyond theoretical knowledge and a sentimental appreciation for the earth to an existential awareness of the Sacred in and beyond the cosmos.[4]

While Nasr's life and perspective are rooted in the Islamic tradition, his writings do not suffer from exclusivism or chauvinism. He is widely regarded as the leading living authority on the *sophia perennis* or the universal wisdom contained at the heart of all orthodox religions. Nasr wrote his magnum opus *Knowledge and the Sacred* on the perennial philosophy for the prestigious Gifford Lectures in 1981. This book is of special interest because the desacralization of knowledge following the Renaissance, Scientific Revolution, and Enlightenment that Nasr carefully documents is intimately linked to the desacralization of nature. Furthermore, from Nasr's perspective man must rediscover the sacred content of the immanent Intellect—and knowledge itself—if he is to behold the Sacred in the cosmos. As soon as we divorce the Sacred from knowledge, our modes of knowing and our very being, there is no way to perceive cosmic realities as so many diverse reflections of Divine qualities, as opposed to simply what can be weighed and measured as pure quantity. In addition to *Knowledge and the Sacred*, Nasr also wrote *The Need for a Sacred Science* and numerous other books and essays on various aspects of the perennial philosophy. His works devoted to the *sophia perennis* demonstrate Nasr's profound understanding of other religions, including Hinduism, Buddhism, Confucianism, Taoism, Judaism, Christianity, and the Shamanic traditions. His critiques of modern philosophy, science, and technology are so striking and persuasive because they make use of the common metaphysical principles and diverse cosmological doctrines of the world's revealed religions, including those in the West where the environmental crisis began. By aiding in the revival of these principles and doctrines, Nasr reminds modern men and

4. For more on Nasr's intimate knowledge of and connection to Sufism, see our review article of his book *The Garden of Truth*, *Sophia* 14, no. 2 (Winter 2008–2009), pp. 185–195.

women that they already have the necessary and sufficient means to live in harmony with the earth.

Concerning Nasr's writings on the environmental crisis, Richard C. Foltz remarks,

> The articulation of an Islamic environmental ethic in contemporary terms—recognizing the urgency of the global crisis now facing us all—is quite new. The first Muslim intellectual to do so was the American-trained Iranian Shīʿite philosopher Seyyed Hossein Nasr, a proponent of the *philosophia perennis* associated with Frithjof Schuon, Titus Burckhardt, and René Guénon, in which timeless truths are seen as being expressed in a variety of historical, cultural and philosophical traditions. Nasr's environmental critique of Western modernity began with a series of lectures at the University of Chicago in 1966, which were published the following year as *Man and Nature: The Spiritual Crisis of Modern Man.* Nasr has continued to explore the spiritual dimension of the environmental crisis over the past four decades through further articles, lectures, and his 1996 book *Religion and the Order of Nature.*[5]

While attempting to outline Nasr's defense of the natural environment, we look primarily at his books *Man and Nature* and *Religion and the Order of Nature*, while occasionally making reference to his other works, such as *Knowledge and the Sacred.* It would not be an exaggeration to state that Nasr's *Man and Nature* was the first book written to address the current environmental crisis from the traditional point of view, taking into account metaphysics, cosmology, anthropology, symbolism, and the history of modern philosophy, science, and technology. Its foresight and influence is comparable to René Guénon's powerful critique of modernism and scientism in *The Crisis of the Modern World. Man and Nature* influenced such luminaries as E.F. Schumacher, Theodore Roszak and Philip Sherrard, as well as countless Muslims, Christians, and those

5. Richard C. Foltz, Frederick M. Denny, and Azizan Baharuddin, eds., *Islam and Ecology: A Bestowed Trust,* (Cambridge, MA: Harvard Center for the Study of World Religions, 2003), p. xxxviii.

from other traditions who have begun to rediscover their respective eco-theologies.[6]

A Critique of Modern Philosophy and Science

The essential content of Nasr's response to modernism and scientism can be traced back to the writings of René Guénon, A.K. Coomaraswamy, and Frithjof Schuon. Of the three founders of the Traditionalist School, however, only Coomaraswamy was trained at an advanced level in the modern sciences. Therefore, Nasr's study of physics at M.I.T., and geology, geophysics, and the history of science at Harvard, made him an ideal candidate to question many of the foundations and philosophical assumptions of modern science, and to apply the traditionalist critique of modern science to the environmental crisis. Nasr's detailed analysis of the roots of the environmental crisis looks primarily at philosophy and science in the West, where the crisis began. For Nasr, the turning point in the West was the Renaissance, which saw the revival of Greek rationalism, naturalism, and humanism or what Nasr has called "Promethean Man."[7] Nasr states,

6. Seyyed Hossein Nasr, *Man and Nature: The Spiritual Crisis of Modern Man*, (Chicago: ABC International Group, Inc., 1997), p. 9; originally published as *The Encounter of Man and Nature: The Spiritual Crisis of Modern Man* (London: George Allen & Unwin Ltd., 1968). See also, E. F. Schumacher, *Small is Beautiful* (New York: Harper & Row, Publishers, Inc., 1973); Theodore Roszak, *Where the Wasteland Ends* (New York: Anchor Books, 1973); and Philip Sherrard, *The Rape of Man and Nature* (Ipswich, Suffolk: Golgonooza Press, 1987). The well-known American Muslim scholar Hamza Yusuf writes, "Dr. Nasr was perhaps the first person to identify the *causa profundis* of the current environmental crisis, and in the mid-sixties he was a lone voice in the wilderness calling people's attention to the grave danger that we now all recognize we are in. We ignore him to our own peril. He has much to teach us, and in an age that lacks wisdom, he is surely one of our great sages." William Chittick, ed., *The Essential Seyyed Hossein Nasr*, front material. Huston Smith, the leading academic authority of comparative religion in the West, states that Nasr's *Religion and the Order of Nature* is "The most comprehensive and intelligent treatment of its topic that has been written. . . ." Seyyed Hossein Nasr, *Religion and the Order of Nature*, back cover.

7. Seyyed Hossein Nasr, *Knowledge and the Sacred*, pp. 160–188; *Religion and the Order of Nature*, pp. 169–185.

> With the Renaissance, European man lost the paradise of the age of faith to gain in compensation the new earth of nature and natural forms to which he now turned his attention. Yet it was a nature which came to be less and less a reflection of a celestial reality. Renaissance man ceased to be the ambivalent man of the Middle Ages, half angel, half man, torn between heaven and earth. Rather, he became wholly man, but now a totally earth-bound creature. Freedom for him now became quantitative and horizontal rather than qualitative and vertical, and it was in this spirit that he went on to conquer the earth and with it open new horizons in geography and natural history. However, there still existed a religious significance in the wilderness and nature that had come down through the Christian tradition.[8]

There is a great disparity between the traditional conceptions of man held in the world's religions in a variety of forms, but which are nonetheless unanimous in maintaining our dependence on the Divine Principle, and Promethean humanism that was revived during the Renaissance, which envisages man as the ultimate measure of all things, free to mold himself, society, and his environment outside of the intellectual, spiritual and aesthetic principles, as well as the laws and ethics of revealed religion. In order to live in harmony with the earth, men and women must question the ephemeral independence and individualism that humanism posits, but which is in reality a form of bondage to the egocentric soul and its insatiable appetite, and realize the true freedom that comes from an attachment to the Divine Reality through the outward and inward dimensions of revealed religion. God is the ultimate source of all Divine Qualities, such as Majesty, Beauty, Peace, and Justice. In order to reflect these qualities in the cosmic order we must avail ourselves of the modalities of revelation that communicate the Sacred and, through our participation in the Divine descent, transfigure and sacralize both the human being and the natural world. The rebel against Heaven has no right to act as a steward of creation here on earth and he in fact lacks the intelligence, dignity and grace to do so without an authentic connection to the Source of these qualities.

8. *Man and Nature*, p. 64.

According to Nasr, many authentic esoteric currents and groups in the West were also destroyed or marginalized during the Renaissance, such as the Rosicrucians, as well as many of those who cultivated the study of Hermeticism, the Kabbalah, and the arcane sciences.[9] These currents provided certain western men and women with the necessary metaphysical and cosmological knowledge to see themselves and nature as reflections of the Sacred. Without access to the gnostic dimension of religion, which became mostly eclipsed and forgotten in Western Christianity, the western intelligentsia developed a secular philosophy and science that reduced nature to a machine. Nasr states,

> The scientific revolution itself came not in the Renaissance but during the seventeenth century when the cosmos had already become secularized, religion weakened through long, inner conflicts, metaphysics and gnosis in the real sense nearly forgotten and the meaning of symbols neglected, which can be seen in the art of this period.[10]

The Scientific Revolution is characterized by the ideas of several key figures such as Descartes, Galileo, and Newton. Cartesian bifurcation created a separation between the mind and the body (the latter being our primary link to the world of nature), as well as the knowing subject and the known object, including God and the cosmos. Descartes also reduced the physical world to quantity alone, ignoring the qualitative dimensions of reality, which enabled the mechanization and desacralization of the earth to occur.[11] Regarding Galileo, Nasr writes,

> By destroying the significance of what he called "secondary qualities" or qualities as such and emphasizing only the "primary qualities," which for him were none other than pure quantity, Galileo also rejected the religious understanding of the order of nature.[12]

9. Ibid., p. 64.

10. Ibid., p. 69.

11. *Religion and the Order of Nature*, pp. 102–103, 139–140. See also, *Knowledge and the Sacred*, pp. 41–42.

12. *Religion and the Order of Nature*, p. 136.

Galileo's physics emphasized the mathematical structure of the cosmos and denied the symbolic doctrines and sciences of nature in Judaism, Christianity, and the Greek philosophical heritage. His worldview represents a radical break and ontological reduction from the hierarchically structured heavens inhabited by angelic beings and an earth that is a reflection of the Sacred, to a materialistic view of the cosmos devoid of any meaningful category or space for sacred qualities. By flattening existence to the material level alone and reducing that level to its most outward dimension, Galileo essentially cut off the earth from the higher levels of existence, including the psychic, imaginal, and spiritual or intelligible worlds, at the center and summit of each is the Divine Reality. When the materialist no longer sees the earth as a reflection of Paradise, but simply as an amalgam of dead matter, what motivation does he have to walk gently upon it with a sense of reverence and awe?[13] Nasr states,

> No event in modern European history is more significant than the trial of Galileo in replacing the religious understanding of nature with the new "mechanical philosophy," which not only claimed to be a science of nature but also to be the *only* legitimate science of the natural world.[14]

This critique of scientism did not come from a religious fundamentalist, but a trained scientist and philosopher who also champions traditional cosmologies as legitimate ways of gaining objective knowledge of nature. Nasr is not against science as such, but the philosophical assumptions and reductionism associated with scientism, whose adherents claim to be the sole possessors of knowledge of the cosmos. Indeed, scientism is a form of fundamentalism that has proven far more narrow-minded and destructive than any

13. One wonders if the instinct of self-preservation is strong enough in modern man to change his relationship with the earth? It is in fact impossible for this change to occur in the absence of true metaphysical and cosmological knowledge, although the current environmental crisis may propel some souls to look for a solution in pre-modern civilizations and their traditional sciences.

14. *Religion and the Order of Nature*, pp. 137–138.

form of religious fundamentalism. Concerning Isaac Newton, Nasr writes,

> The genius of Newton was able to create a vast synthesis from the works of Descartes, Galileo and Kepler and to present a picture of the world which Newton, himself a religious man, felt was a confirmation of a spiritual order in the Universe.... Yet the Newtonian world view led to the well-known mechanistic conception of the Universe and totally away from the holistic and organic interpretation of things. The result was that after the seventeenth century science and religion became totally divorced. Newton was one of the first to realize the adverse theological effects of his discoveries. We must not forget how much effort he spent and how many pages he wrote on the alchemical and Kabbalistic sciences of his day. Perhaps for him the new physics, with its eminent success on the mathematico-physical level, was just a science of material things. For those who followed him it became *the* science, the only legitimate knowledge of the objective world.[15]

This passage gets to the heart of Nasr's view of modern science. From his point of view, there is nothing wrong with the quantitative sciences. The problem with modern science or empiricism is that most of its proponents claim that all that can be known about the reality of the cosmos is exhausted by modern science, while rejecting the traditional sciences and their methodologies as archaic and fanciful. Therefore, most modern philosophers and scientists marginalize the qualitative views of the cosmos held in traditional civilizations, which see nature as a harmonious reflection of Divine archetypes that should be revered and protected as much as their sacred books and places of worship. This materialistic view of the cosmos reduced nature to a machine and blinded modern humanity to the earth's and our own spiritual substance. Without the aid of traditional metaphysics and cosmology and our higher intellectual and spiritual faculties humanity no longer saw the earth as sacred and felt free to plunder what seemed to be an endless amount of material resources.

One of the early influential philosophers in Europe to link the

15. *Man and Nature*, pp. 69–70.

new scientific worldview and method to material progress and power was Francis Bacon. According to Nasr,

> Bacon was important in popularizing the new science and defining its role as a search for power to dominate over nature and not only to understand it. In him can be found the genesis of that aspect of modern science which is concerned not so much with understanding the order of nature as with dominating over it, with the result of imposing upon nature a purely human order aimed at the attainment of material goals.[16]

For all intents and purposes, God is absent from the universe that is studied by modern science. One often hears assertions that modern science is amoral and agnostic, while individual scientists can be, as some indeed are, devout and pious believers. Yet when one examines the history of modern philosophy, science, and technology—as Nasr does in a thorough and well-documented manner—it is clear that the scientism or materialism of our day is responsible for creating a worldview that reduced nature to an inanimate object devoid of spirit and meaning. From this bleak vantage point there was and is one simple step to the destruction of the natural world. When men and women no longer see nature as so many symbols that reflect and embody higher archetypes and realities—including the Divine Reality—they begin to view the earth solely as a source of material gain and profit.

A few words must be said about the close relationship between scientism and technology. Technology and industry are also closely wed to modern philosophy and science. Man would not be able to mow down forests, hallow out mountains, or pollute the oceans and sky with such callous efficiency if he did not have the tools and profit motive to do so, both of which rely on a purely materialistic and humanistic worldview that is blind to the meaning of life and our final end. Furthermore, the encroachment of urban cities into rural areas and virgin nature continues to lead more species into extinction. Overpopulation itself is a unique and unforeseen consequence of modern medicine, the idea of progress, and the never-ending

16. *Religion and the Order of Nature*, p. 135.

development of human civilizations. Global warming caused by carbon emissions is now gaining wider attention. The excessive use of fossil fuels, however, continue to be drilled and mined for greater profits by the stewards of industry.[17] Meanwhile, modern engineers and scientists continue to create new forms of technology and transportation for its use, while the public puts its faith in the creation of new forms of alternative energy technology and fuel efficient vehicles, with little or no criticism directed at the scientific and technological paradigm that created the problem to begin with. In a recent interview Nasr stated,

> There are technologies which can reduce pollution, but I do not believe that those technologies alone will save us from this crisis. We have to have an inner transformation. We have to have another way of looking at ourselves, at the purpose of human life, at what satisfies us, what makes us happy, and not turn over to consumption as the only way to be happy, seeking satiation of our never-ending thirst and satisfaction of endless wants that are then turned into needs.[18]

A Defense of Nature

One of the central themes in Nasr's books on the environment is Pontifical Man or to use an Islamic term "God's vicegerent on earth" (*khalīfat Allāh fi'l-arḍ*), who acts as a bridge between Heaven

17. Moreover, military technology—which is the origin of most popular forms of modern technology from our modes of transportation to those of impersonal communication—is responsible for the destruction of entire cities by the atomic bomb, such as Hiroshima and Nagasaki in World War II, and continues to threaten the existence of life on the planet. Other forms of chemical warfare developed by modern scientists in the twentieth century—such as Agent Orange used by the United States during the Vietnam War to defoliate jungles and depleted uranium also used by the United States in the Iraq Wars—have left toxic and carcinogenic traces that will remain in the environment, affecting the human, animal and plant populations long after the end of the conflicts in which they were used.

18. Seyyed Hossein Nasr and Muzaffar Iqbal, *Islam, Science, Muslims, and Technology*, (Kuala Lumpur: Islamic Book Trust, 2007), p. 131. Nasr states in the same conversation, "I do not believe that any cosmetic change can cure the crisis; it is as if a cancer patient is dying of cancer and you put powder on her face so that she looks pretty. That is not going to save the patient. We need a deep transformation

and earth and represents and reflects the Divine Principle in the cosmic order by virtue of surrendering his or her limited ego before God. Nasr was perhaps the first person to examine and apply the traditional understanding of the human being—as a theomorphic being created in the image of God and not as a usurper of Divine sovereignty—to the current environmental crisis. In *Man and Nature* and *Religion and the Order of Nature* one finds detailed expressions of the traditional doctrine of man (by which he of course means man and woman) in the world's religions, as well as corresponding metaphysical and cosmological doctrines. Pontifical Man's inner being is intellectually and existentially linked to the Divine Principle and the cosmos as manifestation. He is the guardian of nature because he sees the universe as an extension of his own being and a reflection of the Sacred.

What must be stressed is that Pontifical Man, or to use another Islamic term "the Universal Man" (*al-insān al-kāmil*), does not seek simply to unite with nature. Rather, as a result of direct knowledge of the Metaphysical Reality or Self, he realizes his primordial connection to both God and the cosmos. In Nasr's own words,

> The purpose and aim of creation is in fact for God to come 'to know' Himself through His perfect instrument of knowledge that is the Universal Man. Man therefore occupies a particular position in this world. He is at the axis and centre of the cosmic *milieu* at once the master and custodian of nature. Being taught the names of all things he gains domination over them, but he is given this power only because he is the vicegerent (*khalīfah*) of God on earth and the instrument of His Will. Man is given the right to dominate

of our understanding of nature and of the human state, of who we are, of what our relationship is with God and the natural environment which is His creation. And all of this implies a radical change in the worldview that dominates much of the globe today. . . . It is true that we have to take some immediate practical measures such as having more public transportation, using natural gas rather than petroleum, and so forth. . . . Such actions are well and fine, and one should do what one can along these lines, but that is not going to solve the problem in the long run. Such actions are going to give us more time in which to try to solve the problem. So I am in favor of immediate solutions on a technological or economic level, but I do not believe that is going to solve the crisis if we insist on pursuing our present course." Ibid., pp. 127–129.

> over nature only by virtue of his theomorphic make-up, not as a rebel against heaven.[19]

In Islam, all of the prophets from Adam to Muḥammad are the vicegerents of God on earth by first becoming His servants. Their authority here below is a result of their submission to the Will of God and their knowledge of the archetypes of all things. We read in the Quran: "And He taught Adam the names, all of them. . . ." (2:31) The names include the Divine Names and therefore imply not only nominal designations, but the higher principles or archetypes of both man and the world—a knowledge which is itself the bestowal of authority and centrality in the cosmic order. Diverse examples of this traditional anthropological doctrine are given in *Man and Nature* and *Religion and the Order of Nature.* Nasr cites the neo-Confucian sage Yi Hwang:

> *Chi'en* [Heaven] is called the father and *K'un* [Earth] is called the mother. I, this tiny being, am commingled in their midst; therefore what fills up all between Heaven and Earth, that is my body, and that which directs Heaven and Earth is my nature.[20]

Nasr also cites the examples of *purusha* in Hinduism who is "the primordial cosmic being and celestial prototype of man,"[21] and the Logos in Christianity.[22] Nasr focuses extensively on the resacralization of man and the cosmos in the Christian tradition, which is crucial if the majority of western men and women hope to abandon their materialistic view of nature. In *Religion and the Order of Nature* Nasr summarizes the perspective of the Orthodox Christian scholar Philip Sherrard:

> What was lost [in Western Christianity] is what Sherrard calls the theoanthropocosmic vision; henceforth, the sonship of the Divine Logos was envisaged primarily in the historical Jesus and not in the world of Creation.... In reality, however, according to Sherrard, Christ is only one form of the embodiment of the Divine

19. *Man and Nature*, p. 96.
20. *Religion and the Order of Nature*, pp. 41–42
21. Ibid., pp. 43–44.
22. Ibid., p. 56.

> Logos, the cosmos being the other. Creation of the world is linked to the eternal generation of the Son, both of whom are aspects of a single Divine Act.[23]

Before Sherrard's masterful text *The Rape of Man and Nature*, Nasr lent profound expression to traditional Christian metaphysics and cosmology in *Man and Nature* and *Knowledge and the Sacred* through his detailed critique of modern science and philosophy, as well a penetrating survey of classical Christian views of nature, the human being, and knowledge. As mentioned earlier, Nasr documents the gradual secularization of philosophy, science, and the cosmos, as well as the existence of those faithful Christian philosophers, theologians, and mystics who championed the sacred quality of nature. Furthermore, Nasr points out that Eastern Orthodox Christianity did not follow the same trajectory as Western Christianity, which came to view nature as participating in the fall of man, as opposed to a reflection of Eden.[24] Nasr writes,

> Among the early fathers also the Greek fathers like Origen, Irenaeus, Maximus the Confessor and Gregory of Nyssa who were so influential in the formation of Orthodox theology developed a theology of nature. Origen and Irenaeus are, particularly important since they applied the Logos doctrine not only to man and his religion but also to the whole of nature and all creatures. Their followers likewise showed much sympathy for a spiritual vision of nature. The Latin fathers, however, did not for the most part show great interest in nature to the extent that the most famous among them, St Augustine, in the *City of God* considers nature as fallen and not yet redeemed.[25]

Western Christianity was not, however, devoid of visionaries who saw the *vestigia Dei* in nature. Nasr cites the contributions of Johannes Scotus Erigena, Hildegard of Bingen, Roger Bacon, St. Francis of Assisi, Dante, Jacob Böhme, and numerous other Christian saints and sages.[26] What is unfortunate, and very likely allowed

23. Ibid., p. 202.
24. *Man and Nature*, p. 100.
25. Ibid., p. 100.
26. Ibid., p. 100–106.

the environmental crisis to occur, is that mainstream Western Christian theologians, philosophers and scientists retreated and capitulated to the advances of modern philosophy and science after the trial of Galileo. It is therefore imperative to reexamine, as many contemporary Christian theologians have done in recent decades, the sacred views of nature held by the aforementioned as well as other Christian mystics in the Western and Eastern Orthodox Christian traditions.

The Principle and its cosmic manifestations do not, however, take on the same form in various religions. Concerning the Native American traditions, Nasr writes:

> The views of the Native Americans concerning the order of nature indicate not only the perspective of one of the best kept branches of primordial Shamanism toward the natural world, but also at once a powerful challenge and a stark contrast to the mechanistic view of the order of nature underlying the modern technological worldview and the attitude toward nature of that civilization which conquered and crushed the Native American world. Paradoxically, this primordial attitude made possible the preservation of a whole continent in the state of an almost Edenic perfection before the advent of the Europeans and the gradual destruction of the natural environment, with an accelerated pace ever since. It is not accidental that with greater awareness of the environmental crisis the white man's views of the Native Americans' understanding of nature has gone from its earlier total rejection as "animism," "totemism," or "pantheism" understood in their most pejorative sense, to praise and adoration in many circles today. In any case the Native American understanding of the meaning of the order of nature is a most important and precious element in the current global religious response to the acute crisis between man and the natural environment.[27]

Perhaps even more than later manifestations of Tradition, the Native American, Aboriginal, African tribal religions, and other branches of the primordial tradition, possess what Frithjof Schuon

27. *Religion and the Order of Nature*, p. 35.

has called "the symbolist outlook."[28] Each phenomenon in nature, such as an eagle, a tree, or the sun, is linked to the soul and Spirit or Intellect of man, as well as higher levels of Being.[29] Moreover, the signs and symbols in the cosmos are so transparent to primordial man that he directly approaches the Divine Principle through them and nature is for him a direct revelation. It is no wonder that the various worldviews associated with these great traditions have enabled vast civilizations to live in harmony with nature for thousands of years, while modern man has managed to destroy countless species and even put his own existence in jeopardy in only a few hundred years.[30]

The common thread that unites Nasr's defense of nature, whether he is referring to his own tradition—Islam—or other religions and their respective cosmologies and symbolic doctrines, is metaphysics or *scientia sacra*. We can only act as a channel of grace for the natural world if we know and remain connected to the Source of grace, which is the Absolute and Infinite Reality. Furthermore, gnostic realization requires a veritable revelation and tradition from Heaven, to use Abrahamic terminology. Here we are not referring only to a sentimental appreciation of the world's great religions, but adherence to a particular orthodox religion in its totality, including its exoteric and esoteric dimensions. The forms of each religion, including their rites, rituals, liturgies and sacred art are so many openings to Heaven. We must employ these forms, as well as the esoteric aspects of tradition, such as an initiatic way, contemplation, and quintessential invocation or the prayer of the heart, to realize and in turn reflect the Divine Reality in the world.[31]

28. Frithjof Schuon, "The Symbolist Mind," *The Feathered Sun* (Bloomington, IN: World Wisdom, Inc., 1990), pp. 3–13.

29. "One wonders who knows more about the coyote, the zoologist who is able to study its external habits and dissect its cadaver or the Indian medicine man who identifies himself with the "spirit" of the coyote?" *Knowledge and the Sacred*, p. 193.

30. Tragically, like nature, these civilizations and their modalities of knowing and being remain under siege through the globalization of the modern European materialistic worldview, which has been enforced through coercive measures around the world for over five hundred years.

31. For a detailed and penetrating overview of metaphysics, see Seyyed Hossein Nasr, "Scientia Sacra" in *Knowledge and the Sacred*, p. 130–159.

> By virtue of being the *khalīfah* of God on earth and occupying the central position he does hold, man is the channel of grace for nature. The spiritual man is the means whereby nature breathes of the spiritual life and is prevented from suffocation and destruction, as also confirmed by Western Hermetical and alchemical writers like Flamel and Jacob Böhme. Were man to cease completely to follow the spiritual life and lose contact with the spiritual world, he would cease to be a source of light for nature and in fact would turn toward the destruction and vilification of nature.[32]

Nasr's own life and work bear witness to his full dedication to his own tradition—including Sufism, Islam's mystical dimension—while being intellectually open to the doctrines of other traditions and encouraging seekers from other traditions and civilizations to maintain fidelity to their own religion. His defense of nature crosses religious frontiers for metaphysical reasons and because of the fact that the crisis we are now facing is truly global. While demonstrating the reality of the common and unique metaphysical Principle that shines through nature in the various cosmologies of the world's religions, Nasr also looks closely at the Islamic tradition and the wealth of knowledge pertaining to God, the human being, and the various levels of the cosmos described in the Quran, *Ḥadīth* literature, and the wisdom of Muslim scientists, philosophers and Sufis. Nasr writes,

> When we turn to Islam we find a religious tradition more akin to Christianity in its theological formulations yet possessing in its heart a gnosis or *sapientia* similar to metaphysical doctrines of other Oriental traditions. In this, as in many other domains, Islam is the 'middle people', the *ummah wasaṭah* to which the Quran refers, in both a geographical and metaphysical sense. For this reason the intellectual structure of Islam and its cosmological doctrines and sciences of nature can be of the greatest aid in awakening certain dormant possibilities within Christianity.[33]

Nasr goes on to remind us that Islamic metaphysics and cosmol-

32. *The Essential Seyyed Hossein Nasr*, p. 67.
33. *Man and Nature*, p. 93.

ogy are based on the doctrine of Divine Unity (*al-tawḥīd*), which is the central reality and leitmotif of the Quran and *Ḥadīth*.[34] In Islam, the Absolute and Infinite Unity of God radiates into the cosmos through a gradation of Being (*wujūd*) or Light (*Nūr*), which refers to the Divine Reality in the language of Muslim philosophers and Sufis. As such, everything in existence is seen as a theophany or symbol of the Names and Attributes of God. Concerning the Quran, Nasr writes,

> In Islam the inseparable link between man and nature, and also between the sciences of nature and religion, is to be found in the Quran itself, the Divine Book which is the Logos or Word of God. As such it is both the source of the revelation which is the basis of religion and the macrocosmic revelation which is the Universe. It is both the recorded Quran (*al-Qur'ān al-tadwīnī*) and the 'Quran of creation' (*al-Qur'ān al-takwīnī*) which contains the "ideas" or archetypes of all things. That is why the term used to signify the verses of the Quran or *āyah* also means events occurring within the souls of men and phenomena in the world of nature.[35]

Moreover, Nasr states that these three books (revelation, man, and the cosmos) have inner and outer meanings. Full knowledge of these books—including nature—requires an esoteric or symbolic hermeneutical approach that reveals their common principles and archetypes, and ultimately the Principle as such.[36] As man loses knowledge of the inner meaning of sacred scripture, which occurred in the West during the Renaissance through the rise of humanism and during the Scientific Revolution and its aftermath through scientism, the inner reality of the other books, that is man and nature, also became obscured. It is not at all a coincidence that the inner knowledge of the book of nature was lost at the same time that western man began to marginalize the cosmological and symbolic teachings in the Bible (including the Kabbalah), as well as the traditional understanding of man held in Christianity. What was left was a sentimental appreciation of nature, religion and man that

34. Ibid., p. 94.
35. Ibid., pp. 94–95.
36. Ibid., p. 95.

flowered during the Romantic period, but which had no power to influence the dominant philosophical and scientific paradigm of the day which was based on a mechanistic view of the cosmos.

Returning to Islam, the Muslim is called to reflect upon the signs of God in the Quran as well as those in his own being in order for nature to reveal Divine beauty and majesty to him.[37] In addition to illuminating the significance of nature through the Quran and *Ḥadīth*, in *Man and Nature* and *Religion and the Order of Nature* Nasr also cites the metaphysical, cosmological and anthropological doctrines of numerous Muslim sages, such as the Ikhwān al-Ṣafā', Ibn Sīnā, Ibn 'Arabī, and 'Abd al-Karīm Jīlī.[38] In Islam, man—as God's vicegerent on earth—has certain rights and responsibilities that can only be fully realized when he surrenders to God as his servant and faithfully reflects and radiates the Divine Names and Presence on earth. Nasr writes,

> In fact man is the channel of grace for nature; through his active participation in the spiritual world he casts light into the world of nature. He is the mouth through which nature breathes and lives. Because of the intimate connection between man and nature, the inner state of man is reflected in the external order. Were there to be no more contemplatives and saints, nature would become deprived of the light that illuminates it and the air which keeps it alive. It explains why, when man's inner being has turned to darkness and chaos, nature is also turned from harmony and beauty to disequilibrium and disorder. Man sees in nature what he is himself and penetrates into the inner meaning of nature only on the condition of being able to delve into the inner depths of his own being and to cease to lie merely on the periphery of his being. Men who live only on the surface of their being can study nature as something to be manipulated and dominated. But only he who has turned toward the inward dimension of his being can see nature as a symbol, as a transparent reality and come to know and understand it in the real sense.[39]

37. See, Quran 41:53; and 51:20–21.

38. See also, *An Introduction to Islamic Cosmological Doctrines: Conceptions of Nature and Methods used for its study by the Ikhwān al-Ṣafā', al-Bīrūnī, and Ibn Sīnā.*

39. *Man and Nature*, pp. 96–97.

To penetrate into the inner reality of nature, we must first reach the inner reality of our own being through prayer and contemplation. Our relationship with the world around us is a direct reflection of the state of our own soul. If the soul is cluttered and chaotic, we will produce cities and works of art that reflect that disorder and impose it upon the natural world. If the soul is at peace and ordered, however, we will be able to preserve the vestiges of nature that remain and build homes and other spaces that are in harmony with the world around us. Japanese Zen gardens and traditional Islamic mosques, for example, were built by craftsmen who followed the inner and outer teachings of the Buddha and the Prophet. As a result, these spaces mirror the inner substance of the founders of these religions, which are based on the realization of emptiness or the void (*sūnyatā*) and spiritual poverty (*faqr*). Through making space within for the Presence of the Real, men and women will inevitably be able to create and preserve space in the world around them, including in their homes, places of worship, schools and cities, for the void, which also manifests in the most immediate manner in the natural world.[40] In is not an accident that some of the most beautiful traditional mosques and temples throughout the world integrate the features of nature into their very structure, including the sky, water and plant life, as well as the use of natural materials in their construction. Moreover, by realizing the void within, we will be able to behold it in nature. The blue sky and the air that we breath from our lush forests, as well as what remains of our untouched terrains from vast desert plains to pristine mountain tops, all manifest the void and symbolize paradisal realities. Only by realizing our own virgin nature will we be able to perceive the true value of virgin nature on earth. It is upon this sacred ground within and without—which is in reality the realization of the insubstantial and perishing nature of both psychic and corporeal existence—that God can manifest His enduring Presence and Reality to us. A glance at the skylines of Tokyo or Mecca is evidence of how far some modern Buddhists and Muslims have fallen from the ideals established

40. Seyyed Hossein Nasr, *Islamic Art and Spirituality*, pp. 185–191; and Titus Burckhardt, *Mirror of the Intellect*, pp. 231–235.

by their ancestors by creating skyscrapers with the façade and illusion of permanence. These structures also mirror the inner being of modern man—his ignorance of reality and hubris—that obstructs a true vision of the impermanence of the world and the ego and the abiding Reality of the One. Due to their transparency, sacred and traditional art and nature both reveal higher metaphysical archetypes. By approaching these archetypes through religion and the space created within our own being, we begin to recognize their manifestations as so many sacred symbols. In addition to an inward reorientation and transformation, among the most important aids in harmonizing our relationship with the earth is the building and preserving of sacred spaces that are so many extensions of nature and reflections of Paradise itself.

Other practical solutions to the environmental crisis, such as the preservation of endangered plant and animal species, stopping the pollution of the air and water, the use of alternative energy to prevent global warming, recycling, the reduction of waste, and a return to organic farming, for example, will only be employed once we recognize the earth and all life upon it as Sacred and have the moral discipline and will to act upon that vision. Such a change requires the radical paradigm shift and spiritual reorientation that Nasr has insisted upon throughout his life and writings. Nasr's defense of nature is inextricably linked to his defense of Tradition, understood in its most universal sense, as well as traditional or Pontifical Man. All of the authentic religions of the world contain a metaphysical vision of the transcendent Principle whose reality is known objectively through nature and subjectively within the heart of man. Nasr has helped to revive an awareness of the sacred character of nature, as well as criticize the philosophical reductionism associated with the quantitative and mechanical cosmology of modern science. From Nasr's perspective, humanity will not take the necessary practical steps to avert the apocalyptic consequences that will likely result from the abuse of the planet unless the Sacred is rediscovered and seen in the theophany that is nature. Modern man will not possess this gnostic vision of the cosmos and have the will to act upon it unless he embraces with his whole being a veritable revelation and tradition sent from Heaven. Each tradition contains the power to reawaken the Intellect or the eye of the heart, and in doing so facilitates the vision of the Sacred and the signs of God in the natural world. Only when this inner vision is restored will modern man be able to witness natural phenomena as so many transparent veils that reveal the Face of God here on earth. Nasr concludes his *Man and Nature* with the following words:

> In the end what we can say with certainty is that there is no peace possible among men unless there is peace and harmony with nature. And in order to have peace and harmony with nature one must be in harmony and equilibrium with Heaven, and ultimately with the Source and Origin of all things. He who is at peace with God is also at peace with His creation, both with nature and man.[41]

Nasr's corpus on the environment, as well as his works that deal with Islamic philosophy, science, esoterism, and Tradition in general, provide a masterful vision and prescription that must be understood and heeded if we are to change our relationship with the earth. Moreover, Nasr's precious writings on nature and the environmental crisis demonstrate the relevance and vitality of the Islamic sapiential tradition in the modern world, which can still provide answers to age-old existential questions and new problems that humanity faces at this late hour. Following closely in the footsteps of the prophets, the true vicegerents of God on earth among the saints and sages transmit sacred knowledge that relates to all of the essential aspects of the human condition.[42]

41. Ibid., p. 136.

42. In addition to the writings of Nasr and the other Muslim traditionalists cited in chapter one, we would also recommend the following works that start from the point of view of traditional principles to ask and answer the existential questions that we all face, and also apply these principles to the contingencies and challenges of the modern life: William Chittick, *Science of the Cosmos, Science of the Soul: The Pertinence of Islamic Cosmology in the Modern World*; *Islam, Fundamentalism, and the Betrayal of Tradition*, Joseph E. B. Lumbard, ed.; M. Ali Lakhani, *The Timeless Relevance of Traditional Wisdom* (Bloomington, IN: World Wisdom, Inc., 2010); James S. Cutsinger, *Advice to the Serious Seeker: Meditations on the Teaching of Frithjof Schuon* (Albany, NY: State University of New York Press, 1997); and Huston Smith, *Why Religion Matters: The Fate of the Human Spirit in an Age of Disbelief* (New York: HarperCollins Publishers Inc., 2001).

8

The Wisdom and Forms of Islam

> I am a slave of the Quran if I have a soul
> I am the dust of the road of Muḥammad, the Chosen
> If anyone quotes from my sayings other than this
> I have nothing to do with him and I have nothing to do with his words.[1]
> —Jalāl al-Dīn Rūmī

> Though Islamic mysticism, as it persists ... down to the present day, may be compared in many respects with Christian mysticism—and in other respects with Hindu and Far-Eastern mysticism—it is nevertheless founded entirely on the religious form specific to Islam.[2]
> —Titus Burckhardt

Many people in the West and other parts of the globe are now familiar with and even conversant in the revealed and inspired wisdom of both the East and the West, yet think that the acceptance of all religions is a sufficient end in and of itself. To be able to marvel at the wisdom of the Bhagavad Gita and the Tao te Ching, the Bible and the Quran, or the writings of Plato, Shankara, Rūmī and Eckhart is a wonderful and necessary compensation for many in the time that we live, but an awareness of the universal Truth at the heart of all religions will not change our condition unless we accept the discipline of a particular religion that God has revealed to humanity. In this volume we have presented the universal wisdom of Islam, yet the religion also contains its own particular wisdom and forms that are in many ways more central and meaningful to Muslims in their

1. Michelle Kimball, "Jalalo'd-Din Rumi's Views on the *Shari'at*," *Sufi* 17 (1993), p. 25.
2. *The Essential Titus Burckhardt*, p. 259.

day-to-day lives, as well as for their expected posthumous encounter with the Divine Reality. As we have discovered, the Quran and the Prophet Muḥammad synthesize all pre-Islamic revealed books and prophets in their own particular forms. Moreover, the primary Islamic sources, as well as the central rites and spiritual dimensions of the religion are direct openings to Universal Wisdom, Love, Peace and Beauty—precisely through a Muslim's exclusive devotion to God through the forms of Islam. The Islamic tradition is not unique in this regard, but a failure to recognize the Universal through the particulars of religion would be an oversight in any study of pluralism. Here it is not possible to provide an exhaustive account of the Islamic tradition, but we underscore those elements of doctrine and praxis that constitute the heart of the religion.[3]

The beginning and end of Islam is the *shahādah*, which a born Muslim hears upon entering the world or a convert proclaims when accepting the faith, both of whom live their days hoping to be able to pronounce it at the moment of death. The affirmation of faith is expressed in Islam through the words, *Lā ilāha illa'Llāh*, followed by, *Muḥammadun rasūl Allāh*. The outward meaning alone, "There is no god but God" and "Muḥammad is the Messenger of God" brings an awareness of the One into the lives and hearts of Muslims, as well as the means of accessing the One through the Prophet. Muslim philosophers and Sufis have also seen in the *shahādah* its inner meaning, which is "There is no reality but God," and that therefore "Muḥammad—and all of creation—is a Manifestation of God." The doctrine of Unity is not unique to Islam, as all revealed religions articulate the Unity of the Supreme Principle in one form or another, even though this principle is reaffirmed in a particular manner with insistence in the Islamic tradition. To accept that

3. For an overview of the Islamic tradition as a whole see Frithjof Schuon, *Understanding Islam*; Seyyed Hossein Nasr, *The Heart of Islam*; Seyyed Hossein Nasr, *Ideals and Realities of Islam*; Sachiko Murata and William Chittick, *The Vision of Islam* (St. Paul, MN: Paragon House, 1994); Victor Danner, *The Islamic Tradition: An Introduction* (Hillsdale: NY: Sophia Perennis, 2005); Joseph Lumbard, *Submission, Faith, and Beauty: The Religion of Islam*; Charles Le Gai Eaton, *Islam and the Destiny of Man*; and Annemarie Schimmel, *Islam: An Introduction* (Albany, NY: State University of New York Press, 1992).

Muḥammad is the Messenger of God, however, is unique to Islam and Muslims, even if one can find numerous prophets and avatars that play analogous roles in other religions. To accept the Messenger of God is to accept his Message—the Holy Quran or the Word of God in the Arabic tongue.[4] As we have discovered, it means that one must also accept the Biblical prophets mentioned in the Quran, such as Adam, Noah, Abraham, Moses, David and Jesus, as well as the revealed nature of the Torah, Psalms and Gospel. It means that one must also accept that "for every community there is a messenger." (10:47) The particular wisdom of the Quran is in fact an affirmation of the universal wisdom of humanity. The Quran also insists that the Prophet Muḥammad is the "Seal of the prophets," which means that he is the last prophet of God sent to humanity with the final Revelation and religion. Such a claim may appear bold, but one must only reflect upon the fact that no major world religion—complete with a revealed book, prophet, sacred art and saints—has appeared since the rise of Islam. In the nineteenth and twentieth centuries new religions appeared on the scene, but these are usually offshoots of an existing religion or simply man-made constructs, which cannot guarantee salvation or sanctity in the absence of a vertical revelation and orthodox traditional framework.

Closely related to the Quran's emphasis on Divine Unity is the doctrine of the most beautiful Names (*al-asmā' al-ḥusnā*) of God, numbered ninety-nine by tradition.[5] The Holy Quran provides an incredibly rich description of the Divine Reality through the beautiful Names that punctuate its chapters and verses and consequently

4. Among the best translations of the Quran into English are *HarperCollins Study Qur'ān*, trans. Seyyed Hossein Nasr; *The Message of the Quran*, trans. Muhammad Asad (Gibralter, Dar al-Andalus, 1980); *The Sublime Quran*, trans. Laleh Bakhtiar (Chicago, Kazi Publications, 2007); *The Meaning of the Glorious Koran*, trans. Muhammad Marmaduke Pickthall (New York: The New American Library, 1963); and *The Koran Interpreted*, trans. A.J. Arberry (London, Allen & Unwin, 1955).

5. Shams Friedlander and al-Hajj Shaikh Muzaffereddin, *Ninety-Nine Names of Allah: The Beautiful Names* (New York: HarperCollins Publishers, 1993); and Shaykh Tosun Bayrak, *The Name & the Named: The Divine Attributes of God* (Louisville, KY: Fons Vitae, 2000).

the life of the Muslim whose awareness of God is expanded by his study and recitation of the Book. It is through remembering and reflecting upon these Names that Muslims can approach and recognize the Qualities of the Sacred during prayer and witness their presence and reality within the heart and in the world. We read in the Quran, "Unto God belong the most beautiful Names; so call on Him by them. . . ." (7:180) Among these Names include the One (*al-Wāḥid*), the Truth (*al-Ḥaqq*), the Light (*al-Nūr*), the Living (*al-Ḥayy*), the Self-Subsisting (*al-Qayyūm*), the All-Embracing (*al-Wāsi*ʿ), the Just (*al-ʿAdl*), the Wise (*al-Ḥakīm*), the King (*al-Malik*), the Witness (*al-Shahīd*), the Peace (*al-Salām*), the Loving (*al-Wadūd*), the Friend (*al-Walī*), the Outward (*al-Ẓāhir*), the Inward (*al-Bāṭin*), and, among the most central, the Infinitely Good (*al-Raḥmān*) and the All-Merciful (*al-Raḥīm*), which begin all but one of the chapters of the Quran and are recited by Muslims throughout their lives during the five daily prayers. The Quran in fact synthesizes the diverse ways that God has revealed Himself to humanity throughout the ages through the beautiful Names, including the all-encompassing Name Allah. While all religions refer to the Qualities of God, too few of us in the modern world realize the power a revealed Name has in its original language, such as Arabic, Hebrew, or Sanskrit, to communicate the Reality it denotes. Indeed, a sacred language is a medium of Divine revelation no less direct than a physical or spiritual encounter with Jesus or the Buddha. The Names contained in the Arabic revelation therefore help us to recognize the Identity of God and also transmit a measure of that Identity in their very forms. While in Islam God is not anthropomorphic, the doctrine of the most beautiful Names provides Muslims with very personal and meaningful ways to relate to God. Wherever one of these Names or Qualities is found—in the diverse forms of Revelation, the beauty and majesty of nature, the love of a parent for their child, the light and sanctity of a prophet or saint, and in vocal or silent prayer—its origin is ultimately in God, whose Essence and Qualities nevertheless transcend creation.

In Islam, God is transcendent and incomparable (*tanzīh*) vis-à-vis creation and also immanent and similar (*tashbīh*). The doctrine of *tawḥīd* avoids abstracting God as a conceptual reality somewhere above us and also of limiting God to His signs in creation alone. The Divine Reality and Presence is ubiquitous and infinite and therefore embraces and transcends man and the world. As the Outward (*al-Ẓāhir*), He reveals Himself through creation as so many Self-disclosures, and as the Inward (*al-Bāṭin*), He veils the fullness of His Being lest it consume and annihilate the world. He is "nearer to [man] than his jugular vein" (50:16), while being simultaneously transcendent. This is possible because God transcends our ordinary experience of the world and ourselves precisely through His immanence. Only in the heart—the locus of the Divine Reality—is God neither near nor far. Yet most of us are far removed from the Divine Center where we can experience God beyond all mental concepts and images as That (*al-Dhāt*) which radiates knowledge and love like the light and warmth of the Sun. The Prophet proclaimed that, "The heart of the faithful is the throne of the All-Merciful (*al-Raḥmān*)." The place where Unity and the Names are known and realized is the inner heart and the methods of Islam and Sufism can orient us towards and eventually help us enter the heart. Jesus himself revealed the mystery of the heart when he said, "The kingdom of God is within you." (Luke 17:21)

Rotating around the axis of Divine Unity and the beautiful Names, the Quran contains other leitmotivs, including the reality of higher levels of existence, such as the Unseen, the existence of angels and other celestial beings, the need for men and women to accept Divine guidance through Revelation and prophecy, and the soul's accountability before God now and on the Day of Judgment. The Quran reminds us that God knows all that we do and that our actions and words are recorded and will be recounted to us on the Day of Judgment. The Revelation also describes in lucid detail the realities of heaven and hell and brings these images into the immediate awareness of whoever reads the Book. We are ultimately responsible for the condition of our soul and its posthumous state. It is only through sincere and faithful adherence to a revealed religion—which communicates the Wisdom, Mercy and Will of God—that we can be assured of Paradise in the hereafter. Of course God is Merciful, but human nature is also weak and without being guided by religion and reminded of the Justice of God in the hereafter many more men and women would violate the sanctity of their neighbors' lives, property and honor and ignore the One who has given us life to begin with.

The reader approaching the Quran for the first time should also be aware that it, like other holy books, contains many levels of meaning. The Reality that is Being or Existence itself contains many levels—while being One in God—and the Book therefore reflects and inculcates an awareness of these levels, including the corporeal, psychic, imaginal, angelic and Divine levels of reality. To flatten the Book to one meaning is analogous to flattening existence to the material level alone. Each time we read the Quran a new meaning is in fact revealed to us based upon the condition of our soul and the circumstances that we find ourselves in. The prophets and their adversaries, such as Moses and Pharaoh, are not only historical figures to be venerated and despised, but also aspects within the inner being of all men and women. Through a meta-historical reading on the Book, we can begin to recognize within ourselves higher faculties, such as the Intellect and Spirit, that resemble the prophets, and lower faculties, such as the egocentric soul and its pride, that resemble the unbelievers. The Quran is a living book and mirror that describes and reflects all that is in us, as well as those we interact with in the world. Part of the alchemical power of the Arabic revelation to transform souls is through its ability to clearly communicate the sacred stories of the prophets in a manner that is meaningful to all men and women in all times and places. Furthermore, the highest level of the Quran remains the most outward, for God Himself is speaking through each verse and we must only be attentive and pure of heart to hear the Voice of God as we recite the Revelation. It is only through attaining a measure of the spiritual purity of the Prophet that we can perceive the perpetual descent of the Book.

With unsurpassed power and eloquence, God also transmits wisdom through so many rhetorical questions. Certain existential arguments are advanced by God in the Quran, encouraging the reader to reflect upon his origin, the origin of the universe and the eternal nature of the Supreme Principle in a Socratic manner. The Quran is in fact the primary source of the tradition of prophetic philosophy that has flourished throughout Islamic history and remains a living tradition in Iran, Turkey, Pakistan, India, Malaysia, and parts of the Arab world and even the West.[6] By reflecting upon the Book, Muslim philosophers gained Divine insight into the questions they posed, including the primacy of existence or quiddity, cosmogony, spiritual psychology and eschatology, some of which would remain unanswered if left to the resources of the rational faculty alone. Be that as it may, the Quran enjoins men and women to use their Intellect, which refers to both the suprarational faculty of intelligence centered in the heart and its reflection in the mind. As such, Muslims sages saw in the Greek philosophical heritage a powerful support in their own quest for sacred knowledge.

The Quran is also a book of law, ethics and virtue, calling men and women to live together before God in peace and justice. Like the Decalogue, it forbids idolatry, murder, theft, adultery, lying and other transgressions, while also inculcating faith, honesty, compassion, humility and gratitude. While it is not possible for every Muslim to be an expert in Islamic Law, the basics of the *Sharī'ah* are described in an intelligible manner in the Quran and the *Sunnah* of the Prophet Muḥammad and brought out in more detail in the Sunni and Shī'ite schools of jurisprudence.[7] It is by conforming one's life to the *Sharī'ah* to the best of one's ability that one is truly a Muslim. Islamic Law not only details what God has prohibited for Muslims, including such well-known dietary restrictions as pork and alcohol, but also describes the central pillars (*arkān*) of the religion such as the testimony of faith, prayer, alms, fasting and the pilgrimage, which are discussed in more detail below. Moreover, the

6. Seyyed Hossein Nasr, "The *Qur'ān* and *Ḥadīth* as source and inspiration of Islamic philosophy," in Seyyed Hossein Nasr and Oliver Leaman, eds., *History of Islamic Philosophy* (London: Routledge, 2003), pp. 27–39.

7. Seyyed Hossein Nasr, "The *Sharī'ah*—Divine Law—Social and Human Norm," *Ideals and Realities of Islam*, pp. 85–113; 'Abd al-Raḥmān al-Jazīrī, *Islamic Jurisprudence According to the Four Sunni Schools (Al-Fiqh 'Alā al-Madhāhib al-Arba'ah)*, vol. I, trans. Nancy Roberts (Louisville, KY: Fons Vitae, 2009); Mohammad Hashim Kamali, *Principles of Islamic Jurisprudence* (Cambridge: Islamic Texts Society, 1991); and Muhammad Baqir al-Sadr, *Principles of Islamic Jurisprudence: According to Shi'i Law*, trans. Arif Abdul Hussain (North Haledon, NJ: Islamic Publications International, 2003).

Sharī'ah embraces all aspects of life, including the rights and responsibilities of Muslims and minority religious groups, marriage, social and business interactions, and the principles of good governance and just war. While it is beyond the power of most of us to mold our societies based upon the Laws of Moses, Manu or Muḥammad, we can attempt to order our own lives based upon the Will of God as expressed in one of His Revelations and by one of His prophets.[8] Furthermore, from our point of view, the *Sharī'ah* can be essentialized for contemporary Muslim men and women whose circumstances often necessitate a broader and more flexible approach. We are not advocating that Muslims steal or consume alcohol—what is permissible (*ḥalāl*) and forbidden (*ḥarām*) in Islam is clear in our sources—but we should be able to apply the easiest traditional interpretations of the Law and the religion in general to our lives.[9] For some this may mean practicing the five pillars alone and avoiding sin to the best of one's ability—an approach to Islam that has precedence and is sanctioned in the very *Ḥadīth* of the Prophet.

8. Strictly speaking, in Islam God Himself is the Supreme Legislator (*al-Shār'*) through His Will expressed in the Quran, while the Prophet Muḥammad's *Sunnah* acts as the secondary—yet necessary—source of Islamic Law. This is also true of the Mosaic Law, as God revealed the Decalogue through the prophet Moses to the Jewish people.

9. Ibn 'Arabī states, "God has made the divergence in legal questions a mercy for His servants and a broadening (*ittisā'*) of what He has prescribed they should do to testify to their adoration. But in the case of those who follow the jurists of our time, these jurists have prohibited and restricted what the sacred Law had broadened in their favour. They say to the person who belongs to their school, if for example he is a Ḥanafite: 'Don't go looking for a *rukhṣa* (an alleviation or exemption) from Shāfi'ī regarding this problem you are faced with'; and so on with all of them. This is one of the greatest calamities and heaviest constraints in the matter of religion. God himself has said: 'In religion he had not imposed anything difficult on you' (Quran 22:78). The Law has affirmed the validity of the status of anyone who makes a personal effort at interpretation for himself and for those who follow him. But in our days the jurists have condemned this effort, claiming it encourages people to make a mockery of religion. For them to say this is the height of ignorance." Claude Addas, *Quest for the Red Sulphur*, pp. 46–47. Due to the spread of Islamic modernism and fundamentalism in our time, however, one must be cautious of those who attempt to reformulate and in fact violate the *Sharī'ah* through rulings and actions that are opposed to the Law.

> A man asked the Messenger of God (may the Peace and blessings of God be upon him): Do you think that if I perform the obligatory prayers, fast in Ramaḍān, treat as lawful that which is lawful and treat as forbidden that which is forbidden, and do nothing further, I shall enter Paradise? He said: Yes.[10]

The Sacred Law should not be an obstacle but rather an aid to ensure that on the Day of Judgment we will not be ashamed of ourselves before God for having injured our friends, family, and neighbors, and will have given God his due through prayer and other rites of the religion. Moreover, the letter of the Law must be complemented by an awareness of its Spirit. The regulations and restrictions of religion are in place to facilitate the Love of God and love of one's neighbor. The Islamic ideal can be envisaged as a middle path that essentially combines the Law of Moses and the Love of Jesus, expressed in Islam through its own Sacred Law (*Sharīʿah*) and spiritual path (*ṭarīqah*). Many of the excesses that can be witnessed in the Muslim world, the West and other civilizations, are due to a neglect of either the Law or its Spirit.

The Quran also contains numerous directives to reflect upon the signs of God in the natural world. These verses are not intended to simply inculcate reverence for the earth—which they nevertheless do—but to make us aware of our existential situation before God, as all of creation surrenders to God in its own way through following its particular nature according to the Divine command. By reflecting upon the signs of God—the movement of the Sun and Moon, the rain that falls from the sky, and the plant and animal life that grows—we can rediscover our own primordial nature (*fiṭrah*) through which we can also naturally surrender our purpose to God. Moreover, we also become more cognizant of the bounty and grace that God has given humanity through the air we breathe, the water we drink, the food we eat, and the materials we use for travel and shelter—as well as what these symbolize spiritually. Reflecting upon the natural world has the power to inculcate the imperative virtue of gratitude. To be reminded that all that we are given in this

10. *Forty Hadith*, trans. Ezzeddin Ibrahim and Denys Johnson-Davies (Cambridge: The Islamic Texts Society, 1997), pp. 76–77.

world—indeed all that we are—is from God the Generous (*al-Karīm*), is to possess the faith and joy that can make our journey in this world and the next a blessed one.

The Quran is the primary sacred source for all things Islamic, including the Law, theology and philosophy, as well as the spiritual dimensions of Islam discussed below. The descent of the Book is, however, closely wed to the historical person and spiritual substance of the Prophet Muḥammad, without whose example the Quran would remain a closed book.[11] In the same way that one cannot imagine Jesus without the Virgin Mary, it was through the unlettered Prophet that God revealed His final Word to humanity in the form of the Holy Quran. Not only did he faithfully transmit the successive verses of the Revelation, despite being ostracized and persecuted by the Meccan aristocracy and being forced into exile in Medina, but his own life, teachings and character act as the essential commentary on the Quran for Muslims. The Quran tells us to pray, but it is the *Sunnah* or Wont of the Prophet that tells us how to pray.[12] Like the Quran, the *Sunnah*—which includes his sayings or *Ḥadīth*—pertains to practical matters like business interactions and hygiene to the most sublime discussions on spirituality and philosophy recalled throughout this book. It is upon the basis of following the *Sunnah* that a Muslim is guided and draws near to God. The Quran states, "Say [Muḥammad], 'If you love God, follow me, and God will love you and forgive you your sins. And God is Forgiving, Merciful.'" (3:31)

The Prophet's example teaches Muslims about the nature of Reality and the soul; the inner and outer dimensions of prayer and the other rites of religion; to treat one's parents—especially one's mother—with respect and kindness; to care for the poor, the sick, orphans and the elderly; to respect animal and plant life; to handle one's business interactions in a fair and just manner; to protect the weak from violence and injustice; and to see all races, nations, and

11. See Martin Lings, *Muhammad: His Life Based on the Earliest Sources*; and Seyyed Hossein Nasr, *Muhammad: Man of God*.

12. S.H. Nasr "The Prophet and Prophetic Tradition—the Last Prophet and Universal Man," *Ideals and Realities of Islam*, pp. 57–83.

tribes as equal in the eyes of God. The Prophet Muḥammad was and is "a mercy unto the worlds" (21:107), a mercy that is perpetuated in the world by Muslims who follow his *Sunnah* and also through the Prophet's own living spiritual presence. It is meritorious to follow the *Sunnah* in its smallest details, from how the Prophet dressed and ate to the particular acts of kindness that he displayed, such as removing an obstruction from a path for those who might follow. However, for many of us it may be difficult to put all of these details into practice, especially in societies that are hostile to outward displays of religiosity. As such, the quintessential dimension of the *Sunnah*—which is his character or virtues—can be emphasized in all times and places. His primary virtues consist of humility or spiritual poverty, generosity or magnanimity, and sincerity or truthfulness. All of the prophets of humanity are known for certain virtues, while possessing them all in principle, while the Prophet of Islam is characterized by his selflessness vis-à-vis his own ego, his generosity towards others, and the equilibrium or perfection of these two in perfect sincerity towards God, which ensures that ascetic and generous acts are done for the sake of earning God's pleasure and not to be seen by others.[13] The virtues are cosmic reflections of the Divine Names and Attributes, which the Prophet was oriented towards through his devotion to God, reception of the Word of God, and his own pure nature. Even where it is possible to practice the supererogatory aspects of the *Sunnah*, man must not lose sight of the purpose of these details, which is to live with a measure of prophetic virtue that makes one a suitable container for the Divine Word and ultimately the Divine Reality and Presence.

According to Islam, the purpose of human existence is to worship and know God. We read in the Quran, "I did not create jinn and humanity save to worship Me." (51:56) God also states through the Prophet in a *ḥadīth qudsī*, "I was a Treasure but was not known. So I loved to be known, and I created the creatures and made Myself known to them. . . ." Islam is therefore centered on prayer, first and foremost the five obligatory canonical prayers know as *ṣalāh*,

13. Frithjof Schuon, "The Prophet," *Understanding Islam*, pp. 91–95.

through which we can know God.[14] During the times of prayer all Muslims recite at least the *Fātiḥah* or the opening chapter of the Quran and in certain cycles additional verses or short chapters of the Book. It is said that the entire Revelation is summarized in the *Fātiḥah*, which is translated in English as follows:

> In the Name of God, the Infinitely Good, the All-Merciful.
> Praise be to God, the Lord of the worlds,
> the Infinitely Good, the All-Merciful,
> Master of the Day of Judgment.
> Thee alone we worship and from Thee alone we seek help.
> Guide us upon the straight path,
> The path of those upon whom is Thy Grace,
> not of those who incur wrath,
> nor of those who are astray. (1:1–7)

Through punctuating their days with the daily prayers, Muslims are reminded of the essential Nature of God, as Good and Merciful; we inculcate gratitude through our praise of Him; remember His Sovereignty now and on the Day of Judgment; and beseech Him for His help and guidance on the straight path that makes our journey through this world and the next safe and felicitous. Moreover, when we pray, spiritual grace, protection, and joy descend upon us through the living words of the Revelation, the Presence of God, and the invisible company of the angels who pray with us. The culmination of the prayer is the rite of prostration through which men and women humble themselves before God in a physical manner. Through prostration we negate our ego and very existence and can begin to behold the ubiquitous Reality of the One in and around us. It is impossible to overstate the significance of prayer, which is the greatest blessing that God has given to humanity. Only through the regular practice of the rite, however, can we begin to perceive the subtle, yet powerful affect of prayer to bring the Presence of God into our lives and transform and even transport the soul to Paradise and the Divine Throne. The Prophet said, "The key to Paradise is

14. Among the most accessible works on the meaning and forms of *ṣalāh* in English is Coleman Barks and Michael Green's *The Illuminated Prayer: The Five-Times Prayer of the Sufis* (New York: Ballantine Books, 2000).

prayer." And also, "Prayer is the *mi'rāj* of the believer." In another tradition we are told, "To worship God as if you see Him, for even if you do not see Him, He sees you." We are ultimately brought face to Face with God through prayer and only need to awaken our inner faculties to perceive the Countenance of the Real through mindfulness during the rite and the perpetual remembrance of God at other times during the day. The regular orientation in the direction of Mecca during prayer can lead a Muslim to the realization that "To God belong the East and the West. Whersoever you turn, there is the Face of God. God is All-Encompassing, Knowing." (2:115)

Other essential pillars of the religion support the prayer of the believer. Muslims are called to give at least 2.5% of their extra annual income in charity or *zakāh*. For we are warned in the Quran,

> Hast thou seen the one who denies religion?
> That is the one who drives away the orphan,
> And does not urge feeding the indigent.
> So woe unto performers of prayer
> Who are heedless of their prayers—
> Those who strive to be seen,
> Yet refuse small kindnesses. (107:1–7)

Muslims also fast from food and water during the Islamic lunar month of Ramaḍān, which is known as *ṣawm*, and is also a fast from the passions and appetite of the lower self and the world in general. The space created in the body and soul is then filled by the pious Muslim with prayer and the remembrance of God. Those that are able are also called to make the pilgrimage to the Ka'bah in Mecca at least once during their life, which is the *ḥajj*. Following in the footsteps of the prophets Abraham and Muḥammad, Muslim pilgrims during the annual *ḥajj* wear simple white garments, abstain from all argumentation and especially violence, and remember God through so many rites, the first and last of which are the circumambulation of the Ka'bah. The *ḥajj* is one of the great manifestations of the unity of the Muslim community, where believers from all parts of the globe come together to remember God and return home with something of the grace (*barakah*) from the House of God for their families and communities. The Ka'bah is also a symbol for the

Throne of God and the inner heart. It is said that the one who truly performs this rite enters the heart where God resides; he has died to the world and already been resurrected before God.

Upon the basis of the sincere and regular practice of the rites of Islam and the observance of other essential aspects of Islamic Law, Muslims who yearn to know God here and now can also embark on the spiritual path or *ṭarīqah*, which is a synonym for Sufism or *taṣawwuf*.[15] Sufism also derives from the Quran and *Sunnah* of the Prophet, even if one can find analogous spiritual or contemplative paths in other religions. In addition to the exoteric rites of Islam, Muslim aspirants on the Sufi path practice additional esoteric rites under the guidance and direction of a spiritual master or shaykh, who also transmits the initiatic power (*walāyah*) of the Prophet of Islam that makes our journey to the One possible. Although there are numerous practices that have varying degrees of emphasis in the different Sufi orders or *ṭuruq* (pl. of *ṭarīqah*)—such as the spiritual retreat (*khalwah*), communal gatherings (*majālis*), sacred music and dance (*samāʿ*), the recitation of a litany (*wird*) derived from certain Quranic verses and meditation (*fikr*)—the most important Sufi practice is the remembrance or invocation of God known in Arabic as *dhikr Allāh*.[16] The Quran states,

> Recite that which has been revealed unto thee of the Book, and perform the prayer (*al-ṣalāh*). Truly prayer prevents against indecency and abomination, but the remembrance of God (*dhikr Allāh*) is surely greater. And God knows whatsoever you do. (29:45)

15. See Seyyed Hossein Nasr, *The Garden of Truth*; Seyyed Hossein Nasr, *Sufi Essays*; Seyyed Hossein Nasr, ed., *Islamic Spirituality*, 2 vols.; Martin Lings, *What is Sufism?*; Titus Burckhardt, *An Introduction to Sufi Doctrine*; William Chittick, *Sufism—A Short Introduction* (Oxford: One World, 2000); Annemarie Schimmel, *Mystical Dimensions of Islam* (Chapel Hill, NC: The University of North Carolina Press, 1975); and Jean-Louis Michon and Roger Gaetani, eds., *Sufism: Love & Wisdom*.

16. Ibn ʿAṭāʾ Allāh al-Iskandarī, *The Key to Salvation: A Sufi Manual of Invocation* (*Miftāḥ al-falāḥ wa miṣbāḥ al-arwāḥ*); and David Dakake, "The Practice of *dhikr* in the Early Islamic Community," in Zailan Moris, ed., *Knowledge is Light: Essays in Honor of Seyyed Hossein Nasr* (Chicago, IL: ABC International Group Inc., 1999).

The Shaykh transmits a particular Divine Name or formula from the Quran to the disciple and instructs him or her to invoke it at certain times each day. One cannot simply read about Sufism in books and choose practices and invocations for oneself, which is analogous to someone ignorant of medicine and pharmacology self-medicating and even mixing various remedies and drugs. Sufism is an oral tradition that is received from a physician of the soul after he or she has diagnosed our spiritual illnesses. We can be introduced to some of its profundities through the writings of its greatest masters such as Ibn ʿArabī or Rūmī, but we cannot reach their spiritual station and a direct vision of Ultimate Reality in the absence of a living master—the exceptions only proving the rule. In any case, a spiritual master prescribes a particular Quranic Name or formula to invoke, such as Allah (God), *Hū* or *Huwa* (He), *Lā ilāha illa'Llāh* (There is no god but God), *al-Raḥmān* (the Infinitely Good), or *al-Ḥaqq* (the Truth), for example. Through the invocation of the Name with the tongue, the Presence of the Name begins to penetrate into our awareness and being, moving from the tongue and mind to the heart, where it is said that God Himself invokes within us. Gradually we begin to exclusively concentrate on the Name and gain an awareness that only God is Real. The psychic and physical dimensions that we normally imagine to be real are seen to be ephemeral and ultimately non-existent before the true Reality or Self that discloses itself to us through the Name. However, it matters little whether or not Reality is unveiled through spiritual praxis. The goal of the path is not some great epiphany—which is in any case God's to give or withhold—but the perpetual devotion to God that communicates a measure of His Peace and Presence and has the power to transform our soul and help us lead more virtuous lives. Thus, the Prophet defined Islamic spirituality through the following maxim: "Qualify yourself with the Qualities of God" (*takhalluqū bi-akhlāqi'Llāh*).

Sufism, like Islam in general, is based on the love (*maḥabbah*) and knowledge (*maʿrifah*) of God. Those who intuit the possibility of a vision of and union with the Beloved can have no other goal in mind. However, as we said this is in God's Hands and, whether this happens in this world or the next, all we can do is to prepare the soul for this beatific vision and encounter. Thus, traditionally Sufi teachers emphasize a dedication to the rites of Islam and other essential aspects of the *Sharī'ah*, the reverential fear of God (*makhāfah*), repentance (*tawbah*), spiritual poverty (*faqr*) and the virtues (*akhlāq*) in general, respect or spiritual courtesy (*adab*), the reliance upon God (*tawakkul*), and attentively following the prescriptions of one's shaykh to make the soul worthy for spiritual realization. The Sufis often call this realization *fanā'* and *baqā'* or annihilation in and subsistence through God. We cannot reach the end of the path without the means or reach the kernel of religion without possessing the husk, which for Muslim aspirants on the spiritual path means that the forms of the Islamic religion are necessary at every step along the way. In reality, Sufism is the culmination and perfection of Islam or submission to God and *īmān* or faith.

Moreover, it is through the initiation and guidance of a living master that one can follow the spiritual *Sunnah* of the Prophet of Islam. Ultimately, it is through following this *Sunnah* that we rediscover our own inner heart (*qalb*) and the Light of the Prophet (*al-nūr al-muḥammadiyyah*) contained therein, for "The Prophet is closer to the believers than are they to themselves. . . ." (33:6) It is through the Prophet—his Light, station (*maqām*) and character—that we can truly realize the inner meaning of *tawḥīd*, which is "There is no reality but God; no self but the Self." No man or woman is a prophet after the Prophet of Islam, but we can each attain nearness to God through the spiritual Light that he conveyed to his family members and close companions and which has reached humanity through the Sufis and other Muslim gnostics. Even though the corporeal life of the Prophet has passed, the Spirit of the Prophet is alive. To walk in the footsteps of the Prophet is to be guided by him directly or else follow a master who has such a spiritual connection. There is no other way to God in Islam except through the door that is the beloved of God. The presence of pre-Islamic prophets, including those studied in this book, such as Jesus, Elias, Khiḍr, and Hermes, remain accessible to Muslims through the universal nature of the Prophet of Islam and the Holy Quran, which open a spiritual universe for Muslims in which all of the prophets of humanity are alive. Even the Muslim whose knowledge of religion is "limited" to the Quran and the Prophet Muḥammad, knows all Divine revelations and prophets in principle because the primary sources of Islam synthesize what came before them.[17]

It must be noted that some realized Sufi teachers in the West, as in India and other lands, do instruct both Muslim and non-Muslim disciples. In special circumstances—which are perhaps more common in our own time—Jews, Christians, Hindus, Sikhs, and others have been able to deepen their knowledge of and devotion to God through contact with a Sufi master. Conversely, some Muslims throughout history have taken knowledge and guidance from Christian or Hindu saints, for example. It must be stressed, however, that Sufism finds its origins in the Quran and Prophet Muḥammad. Moreover, traditionally most Sufi teachers and disciples were practicing Muslims and this remains normative in most contexts. Non-Muslims seeking to approach the Divine through the counsel and presence of a Sufi master should be aware of Sufism's intrinsic connection to Islam—the universal dimensions of which make esoteric ecumenism in such contexts possible. We are of the opinion that Islamic spirituality or Sufism can aid not only Muslims, but also some serious Jewish, Christian and other spiritual seekers in our time. One cannot rule out such possibilities if done with care and discernment by the teacher and the disciple.[18] In the words of Jalāl al-Dīn Rūmī,

> I was speaking one day amongst a group of people, and a party of non-Muslims was present. In the middle of my address they began

17. Annemarie Schimmel, *And Muhammad is His Messenger—The Veneration of the Prophet in Islamic Piety* (Chapel Hill, NC: The University of North Carolina Press, 1985); *Muhammad: Man of God*; and "The Prophet," *Understanding Islam*, pp. 87–105.

18. I am indebted and grateful to Dr. Pir Zia Inayat-Khan for helping me to understand some of the nuances involved in these questions, including the accessibility of Sufi teachings in the West for both Muslim and non-Muslim spiritual seekers. See also, S.H. Nasr, "The Spiritual Needs of Western Man and the Message of Sufism," *Islam and the Plight of Modern Man* (Lahore: Suhail Academy, 1988), pp. 47–66.

> to weep and to register emotion and ecstasy. Someone asked: What do they understand and what do they know? Only one Muslim in a thousand understands this kind of talk. What did they understand, that they should weep? The Master [i.e. Rūmī himself] answered: It is not necessary that they should understand the form of the discourse; that which constitutes the root and principle of the discourse, that they understand. After all, everyone acknowledges the Oneness of God, that He is the Creator and Provider, that He controls everything, that to Him all things shall return, and that it is He who punishes and forgives. When anyone hears these words, which are a description and commemoration (*dhikr*) of God, a universal commotion and ecstatic passion supervenes, since out of these words come the scent of their Beloved and their Quest.[19]

The spirituality of Islam is also expressed in an immediate manner through the sacred and traditional art forms of the religion.[20] The Prophet of Islam said, "God is beautiful and He loves beauty." And also, "God hath written beauty upon the face of all things." There is a hierarchy of beauty and art in Islam. God is the Beautiful (*al-Jamīl*) and ultimately all beauty in the world is a reflection of His Beauty. On earth this beauty is most radiant in the Quran and other revelations. In their different forms, the sacred arts of Quranic recitation and calligraphy are the sonoral and visible manifestations of the Word of God. This beauty is complemented by the beauty of the Prophet of Islam or the Universal Man, whose physical form, character and Spirit are perfect embodiments of inward and outward beauty—the former relating to the virtues. Each believer reflects this beauty to some degree by following the *Sunnah*, while the saints of Islam are themselves Divine masterpieces of sacred art. Traditional mosques are also high in the hierarchy of art in Islam. Not only are they decorated with verses of the Quran and geometric and arabesque patterns, but the empty space or void within mosques is complemented by recitation of the Quran—the true form and Presence of the Word of God. The mosque is there-

19. Trans. by Reza Shah-Kazemi, *The Other in the Light of the One*, p. 270.
20. Titus Burckhardt, *Art of Islam*; S.H. Nasr, *Islamic Art and Spirituality*; and Samer Akkach, *Cosmology and Architecture in Premodern Islam*.

fore like the soul of the Prophet and by extension all believers who are empty or pure enough to receive the Word. We must also mention in summary the Islamic arts of poetry and prose, music and dance, and the weaving of rugs and other arts and crafts. As in other traditional civilizations, the simplest of objects in the traditional Muslim home are characterized by both their practical utility and their beauty. Not unrelated is the art of dress for both Muslim men and women. When possible, dressing according to the *Sunnah* of the Prophet radiates something of his very presence into our lives, while also facilitating prayer and bearing the mark of dignity and beauty that characterizes all traditional dress. The purpose of Islamic art is not luxury or the air of sophistication as we find among many modern aesthetes, but to allow Heaven to touch earth through illuminating and ennobling the materials the artist works with, including his or her own soul. To create and live in an ambience that is based on the principles of Islamic aesthetics is to be constantly reminded of the Truth and Beauty of God. The doctrine and rites of the religion and the Reality and Presence that they convey are prolonged through Islamic art.

It is also necessary to say a few words about the Muslim family, where Islam manifests most clearly and directly. The Prophet Muḥammad himself declared that, "Marriage is half of religion." The soul is brought into equilibrium and perfection through interacting with one's spouse, which while being among the greatest blessings that God may give us, also requires a great amount of patience, forbearance and mildness from both partners. The religious education of children also begins in the home and the mother is most often our first teacher. The Prophet said that, "Heaven lies at the feet of mothers." The Islam of the Prophet Muḥammad was a community of men, women and children that began with him and his wife Khadījah in Mecca and grew to embrace thousands of souls from his home and mosque in Medina. All too often in the Muslim world and even in parts of the West, women are given the impression that their presence is not required nor even welcome in mosques and other traditional institutions. Traditional Islam does not advocate a radical form of feminism that opposes men, but the feminine is as integral to Islam as the masculine and an opposition to the exclusion of women by some men is needed in our time. Muslim women have been among the greatest scholars, saints, artists, entrepreneurs, and even political leaders in Islamic history—possessing an equal share of the gifts and perfections of the human state.[21] Those men who reached spiritual perfection rarely did so without the influence of a wise, supportive and virtuous woman at some point in their lives—whether a mother, sister, spouse, friend, or teacher. Muslim women represent and give expression to all that is beautiful in Islam, including the religion itself, its spiritual path, schools of philosophy, artistic forms, and even the generous nature of God. The lack of a significant role for Muslim women in some Muslim societies is highly indicative of a general imbalance, where the outward or masculine dimensions of Islam have almost entirely eclipsed the feminine. Be that as it may, traditional Muslims cherish the exalted status of mothers and women in general, who wield considerable power over men and society through the home and are fully capable of lending their wisdom and gifts to society at large when given the opportunity.

If we have focused on the imbalance between men and women in some Muslim societies, it does not imply that we see all western models of gender relations as ideal solutions. Women face as many problems in the West as they do in the East, even if their struggles sometimes take on different forms. It is the inclusion of the voices and presence of traditional Muslim women in their societies that will facilitate the harmony between men and women that we have in mind and not the intrusion of foreign solutions that often come in the form of violence, such as one of the ostensible and retrospective justifications for the U.S. war in Afghanistan that has led to the deaths of more women and children than real or apparent terrorists. We cannot succeed in bombing the burqas off of women without killing the women we are claiming to liberate. Neither will

21. Maria Massi Dakake, "'Walking upon the Path of God like Men'? Women and the Feminine in the Islamic Mystical Tradition," in *Sufism: Love & Wisdom*, pp. 131–151; Camille Adams Helminski, *Women of Sufism: A Hidden Treasure*; Annemarie Schimmel, *My Soul Is a Woman: The Feminine in Islam*; and Michelle R. Kimball and Barbara R. von Schlegell, *Muslim Women Throughout the World: A Bibliography* (Boulder, Colorado: Lynne Rienner Publishers, 1997).

Muslims accept the sexual objectification and exploitation of women so pervasive in western media and societies that many serious feminists in the West also strongly object to. There are various forms of traditional dress across the Muslim world, taking into account the different cultures and climates, that both men and women should not be forced nor denied the freedom to wear. Islam is a balanced and moderate religion that is opposed to the excesses of both secular modernists and religious fundamentalists. It requires the contributions and wisdom of both men and women for a society to thrive and beget new life. The One God is both Majesty (*Jalāl*) and Beauty (*Jamāl*)—Rigor and Mercy—and thus the Unity or Perfection (*Kamāl*) of all masculine and feminine qualities.[22] An awareness of one without the other leads to the many imbalances that we see in the world.

Due to the fact that Islam is such a diffuse phenomenon in the modern world, by which we mean not only geographically but primarily in terms of perspective, it is necessary to more clearly differentiate traditional Islam from both Islamic modernism and fundamentalism.[23] Traditional Muslims are characterized primarily by their fidelity to God, the Quran and *Sunnah*, the Sacred Law, spiritual path, traditional theological and philosophical perspectives, and the beauty of the religion expressed externally by sacred and traditional art and internally by the virtues. Modernists and fundamentalists in the Muslim world on the other hand justify their respective betrayals of the principles of Islam by attaching the adjective "Islamic" to their essentially secular ideologies, motives and actions. For modernists this may take the form of Islamic capitalism, socialism, rationalism, scientism, as well as the importing of western forms of technology, art and architecture. Nearly every theory, fad and gadget from the West is accepted without critically examining it based upon Islamic principles. Even where traditional Muslims would agree with the socialist critique of the excesses of

22. Sachiko Murata, *The Tao of Islam*; and Seyyed Hossein Nasr, *Islam in the Modern World*, pp. 62–72.

23. Ibid.; and Joseph E.B. Lumbard, ed., *Islam, Fundamentalism, and the Betrayal of Tradition*.

capitalism, the capitalist critique of socialism, the useful function of reason and logic, and the discoveries of modern science, they would not accept these worldviews in their totality, nor the secular programs they advance that are in opposition to traditional principles and civilizations. Because the Muslim world is politically and militarily weaker than the West, Islamic modernists often have an inferiority complex vis-à-vis the West and as a result accept its many ideologies and discoveries in the name of their own material progress. Islamic modernists, most of whom are among the western educated elites, fail to see the havoc modernism has wreaked in the West itself, including the loss of meaning and faith for many people, widespread crime and corruption, the diminished influence and reality of the family, the destruction of traditional cities and the natural world, and the development of new forms of military technology capable of destroying all life on the planet. Islamic fundamentalists on the other hand often reduce Islam to its most outward and political dimensions alone, while sometimes even betraying the *Sharīʿah* itself through acts of violence that take innocent life and are in reality modes of modern warfare and military tactics taken from the examples of western governments or revolutionary guerrilla movements as opposed to the *Sunnah* of the blessed Prophet. According to the Quran,

> O you who believe! Be steadfast for God, bearing witness to justice, and let not hatred for a people lead you to be unjust. Be just, that is nearer to reverence. And revere God. Surely God is Aware of whatsoever you do. (5:8)

> Whosoever slays a soul—unless it be for another soul or working corruption on the earth—it is as though he slew all mankind, and whosoever saves the life of one, it is as though he saved the life of all mankind. . . ." (5:32)

Only a heartless or ignorant person could be unmoved by the plight of the those Muslims who are attacked and oppressed throughout the world—including those in Palestine, Iraq, Afghanistan, Chechnya and parts of China, for example—but Muslims seeking to defend their lives and homelands have already lost the battle if, by taking innocent life, they for all intents and purposes mirror the identity of their enemies. Realizing that Muslims cannot successfully wage modern wars without betraying the principles of the Sacred Law and endangering their own communities, some prominent Muslim spiritual leaders have advocated and practiced non-violence when faced with colonial governments, foreign occupation or oppressive domestic governments, including Aḥmadū Bāmbā (d. 1927) in Senegal and 'Abd al-Ghaffār Khān (d. 1988) in India, as well as a number of leaders and movements in the Arab world in recent years.[24] Joseph Lumbard writes,

> Patience and non-violence are what is recommended for confronting such calamities [during the end times]. As the Prophet Muḥammad has said, "Who comes upon a man from my people in order to slay him, let him slay. For the slayer is in the fire and the slain is in paradise."
>
> In an account that sums up the nature of such times and the proper reaction to it, the Prophet Muḥammad says:
>
> "At the time when the Hour comes there are trials like the pitch dark of night. During such trials a man rises as a believer and retires as an unbeliever, and rises as an unbeliever and retires as a believer. The one sitting at such times is better than the one standing, and the one walking is better than the one running. So break your hardness, cut off your desires, and break your swords upon a rock. And if anyone enters upon you, then be like the better son of Adam."
>
> Thus, one should be like Abel, who said to his brother Cain,
>
> "Even if you extend your hand to kill me, I will not extend my hand to kill you. Truly I fear God the Lord of the worlds." (5:28)[25]

Islam and Muslims have a history of non-violence that dates back to the Meccan period during the Prophet Muḥammad's life and the general amnesty that he declared before his passing in Medina. It is

24. Michelle R. Kimball, "Shaykh Ahmadou Bamba's Nonviolent Jihad of the Pen," *Sophia* vol. 15 no. 1 (Summer 2009), pp. 122–141; and Eknath Easwaran, *Nonviolent Soldier of Islam: Badshah Khan, A Man to Match His Mountains* (Tomales, CA: Nilgiri Press, 1999).

25. *Submission, Faith, and Beauty*, pp. 77–78.

true that the Prophet, his family and companions were also warriors during certain circumstances where they were forced to choose between self-defense or the annihilation of the nascent religion and community, but so were Krishna, Arjuna, David and Solomon. No religion has a monopoly on peace or war. The fact that most people in the West know the names of Gandhi and the Dalai Lama, but not those of Bāmbā or Khān is indicative of the pervasive and successful anti-Islamic propaganda in the West that would prefer and insist we identify Islam with Osama bin Laden—an image that has provided considerable mileage to justify the West's own dubious wars in the Muslim world. It was in fact initial support from western governments that gave power and prominence to some of the most well-known manifestations of Islamic fundamentalism, including Bin Laden, the Taliban, and Wahhābism. Thus, Islamic fundamentalism is as much a product of the West as it is the Muslim world, which is true even where there is no political or military support from the West at the genesis of such a movement because they most often come into being as a reaction to western wars, colonization, occupation or influence, which have been commonplace in the Muslim world since Napoleon's occupation of Egypt beginning in 1798. By and large, the vast majority of Muslims have demonstrated incredible self-restraint, patience, and reliance upon God and the principles of their religion in the face of open hostility and aggression. Even most Muslim fundamentalists—who themselves make up less than 5% of the world's estimated 1.6 billion Muslims—cannot be considered militants, and among those that can far less can be labeled terrorists. A recent study in fact found that a significantly larger percentage of Americans compared to those in the Muslim countries surveyed think that attacks in which civilians are targeted are justified—which can also be discovered by counting the civilian deaths among Americans and Muslims through the acts of terrorism and war in recent years.[26] For some reason, however, peace-lov-

26. John L. Esposito and Dalia Mogahed write, "A recent study shows that only 46% of Americans think that 'bombing and other attacks intentionally aimed at civilians' are 'never justified,' while 24% believe attacks are 'often or sometimes justified.' Contrast this with data taken the same year from some of the largest majority Muslim nations, in which 74% of respondents in Indonesia agree that terrorist

ing Muslims are forced to apologize for the criminals in their societies, while both religious and secular people in the West rarely have to even question the violence that their elected leaders and governments commit in their name around the world. So while we are forced by circumstance to address modernism and fundamentalism among Muslims here, it is useful to recall that these aberrations are not confined to any one civilization or religion, and that they in fact began and persist in the West. In any case, Muslim modernists and fundamentalists usually have little interest in the intellectual and spiritual dimensions of Islam, the art of the religion or virtue—indeed also things beautiful and feminine—and fill this lacuna with secular paradigms and actions dressed in Islamic garb. Moreover, both groups invariably put ideology and activism in the place of religion and contemplation. One cannot act in the service of Truth and Justice unless one knows what these principles are. Acting without being oriented towards spiritual and ethical principles will inevitably lead to error and injustice. When faced with such a situation, we must cultivate a measure of discernment to see who has remained faithful to the principles of the tradition and not simply accept every theory or movement that attaches the sacred name of Islam to it—or Judaism, Christianity, Hinduism or Buddhism for that matter. Although the forms of traditional Islam vary

attacks are 'never justified'; in Pakistan, that figure is 86%, In Bangladesh, 81%; and in Iran, 80%. Similarly, 6% of the American public thinks that attacks in which civilians are targeted are 'completely justified.' As points of comparison, in both Lebanon and Iran, this figure is 2%, and in Saudi Arabia, it's 4%. In Europe, Muslims in Paris and London are no more likely than their counterparts in the general public to believe attacks on civilians are justified and are as likely to reject violence, even for a 'noble cause.' Many continue to ask: If Muslims truly reject terrorism, why does it continue to flourish in Muslim lands? What these results indicate is that terrorism is as much an 'out group' activity as any other violent crime. Just as the fact that violent crimes continue to occur throughout U.S. cities does not indicate Americans' silent acquiescence to them, the continued terrorist violence is not proof that Muslims tolerate it. An abundance of statistical evidence indicates the opposite." *Who Speaks for Islam?: What a Billion Muslims Really Think* (New York: Gallup Press, 2007), p. 95. See also, Naveed S. Sheikh, *Body Count: A Quantitative Review of Political Violence Across World Civilizations* (Amman: The Royal Aal al-Bayt Institute for Islamic Thought, 2009).

among the diverse Muslim peoples, the quality of serenity stands out among all traditional Muslims and its presence or absence is a good litmus test for who—regardless of what they claim—truly represents Islam in these uncertain times. Be that as it may, the vast majority of Muslims throughout history and in the contemporary period remain faithful to traditional Islam. It is only a small but vocal minority among the modernists and fundamentalists who have gained power and influence because of their indiscriminate acceptance or superficial rejection of all things western.

It is also necessary to state that traditional Muslims are opposed to sectarianism.[27] Not only does the Quran and the *Sunnah* of the Prophet inculcate an awareness of the essential unity of humanity in general, but also of the Muslim *ummah* or community. The two main branches of the Islamic tradition are Sunnism and Shīʿism, both of which are, despite their differences, completely orthodox manifestations of the religion.[28] Sunnis are referred to in Arabic as the *Ahl al-Sunnah wa'l-jamāʿah* or the People of the *Sunnah* and the majority. In addition to the foundational aspects of Islam men-

27. Among the most inclusive and conclusive assertions of Sunni and Shīʿite unity is *The Amman Message* that was signed by leading scholars and representatives of both branches of Islam from around the world. The signatories of *The Amman Message* agreed to the following: "Whosoever is an adherent to one of the four *Sunni* schools (*Madhāhib*) of Islamic jurisprudence (*Ḥanafī, Mālikī, Shāfiʿī* and *Ḥanbalī*), the two *Shīʿī* schools of Islamic jurisprudence (*Jaʿfarī* and *Zaydī*), the *ʿIbādī* school of Islamic jurisprudence and the *Ẓāhirī* school of Islamic jurisprudence, is a Muslim. Declaring that person an apostate is impossible and impermissible. Verily his (or her) blood, honour, and property are inviolable. Moreover, in accordance with the Shaykh Al-Azhar's *fatwā*, it is neither possible nor permissible to declare whosoever subscribes to the *Ashʿarī* creed or whoever practices real *taṣawwuf* (Sufism) an apostate. Likewise, it is neither possible nor permissible to declare whosoever subscribes to true *Salafī* thought an apostate. Equally, it is neither possible nor permissible to declare as apostates any group of Muslims who believes in God, Glorified and Exalted be He, and His Messenger (may peace and blessings be upon him) and the pillars of faith, and acknowledges the five pillars of Islam, and does not deny any necessarily self-evident tenet of religion." *The Amman Message* (Amman: The Royal Aal al-Bayt Institute for Islamic Thought, 2008), pp. 16–17.

28. "Sunnism and Shiʿism—Twelve-Imam Shiʿism and Ismāʿīlism," *Ideals and Realities of Islam*, pp. 141–174.

tioned above, which both Sunnis and Shī'ites adhere to in one form or another, Sunnis also accept the first Four Caliphs after the death of the Prophet Muḥammad as "rightly guided" (*rāshidūn*), including Abū Bakr, 'Umar, 'Uthmān, and 'Alī. Moreover, traditional Sunnis generally follow one of their four main schools of jurisprudence (*fiqh*), the Mālikī, Ḥanafī, Shāfi'ī, or Ḥanbalī; a particular orthodox school of theology (*kalām*), such as the Ash'arī or Māturīdī; and, for those who are called, one of the orders of Sufism (*taṣawwuf*), such as the Qādiriyyah, Shādhiliyyah, or Naqshbandiyyah, to name only a few of the most well-known. Shī'ites, on the other hand, are the minority branch of the religion who take their name from the Arabic term *Shī'at 'Alī* or the Partisans of 'Alī, the cousin and son-in-law of the Prophet. The major groups of Shī'ites are the Ithnā 'asharīs, Ismā'īlīs, and Zaydīs, who all believe that the Muslim community must be guided by a living Imam. The Ithnā 'asharīs or Twelvers constitute the main body of Shī'ites and believe that the guidance and light of the Prophet of Islam was transmitted to twelve successors, including 'Alī ibn Abī Ṭālib, Ḥasan ibn 'Alī, Ḥusayn ibn 'Alī, Zayn al-'Ābidīn, Muḥammad al-Bāqir, Ja'far al-Ṣādiq, Mūsā al-Kāẓim, 'Alī al-Riḍā, Muḥammad al-Taqī, 'Alī al-Naqī, Ḥasan al-'Askarī, and Muḥammad al-Mahdī. The Twelvers follow their own school of jurisprudence known as the Ja'farī school, which takes its name from the Sixth Imam. They also have their own theological perspective that became systematized through the works of Naṣīr al-Dīn Ṭūsī and other Shī'ite theologians. Moreover, there are a number of manifestations of Islamic spirituality in Shī'ism, including the devotional structure of the religion itself, teachers and circles of *ḥikmah* and *'irfān*, as well as Sufi orders, such as the Ni'matullāhiyyah and Dhahabiyyah. The primary sources of jurisprudence, theology, philosophy and spirituality for Shī'ites remain the Quran and *Sunnah*, but they add to these the sayings and actions of the Imams.

There are certain differences between Sunnis and Shī'ites that need not be ignored for both groups of Muslims to live together in peace and harmony. Although Sunnis and Shī'ites have preserved many of the same *aḥādīth* or sayings of the Prophet, their canonical collections are not identical. The major Sunni books of *Ḥadīth* include the *Jāmiʿ al-ṣaḥīḥ* of Bukhārī, the *Ṣaḥīḥ* of Muslim, the *Sunan* of Abū Dāʾūd, the *Jāmiʿ* of Tirmidhī, the *Sunan* of Dārimī, and the *Sunan* of Ibn Mājah, while the most authoritative Shīʿite books of *Ḥadīth* are the *Uṣūl al-kāfī* of Kulaynī, the *Man lā yaḥḍuruhuʾl-faqīh* of Ibn Bābūyah, and the *Kitāb al-istibṣār* and *Kitāb al-tahdhīb* of Muḥammad Ṭūsī. Sunnis also believe that all four of the first Caliphs were rightly guided, while Shīʿites maintain that ʿAlī and his descendents are the legitimate political and spiritual heirs of the Prophet. Sunnis also make certain allowances for those companions of the Prophet who fought ʿAlī in battle after the Prophet's death, while Shīʿites consider this to have been a transgression. Moreover, while both Shīʿites and Sunnis remember the martyrdom of Ḥusayn at Karbalāʾ, this event is undoubtedly more central in Shīʿism and may even be regarded as among its most defining characteristics.

Despite these differences and others, both Sunnis and Shīʿites read the same Quran, venerate and follow the same Prophet, prostrate in same direction five times a day, and ultimately worship and seek to know the same God. The differences that separate the Shīʿite and Sunni schools of jurisprudence are not much greater than those that separate the four main Sunni schools. Even the spirituality of both branches is largely based on what the Prophet Muḥammad transmitted to ʿAlī, even though Sunnis also regard other companions, such as Abū Bakr, as among the early representatives of Islamic spirituality.[29] The names of the first eight Imams are in fact on the chains of transmission of several Sunni Sufi orders. Here they are not regarded as *Shīʿite* Imams, but as poles of proto-Sufism. Moreover, the works of some of the greatest Sunni Sufis in history, such as Ghazzālī, Rūmī and Ibn ʿArabī, are central among masters and students of *ʿirfān* or Sufism in the Shīʿite world. There is thus a greater degree of unanimity and cross-fertilization among Sunnis and Shīʿites concerning their inner doctrine and rites as opposed to their perspectives on early Islamic history or political succession. In any case, a Sunni has the right to remain a Sunni and a Shīʿite a

29. "Shiʿism and Sufism: their Relationship in Essence and in History," *Sufi Essays*, pp. 104–120.

Shīʿite. Their different perspectives and interpretations of Islam are both legitimate archetypes and possibilities that God willed to manifest to allow a greater number of souls to integrate their lives into the religion. As we read in a *ḥadīth*, "Differences between the scholars of my community are a mercy from God." The diversity of Muslims does not detract from the essential unity of the *ummah*. Islam is based on the realization of the doctrine of *tawḥīd* through following the Quran and *Sunnah* of the Prophet. The fact that Ibn ʿArabī realized the heights of Divine Unity as a Sunni and Mullā Ṣadrā as a Shīʿite, for example, proves that both branches of Islam are orthodox and can lead to the highest stations of wisdom and sanctity. In addition to the presence of countless sages and saints in both branches of Islam, one can also point to the manifestations of Ottoman and Safavid art and architecture and many other peaks of Islamic art in both the Sunni and Shīʿite worlds. A heterodox sect devoid of Truth and Beauty cannot reflect Heaven on earth in the way that both communities have been able to do so through men and women of sanctity and sacred and traditional art. Ultimately, both groups of Muslims accept the *shahādah* and essentially differ regarding who they think best represents the Prophet after his passing. Given the centrifugal forces in the world, only during the lifetime of the Prophet were all Muslims truly united, but we can at least aspire towards greater unity and understanding through remaining faithful to our own understanding of Islam—be it Sunni or Shīʿite—and respecting the other branch of the tradition and our Muslim brothers and sisters who practice it. For both branches represent a veritable manifestation of Islam, a possible and an orthodox interpretation of the Quran, and even accentuate an aspect of the Prophet's own soul.[30] While the One can be realized through either Sunni or Shīʿite Islam, we can expand our understanding of God, His Revelation and Prophet, and the Islamic tradition as a whole by including the so-called other into our understanding of the Prophet's *ummah*. Ultimately, there is no simple answer to this dilemma that does not involve the anathema of one group by the

30. Frithjof Schuon, "Seeds of a Divergence," *Islam and the Perennial Philosophy*, pp. 91–110.

other.[31] Therefore, the Quranic decrees concerning interfaith relations and questions also hold true for intrafaith matters, despite the fact that Sunnis and Shīʿites constitute one community:

> For each among you We have appointed a law and a way. And had God willed, He would have made you a single community, but [He willed otherwise], that He might try you in that which He has given you. So vie with one another in good deeds. Unto God shall be your return, all together, and He will inform you of that wherein you differed. (5:48)

It has not been possible in this brief survey of the particular wisdom and forms of Islam to be exhaustive. Instead of writing an academic survey of the religion in this chapter we have simply tried to convey a few reasons why Islam is meaningful to Muslims. We have been forced to leave much out, including the role of the Muslim community and its various geographic, cultural and ethnic expressions from Senegal to Indonesia, as well as the various theological and philosophical schools and perspectives and many other principles and historical realities of the religion. However, we hope the reader will have gained some awareness of the particular fragrance of Islam which, while synthesizing the wisdom that has flourished on earth throughout the ages, also possesses its own subtle power and beauty to inculcate the nostalgia for Paradise and the Beloved. Islam is based on the Unity of the Supreme Principle, which embraces God, the angels, the revealed books, the prophets, and the origin, history, present and posthumous destiny of humanity and all of creation. We can gain a measure of awareness of Divine Unity through actively following a revealed and prophetic path. Islam descended from Heaven as the final Divine message to confirm what came before it and to provide those souls who are destined to receive it a particular path that opens onto the Universal.

Innā li'Llāhi wa-innā ilayhi rājiʿūn
"Truly we are God's, and unto Him we return." (2:156)

31. The most important statement we have read that articulates the need for both unity and distictness among Sunnis and Shīʿites is Seyyed Hossein Nasr's preface to ʿAllāmah Ṭabāṭabāʾī's *Shīʿite Islam*, pp. 3–26.

Sources*

1. "Muslim Intellectuals and the Perennial Philosophy," *Sophia* 13, no. 2 (Winter 2007–8), pp. 87–140.

2. "Lovers of Sophia: Srī Ramakrishna and Muḥyī al-Dīn ibn 'Arabī" *Luvah* vol. 1, no. 2 (August 2012), pp. 20–42.

3. "Thou art *Dhāt*: Metaphysical Expressions of Non-Duality in Islam," *Sacred Web* 22 (January 2009), pp. 91–117.

4. "Jesus and Christic Sanctity in Islam," *Sophia* (forthcoming).

5. "The Eliatic Function in the Islamic Tradition: Khiḍr and the Mahdī," *Sacred Web* 25 (June 2010), pp. 47–74.

6. "Hermetic Wisdom in Islam," *Sacred Web* 29 (July 2012), pp. 87–107.

*All selections have been revised and expanded for this volume.

INDEX

A Common Word 9–10
Aaron (Hārūn) 30, 147, 200, 272
'Abd al-Raḥmān ibn 'Awf 241
Abdul Rauf, Feisal 113
Abel (Hābīl) 327
Abraham (Ibrāhīm) 3, 6, 21, 30, 35, 37, 40, 77, 139, 187, 197–198, 257, 272, 307, 317
Abu Bakr al-Ṣiddīq 138, 170, 233, 331–332
Abū Dā'ūd al-Sijistānī 241, 332
Abū Dharr al-Ghifārī 36, 200, 216–217
Abū Dujāna al-Anṣarī 252
Abū Ḥanīfah al-Nu'mān 242, 331
Abū Hurayrah 'Abd al-Raḥmān 216, 241
Abū Sufyān ibn Ḥarb 205
adab 232, 320
Adam 3, 21, 30–35, 41, 52, 56, 194, 195, 197, 257, 267, 272, 295, 307, 327
Addas, Claude 127, 131, 181, 197, 235, 312
Advaita Vedānta 14–16, 83, 87, 122–123, 144–192
afrād 199, 229, 235
Afsaruddin, Asma 11
Aguéli, Ivan Gustaf 77, 114, 228
Aḥrār, 'Ubayd Allāh 200
'Ā'ishah bint Abī Bakr 202–203
Akbarī school 21, 51, 55, 69, 77, 127, 180, 185, 188
akhlāq 315, 319–320
Akkach, Samer 113, 264, 322
'ālam al-khayāl 199, 183–184, 290, 310
'ālam al-mithāl 243
'Alawī, Aḥmad 31, 83–87, 90, 100, 111, 200
'Alawiyyah 87–88
alchemy 15, 55, 91, 92, 94, 257, 260–263, 268, 269, 274–280
'Alī ibn Abī Ṭālib 22, 67–69, 138, 170–172, 174, 200–201, 203–205, 216–217, 229, 233, 241–243, 246, 250, 253, 255, 331–332
'Alī al-Naqī 331
'Alī al-Riḍā 170, 243, 331
Allah 3, 53, 85, 121, 124–125, 128–129, 131, 146, 159–160, 162, 164, 167, 236–237, 208–309, 318–319
Allawi, Ali 113
'Āmilī, Bahā' al-Dīn 55
Amīnrazavī, Mehdī 103
Amir-Moezzi, M.A. 202, 209–210, 249–250, 253
The Amman Message 330
Āmulī, Ḥaydar 55
ānanda 136, 147, 159
Anas ibn Mālik 241
Anti-Christ (al-Dajjāl) 249, 252
'aql 5, 41, 138, 169, 209–210, 251, 267
Aristotle 42, 46–47, 56, 268
Arjuna 148–149, 151, 170, 328
arkān 311–312, 315–318
Ash'arism 46, 330–331

Āshtiyānī, Jalāl al-Dīn 103
'Āshūrā' 205–211, 221
Āsiyah bint Muzāḥim 139, 203
'Askarī, Muḥammad Ḥasan 242, 331
asmā' al-ḥusnā 50–55, 69–70, 81, 121, 124, 127–136, 142, 144, 159–167, 172–173, 181–186, 191, 236, 251, 265, 295, 300, 307–309
'Aṣṣār, Muḥammad Kāẓim 103
astrology 15, 91, 94, 260–262, 268–274
Ātman 121, 123, 144–156, 159–160, 167, 189
'Aṭṭār, Farīd al-Dīn 21, 57–60, 109, 139, 146, 177–178, 202, 215, 217, 231, 234, 255
Augustine 296
A'vānī, Gholām Rezā 103, 113
awtād 235
āyat Allāh 4, 33–35, 158, 251, 264–265, 268, 270, 274, 298, 300–301, 313
'ayn al-qalb 5, 41, 92, 100, 148, 166, 172–176, 209–210, 238, 251, 263, 304
Azhar 78, 103, 213, 330

Bacon, Francis 291–292
Bacon, Roger 296
Badawī, 'Abd al-Raḥmān 213
Badr 166
Bakar, Osman 103, 113
Bakhtiar, Laleh 114
Bālīnūs 261
Balkhī, Abū Ma'shar 261–262
Balyānī, Awḥad al-Dīn 182, 184–185
Bāmbā, Aḥmadū 86, 327–328
baqā' 57, 150, 182, 216, 218, 320
Baqlī, Rūzbihan 233
barakah 87, 98, 112, 141, 162, 177, 219, 232, 317
barzakh 183, 230, 258
Baṣrī, Ḥasan 170, 216, 242
Basṭāmī, Bāyazīd 47, 146, 173–174, 183
Bayman, Henry 114
Benedict XVI, Pope 9–10
Bhagavad Gita 4, 7, 86, 89, 144–146, 148–149, 151, 170, 305
Bible 4, 7, 30–32, 44, 79, 86, 103, 139–141, 151, 172, 190, 198, 205, 209, 214, 216, 224–225, 238, 241, 249, 255, 257–258, 300, 305, 307, 309
Bill, James 203–204, 213, 221
Bin Muhammad, H.R.H. Prince Ghazi 9
Bint al-Muthannā, Fāṭimah 131
Bīrūnī, Abū Rayḥān 150, 262, 284
Blackhirst, Rodney 113
Bladel, Kevin Van 258
Böhme, Jacob 296, 299
Bonaparte, Louis Napoleon 72
Brahman 3, 119–121, 123–124, 144–156, 159, 171
Brahmasūtras 146
Brown, Joseph Epes 82, 112–133
Buddha 3, 31, 33, 234, 302, 308
Buddhism 11, 21, 53, 66, 83, 91–92, 97, 255, 285
Bukhārī, Muḥammad 216, 230, 332
burāq 39
Burckhardt, Titus 8, 20–22, 53, 82, 88, 91–96, 109, 116, 245, 255, 261, 269, 271–272, 275–276, 278, 286, 305
burhān 46, 57
Būzarjumihr 45, 48

Cain (Qābīl) 327
Cairo 75, 78, 201
Caldecott, Stratford 220
Çelebī, Ḥusām al-Dīn 61, 237
Charles, H.R.H. the Prince of Wales 101
Chittick, William 8, 10, 103, 197, 252, 268
Chodkiewicz, Michel 114, 182–183, 199, 219–220, 235, 246,
Christianity 5, 9, 11–12, 15–16, 21, 23, 25, 34, 36, 59–60, 63–65, 75, 81, 83, 86–87, 91–92, 96–97, 104, 123–124, 134, 140–141, 193–223, 227, 229, 250, 254, 259, 283, 285, 287–293, 295–297, 299–300, 329
cit 136, 147, 159
Coomaraswamy, Ananda K. 26–27, 78, 91–92, 102, 104, 111, 115, 124, 142, 155, 287
Coomaraswamy, Rama 115
Confucianism 66
Confucius 3
Constitution of Medina 38
Corbin, Henry 103, 114, 138, 235–236, 243, 248, 250–251
Cornell, Vincent 55, 114
cosmology 15, 33–35, 48, 110, 128–133, 145, 189–190, 257–304
Critchlow, Keith 93, 103
Cutsinger, James 9, 82, 115

Dagli, Caner 103, 113
Dakake, David 103, 113
Dakake, Maria Massi 129, 324
Danner, Victor 88, 112
Dante Alighieri 49, 133, 296
Dārimī al-Samarqandī 332
Darqāwī, Mūlay al-ʿArabī 94, 165
David (Dā'ūd) 3, 30, 139, 197, 245, 307, 328
Dawānī, Jalāl al-Dīn 267
Decalogue 311–312
Descartes, René 289, 291
Deutsch, Eliot 149
Dhahabiyyah 331
Dhāt 130, 141–192, 244–245, 309
dhikr 35, 50, 62, 85, 100, 161–162, 236, 256, 308, 318–319, 322
Dhu'l-Kifl 31
Dieye, Abdoulaye 85, 114
al-dīn al-ḥanīf 21, 35, 251, 257
al-dīn al-ḥaqq 41

Eaton, Charles Le Gai 74, 82, 90, 96, 107, 112
Eckhart, Meister 193, 220–221, 305
El-Ansary, Waleed 103
Eliade, Mircea 78, 115
Elias/Elijah ('Ilyās) 172, 224–256, 258, 320
Elisha (Alyasaʿ) 224–225
Elliot, T. S. 82
Emre, Yūnus 217
environmental crisis 13, 110, 251, 282–304
epistemology 5–6, 25, 41, 43, 46, 56–57, 209–210, 238, 283, 310–311
Erigena, Johannes Scotus 296
Erndl, Kathleen 120
eschatology 31, 48, 56–57, 104, 215, 224–256, 267, 274, 311, 313, 316
esoteric ecumenism 60, 64, 222, 250–251, 321
esoterism 29, 40, 50–52, 56, 59–60, 76, 87, 89, 94, 108, 114, 126, 128, 130, 148, 153–154, 158, 162, 164, 170, 177, 222, 226, 231–232, 238–239, 255, 284, 304

Faghfoory, Mohammad 17
fanā' 57, 100, 125, 150, 182, 216, 218, 320
faqr 182–183, 190, 194, 222, 234, 302, 315, 320
al-Fārābī, Abū Naṣr 42–43, 46
Faruqi, I. H. Azad 122–123, 125–126
Fāṭimah bint Muḥammad 50, 138, 201–204, 210, 242
fikr 318
fiqh 311–312, 331
Flamel, Nicolas 299
Foltz, Richard 286
Foucault, Charles de 53
Francis of Assisi 221, 296
Friedlander, Shems 96
Fulgentius 258
futuwwah/javānmardī 22, 67–74, 205–211, 245–249, 252, 326–328

Gabriel (Jibra'īl) 39, 48, 137, 194–195, 239, 266
Galileo Galilei 289–291, 297
Gauḍapāda 149
Geoffroy, Éric 114, 229
Ghazzālī, Abū Ḥāmid 46, 48, 56, 79, 127, 164–165, 195–196, 217, 268, 275, 332
Godlas, Alan 114
Gospel 4, 9, 31, 32, 44, 79, 103, 155, 190, 205, 209, 214, 216, 224–225, 249, 255, 307, 309
Govinda 149
Govinda Rai 123, 125
Greek philosophy 5, 7, 15–16, 21, 25, 40–49, 55–58, 66, 115, 142–143, 257–281, 287, 290, 311
Gregory of Nysaa 296
Guénon, René 8, 10–11, 20–22, 26–27, 75–80, 83, 86, 88, 91, 94, 96–97, 103–104, 110–111, 114–116, 144, 146, 152–156, 169, 191, 220, 238–239, 255, 286–287
Gupta, Mahendranath 119

Ḥadīth 5–9, 11, 32, 37–39, 42, 68, 127–128, 135, 137–138, 144, 148, 154, 158, 164, 167–169, 172, 178, 183, 185, 193 195, 198, 200, 204, 208, 215–216, 230, 241–242, 252, 265, 273–274, 281, 309, 312–317, 319, 322–323, 327, 331–333
Ḥadīth qudsī 128, 144, 148, 164, 167–169, 185, 216, 315
Haeri, Fadhlalla 114
Ḥāfiẓ Shīrāzī 22, 58, 64–65, 102
Hagar (Hājar) 139
ḥajj 317–318
Halakhah 36, 193
Halevy, Yehudah 227
Ḥallāj, Manṣūr 19, 47, 66–67, 154, 160–161, 174–175, 183, 190, 199, 202, 210–222, 276
Hamadānī, 'Alī 139
Hamadānī, 'Ayn al-Quḍāt 200, 219
Ḥamūyah, Sa'd al-Dīn 244
ḥaqīqah 28, 34, 94, 130, 209, 277
Haqqani, Nazim 114
Ḥasan al-'Askarī 242, 331
Ḥasan ibn 'Alī 174, 203–206, 217, 242, 331
Hasany, Aasim 224
Helminski, Camille 114, 203
Helminski, Kabir 114
Henry-Blakemore, Virginia Gray 96
Hermes/Enoch (Idrīs) 3, 15, 41–42, 47–48, 56, 197, 228, 235, 238, 243, 257–281, 320

Hermeticism 15, 48, 257–264, 281, 289
Hesychasm 65, 87
ḥijāb 165
ḥikmah 6–7, 25–26, 40–41, 45, 47, 55–58, 141, 196, 204, 229–230, 244, 257, 259–261, 267–268, 331
al-ḥikmat al-ʿatīqah 47
al-ḥikmat al-khālidah/jāvīdān khirad 20, 25–26, 45
al-ḥikmat al-ladunīyah 47, 229–230
al-ḥikmat al-mutaʿāliyah 55–58, 267
Hildegard of Bingen 296
Hiltebeitel, Alf 120
Hinduism 5, 21, 29, 33–35, 49, 53, 55, 66, 75, 83, 87, 91–92, 97, 118–126, 136, 142, 144–156, 158–162, 165, 169–171, 174, 187–188, 191, 250, 255, 276, 285, 295, 329
Hixon, Lex 114,
Ḥudaybiyyah 166, 246
Hujwīrī, ʿAlī 234–235
Ḥusayn ibn ʿAlī 174, 201–211, 217, 219, 221–222, 242–243, 331–332
Hyde, Bilal 114

Iamblichus 258
Ibn Abī Jumhūr Aḥsāʾī 55, 218
Ibn Adham, Ibrāhīm 233–235
Ibn ʿArabī, Muḥyī al-Dīn 6–8, 10, 21, 30, 32, 40, 49–57, 60, 67, 69, 71–72, 77, 79, 93–94, 108, 117–119, 122, 125–137, 139–140, 142–143, 146, 149, 180–186, 189, 196–203, 219–222, 232–233, 235–236, 243, 246–248, 250–251, 255, 263, 272–273, 275, 277, 279–280, 301, 312, 319, 332–333
Ibn ʿAṭāʾ Allāh Iskandarī 6, 141, 229
Ibn Bābūyah al-Qummī 332
Ibn Ḥasan Raḍī, Salāmah 77
Ibn Ḥayyān, Jābir 43, 262, 277, 279
Ibn Isḥāq, Muḥammad 38
Ibn Kathīr, Ismāʿīl 230
Ibn Khaldūn, ʿAbd al-Raḥmān 229
Ibn Mājah al-Qazwīnī 332
Ibn Miskawayh, ʿAlī Aḥmad 45
Ibn Muthlih, Ḥasan 233
Ibn al-Nadīm, Muḥammad 261
Ibn Sīnā, Ḥusayn (Avicenna) 21, 40, 46–47, 55–56, 108, 180, 266, 284, 301
Ibn Ṭāhir Azdī, ʿAbd Allāh 66–67
Ibn Taymiyyah, Aḥmad 218
Ibn Turkah Iṣfahānī 55
Ibn Umayl, Muḥammad 262
Ibn Waḥshiyyah, Abū Bakr 261
Ibn Yazīd, Khālid 262
iḥsān 7, 49, 193, 257, 317, 320
Ikhwān al-Ṣafāʾ 7, 43–44, 46, 180, 263, 269–270, 284, 301
ʿIlaysh al-Kabīr, ʿAbd al-Raḥmān 76–77, 97
ilhām 210
ʿilm al-ḥurūf 160, 269
Imāmī, Sayyid Ḥasan 87
īmān 171, 209, 257, 320
Inayat Khan, Hazrat 114
Inayat-Khan, Zia 114, 321
al-insān al-kāmil 23, 51, 77, 128, 140, 164, 185–188, 202, 209, 220, 244–245, 248, 263, 294
Iqbal, Muzaffar 293
Irenaeus 24, 296
ʿirfān-i naẓarī 146, 180
Isaac (Isḥāq) 30, 40, 67
ʿĪsawī Sufis 139, 193–223
Iṣfahānī, Hatīf 65

Isherwood, Christopher 123
Ishmael (Ismā'īl) 30, 40
Ishrāqī school 21, 47–49, 55, 188, 266–267
Islamic art 53, 91–95, 101, 109, 322–323
Islamic philosophy 6–7, 40–49, 55–58, 102–112, 136–143, 188–190, 257–281, 300, 310–311
Ismā'īl ibn Ja'far 242
Ismā'īlī Shī'ism 44, 169, 242, 331
Ithnā 'asharī Shī'ism 138–139, 169, 201–211, 241–244, 253–254, 330–334
Izutsu, Toshihiko 103, 114

Jacob (Ya'qūb) 30, 40, 67,
Ja'far al-Ṣādiq 172–173, 242, 245–247, 251–252, 262, 279, 331
Jafri, S.H.M. 207
Jameelah, Maryam 113
Jāmī, 'Abd al-Raḥmān 61, 217
Jazā'irī, 'Abd al-Qādir 22, 54, 69–74, 218, 255
Jenar, Siti 200, 219
Jerusalem 39, 141, 233, 252
Jesus ('Īsā) 3, 9, 15–16, 24, 30, 33–34, 37–38, 40, 52–53, 62–65, 72, 82, 85, 124, 139, 164, 183, 193–223, 225–228, 232, 235, 241, 249–250, 252, 254–255, 257–258, 272, 281, 295–296, 307–309, 313–314, 320
Jifri, Habib Ali 9
al-jihād al-akbar 67–69, 205–206, 245–246
Jīlī, 'Abd al-Karīm 51, 54–55, 94, 128–129, 146, 150–151, 180, 185–189, 244–245, 252, 263, 301
Joan of Arc 207, 221
Job (Ayyūb) 30
John (St.) 103, 205, 209, 216, 225, 238
John the Baptist (Yaḥyā) 225–226, 228, 241
Jonah (Yūnus) 30, 38
Joseph (Yūsuf) 67, 272
Joshua (Yūsha') 252
Judaism 15, 21, 25, 34, 66, 75, 83, 91, 97, 104, 113, 134, 193, 198, 212, 224–229, 231, 246, 266, 285, 290, 329
Julian 258
Juma'a, 'Alī 96–97, 113
Junayd, Abu'l-Qāsim 211, 276

Ka'bah 34, 37, 50, 58, 118, 128, 134, 140, 169, 183, 277, 317–318
Kabbalah 113, 227, 231, 289, 300
Kabīr 150
kalām 4–5, 11, 15, 33–35, 53, 130, 163–164, 257, 308–309, 331
Kali 5, 118–126, 142
Kalin, Ibrahim 103, 113
Karbalā' 201–203, 206–208, 332
Karkhī, Ma'rūf 170, 216, 243
Kāshānī, Afḍal al-Dīn 261, 267–268
Kāshifī, Wā'iẓ 67
Kashmir Shaivism 145
Keeble, Brian 93
Keller, Nuh Ha Mim 10–11, 113–114
Kepler, Johannes 291
Khadījah bint Khuwaylid 38, 137–138, 203–204, 323
Khalidi, Tarif 196
khalīfah 187, 245, 282, 293–295, 299
Khalil, Mohammad Hassan 9, 11, 54
khalwah 56, 236, 318
Khān, 'Abd al-Ghaffār 327–328

Khiḍr/al-Khaḍir 56, 218, 224, 226, 228–240, 253–254, 258, 320
Kimball, Farah Michelle 16, 61, 305, 324, 327
Kindī, Ya'qūb 41–42, 261
Kingsley, Peter 43, 96, 115, 142
Kirmānī, Muḥammad Karīm-Khān 248
Krishna 3, 144, 148–149, 151, 170, 328
Kulaynī, Muḥammad 332

Lakhani, M. Ali 17, 112, 304
Lao Tzu 3
Laude, Patrick 8–9, 85–86, 90, 114, 138
laylat al-qadr 24, 162
le point vierge 221
Legenhausen, Muhammad 10
Leibnitz, Gottfried von 20, 24, 45
Lewis, C.S. 96
Lewisohn, Leonard 17, 64, 114
Lincoln, Abraham 73
Lindbom, Tage 112
Lings, Martin 8, 20–22, 37, 82, 88, 95–103, 113–114, 116, 132–133, 137, 153, 160, 174, 213, 215, 255
Logos 23, 27, 39, 62, 81–82, 106, 138, 162–164, 194, 208–209, 265, 278, 295–296, 300
Lumbard, Joseph 7, 49, 103, 113, 304, 327

maḥabbah 126–127, 148, 319
Mahābhārata 148
Maharshi, Ramana 123
mahāvākyas 147, 191
Mahdī/Twelfth Imam 194, 215, 224, 226–228, 239–256, 331
Maḥmūd, 'Abd al-Ḥalīm 78–79, 92, 213
Mahmutcehajic, Rusmir 78, 113
Maimonides, Moses 227
Majlisī, Muḥammad Bāqir 261
makhāfah 148, 320
Mālik al-Ashtar 252
Mālik ibn Anas 242
maqām 182, 320
ma'rifah/*'irfān* 6, 41, 100, 126, 148, 210, 228, 232, 244, 319
Māriyah al-Qibṭiyyah 137
Mary (Maryam) 34, 37, 50, 53, 87–88, 138–140, 194–195, 202–204, 210, 226, 228, 314
Maryamī 139–140, 203–204
Maryamiyyah 87–88, 139
Mason, Herbert 211
Massignon, Louis 138, 174, 211–214, 216, 219, 221
Maximus the Confessor 296
māyā 139, 150, 165, 189, 251
maẓhar 165, 186
Mecca 33–34, 39, 58, 116, 132, 141, 205, 219, 246, 302, 317, 323
Medina 5, 38–39, 141, 243, 314, 323, 327
Melchizedech 238
Merton, Thomas 82, 115, 213, 221
metaphysics 20, 24, 39, 41, 45, 48, 51–53, 57, 59, 65, 67, 69–71, 76, 80–84, 86, 89, 91, 95, 100, 104, 106, 109–110, 123–125, 136, 141, 143–192, 215–218, 228, 244–245, 278, 299–300, 306–309
Metatron 238, 258, 266
Michon, Jean-Louis 96, 112
Minnaar, Clinton 98
Miqdād ibn al-Aswad 252
Mīr Dāmād 55

Mīr Findiriskī 55, 151, 262
mi'rāj 24, 39–40, 57, 162, 273, 317
Miṣrī, Dhu'l-Nūn 47, 262, 276
Moris, Zailan 103, 113
Morris, James 103, 114
Moses (Mūsā) 3, 30–31, 33–34, 37–38, 40, 52, 62, 137, 193, 197–198, 200, 225–226, 230–233, 257, 272, 307, 310, 312–313
Mu'āwiyah ibn Abī Sufyān 205
Muhaiyaddeen, M.R. Bawa 114
Muḥammad 4–7, 15–16, 19, 21–22, 24, 30, 32–40, 42, 48, 50–53, 57, 60–63, 68, 70, 76–77, 88, 98–99, 106, 109, 112, 116, 125, 127, 129, 131, 134–135, 137–140, 148, 154, 156–158, 162, 164, 166–170, 172–173, 175, 177, 178, 182–185, 191, 193–195, 197–206, 208–209, 211, 213, 215–216, 219–222, 228–233, 235, 238–239, 241–248, 252–253, 255, 257–258, 260, 265–266, 273–274, 277, 279, 281, 295, 302, 306–307, 309–323, 326–328, 330–333
Muḥammad al-Bāqir 210, 249, 331
Muḥammad al-Taqī 331
Muḥāsibī, Ḥārith 216
Muḥsin ibn 'Alī 203
Murata, Sachiko 8, 103, 114, 129, 143, 259, 273
Mūsā al-Kāẓim 242, 331
Muslim ibn Ḥajjāj 332
Muṭahharī, Murtaḍa 103

nafs 103, 159, 194, 204–205, 252, 265, 267
Nahj al-balāghah 170–171
Naqshbandiyyah 69, 170, 331
Narjis Khātūn 138–139, 242
Nasr, Seyyed Hossein 4, 6–9, 16, 20–22, 24, 27, 28, 30–31, 41–42, 46–47, 49, 51, 57–60, 67–68, 78, 82, 87–88, 90, 93, 96, 102–114, 116, 129, 133, 142–143, 153, 161, 163, 169–170, 173–174, 178, 180, 187, 196, 204, 211–214, 218, 226, 239–240, 249–250, 253, 255, 261–262, 270–271, 276–277, 279, 282–304
Nawawī, Yaḥyā 10
Needleman, Jacob 82, 103, 116
Newton, Isaac 289, 291
Nicholas of Cusa 24–25
Nicomachus 43
Niffarī, Muḥammad 175–176
Ni'matullāhiyyah 331
Niẓām 49–50, 118–119, 126, 130, 132–136, 142, 199–200
Noah (Nūḥ) 3, 30, 56, 197, 267, 307
Northbourne, Lord 112
nubuwwah 15, 67
Nurbakhsh, Javad 114

O'Brien, Katherine 17, 105
Oldmeadow, Harry 116
Om 162
Origen Adamantius 296
orthodoxy 4–5, 10, 23, 26, 58, 78, 83, 108, 117, 130, 213, 232–233, 238
Ozak, Muzaffer 114

Pallavicini, 'Abd al-Wahid 78, 113
Pallis, Marco 78, 115, 156
Parmenides 142–143
Paul 155
People of the Book (*ahl al-kitāb*) 3–4, 25, 31, 36–37, 53, 187, 261
perennial philosophy 8, 19–117, 119, 143–144, 146–156, 260, 282, 285

Perry, Whitall 112
Peyre, Henri 264
Pharaoh 139, 190, 310
Pio of Pietrelcina 221
Plato 41–44, 47–48, 56, 79, 86, 149, 305
Platonism 46, 48, 258
Plotinus 42
Pontius Pilate 205
Poshtmashhadī, Moḥammad Taqī 102
Pourjavādī, Naṣrollāh 103
Primordial Tradition 28, 35, 251, 257, 297–298
Psalms 4, 30–31, 307
Pythagoras 3, 41–43, 47

Qāḍī, Mīrzā 'Alī 280
Qādiriyyah 69, 170, 201, 331
qalb 5, 41, 50, 100, 110, 118, 125, 134–136, 140–141, 144–145, 167, 169, 171, 173–175, 196, 209–210, 230, 235–238, 249, 251, 263, 274, 278, 304, 309, 318, 320
Qayṣarī, Dā'ūd 250
Qazwīnī, Abu'l-Ḥasan 103
Qūnawī, Ṣadr al-Dīn 54, 263
Quran 3–4, 6, 16, 19–24, 29–37, 40, 48, 50, 52–63, 67, 69–70, 74, 84, 91–92, 99, 109, 113, 116, 118, 125, 127–129, 134, 139, 141–142, 146, 148, 151–152, 159–169, 172–174, 183, 191, 193–197, 203, 206–208, 213–215, 219, 221–222, 224, 226, 229–232, 239, 246–249, 251, 257–260, 265, 268–269, 274, 278, 282, 295, 299–301, 305, 307–322, 326, 322, 334
quṭb 201, 230, 235, 243, 246, 253, 258, 272, 279–280

Raine, Kathleen 82
Rama 3, 124
Ramaḍān 208, 233, 313, 317
Ramakrishna 5, 13, 61, 74, 118–126, 135–137, 142–143, 150
Rāzī, Abū Ḥātim 44
Rāzī, Fakhr al-Dīn 46
Rāzī, Muḥammad 262
religio cordis 50, 134
Revelation 6, 12, 28, 30–31, 33–35, 42–44, 46, 69–70, 80–82, 89, 141–142, 148, 157, 194, 213, 251, 260, 263, 265–266, 288, 298, 300, 307–309, 312, 321–322
rijāl al-ghayb 226, 229, 240, 253–254
Roszak, Theodore 286
rūḥ 34, 48, 159, 194, 239, 252, 258, 273
Rūmī, Jalāl al-Dīn 13, 60–63, 68, 102, 109, 126, 178–179, 190, 196, 201, 206–207, 217–218, 236–237, 243, 305, 321–322

Saadya Gaon 227
Sabians 15, 31, 84, 261
Ṣafiyyah bint Huyayy 137
Sāī Bābā 150
sakīnah 141
ṣalāh 39–40, 97, 100, 182, 273, 315–318
Ṣāliḥ 34
Salmān al-Fārsī 138, 252
samā' 318
sanatāna dharma 25–26, 28, 119
Sarada Devi 122
Sarah 139
Sarasvatī 122
sat 136, 147, 159
Satan 157, 195

Ṣāwī, Ṣalāh 105
ṣawm 317
Schaya, Leo 113, 224–228, 237–238, 255–256
Schimmel, Annemarie 82, 93, 114, 202
Schleifer, Abdallah 96
Schumacher, E. F. 286
Schuon, Frithjof 10–11, 26–27, 50, 61, 64, 78, 80–91, 94–98, 100, 102–105, 108, 111, 114–116, 130, 132, 139–140, 152–158, 160, 170, 191, 194–196, 203, 208–209, 222, 225, 237–238, 255–256, 278, 280, 282, 286–287, 297–298
Sedgwick, Mark 10, 90
Seth (Shīth) 52, 56, 267
Shabistarī, Maḥmūd 63–64, 180
Shādhilī, Abu'l-Ḥasan 217–218, 233
Shādhiliyyah 69, 76–77, 79, 82, 86–88, 139, 170, 201, 218, 331
shahādah 3–4, 33, 51, 89, 95, 109, 146, 149, 154, 156–163, 180–181, 184, 190–191, 202, 306–307, 333
Shah-Kazemi, Reza 8, 11, 31, 39, 71–73, 82, 96, 112, 153, 170
Shahrbānū 138
Shakespeare 95, 101–102, 116
Shakir, Zaid 32, 36
Shamanism 33–35, 297–298
Shāmil Dāghastānī 73
Shams al-Dīn Tabrīzī 61, 178, 236
Shams Umm al-Fuqarā' 131
Shankara 145, 147, 149–150, 158, 175, 191, 305
Sharī'ah 4–5, 12, 28, 31, 34, 53, 57, 64, 74, 76, 85, 94–95, 107, 128, 182, 193, 231–232, 244–245, 247, 257, 311–313, 318, 320, 326
shaṭḥiyyāt 146, 173–175, 212
Shaykh-i Ṣan'ān 58–60, 139
Sheba (Bilqīs) 139
Shelton, Mahmoud 113
Sherrard, Philip 115, 286, 295–296
Shiblī, Abū Bakr 217–218
Shī'ism 49, 55–58, 68, 88, 103–104, 108–109, 138–139, 169–173, 188–189, 201–211, 214, 218, 228, 233, 238, 241–255, 258, 330–334
Shikūh, Dārā 146, 151–152, 255
Shimr al-Kalbī 206
Shīrāzī, Quṭb al-Dīn 55, 267
Shīrāzī, Ṣadr al-Dīn 49, 54–58, 188–190, 218, 262, 267–268, 280, 333
shirk 35, 158, 161, 167, 182–183, 218
Shiva 120–121
shruti 148
Shushtarī, Abu'l-Ḥasan 176–177
Sijzī, 'Abd al-Jalīl 262
Sikhism 150, 321
silsilah 76, 94, 170
Sīmurgh 58, 60, 64, 177–178
al-ṣirāṭ al-mustaqīm 232, 316
sirr 145, 160, 175, 177, 184, 191, 210–211, 217, 221
Smith, Huston 1, 5, 16, 78, 82, 92–93, 103, 105, 116, 287
Smith, Wolfgang 115
smrti 148
Snodgrass, Adrian 264
Socrates 207
Solomon (Sulaymān) 30, 58, 141, 238, 328
Steuco, Agostino 20, 24–25, 45
Stoddart, William 93, 158
Sufism 6, 41, 43, 46, 49–55, 58–75, 82–83, 87–89, 94–95, 98–103, 108–109, 111, 113–114, 125–137, 144, 148, 154, 160, 162, 173–188,

190–193, 196–202, 209–223, 229–240, 242–248, 250, 253, 258, 260, 268, 275–276, 278–279, 281, 284–285, 309, 318–322, 330–332
Suhrawardī, Shihāb al-Dīn 6, 46–49, 180, 217, 251, 255, 266–267, 279
Sunnah 21, 32, 37–40, 61, 70, 99, 116, 134–135, 166–169, 197, 221, 232, 245, 273, 275, 314–315, 318, 320, 323, 326, 330–331, 333
Sunnism 11, 68, 88, 108–109, 138, 169–170, 201–202, 205, 207, 241–243, 311, 330–334
sūnyatā 302
symbolism 15, 34–35, 37, 85, 95, 97–98, 100, 132–133, 158, 184, 220, 248–249, 251, 264–265, 269–273, 276–278, 281, 292, 297–298, 300

Ṭabāṭabā'ī, Muḥammad Ḥasan 280
Ṭabāṭabā'ī, Muḥammad Ḥusayn 103–104, 108, 113, 206–207, 280
Tabula Smaragdina 257, 261, 264–265, 279
tajallī 165
Ṭalḥah ibn 'Ubayd Allāh 241
Tantra 122–123, 125, 132, 276
tanzīh 157, 308–309
ta'ziyah 208
Tao te Ching 4, 103, 305
Taoism 33–34, 57, 66, 75–76, 92, 255, 285
ṭarīqah 4, 28, 57, 63, 75, 87–88, 128, 139–140, 170, 181, 193, 232, 257, 313, 318–322
taṣawwuf 229, 232, 318–322, 330–331
tashbīh 157, 308–309
tawakkul 320
tawbah 234, 320
tawḥīd 3, 15, 20–21, 26–27, 30, 51, 53, 67, 76–77, 83–84, 92, 95, 106, 145, 151–152, 154, 159, 163, 167, 181, 185, 188, 190–191, 217, 244, 250, 281, 300, 308–309, 320, 333
ta'wīl 250–251, 265
tetragrammaton 246, 256
theology 5, 11, 15, 33, 53, 64, 130, 308–309, 331
Ṭībāwī, A. L. 44
Tirmidhī, Muḥammad 332
Tirmidhī, Ḥakīm 127, 233
Toorawa, Shawkat M. 233
Torah 4, 31–32, 34–35, 44, 50, 118, 134, 249, 307, 311–312
Tota Puri 123
Tradition 27–28, 75–80, 100, 105
traditional Islam 107, 305–334
Traditionalist School 8–9, 26–29, 41, 75–117, 139–140, 152–155, 255, 282–287, 304
Ṭūsī, Muḥammad 332
Ṭūsī, Naṣīr al-Dīn 55, 218, 331
Tustarī, Sahl 47, 211, 233

'ubūdiyyah 181–182
'Umar ibn al-Khaṭṭāb 138, 241, 331
Umar, Muhammad Suheyl 8, 113
Umm al-kitāb 141–142, 260
Umm Salamah bint Abī Umayyah 241
ummah 12, 37, 39, 97, 138, 210, 242, 299, 330, 333
Upanishads 103, 144–147, 151–152, 160
Upton, Charles 10, 113, 254
'Uryabī, Abu'l-'Abbās 199, 235–236

'Uthmān ibn 'Affān 37, 241, 331
Uways al-Qaranī 229, 255
uwaysī 229, 238–239
Uždavinys, Algis 43, 115

Vaishnavism 123–124
Valad, Sulṭān 236
Vâlsan, Michel 78, 112
Vedas 86, 146–149, 151–152, 187–188, 192
Vivekananda 119

Wahb ibn Munabbih 258
waḥdat al-adyān 23, 67
waḥdat al-wujūd 23, 51, 61, 67, 70, 100, 135, 159, 180–181, 188–189, 202, 263
wajd 159
wajh Allāh 4, 165
walāyah 204, 220, 248, 279, 318
wijdān 159
Williams, John 203–205, 213, 221
Williams, Rowan 9
wird 318
wuḍū' 100

Yaḥyā, 'Uthmān 213
Yashruṭiyyah, Fāṭimah 93, 113
Yazīd ibn Mu'āwiyah 201, 205–208
Yi Hwang 295
yoga 148
Yoga Vasíshtha 55, 146, 151
Yogīshwarī, Lalla 139
Yusuf, Hamza 32, 36, 96, 113, 287

Zachariah (Zakariyyā') 203
zakāh 317
Zakariyah, Mohamed 96
Zaydī Shī'ism 169, 330–331
Zayn al-'Ābidīn 207, 331
Zaynab bint 'Alī 207–208
Zinner, Samuel 114, 142
Zolla, Elémire 115
Zoroaster 3
Zoroastrianism 14–16, 21, 25, 31, 48, 66, 97, 99, 103–104, 138
Zosimus 258

www.ingramcontent.com/pod-product-compliance
Lightning Source LLC
Chambersburg PA
CBHW020323170426
43200CB00006B/248
* 9 7 8 1 5 9 7 3 1 1 3 9 7 *